HOUGHTON MIFFLIN SOCIAL STUDIES

Across the
Centuries

*W*e have not journeyed all this way
across the centuries,
across the oceans,
across the mountains,
across the prairies, because
we are made of sugar candy.

Winston Churchill

Beverly J. Armento
Gary B. Nash
Christopher L. Salter
Karen K. Wixson

Across the
Centuries

Houghton Mifflin Company • Boston

Atlanta • Dallas • Geneva, Illinois • Princeton, New Jersey • Palo Alto • Toronto

Consultants

World History Consultant
Scott Waugh
Associate Professor of History
University of California—Los Angeles
Los Angeles, California

Program Consultants
Edith M. Guyton
Associate Professor of Early
  Childhood Education
Georgia State University
Atlanta, Georgia

Gail Hobbs
Associate Professor of Geography
Pierce College
Woodland Hills, California

Charles Peters
Reading Consultant
Oakland Schools
Pontiac, Michigan

Cathy Riggs-Salter
Social Studies Consultant
Hartsburg, Missouri

Alfredo Schifini
Limited English Proficiency Consultant
Los Angeles, California

George Paul Schneider
Associate Director
  of General Programs
Department of Museum Education
Art Institute of Chicago
Chicago, Illinois

Twyla Stewart
Center for Academic Interinstitutional
  Programs
University of California—Los Angeles
Los Angeles, California

Teacher Reviewers

David E. Beer (Grade 5)
Weisser Park Elementary
Fort Wayne, Indiana

Jan Coleman (Grades 6–7)
Thornton Junior High
Fremont, California

Shawn Edwards
  (Grades 1–3)
Jackson Park Elementary
University City, Missouri

Barbara J. Fech (Grade 6)
Martha Ruggles School
Chicago, Illinois

Deborah M. Finkel
  (Grade 4)
Los Angeles Unified
  School District,
  Region G
South Pasadena,
  California

Jim Fletcher (Grades 5, 8)
La Loma Junior High
Modesto, California

Susan M. Gilliam
  (Grade 1)
Roscoe Elementary
Los Angeles, California

Vicki Stroud Gonterman
  (Grade 2)
Gibbs International
  Studies Magnet School
Little Rock, Arkansas

Lorraine Hood (Grade 2)
Fresno Unified School
  District
Fresno, California

Jean Jamgochian
  (Grade 5)
Haycock Gifted and
  Talented Center
Fairfax County, Virginia

Susan Kirk-Davalt
  (Grade 5)
Crowfoot Elementary
Lebanon, Oregon

Mary Molyneaux-Leahy
  (Grade 3)
Bridgeport Elementary
Bridgeport, Pennsylvania

Sharon Oviatt
  (Grades 1–3)
Keysor Elementary
Kirkwood, Missouri

Jayne B. Perala (Grade 1)
Cave Spring Elementary
Roanoke, Virginia

Carol Siefkin (K)
Garfield Elementary
Sacramento, California

Norman N. Tanaka
  (Grade 3)
Martin Luther King Jr.
  Elementary
Sacramento, California

John Tyler (Grades 5, 8)
Groton School
Groton, Massachusetts

Portia W. Vaughn
  (Grades 1–3)
School District 11
Colorado Springs,
  Colorado

Acknowledgments

Grateful acknowledgment is made
for the use of the material listed below.

The material in the Minipedia is
reprinted from *The World Book*
Encyclopedia with the expressed permission of the publisher. © 1990 by World
Book, Inc.

–*Continued on page 557.*

From Your Authors

*S*ilk robes flowing, an aged man hurries through the dark streets of Luoyang, capital of the Chinese Empire during the late Han Dynasty. It is a crisp autumn morning in A.D. 220. He moves swiftly along the broad boulevard, over the marble bridge, through the gardens, into the Outer Court.

So begins an account of a real event in ancient China's history. The man was on his way to court to meet the Chinese emperor and to tell him that nomadic horsemen were attacking the northern frontier. In Chapter 8 of this book, you will read more about Chinese court life and the problems of keeping such a large empire together.

Most of the people you will meet in this book lived long ago in places that may seem very far away from home. But they all had feelings just like yours and faced many of the same challenges you will face in your life. And whether they were great leaders or ordinary people, their decisions and actions helped shape the world you live in.

As you read about these people, places, and events, we hope you will ask many questions. Some questions may be about history: "What caused these people to make the decisions they did?" or "How do we know about these events?" Other questions may be about geography: "What are the land and weather like in that place?" or "Why did people choose to settle there?" Still other questions may be about economics: "How did people meet their needs for food and shelter?" or "How did people work out ways for using scarce resources?"

Most of all, we hope you catch the excitement of thinking, questioning, and discovering answers about your world— now and in the 21st century.

Beverly J. Armento
Professor of Social Studies
Director, Center for Business and
Economic Education
Georgia State University

Christopher L. Salter
Professor and Chair
Department of Geography
University of Missouri

Gary B. Nash
Professor of History
University of California—Los Angeles

Karen K. Wixson
Associate Professor of Education
University of Michigan

Contents

Understanding Skills

Each "Understanding Skills" feature gives you the opportunity to learn and practice a skill related to the topic you are studying.

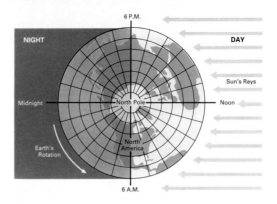

Understanding Concepts

Each "Understanding Concepts" feature gives you more information about a concept that is important to the lesson you are reading.

Exploring

The story of the past is hidden all around you in a world of the present. "Exploring" pages tell you the secrets of how to find it.

Making Decisions

Much of history is made of people's decisions. These pages take you step-by-step through fascinating problems from history and today. What will you decide?

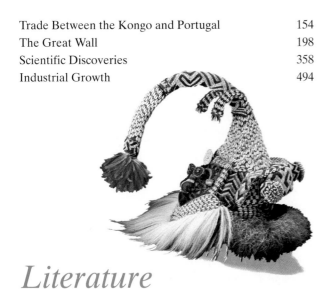

Literature

Throughout history people have expressed their deepest feelings and beliefs through literature. Reading these stories, legends, poems, and shorter passages that appear in the lessons will help you experience what life was like for people of other times and places.

Primary Sources

Reading the exact words of the people who made and lived history is the best way to get a sense of how they saw themselves and the times in which they lived. You will find more than 50 primary sources throughout this book including the following:

A Closer Look

Take a closer look at the objects and pictures spread out on these special pages. With the clues you see, you'll become a historical detective.

A Moment in Time

Someone or something from the past is frozen at an exciting moment. You'll get to know these people or things by reading about where they are and the objects around them.

Making a Hypothesis

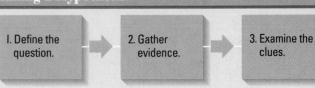

1. Define the question. → 2. Gather evidence. → 3. Examine the clues.

Charts, Diagrams, and Timelines

These visual presentations of information help give you a clearer picture of the people, places, and events you are studying.

Maps

The events of history have been shaped by the places in which they occurred. Each map in this book tells its own story about these events and places.

Russia, Prussia, and Austria in 1780

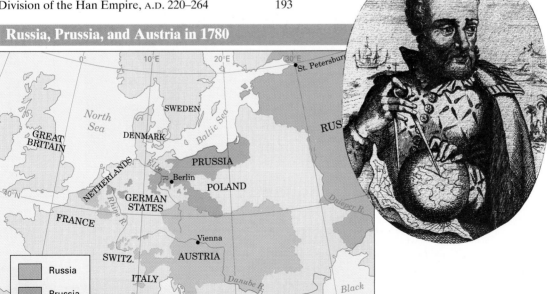

Russia
Prussia
Austria

0 200 400 mi.
0 200 400 km
Azimuthal Equidistant Projection

Starting Out

What makes this textbook so much more interesting than others you've used? In this book, the people of the past speak directly to you, through their actual words and the objects they used. You'll walk inside their houses and look inside their cooking pots. You'll follow them as they go to school, build cities, fight wars, work out settlements for peace.

Unit 6
Europe: 1300–1600

1300

1600

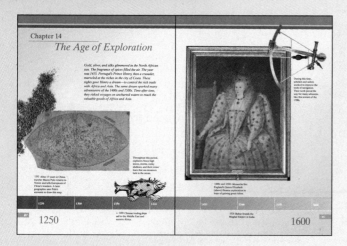

Chapter 14
The Age of Exploration

1250

1600

The titles outline the lesson. The red titles tell you the main topics discussed in the lesson on "Exploring, Trading, and Converting." The blue titles tell you the subtopics.

When and what? The timeline at the beginning of each lesson tells you when these events took place. The lesson title tells you what the lesson is about.

From unit to chapter to lesson—each step lets you see history in closer detail. The photos show you where events happened. The art introduces you to the people.

Right from the beginning the lesson opener pulls you into the sights, the sounds, the smells of what life was like at that time, in that place.

Like a road sign, the question that always appears here tells you what to think about while you read the lesson.

Look for these key terms. They are listed here so that you can watch for them. The first time they appear in the lesson they are shown in heavy black print and defined. Key terms are also defined in the Glossary.

1250

1600

Finding the Way

Significant advances
making enabled explorer
Vasco da Gama to under
voyages. Between the lat
and 1500, geographers be
produce a more accurate
of the world. They also
new theories about its sha
size. And new information
ered by earlier world trav
about the riches of farawa
kindled the desire for tra
exploration.

Early Exploration

Interest in exploration
greatly stimulated in Eur
Marco Polo's accounts of
els to China in the late 12
Italian merchant's tales o
lands, great riches, and po
profits captured the imagi
of kings and commoners

Firsthand observation
people such as Marco Pol
Ibn Battuta, an Arab trav
writer, also provided map
with valuable geographic
tion. By the 1300s, sailors
using coastal charts, or po
that had been prepared ac
to information supplied by
ship captains. These charts
the sailing courses, ports,
chorages that were mainly
traders in the Mediterrane
Portolan charts eventually
passed earlier maps in acc
and reliability.

Although the quality
tolan charts was improving
time, travelers needed still

LESSON 1

Exploring, Trading, and Converting

*T*he seas rose towards the sky and fell back in heavy showers which flooded the ships. The storm raging thus violently, the danger was doubled, for suddenly the wind died out, so that the ships lay dead between the waves, lurching so heavily that they took in water on both sides; and the men made themselves fast not to fall from one side to the other; and everything in the ships was breaking up, so that all cried to God for mercy.

Gaspar Correa,
from *Lendas da India,* 1561

That is how the Portuguese chronicler Gaspar Correa recorded the dramatic events of Vasco da Gama's voyage. The Portuguese explorer sailed around the Cape of Good Hope at the southern tip of Africa to India in the late 1490s.

The voyage took tremendous courage. At one point, da Gama's four ships lost sight of land for 96 days. The sailors thought they were lost. The crew was panic-stricken with fear, and murmurings of mutiny worried the captain.

But da Gama did not turn back, despite storms, sickness, and food shortages. He reached India in May 1498, after 14 months at sea. In 1499, when he finally returned to Portugal, only 44 of the original 170 sailors still survived.

THINKING FOCUS

Why did explorers in the 1400s risk their lives to explore unknown parts of the world?

Key Terms

- monopoly
- balance of trade
- bullion

➤ *This print of Vasco da Gama is based on an unknown artist's painting.*

364

Every map tells a story. The maps in this book tell the story of where traders like the Italian merchants went and what their travel routes were like.

Take a closer look, in this case at the spice trade. Look at the seeds and berries that became as valuable as gold, and at the ships that delivered them to Europe.

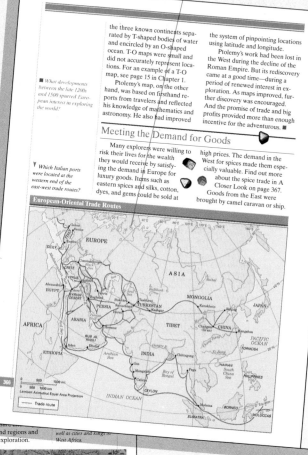

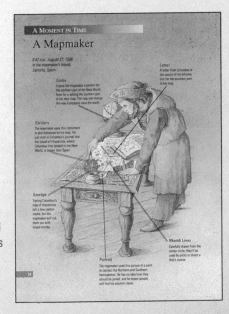

Giving you the inside story is the purpose of two special paragraphs. Across Time & Space connects what you're reading to things that happened centuries ago or continents away. Its companion, How Do We Know?, tells you where information about the past comes from. (See page 379 for an example.)

Frozen at a moment in time, the Spanish mapmaker extends your knowledge of the world. You learn all about him, through his equipment, his clothes, the place he's working.

Continuing On

As you get to know the people of the past, you'll want ways of understanding and remembering them better. This book gives you some tools to use in learning about people and places and remembering what you've learned.

Charts and graphs help you understand difficult information—in this case the cost of spices then and now. Other illustrations, diagrams, and charts tell you how things work and how one bit of information relates to another.

Every age has its great storytellers. Each chapter includes short examples of fine writing from or about the period. The literature is always printed on a tan background with a blue initial letter and a multicolored bar.

Costs of Spices, c.1350 and Today

A.D. 1350 at Master Craftsperson's Wages

One Pound: Cinnamon, Ginger, Pepper

Days: 0 1 2 3 4 5 6 7 8 9 10 11 12 13 14

Today at Minimum Wage

83 minutes   38 minutes   123 minutes

▲ *This chart compares the amount of time it would have taken to earn enough money to buy these luxury items in 1350 with the amount of time it takes today. Which item remains the most expensive?*

■ *How did Europeans obtain goods from the East?*

In the bustling Mediterranean ports, cargoes from the East were loaded onto Italian merchant ships for the passage to Europe. Italian port cities such as Venice and Genoa played a key role in east-west trade.

Because their location was central to Mediterranean markets, the Italian city-states had long been home to the best seafarers, navigators, and shipbuilders in the West. Moreover, Italian merchants had long been involved in overseas trade with commercial centers in Muslim countries. As a result, Italian cities had flourished since the 1100s.

Venice was all-powerful in the eastern Mediterranean, while Genoa dominated western Mediterranean trade in the early 1300s. However, in the late 1300s, the two cities waged war to determine which of them would command trade on the Black Sea and the Aegean Sea. Despite some crushing defeats in battle, Venice maintained a **monopoly,** or complete control, over trade with the East. ■

Along the way to ports such as Antioch and Alexandria the goods changed hands many times. Each trader covered only a portion of the route and then sold his cargo to the next trader.

Each Muslim, Arab, or Persian trader along the way raised the price of the items. Thus, by the time a piece of silk reached the Mediterranean, it might cost more than 100 times its original price.

Carrying Christianity Across the Sea

Europeans sought goods and profit, but they also wanted to spread Christianity among nonbelievers in other parts of the world. Some Christian explorers also hoped to find a mythical king named Prester John, who was rumored to rule a Christian kingdom in Africa. According to legend, Prester John had successfully defended his kingdom from Muslim attack. From the 1100s on,

the Portuguese spent great amounts of time, energy, and resources looking for this potential ally in the fight against the Muslims.

The Spanish and Portuguese had long been waging religious warfare against Islam. Since the early 700s, Muslims had invaded and occupied much of Spain and what would later become Portugal. Many battles were fought against the Muslims, but they were not finally driven out of southern Spain until 1492.

These religious wars influenced Spanish and Portuguese exploration. If people in newly discovered regions converted to Christianity, Spain and Portugal would have new allies in the fight against Islam. This was one reason missionaries usually accompanied the expeditions that explored or settled new regions.

Missionaries used education to convert the nonbelievers to Christianity. In the 1600s, Jesuit missionaries in China studied Chinese language and culture to better understand the people they wanted to convert. They also helped teach the Chinese and Europeans about each other's civilizations.

However, other missionaries were not so gentle. Some used

torture to subdue nonbelievers in foreign lands. For instance, 16th-century missionaries in Central and South America forced native inhabitants to work on church-owned farms. This outraged many Christians. Bartolomé de Las Casas, a defender of the rights of the natives, wrote a book on acceptable methods of conversion. An excerpt from his work follows.

H earers, especially pagans, should understand that the preachers of the faith have no intention of acquiring power over them through their preaching. . . . [They] should understand that no desire for riches moves [preachers] to preach. . . . In speaking and conversing with their hearers, especially pagans, the preachers should show themselves so mild and humble, courteous and . . . goodwilled that the hearers eagerly wish to listen and hold their teaching in greater reverence.

Las Casas, *The "Only Method" of Converting the Indians, 1530s*

While missionaries on exploratory expeditions sought to make new converts, many of the explorers leading these expeditions were searching for new gold markets. If Spanish and Portuguese explorers could find new sources of gold, their governments might be able to break up the Venetian monopoly on trade. ■

◄ *This 1422 painting is of a Jesuit missionary-astronomer who predicted an eclipse of the sun in China. The Chinese ruler ordered the missionary to teach his people Western science.*

■ *What role did religion play during the new era of European exploration?*

Searching for New Markets

The Venetians delivered their cargoes of spices and other eastern goods by land or by sea to cities

throughout Europe. In exchange for the eastern imports, Europeans exported wool, linen, timber, tin,

---

You're in charge of your reading. See the red square at the end of the text? Now find the red square over in the margin. If you can answer the question there, then you probably understood what you just read. If you can't, perhaps you'd better go back and read that part of the lesson again.

A picture is worth a thousand words. But just a few words in a caption can help you understand a picture, a photograph, a map, or in this case, a painting of an early astronomer in China.

Some tools you'll always use. The Understanding pages walk you through skills that you will use again and again, as a student and later on in life.

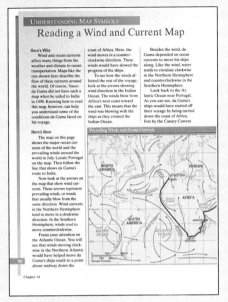

The things people make and use tell a great deal about them. In this book you'll find lots of photographs of the paintings people made, the tools and weapons they used, and the gold they exchanged.

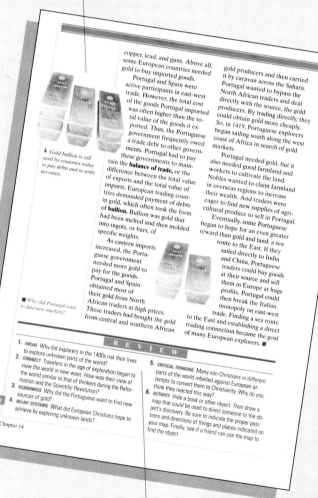

▲ Gold bullion is still used by countries today to pay debts and to settle accounts.

■ Why did Portugal want to find new markets?

A special kind of Understanding page looks at concepts—the big ideas that help put all the pieces together. This section helps you understand ideas like Civilization, Conquest, and in this case, Reform.

Letters, diaries, books—short passages from these primary sources let people from the past speak to you. When you see a tan background, a red initial letter, and a gray bar, you know that the quotation is a primary source.

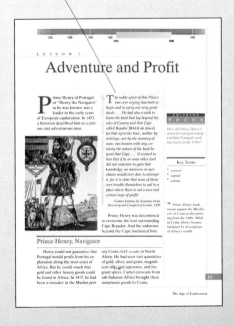

LESSON 2
Adventure and Profit

Prince Henry, Navigator

After you read the lesson, stop and review what you've read. The first question is the same one you started out with. The second question connects the lesson to what you've studied earlier. Other questions and an activity help you think about the lesson you've read. Chapter Review questions help you tie the lessons together. (See pages 394 and 395 for an example.)

Also Featuring

Some special pages show up only once in every unit, not in every lesson in the book. These features continue the story by letting you explore an idea or activity, or read a story about another time and place. The Time/Space Databank in the back of the book brings together resources you will use again and again.

School isn't the only place where you can learn social studies. This feature gives you a chance to explore history and geography outside the classroom—at home or in your own neighborhood.

EXPLORING

Nonverbal
Communication

Or do people need special knowledge in order to understand them, as they would for the signals of the basketball referee?

Move Ahead

Display your sketches of nonverbal messages on the bulletin board. Try to "read" the messages your classmates drew. Can they "read" yours?
Did you find any nonverbal

◄ *Its beacon flashing in the night, this lighthouse transmits information to incoming sailors about conditions close to shore.*

MAKING DECISIONS

The Great Wall

*H*ad the Great Wall not already existed, Yangdi [the second Sui emperor] would certainly have conceived it. As it was, he had to be content with rebuilding it.

Robert Silverberg,
20th-century historian

Background

Records show that Yangdi's rebuilding of the Great Wall in 607 required more than a million workers. Over half of them died of overwork or fled the harsh conditions.

The original building of the Great Wall, begun in 221 B.C., also involved a huge work force. Shihuangdi, the Chinese emperor who conceived of this project, connected shorter walls that had been built along China's northern border centuries before. He also extended the wall for hundreds of miles. The resulting fortified wall was and still is the longest structure on earth.

Benefits and Costs of the Great Wall

The most obvious benefit of building the Great Wall was protection. The wall helped prevent nomadic horsemen from invading China's farms along the northern border. Also, it kept farmers living along the border from joining the nomads.
Building the Great Wall enabled Shihuangdi to get rid of his

enemies. He ordered them to work on distant parts of the wall. He also sent soldiers to work on the wall. As a result, the soldiers could not band together and rise up against the emperor.

However, building Shihuangdi's wall is estimated to have required more than 300,000 workers, most of whom were drafted against their will. Thousands of farmers and merchants were required to supply the workers with food, clothing, tools, and shelter. Most of these supplies never made it

to the work sites; bandits roaming the countryside robbed the supply caravans.

The work of constructing the wall was so difficult and living conditions were so harsh that thousands of workers died. Often they were buried in the wall itself. Thus, the Great Wall of China gained the gruesome title of "the world's longest cemetery."

► *The Great Wall still snakes for thousands of miles across modern China. However, the wall that is still standing is not Shihuangdi's wall, but a later version, built during the Ming Dynasty.*

► *Using a traditional back-strap loom, this Mayan woman weaves patterns used in her village for generations. For the Mayan weaver, snakes symbolize the earth, toads symbolize saints, and eagles symbolize life and death.*

► *These coins, which were issued by Shihuangdi, were the standard currency throughout the empire at the time when the Great Wall was being built.*

Before embarking on any massive work, such as the building of the Great Wall of China, a wise decision maker will try to weigh the benefits and the costs of the project. We can look at historical events to try to compare the benefits and the costs of building the Great Wall of China.

▼ *Sturdy horses, like the one at the left, carried nomads who raided China's northern border. In response, the Great Wall was built, using labor-intensive construction methods as shown. Study the chart for a comparison of the Great Wall's long-range benefits and short-term costs.*

Decision
Build Great Wall

Outcomes

• People are safer	• Many laborers die
• More farmers stay on farms	• People become poorer
• Fewer threats to emperor arise	• Supply caravans often attacked

Decision Point

1. What were the benefits of constructing the Great Wall of China? What were the costs?
2. Do you think these were the only benefits and costs of the Great Wall? Where would you look to find more information about the role of the Great Wall in Chinese history?
3. Based on the information on these pages and any other information you have found,

do you think the benefits and costs of building the Great Wall balanced out? Explain.
4. Collect information from newspapers and magazines about upcoming plans for large government projects in the United States. Discuss the projected benefits and costs of each project. Decide which projects you would support and which you would oppose.

Chapter 15

Chapter 8

198

199

China

What would you do? The Making Decisions pages show you an important decision from the past. Then you practice the steps that will help you to make a good choice.

Stories have always been important parts of people's lives. Each unit in the book has at least one story about the time and place you're studying. In this case, it's a re-creation of Columbus's audience with King Ferdinand and Queen Isabella.

LITERATURE

The Audience

C. Walter Hodges

In Lesson 3 you learned about Columbus's appeal to Ferdinand and Isabella. Here is an imaginative re-creation of his second appearance before that King and Queen.

As you have learned in this chapter, the dream of wealth and the lure of riches drove Columbus and other explorers like him. They undertook journeys of unknown dangers and uncertain outcomes to pursue that dream. But they needed financial support. As you read this story, play the role of the audience—the King or Queen. Would you support Columbus? Why or why not?

*T*he town was taken, the Moors were driven out, the wars were at an end. Now, now at last there must be time to hear Columbus. Now at last the victorious Sovereigns would give him ships to sail in quest of his new horizon.
He went to his friend Alonzo de Quintanilla and implored him to obtain audience for him soon. The Accountant-General promised to do so, and on the following day Columbus was summoned into the presence of Their Majesties.
Father Juan Perez, Luiz de Santangel and I went with him to the audience. The antechamber was full of people, little groups talking in low voices, Court officials, men and

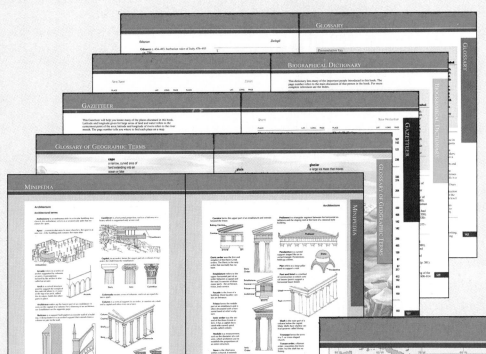

The Time/Space Databank is like a reference section of a library at your fingertips. It's the place to go for more information about the places, people, and key terms you meet in this book.

What's a minipedia? It's a small version of an encyclopedia, one that you don't have to go to your library to use. It's bound right into the back of your book so you can quickly look up its articles, charts, and graphs.

The Atlas maps out the world. Special maps tell you about the languages, religions, climates, and resources of the world. Historical maps let you compare what was going on at the same time in different places.

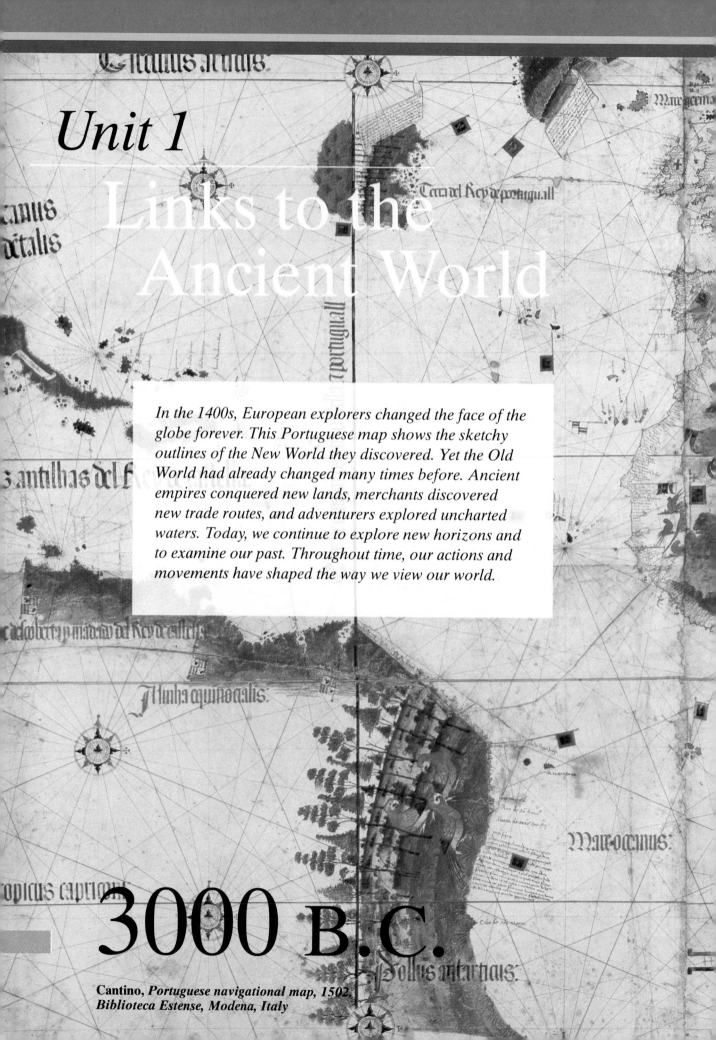

Unit 1

Links to the Ancient World

In the 1400s, European explorers changed the face of the globe forever. This Portuguese map shows the sketchy outlines of the New World they discovered. Yet the Old World had already changed many times before. Ancient empires conquered new lands, merchants discovered new trade routes, and adventurers explored uncharted waters. Today, we continue to explore new horizons and to examine our past. Throughout time, our actions and movements have shaped the way we view our world.

3000 B.C.

Cantino, *Portuguese navigational map, 1502,* *Biblioteca Estense, Modena, Italy*

Today

Chapter 1
A Changing World View

Roman traders who journeyed to the Far East 2,000 years ago measured distance not in miles but in how far they traveled by camel in an hour. As they approached their destination, they neared the edge of their known world. How the world has changed since then! Today, we travel far into space. We also look back, learning about our past. Our world view expands as we explore distant horizons and the evidence of past worlds.

c. 1000 B.C. We travel back in time by examining the objects ancient people left behind. The writing in this bronze dish tells of a border dispute settled by two rival groups in China.

3000	2000	1000

c. 500 B.C. North African people settle in present-day Nigeria and begin making iron tools.

3000 B.C.

During the 1400s, explorers and traders set sail from Lisbon, Portugal, for the far reaches of the known world—the Americas, Africa, and Asia. This illustration of Lisbon, drawn about 1590, helps us see what life in the past was like.

c. 1100 An Arab mapmaker creates this map, showing northern Europe at the bottom. Lacking accurate maps, sailors hug the shore. Today, radar allows travelers to plot courses across seas, over continents, and into space.

B.C.	A.D.	1000	Today

c. 100 B.C. Merchants use camels to transport goods in the arid regions of Asia and the Middle East.

Today

L E S S O N   1

Connections in the Roman Empire

THINKING
F O C U S

How were travel and communication in the Roman Empire different from today?

Key Terms

- electronic communication
- satellite

➤ *What do you know about any of the places on these brochures? How do you know about them?*

P aris, Alexandria, Athens. Would you like to visit these cities? What about Sydney, Nairobi, or Moscow? Which of these names is most familiar to you?

You have probably heard of some, if not all, of these places. Even Sydney, Australia, across the vast Pacific Ocean, is now part of the world view of most Americans.

If you had lived in Rome in A.D. 150, your world view would have been quite different. Paris (then called "Lutetia"), in Gaul; Alexandria, in Africa; and Athens, in Greece, were all part of the Roman Empire. As a merchant or soldier, you might have traveled to these cities.

Sydney? Nairobi? Moscow? These cities did not exist in A.D. 150. More important, the Romans were unaware of cultures in Australia, the Americas, central Africa, and northern Asia. Their limited world view made the world smaller than the one we know today.

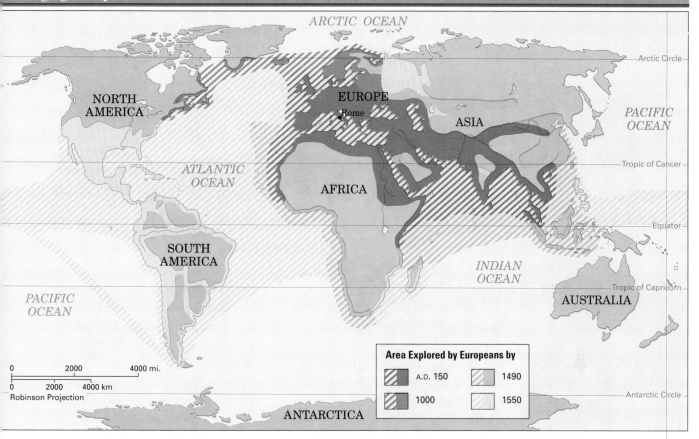

NORTH AMERICA

EUROPE
• Rome

ASIA

PACIFIC OCEAN

ATLANTIC OCEAN

AFRICA

Tropic of Cancer

Equator

SOUTH AMERICA

INDIAN OCEAN

PACIFIC OCEAN

Tropic of Capricorn

AUSTRALIA

ARCTIC OCEAN

Arctic Circle

| 0 | 2000 | 4000 mi. |
| 0 | 2000 | 4000 km |

Robinson Projection

Area Explored by Europeans by

| A.D. 150 | 1490 |
| 1000 | 1550 |

Antarctic Circle

ANTARCTICA

Travel Then and Now

The Romans of A.D. 150 knew of only a small part of the earth's surface, as you can see on the map above. Yet distances within their known world—for example, from Rome to Lutetia—seemed greater to them than they seem to us. That is because the ways we look at and experience the world have changed greatly since Roman times.

If you had to walk three miles uphill to school, would it seem near or far to you? How about if you took an express train and arrived in two minutes? The longer we must travel to get someplace, the farther away it seems to be.

Travel Within the Empire

In A.D. 150, most people in the Roman Empire knew very little about the world away from home. In fact, peasants and members of the lower classes rarely traveled beyond their village.

Those people who did travel went on foot, on horseback, or in horse-drawn carts. More than 50,000 miles of paved highways connected all parts of the empire to Rome. But travel was slow. The public wagons averaged only 60 miles a day, a distance we can now travel in one hour by car!

Roman merchants and government officials sailed in ships to imperial provinces in Spain, North Africa, or the Middle East. Speed varied, of course, with the winds. The voyage from Sicily, at the southern tip of Italy, to Alexandria in North Africa took six days with good winds. Today, many diesel-powered transport ships follow that same route in less than one-third the time.

▲ *Compare your known world with the world known to the Romans in A.D. 150. How are they different?*

How Do We Know?

ECONOMICS *Large numbers of Roman coins found in India show that India and Rome carried on extensive trade. Several Roman coins struck in the late A.D. 100s have been found in a port city in modern Cambodia, and 16 Roman coins have been found in the Chinese city of Shansi.*

5

Travel to Foreign Lands

Roman merchants in A.D. 150 traded gold, textiles, glassware, wine, and papyrus for spices, gems, silk, cotton, and fabric dyes from China, India, and Southeast Asia. Routes to the east, whether by land or sea, were long, difficult, and dangerous.

The overland route from Antioch, on the eastern Mediterranean shore, to Luoyang, capital of China, was over 4,000 miles long. Travelers often climbed frozen mountain ranges and battled rains, sandstorms, floods, and avalanches to reach their destinations.

Merchants with goods bound for India sailed from Alexandria south down the Nile to the town of Coptos. From there, camel caravans carried the merchants' goods east across the desert to ports on the Red Sea. Then traders loaded their cargo onto ships for the two-month voyage to India.

Sea travel was hazardous and often delayed. Captains of sailing ships required favorable winds to reach their desired ports. Also, sailors had no navigational charts or instruments, such as the magnetic compass, to help them find their way. Once at sea, travelers commonly fell victim to, and some even died from, storms, sickness, malnutrition, starvation, and dehydration.

Because of the great distances, discomforts, and dangers involved, very few people ever traveled beyond the boundaries of the empire. Most of those who did sought to trade with or invade foreign lands.

Today, all kinds of people travel all over the world for business and for pleasure. Jet planes, cars, trains, and cruise ships carry travelers in comfort and safety where once only brave soldiers and traders dared to go. ■

▲ *Compare the sizes of a modern ocean liner, the* Queen Elizabeth II, *and a Roman sailing vessel from about A.D. 100. The modern ship measures 963 feet long and the ancient one 120 feet. Hulls of reinforced steel have replaced wooden ones. And with powerful turbine engines, today's captains need not rely on rowers or the wind.*

■ *Describe the main methods of travel within the Roman Empire in A.D. 150.*

Communication Then and Now

Just as travel has become easier and faster, communication has improved. At the time of the Roman Empire, messages could be sent only one way—they were hand carried. Messengers crisscrossed the empire carrying correspondence. Often, people asked travelers to deliver letters to faraway places.

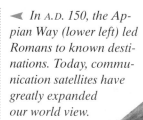

Communication was only as fast as the messenger's transportation. Messengers on foot could cover only about 25 miles a day. The official Roman postal service, which used horses or horse-drawn carriages day and night, covered an average of 100 miles a day. Carried over land and sea, a letter that was sent from a general in Rome could take more than 30 days to reach a legion outpost in Britain.

Today, we can contact people in other parts of the world without anyone having to make a journey.

Electronic communication, which includes such inventions as radio, television, computers, and the telephone, has revolutionized the way we communicate. Communication **satellites** orbit the earth transmitting telephone and television signals. In less than a second, they can relay signals and messages to almost anywhere on earth. We have even launched space probes to explore and send back information about our universe.

Through these many scientific developments, our world view has expanded. At the same time, the earth seems to be much smaller than it seemed to the Romans. Today, our frontiers lie in space rather than beyond a distant ocean or unknown continent. ■

◄ *In* A.D. *150, the Appian Way (lower left) led Romans to known destinations. Today, communication satellites have greatly expanded our world view.*

■ *How has communication changed since* A.D. *150?*

R E V I E W

1. **FOCUS** How were travel and communication in the Roman Empire different from today?

2. **GEOGRAPHY** How do you think a merchant from Lutetia (Paris) would have reached the North African city of Alexandria in A.D. 150?

3. **CRITICAL THINKING** How is space travel today like taking an ocean voyage in A.D. 150?

4. **CRITICAL THINKING** Why would silk clothing have been a sign of wealth in the Roman Empire?

5. **CRITICAL THINKING** Explain this statement: The world shrank on the day when communication no longer depended on transportation.

6. **ACTIVITY** Imagine that you are standing in a major transportation center 1,500 years in the future. Draw a sketch or write a description of the scene. Be sure to include what the destinations might be. Show or describe new methods of travel that you think might exist.

7

A Changing World View

Using Time Zones

Here's Why

Just as there are standard systems that help people around the world communicate about weights and distances, there is also a world standard system to help establish time differences. A time zone map shows the time differences between locations on earth. Because people and information can quickly travel long distances, knowing how to use a time zone map can be a valuable skill.

Here's How

The diagram on page 9 shows that half of the earth's surface is always receiving light from the sun. As the earth rotates on its axis, the part of its surface that receives that light changes. This change provides us with a way to measure time.

The exact time at any place on earth is measured from noon, when the sun is directly overhead. When it is noon for you, the time east of you is a little later, and the time west is a little earlier.

This small difference in time was not very important when people and information traveled slowly. Today, however, people need to communicate immediately with others in distant places. A system of standard time zones was established in

1884, within 10 years of the invention of the telephone.

The earth was divided into 24 time zones, one for each hour of a day, as shown on the map below. Each zone covers about 15 degrees of longitude, the number of degrees the earth rotates in one hour. In some places zone lines are crooked to account for political borders.

The starting point is an imaginary line called the prime meridian, which goes

through Greenwich, England. The time there is called Greenwich mean time or GMT. The time one time zone east of the GMT is one hour later, and the time one zone west is one hour earlier.

The time that divides days is midnight. When it is noon in Greenwich, it is midnight at the International Date Line, which is halfway around the world at the 180th meridian. When you cross the International Date

World Time Zones

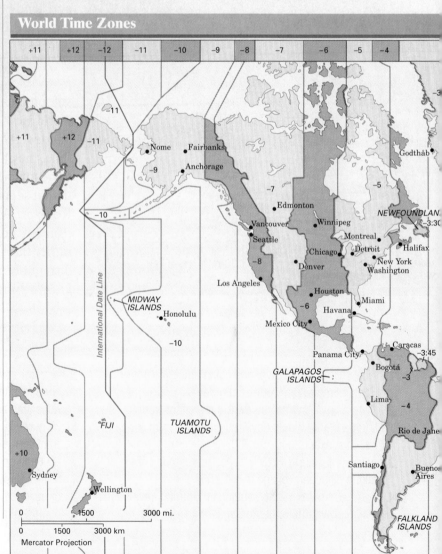

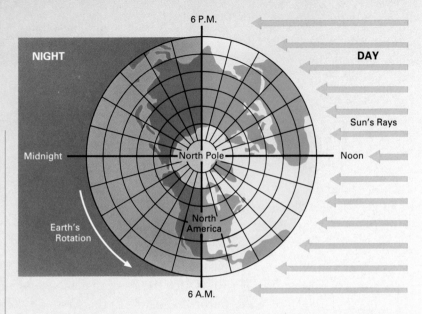

Line going east, you add a day. Going west you subtract a day.

Find Anchorage, Alaska, on the map below, east of the International Date Line. Suppose you are leaving Anchorage at 6 P.M. to fly to Washington, D.C., and you want to set your watch to the correct Washington time. You can see from the map that you will enter four time zones on the trip. To find out what time it is in Washington when you are leaving Anchorage, add one hour to the Anchorage time for each time zone you enter. To have the correct Washington time, you should set your watch to 10 P.M.

If you fly west from Washington, D.C., to Denver, Colorado, subtract one hour for each time zone you enter. When it is 8 A.M. in Washington, it is 6 A.M. in Denver.

If you fly south from Washington, to Lima, Peru, you do not need to change your watch. Although in different hemispheres, both are in the same time zone.

Try It

Use the time zone map to see what time it is in Montreal, Canada, when it is 8 P.M. in Los Angeles, California. What time is it then in Rio de Janeiro, Brazil? How much earlier is it in Stockholm, Sweden, than in Perth, Australia?

Apply It

Suppose you have friends in New York and in San Diego and you want to call them both on your birthday. If you call at 6 P.M., what time is it in each city?

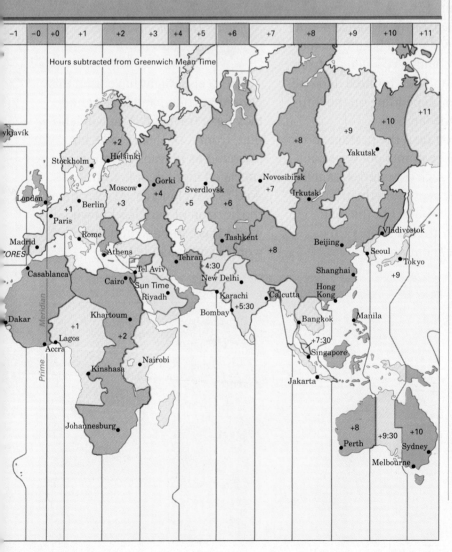

A Changing World View

L E S S O N   2

The Expanding Horizon

How and why did people travel in the years between A.D. 150 and 1500?

Key Terms

- caravan
- stirrups
- lateen sail
- sternpost rudder
- magnetic compass

Isidore of Charax wrote the passage on the right around 10 B.C. for the Roman emperor Augustus. In this first known travel guide, *Parthian Stations*, Isidore describes the trade route from Antioch, on the eastern shore of the Mediterranean Sea, to the borders of India. He names the supply stations and states the distances between them in schoeni *(SKEE nee)*, or the distance people could travel in one hour by camel. Schoeni could vary in length from two and one-half to three and one-half miles, depending on the difficulty of the landscape.

As you read the passage, notice how Isidore points out physical features, such as temples, canals, and villages, to help the traveler follow the route. On the map below, try to find some of the places he mentions.

Then a royal place, a temple of Artemis, founded by Darius, a small town; close by is the canal of Semiramis, and the Euphrates is dammed with rocks, in order that by being thus checked it may overflow the fields; but also in summer it wrecks the boats; to this place, 7 schoeni. Then Allan, a walled village, 4 schoeni. Then Phaliga, a village on the Euphrates (that means in Greek 'half-way'), 6 schoeni.

Who else might have used this particular route, and how would they have traveled? You will learn that, from A.D. 150 to 1500, improvements in transportation encouraged more people to travel. And as travel increased over time, the horizon of people's known world was extended and their world view expanded.

➤ *Compare this map to the maps on pages 524–526 of the Atlas. What has changed? Can you find any of these towns on the modern maps?*

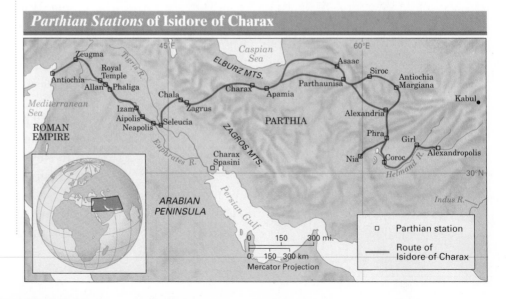

Parthian Stations of Isidore of Charax

Merchants, Soldiers, Explorers, Pilgrims

Many who used Isidore's guide were merchants. But throughout history, people also have traveled on religious quests, to conquer other lands, and to explore unknown realms. And all travelers depended on the means of traveling available in their time.

Merchants

From about 100 B.C., merchants trading in arid regions of Asia and the Middle East used camels to transport their goods. The sure-footed animals could carry up to 1,100 pounds and withstand both intense heat and extreme cold.

Traders often used long halters to tie many camels together to form **caravans.** Great caravans of as many as 5,000 camels trudged along a rugged 4,000-mile route between the Mediterranean Sea and the Chinese capital at Luoyang.

Soldiers

Soldiers and others who also needed swift transportation rode horses. Three inventions improved horseback riding: the stirrup, the bit, and the horseshoe. **Stirrups** are loops that hang down on both sides of a saddle. They hold the rider's feet and make it easier for riders to use their legs to control a horse. By A.D. 400, the Chinese had developed rigid metal stirrups which gave the rider more security in the saddle.

Another invention, the bit, originated in the Middle East, in about 1400 B.C. A bit is a metal piece that fits in the horse's mouth. It is attached to straps, or reins. Pulling on the reins moves the bit and signals the horse to stop or to turn.

The hard, paved roads of the Roman Empire damaged horses' hooves. So to protect their horses, the Romans developed the third invention, horseshoes. At first, Roman soldiers tied an iron plate over each hoof. But by A.D. 100, they nailed on iron shoes.

Though many people traveled on horseback, the most dramatic use of horses was for warfare. For example, the Mongols of central

▲ *People in the deserts of Africa and the Middle East still ride and transport goods on camels. During the 1100s, skillful Mongol horsemen conquered much of Asia. Can you find the stirrups on this Mongol's horse?*

Asia used stirrups to control their horses with their legs so that their hands were free. Experts with bow and arrow, they struck quickly and rode away before their victims could return the attack.

Explorers

Despite fragile ships and the dangers of the open seas, daring explorers set sail to discover what lay beyond the horizon. But, as the Roman Horace wrote in about 65 B.C., "Surely oak and threefold brass surrounded his heart who first trusted a frail vessel to the merciless ocean." Early sailing ships required good weather to reach their destinations. Rigged with rectangular sails, these ships had difficulty sailing against the wind. Also, sailors needed clear skies to see the stars and the shoreline by which they navigated.

Three innovations freed sailors from dependence on the weather: the lateen sail, the sternpost rudder, and the magnetic compass.

Around A.D. 150, a triangular sail known as the **lateen sail** was first used on the Mediterranean Sea. As shown below, the lateen sail enabled ships to sail more easily in any direction, regardless of the direction of the wind.

As early as 200 B.C., the Chinese used the **sternpost rudder** to steer their ships. It was a paddle-like device under the ship that could be moved from side to side. The rudder replaced the steering oar, which was cumbersome and ineffective on large ships. For centuries, sailors were unable to navigate through bad weather. But by the 1100s, the Chinese began to use the **magnetic compass.** A compass needle always points north, so sailors could navigate in any kind of weather.

Such innovations as these revolutionized sea transport.

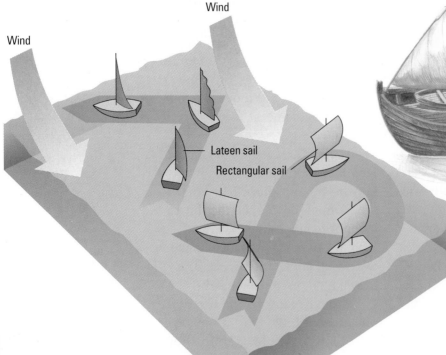

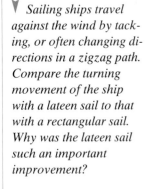

▼ *Sailing ships travel against the wind by tacking, or often changing directions in a zigzag path. Compare the turning movement of the ship with a lateen sail to that with a rectangular sail. Why was the lateen sail such an important improvement?*

Wind

Wind

Lateen sail

Rectangular sail

Longer voyages became safer and more dependable. By the 1400s, adventurous sea captains would sail into unknown regions of the seas. More important, they would find their way back.

Pilgrims

As transportation became safer and more reliable, more people began to travel. Pilgrims and adventurers traveled throughout the world and many wrote about their experiences.

From A.D. 629 to 645, Hsuan-Tsang (shoo ahn DZAHNG), a Chinese pilgrim, journeyed over 5,000 miles from China to India and back to collect Buddhist teachings. He recorded fantastic tales of his adventures. This excerpt describes the Hindu Kush mountains.

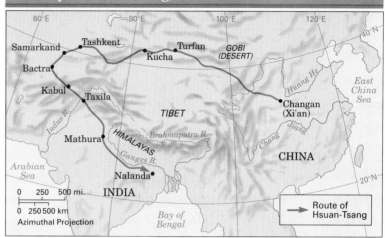

Journey of Hsuan-Tsang, A.D. 629–645

T his mountain pass is very high; the precipices are wild and dangerous; the path is tortuous, and the caverns and hollows wind and intertwine together. At one time the traveler enters a deep valley, at another he mounts a high peak, which in full summer is blocked with frozen ice. By cutting steps up the ice the traveler passes on, and after three days he comes to the highest point of the pass. There the icy wind, intensely cold, blows with fury; the piled snow fills the valleys. Travelers pushing their way through dare not pause on their route.

Another traveler motivated by religious beliefs was Ibn Battuta, a Muslim. In 1325, Battuta left his home in Tangier to journey to the Muslim holy city, Mecca, in Arabia. But the sights he saw and the people he met so fascinated him that he devoted the rest of his life to travel.

For 30 years, Battuta traveled in Arabia, Asia, Africa, and Spain. Like Hsuan-Tsang, he recorded many exciting adventures. These accounts shed new light on the world away from home. Describing a sea voyage, Battuta wrote, "For ten days we never saw the sun, and then we entered on an unknown sea. . . . In this way we passed forty-two days, without knowing in what waters we were."

Mapmakers used information from such travelers to update their own maps of the world. Read A Moment in Time on page 14 to learn more about mapmakers. ■

▲ Hsuan-Tsang's tales of his travels became a popular part of Chinese folklore. What do you think was the most difficult part of his journey? Why?

◄ Hsuan-Tsang is reported to have been a handsome man who liked to wear colorful clothing. This portrait of him, from about A.D. 800, is painted on silk. His backpack is filled with some of the Buddhist writings he brought back to China from India.

■ In what ways did travel become easier between A.D. 150 and 1500?

13

A Changing World View

A Mapmaker

*8:47 A.M., August 27, 1500
In the mapmaker's house,
Santoña, Spain*

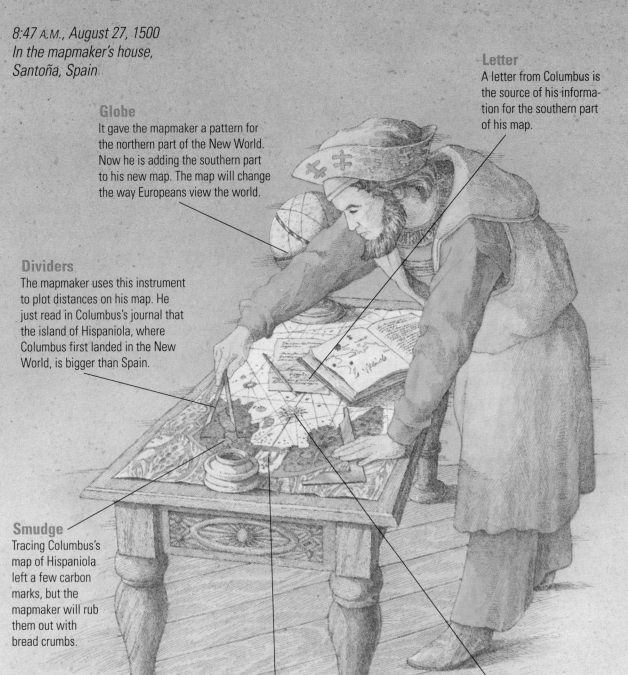

Globe
It gave the mapmaker a pattern for the northern part of the New World. Now he is adding the southern part to his new map. The map will change the way Europeans view the world.

Letter
A letter from Columbus is the source of his information for the southern part of his map.

Dividers
The mapmaker uses this instrument to plot distances on his map. He just read in Columbus's journal that the island of Hispaniola, where Columbus first landed in the New World, is bigger than Spain.

Smudge
Tracing Columbus's map of Hispaniola left a few carbon marks, but the mapmaker will rub them out with bread crumbs.

Rhumb Lines
Carefully drawn from the center circle, they'll be used by pilots to direct a ship's course.

Portrait
The mapmaker used this picture of a saint to connect the Northern and Southern hemispheres. He has no idea how they should be joined, and he hopes people will find his solution clever.

Early Maps

Hsuan-Tsang, Ibn Battuta, and other travelers collected a wealth of information about the geography and people of the places they had visited. Each new journey into unfamiliar lands provided mapmakers with another small piece of the puzzle that was the world. Even so, until about A.D. 1500, people knew little about what lay beyond the region at the center of nearly every map—home.

The greatest geographer and mapmaker during the Roman Empire was Ptolemy *(TAHL uh mee)*, who lived from A.D. 90 to 168. He used information he collected from travelers to draw a remarkably accurate map of the world the Romans knew in 150.

Unfortunately, Ptolemy's work was forgotten as the Roman Empire declined. For the next 1,000 years, maps gave a distorted view of the world. The most common European ones are called T-O maps. They showed the continents of Europe, Asia, and Africa separated by bodies of water that together formed a "T." A vast ocean, which was the "O," was shown encircling the three continents.

Many Christians believed that Paradise lay near India in the East.

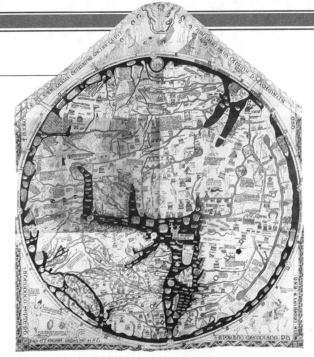

So Christian mapmakers often put the East at the top of their maps. Jerusalem, their holy city, was at the center, as you can see on the map above.

In the early 1400s, scholars found copies of Ptolemy's work. The rediscovery and publication of these manuscripts stimulated a great interest in world geography. Explorers such as Christopher Columbus were equipped with the magnetic compass and other inventions that made ocean travel possible. These adventurers set off on voyages that would change people's view of the world. And when they returned, the mapmakers changed the world on paper. ■

▲ *Find three or four landmarks that appear on this map and on the map on pages 518 and 519. How do their locations here differ from the map in the Atlas?*

■ *How did travelers and explorers change people's view of the world?*

R E V I E W

1. **FOCUS** How and why did people travel in the years between A.D. 150 and 1500?

2. **CONNECT** How would the stirrup, the bit, and horseshoes have affected communications by A.D. 500?

3. **GEOGRAPHY** What areas of early maps were most likely to be accurate? Why?

4. **ECONOMICS** Why did traders choose camels instead of horses as pack animals on trade routes through Asia and the Middle East?

5. **CRITICAL THINKING** Explain this statement: Changes in travel and communications have been more dramatic between 1500 and the present than they were between A.D. 150 and 1500.

6. **WRITING ACTIVITY** Write a "travel guide" telling someone how to get to a certain place. Use physical features, directions, and estimates of time to describe the route. Do not use mileage, number of blocks, road signs, or other modern conveniences.

15

L E S S O N   3

Traveling Through the Past

THINKING

F O C U S

How do historians recon-struct the past?

Key Terms

- history
- prehistory
- archaeology
- primary source
- secondary source

➤ *An Aztec artisan crafted this mask by covering the front of a human skull with pieces of turquoise and lignite.*

> T hen Montezuma . . . pointed out his great city and all the others standing in the water and on the land around the lake.
> That huge . . , temple stood so high that from [the top] one could see over everything: three causeways leading into Mexico . . . the aqueduct of Chapultepec which supplied the city with the finest water, the wooden bridges built certain distances apart on the three causeways through which the lake water flowed. We beheld on that great lake a multitude of canoes loaded with provisions. We saw how it was impossible to pass from house to house . . . except by drawbridges . . . or in canoes. We saw in those cities . . . oratories all gleaming white and wonderful to behold.
>
> From *Cortés and the Conquest of Mexico by the Spaniards in 1521*

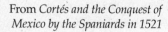

Twenty-seven years after Columbus first landed in the West Indies, a band of Spanish adventurers arrived in Mexico. They had come to find fortunes of gold.

In 1519, the Aztec and their leader, Montezuma, welcomed Hernando Cortés and 650 explorers to their capital at Tenochtitlán *(tay nawch tee TLAN)*. In the above description of the arrival of the Spanish, Spanish explorer Bernal Díaz gives us a look at the astonishing Aztec city, built over the shallow waters of Lake Texcoco.

Just two years later, Tenochtitlán lay in ruins, its once magnificent buildings burnt to the ground, its causeways and canals filled with rubble. Cortés's army had destroyed the city in his quest to conquer the Aztec.

How do we know about the ruined city, the Aztec, Cortés, and the Spanish conquest? The relic on this page tells us, wordlessly, of the Aztec's skill and artistry. The words of the Spanish explorer Bernal Díaz also speak to us, across almost 500 years, of the glorious city.

Studying the Past

Just as early explorers and mapmakers expanded the world view of their time, historians expand our view of the past. **History** is the record of past human events. To reconstruct history, historians must study nonwritten and written sources. To reconstruct the history of the Aztec, they studied both.

Nonwritten Sources

To study **prehistory,** or history before the development of writing, historians must rely on silent remains, such as fossils, ruins, and artifacts. **Archaeology** is the science of finding and studying these physical remains.

Written Sources

Written sources date back only to about 3000 B.C., when writing was developed in the Middle Eastern land of Mesopotamia. A wide variety of written materials exists, including scrolls, tablets, inscriptions, calendars, maps, letters, documents, and books.

Primary sources are those written by people who participated in or observed the events they describe. For example, in the last lesson, Ibn Battuta's account of being lost at sea is a primary source. **Secondary sources** are written after an event, usually with the aid of primary sources. A history of sea travel that retold Ibn Battuta's experience would be a secondary source.

Historians prefer primary sources, because the people who observed or took part in events usually tell a more accurate story. Historians carefully check the accuracy of every source to make sure they get a true view of the past.

In some cases, careful study of historical evidence leads to changes in our view of the past. For example, a document known as the *Donation of Constantine* gave the Roman Catholic popes power over Italy and western Europe. The document was supposedly written during Constantine's reign (c. A.D. 274–337), and for centuries it was considered a genuine primary source. But in 1440, Italian historian Lorenzo Valla carefully studied the document. He discovered that it was a forgery, written hundreds of years after Constantine's death! ∎

Archaeological teams remove and study tiny pieces of earth bit by bit to reveal clues about the past. The workers below are excavating an ancient tomb in Peru.

■ *Explain the difference between primary and secondary sources.*

Interpreting the Past

Like Lorenzo Valla, a good historian has to be a good detective, evaluating the accuracy and the meaning of all sources. A historian must also be a judge, choosing among conflicting interpretations of the past.

Differing Views of the Past

People's backgrounds clearly have an effect on the way they see an event as well as how they choose to tell the story. For example, in Chapter 11 you will read about battles between European Christians and Arab Muslims for control of the city of Jerusalem and the Holy Land. These battles occurred between 1096 and 1291. The Christians called them *crusades* and the Christian soldiers who fought them *crusaders*.

UNDERSTANDING HISTORY

After Cortés's conquest of Tenochtitlán, an Aztec poet lamented the destruction of his city. "The ways are strewn with broken lances," he wrote. "The houses are without roofs." The Aztec poet's name is not known to us, but his words give us a valuable glimpse of Mexican history.

Changing History

History is the study of past events, such as the Spanish conquest of the Aztec. Traditionally, we learn history from the point of view of the winners—in this case, the Spanish. However, hearing an Aztec voice helps us to understand another important part of the story.

The study of history is not just the discovery and listing of facts and events. Historians also attempt to find meaning in those facts and events. But most facts can be interpreted many different ways, so history can never be purely factual. Both the source's and the historian's point of view influence the way history is eventually written.

Future History

Just as history can never be completely objective, a "final" history can never be written. New historians will discover new sources to study and find new questions to ask of the old sources. People will always debate what history means. And as long as people exist, they will be creating history for future historians.

As you might imagine, Christian and Muslim primary sources portrayed the crusaders differently.

Anna Comnena was a Christian. In 1096, when she was 13, Anna watched as the crusaders marched into the city of Constantinople. She later wrote the following in her memoirs:

These people, as though aflame with divine fire, flocked in crowds. . . . Every street swarmed with men whose faces were full of good humor and zeal for their righteous cause.

Less than a century later, Saladin, a Muslim leader, had a less admiring view of the Christian crusaders. In 1174, Saladin wrote a message to the Muslim ruler in Baghdad:

The [Europeans] all used to come, sometimes as raiders, the voracity of whose harm could not be contained and the fire of whose evil could not be quenched.

Historians must ask when, where, why, and by whom a source was written. The answers to these questions help them evaluate how accurate or biased a source is.

Expanding Views of the Past

History has been called a jig-saw puzzle, with some of the pieces missing. As time passes, new pieces are found. Historians continually revisit the past and reinterpret history in light of new information. In doing so, they change our world view as much as the early explorers changed the world's map. ■

■ *How do historians evaluate the accuracy of their sources?*

▼ *Even nonwritten sources can show bias. How might a historian view this portrayal, from about 1340, of an imaginary battle between a Christian crusader (left) and a Muslim knight (right)? What can you tell about the artist's background from this picture?*

R E V I E W

1. **FOCUS** How do historians reconstruct the past?
2. **CONNECT** What kinds of primary sources are being created today with the use of electronic communications devices?
3. **HISTORY** Name three sources from which historians have learned about the Aztec civilization.
4. **CRITICAL THINKING** How do you think changing our view of the past affects our world view today?
5. **WRITING ACTIVITY** Choose an event at your school that could have two or more interpretations. Write either an accurate or a biased account of the event. Then exchange papers with a classmate. As a historian, would you use your classmate's account as a reliable primary source? Why or why not? Give examples to support your decision.

Archaeology: Clues and Connections

P ieces of a bowl, broken tools, rusted coins—when archaeologists dig up things like these, they study them eagerly. Everyday items are clues to the lives of the people who used them: What did they eat and drink? How did they travel? Did they play games?

What people throw out tells as much about a society as what people keep. Mountains of garbage give contemporary anthropologists ample material for study.

Get Ready

Gather items for a "trash" bag from your trash at home. Be sure they are "clean" items, because a classmate will study them to find clues about your family. Rinse out any jars, bottles, or cans. Include anything that gives hints about your family's life—pets, number or age of children, hobbies, or work. Cut the labels off magazines and the address portion off letters.

Find Out

Your teacher will hand out one bag of trash to each student. Make a list of the items in the bag you receive. What does each item tell you? Is there any indication of a family pet: An empty dog-food box? A kitty litter bag? What about ages of

For what purpose might this Peruvian pottery vessel have been created? Note the stone and shell designs pressed into the clay.

the family members: A baby-food jar? A letter from a Cub Scout leader? Did you find anything that suggests work or a hobby: Computer printouts? Pieces of yarn? *Popular Mechanics* magazine? Does anything reveal the family's size: A giant catsup jar? A jumbo container for laundry detergent?

Move Ahead

Make a chart listing the clues you found. Next to each clue, list what you learned or guessed from it. For example:

Clues	Facts and Guesses
cat-food can	pet cat
pieces of yarn	someone knits
baby-food jar	baby in house
sawdust	woodworking

Be sure that every fact or guess is supported by a clue.

Explore Some More

Take a look around the classroom. Suppose it were frozen exactly as it is at this moment. If archaeologists were to dig it up in 1,000 years, what might they conclude? List everything in the room that could be a clue to 20th-century life in your school, in your town, or in the United States.

A Changing World View

Chapter Review

Reviewing Key Terms

archaeology (p. 17)
caravan (p. 11)
electronic communication (p. 7)
history (p. 17)
lateen sail (p. 14)
magnetic compass (p. 14)

prehistory (p. 17)
primary source (p. 17)
satellite (p. 7)
secondary source (p. 17)
sternpost rudder (p. 14)
stirrups (p. 11)

A. On your own paper, explain why each invention below is important.
1. lateen sail
2. stern-post rudder
3. magnetic compass
4. stirrups
5. satellite
6. electronic communications

B. Answer each question below. Use the key term that is in parentheses in your answer.
1. How did merchants of Asia and the Middle East transport goods overland? (caravan)
2. Why was the invention of writing important to our study of the past? (history)
3. How do historians piece together written evidence of the past? (primary sources)
4. What do "silent remains" contribute to our study of the past? (prehistory)
5. How might we discover and describe a lost city of which there is no written record? (archaeology)
6. Why do we need more than just eyewitness accounts of history? (secondary sources)

Exploring Concepts

A. In this chapter, you read how people in the past expanded their view of the world. Copy and complete the cluster diagram below. Add examples from the chapter of inventions, historical events, and other things that helped expand our world view.

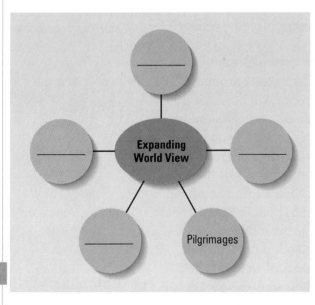

B. Answer each question using information from the chapter.
1. Why did the distance between Rome and Paris, or Lutetia, seem greater in the time of the Roman Empire than it does today?
2. Why was sea travel during the time of the Roman Empire unreliable and dangerous?
3. Compare the speed of communication in the Roman Empire with today.
4. What common role did early soldiers, explorers, merchants, and pilgrims play in expanding the world view of their time?
5. What did travelers such as Ibn Battuta and Hsuang-Tsang contribute to mapmaking?
6. What distinguished Ptolemy's map of the world in A.D. 150 from other maps drawn before 1400?
7. How do historians determine how reliable a primary source is?
8. How do historians affect our world view?
9. Describe how we can "travel" into the past.

Reviewing Skills

1. Use the map at the right to answer the following questions.
   a. When it is 10 A.M. in Seattle, what time is it in Mexico City?
   b. What is the time difference between Detroit and Honolulu?
2. How many time zones does Africa have? Count from Dakar to Nairobi.
3. Twins are born on a ship. The child who is born first has a birth date one day later than the child who is born last. Where is the ship, and in which direction is it traveling?
4. Suppose you are going to fly from Dallas, Texas, to Paris, France. Your itinerary shows that your flight is scheduled to arrive in Paris at 7:58 A.M. What could you use to determine the time your watch will show on your arrival in Paris, if you don't reset it during the flight?

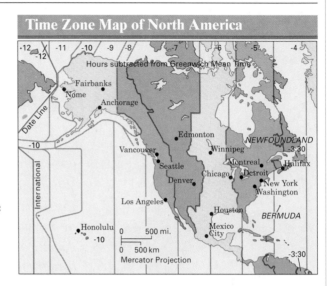

Time Zone Map of North America

Hours subtracted from Greenwich Mean Time

Mercator Projection

Using Critical Thinking

1. A writer has described our world today as a "global village" that has resulted from electronic communications. Based on what you know from the chapter about the limited world view of people of the past and about electronic communications, make an inference about what a global village is. Write a paragraph to explain what led you to this inference.
2. The Romans didn't know that such a place as Australia existed. In fact, they knew nothing of the entire Pacific Ocean. Suppose that somehow a Roman had learned of the existence of the rest of the earth and reported it to the emperor. Imagine the impact such a discovery would have made on Roman society. Now try to imagine what kind of a discovery would have the same impact today. Write a paragraph describing the discovery. Then write another paragraph explaining why you think this discovery would have such an impact.

Preparing for Citizenship

1. **COLLECTING INFORMATION** Read the article on Communication on pages 507–510 in the Minipedia. Notice that the telegraph was one of the first forms of electronic communication. Research the different ways messages were sent before the invention of the telegraph. Make a notebook that shows as many different methods of communication as you can find. Arrange your notebook from the earliest method to the most recent. Be sure to tell where and when each method was used and how it worked.

2. **COLLABORATIVE LEARNING** Read about the history of your community or school and discuss it as a class. Locate a primary source that describes an event in your community or school's history. Form committees. Each committee should write their own description of the historical event based on the information in the primary source. As a class, compare the secondary sources written by the committees. Does each secondary source portray the event accurately? In what ways do they differ?

Chapter 2
Empires of the Ancient World

What was happening to the mighty Roman Empire? The Persians challenged its eastern borders. Wave after wave of barbarian tribes swept down from Europe and central Asia. Political quarrels and economic problems forced leaders to split the empire in two. Even so, conditions in the western half of the empire worsened. But the eastern empire—the Byzantine Empire—prospered. Power in the ancient world was shifting to the east.

Barbarian invaders, shown on the bronze clasps above, overran the Western Roman Empire in the 400s. Yet the empire remained strong in eastern areas like Jordan (left).

527–548 Empress Theodora (above), considered the most powerful woman in Byzantine history, rules with her husband Justinian.

250	B.C.	A.D.		250	500

27 B.C.

c. A.D. 200 West African people called Bantu migrate into central and southern Africa.

300–525 During the Gupta Dynasty, India trades with the Eastern Roman Empire, Persia, and China.

During this period, the Byzantine Empire recaptured Roman lands in the West. This ivory carving shows an emperor, thought to be Justinian, triumphantly returning from battle.

867–1057 The Byzantine Empire expands. This gold and silver container, used in Christian ceremonies, shows the domes typical of Byzantine architecture.

| 750 | 1000 | 1250 | 1500 |

732 Christian forces in France defeat Muslim invaders.

A.D. 1453

LESSON 1

The Fall of the Roman Empire

> *T*he world has grown old and lost its former vigor. . . . Winter no longer gives rain enough to swell the seed, nor summer enough to toast the harvest . . . the mountains are gutted and give less marble, the mines are exhausted and give less silver and gold . . . the fields lack farmers, the seas sailors, the encampments soldiers . . . there is no justice in judgments, competence in trades, discipline in daily life.

THINKING FOCUS

What led to the collapse of the Western Roman Empire?

This description, written in about A.D. 250 by one of the Roman Empire's church leaders, foretells the fate of that mighty empire. Within 200 years of the writing of this description, the Roman Empire would suffer great military and economic crises, weaken, and eventually collapse.

Key Terms

- province
- barbarian

The Empire in Prosperity

From 27 B.C. to A.D. 14, Julius Caesar's adopted son Octavian ruled as Rome's first emperor. Octavian was given the name Augustus, which means the revered or exalted one. As emperor, Augustus put an end to the chaos and power struggles that had occurred within the Roman Empire after Julius Caesar's assassination. During his reign, Augustus also expanded the empire by conquering the territory that ran along the Rhine and Danube rivers.

➤ *Roman emperors were often depicted in military dress. The carved figures on the breastplate of Augustus's armor represent a Roman victory over a Persian army.*

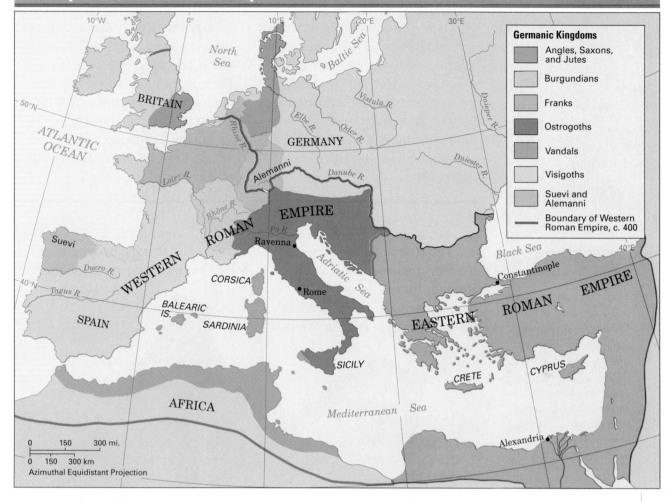

Expanding the Empire

Roman conquests of new territory continued under the emperors after Augustus. By A.D. 117, the Roman Empire had reached its greatest size. It extended from Britain in the north to Africa in the south and from Spain in the west to Syria in the east.

The lands and peoples captured by the empire were organized into **provinces,** or territories, of Rome. Rome maintained peace in its provinces by allowing individuals to continue living and working as usual. However, Roman officials did institute Roman laws in these territories. In addition, they appointed governors to rule the provinces and make sure that Roman law was enforced there.

Profiting from the Provinces

Rome benefited from its empire in many ways. Since enemies could reach Rome only by crossing the provinces, these territories pro-

tected Rome by acting as a buffer zone. They also produced food and other goods for the city of Rome. For example, Egypt and North Africa supplied Rome with most of

As powerful as it was, the Roman Empire did not last. How did its boundaries change as it weakened?

Here Egyptian grain is loaded on a barge for shipment to Rome.

27

Empires of the Ancient World

its wheat. Trade with the provinces brought wealth to Roman citizens. The people in the provinces also paid taxes, which supported the government and the army of about 300,000 men distributed along the empire's frontiers. For a long time, the empire was well fed, strong, and wealthy.

Because Rome was strong, the empire was peaceful and stable, which benefited everyone in it. The government built roads that connected the provinces to Rome. It also funded the construction of aqueducts. Aqueducts were used to pipe drinking water from wells and springs to the people. ■

The Empire in Crisis

The Roman army along the frontiers managed to protect the Romans for many years. But, beginning in A.D. 161, some enemies broke across the frontiers to invade the Roman Empire itself. This became a serious problem for the Romans.

■ *Describe the relation- ship between Rome and its provinces.*

Across Time & Space

The word barbarian *was originally used in the Roman Empire to de- scribe people from out- side the empire who spoke a different lan- guage and had a different culture. Over time, the term* barbarian *has come to mean a person who is uncivilized and warlike.*

▼ *Roman impact on the provinces can be seen in the ruins of a city built by the Romans in Palmyra, Syria.*

A New Type of Art

Justinian's most important contribution to the new Constantinople was the religious art and architecture that he commissioned. Of particular note were the mosaics created during Justinian's reign. The mosaic was an expensive art form, but, with funding from Justinian, artists were able to refine the art of mosaic-making and create masterpieces. **Mosaics** are colored fragments of glass or quartz embedded in plaster. Read A Closer Look on the next page to see how people restore, or repair, mosaics today.

The Byzantines also created architectural masterpieces. None of them was more spectacular than the new Hagia Sophia—Saint Sophia in English—the most important religious structure in Constantinople. After the rioting Greens destroyed the old Hagia Sophia, Justinian had it rebuilt into a magnificent structure. It had columns of spotted green marble, walls of polished marble of many colors, and many glittering mosaics. But the most awe-inspiring

aspect of the Hagia Sophia was its dome. It was 180 feet high and 108 feet wide, and through its stained-glass windows, light flooded the interior of the church.

A New Set of Laws

In 528, Justinian gave 10 men the task of condensing the 1,600 books of classic Roman law. A year later they came up with a well-organized system of 4,652 laws. The new legal system was called the Justinian Code. It extended the rights of women, children, and slaves but also called for harsher penalties for crimes. Criminals could have their property taken away, lose an eye or hand, or even be put to death, depending on their crime. Nevertheless, the laws proved to be very effective.

In fact, Roman law, in the form of the Justinian Code, was so effective that the founders of the United States as well as the peoples of many nations in Europe and Latin America chose to use it as the model for their legal systems.

▲ *Mosaics like these from 547 give us some idea of how the Byzantine emperor Justinian and his empress Theodora actually looked. These mosaics were found in Ravenna, Italy.*

▼ *The wealth that could be found in Constantinople is seen in the chalice, or cup, and bracelets from the city. Gold and jewels combine to create all three items. Note the mosaics of religious figures on the chalice.*

43

Conserving Mosaics

Mosaic art once covered floors and walls in the ancient Roman and Byzantine empires. Today conservators in museums work to make sure the mosaics that survive can still be enjoyed.

Solvent—special chemicals sometimes used to dissolve dirt

Animals of the Nile, a mosaic from Pompeii, c. first century B.C.

Fine-art jigsaw puzzle is one way to describe a mosaic. Mosaics are made of little bits of colored glass, tile, or stone set into plaster. Over time, the pieces may come loose. To repair mosaics, conservators first cover the pieces with cloth and glue to keep them in place. Then they fix the plaster.

Palette knife—used to work with tiny pieces of mosaic

Spatula—used to separate the mosaic from the wall or floor

Sponge—used to apply water or solvent to the mosaic

Some mosaics get flipped over on their faces so that conservators can clean and repair the backs. After repairs, mosaics can be returned to where they were, or moved to museums for display.

A New Empire

Justinian also considered it his duty to recover Roman lands in the West that had been lost, as he said, "through indolence [laziness]." From 533 to his death in 565, Justinian's armies did regain parts of Spain, all of Italy, and North Africa. But, after his death, some lands were lost again to outsiders. What's more, battling over these lands distracted the Byzantine military and distracted it from another more serious enemy, the Persians. ■

▲ *This is a view of the interior of Hagia Sophia.*

The Persian Threat

Although barbarian tribes ultimately regained some lands in the West, the Persians were a greater threat to the Byzantine Empire. The Persians most closely matched the Byzantines in strength. They were also committed to battling the Byzantines for control of Armenia as well as to regaining control of Turkey, Syria, and Egypt. For 500 years, the Persians and Byzantines fought, but neither ever won an advantage for long.

In the early 600s, the Persians made their move. In a campaign lasting 17 years, they conquered part of Mesopotamia, occupied Asia Minor, and finally took Syria, Jerusalem, and Egypt.

This victory was short-lived. In 627, Byzantine Emperor Heraclius *(hehr uh KLY uhs)* defeated the Persian army. The Persians had to give up all the land they had recently won.

Until 1453, the Byzantine Empire was an important center of **commerce,** or trade, and culture. But constant warfare had weakened both empires. The Persians, in particular, soon had trouble mustering the strength to fight off new invaders. ■

■ *What distinctive elements of Byzantine culture developed under Justinian's rule?*

◄ *This cameo shows a Persian ruler taking a Roman emperor prisoner.*

■ *How did the constant battling between Byzantium and Persia affect the two empires?*

R E V I E W

1. **FOCUS** What were some of the accomplishments of the Byzantine Empire?
2. **CONNECT** In what ways was Constantinople like Rome? How was it different?
3. **HISTORY** How has the Justinian Code affected the modern world?
4. **GEOGRAPHY** How did Constantinople's location affect the city's development?
5. **CRITICAL THINKING** Why do you think two countries might battle for centuries over control of a certain territory? What are some of the things people fight about today?
6. **ACTIVITY** Imagine that you have been asked to help revise the laws in your town. In small groups, make a list of laws in existence that you think ought to be changed. Revise each law on your list. Then as a class, vote on the laws to determine which should be added to your legal system.

Chapter Review

Reviewing Key Terms

barbarian (p. 29)   mosaic (p. 43)
commerce (p. 45)   province (p. 27)
dynasty (p. 32)

In each pair of sentences below there are two meanings for one key term. The key term in the first sentence has a different meaning than it does in the second sentence. Explain which sentence describes the key term's meaning as used in this chapter.

1. a. Making laws was the *province* of the Roman emperor.
    b. The captain was assigned to a far-off *province*.
2. a. Caravans kept *commerce* strong.
    b. The Persians and the Indians carried on a vast *commerce* of ideas.
3. a. A family that discovered oil could start a financial *dynasty* in the modern-day Middle East.
    b. Henry Pu-yi was the last ruler of the Manchu *Dynasty*.
4. a. Justinian did not include the *Mosaic* law of the Hebrews in his code.
    b. A popular subject of early *mosaics* was Mary with the Christ child.
5. a. The Greens showed they were *barbarians* by burning and looting.
    b. Marcus knew by the strangers' language that they were *barbarians*.

Exploring Concepts

A. Complete the paragraph by writing in each blank an accomplishment of an early civilization. Two have been completed for you.

Historians and other scholars still study the accomplishments of ancient civilizations. Romans are remembered for the *peace they maintained in their provinces* by allowing people there to live as usual but under Roman law. They are also known for the ___2___ that they built. The Persians are known for the ___3___ they carried on, which enriched their culture. They encouraged trade by establishing a ___4___. Mathematicians today can be grateful to Indians for developing the ___5___. And readers still admire the *poems and folk tales by early Indian writers*. Even today, the Chinese are known in religious art circles for their ___7___, and in commercial circles for their ___8___ trade. The Byzantine Empire influenced modern law with its ___9___ and modern artists with its ___10___.

B. Support each statement with facts and details from the chapter.
1. Rome benefited from having Egypt as a province.
2. Barbarian invasions helped to cause the fall of the Roman Empire.
3. The economies of both India and Persia benefited from safe roads.
4. The Persian navy had the Greeks to thank.
5. Indians made religious and mathematical contributions to other cultures.
6. Law played a key part in the governments of the Roman Empire and the Byzantine Empire.
7. Constantine and Justinian accomplished some similar things during their reigns.
8. The Persians were a greater threat to the Byzantine Empire and weakened it more than the barbarians.
9. Julius Caesar's adopted son, Octavian, was a successful ruler when he took over Rome after his father's assassination.

Using Critical Thinking

1. Many ancient cultures have contributed nuggets of wisdom that sound strangely familiar even today. For example, in the first century a.d., a Roman named Pubilius Syrus wrote the following sayings:
   a. The loss that is unknown is no loss at all.
   b. While we stop to think, we often miss our opportunity.
   c. For a good cause, wrongdoing is virtuous.
   d. When fortune is on our side, popular favor bears her company.
   e. It is a consolation to the wretched to have companions in misery.
   f. Practice is the best of all instructors.
   All of these sayings have counterparts in our language today. List the present-day sayings with similar meanings.
2. Perhaps the Romans should have considered the following Chinese proverb from the fifth century B.C. before they expanded their empire: "To go beyond is as wrong as to fall short." Support this statement with an example from your own life or one from current events. Explain your answer.
3. Read a story from or about India from this century. You might choose one by Rudyard Kipling or Rumer Godden, for example. Do you see any similarities between the story and the literature in Lesson 2? What does the story you chose tell you about Indian beliefs, customs, or way of life?
4. Imagine that the towns in your county cannot agree on where the county seat of government should be located. In order to be selected as the "capital" of the county, your town must prove that it has enough important qualities to merit this honor. Write a one-page report boasting about the strengths of your town that will win it the county seat.

Preparing for Citizenship

1. **COLLECTING INFORMATION** The land that was once known as Persia is called Iran today. Look through newspapers and magazines for stories that answer the following questions about the country of Iran: Is the area still a center of trade? Do the people who live there still borrow ideas from other cultures? What is life like in Iran today? Collect everyone's stories and display them on a bulletin board under headings such as "Persia Yesterday, Iran Today," "Trade in Iran Today," or "Iran and Its Neighbors."
2. **ARTS ACTIVITY** Create a three-dimensional mosaic design that is at least six inches wide and eight inches long. You may use colored cellophane, paper, clay, stones, or other materials to develop a mosaic picture. Your creation could show a person from an ancient civilization, a battle, or just an interesting pattern. As you design and create your mosaic, think about the talent, materials, effort, and imagination that ancient people put into their colorful and often large-scale mosaic pieces. Imagine how much time it took to cover an entire wall or floor in a mosaic pattern.
3. **WRITING ACTIVITY** Write a short, humorous dialogue that takes place between a hostile barbarian armed with a knife and a Roman official. The barbarian fears the conquering Huns and wants to take refuge in the empire. The Roman official is not so sure about the idea and insists on filling out certain paperwork before permitting the barbarian to cross the border. Use what you know about immigration and other government procedures today to write the scene.
4. **COLLABORATIVE LEARNING** As a class project, create a multi-cultural display entitled "Cultural Contributions of the Ancient World." Divide into groups of four and have each member choose one of the following ancient civilizations to research: Rome, Greece, India, or China. Write down as many contributions as you can think of for the civilization you have chosen.

Unit 2
The Growth of Islam

Covered in silver and gold, the walls of the house of worship shimmer in the light. The people turn toward the niche in the wall that tells them they are facing Mecca, their holy city. They pray. These Muslims are carrying on a religious tradition that dates to the A.D. 600s. That was when Arabian peoples united behind a prophet named Muhammad and the Islamic faith began. During the next 800 years, the Islamic Empire grew to rule lands stretching from the Near East to western Europe.

500

Shiite Muslims at prayer, Mashad, Iran. Photograph by Roger Wood

1492

Chapter 3

The Roots of Islam

They lived as desert wanderers, these Arab traders. By about 1000 B.C., their camel caravans were already crossing the desert and grasslands of the Arabian Peninsula. For centuries after that—even as cities grew—most Arab family groups traveled the vast, dry land. Widely separated from each other, these groups developed different beliefs and worshiped different gods. Then, during the A.D. 600s, a religious leader named Muhammad brought them together. His new faith helped turn this land of wanderers into a mighty empire.

Dried fruits, vital for long desert treks, became important trade goods.

500s In the scorching, dry lands of Arabia (above right), Mecca, with its fresh-water well, grows as the most important stop along Arab trade routes.

500	540	580

c. 550 Japanese rulers allow their subjects to practice the Buddhist faith.

500

Muhammad died in 632, but his beliefs lived on. In the painting at the right, followers of the prophet read from the Koran in Mecca. In the background is the Muslim holy building, called the Kaaba.

610 Muhammad begins preaching. Followers later collect his teachings in a book called the Koran. They glorify their holy book with fine works like this Koran stand (above). Even today young believers study the Koran (top).

620

660

700

687 In Europe, Pepin II unites the Franks and rules until 714.

661

LESSON 1

Desert Bloom— Caravan Cities

THINKING FOCUS

What was life in Arabia like in A.D. 500?

Key Terms

- oasis
- nomad
- tribe
- idol
- bazaar
- pilgrimage

▼ *Bedouin lifestyle has changed little since A.D. 500.*

Imagine being a Bedouin in an Arabian desert camp in A.D. 500. In the final hours before dawn, you are keeping guard over the camp, looking out for raiders. Finally in the east, the blood-red sun begins to rise over the dunes. People begin to stir in their tents. Slowly the camp comes to life. The women build fires in front of the tents, using chunks of dried camel dung. Blue smoke drifts into the warming air.

After a breakfast of dates, milk, and bread, you help the others in the camp strap their belongings onto the backs of kneeling camels. The leader of your group climbs into the tasseled saddle of his riding camel. It is time to go. The others line up their camels, now groaning with their burdens.

You begin the day-long journey across the blistering sands. The sun climbs higher, heating the air to over 110°F. After midday, the wind picks up to 60 miles an hour, creating a blinding sandstorm. The camel train stops, and you cover up in a long robe as protection from the stinging grains of sand. After an hour the wind dies down. You shake off the sand and dust and ride on.

As the evening sun begins to set, you glimpse palm trees and high mud walls, enclosing a weathered town. There your group will trade its camel milk and meat for grain, dates, utensils, and weapons. As the sun descends behind the city, you thank your family's god for a safe passage through the desert.

The First Arabs

Although almost completely surrounded by water, the peninsula of Arabia is one of the driest regions of the world. Most of its interior is made up of barren, sandy desert and sparse, rocky, sun-scorched grasslands.

A Desert Oasis

An **oasis** is a small area watered by springs and wells—a welcome relief from desert dryness. Oases dot Arabia's interior. The oases were the only source of life-giving water and green pasture for the camel herds. The herding families moved routinely from one oasis to the next, seeking pasture for the camels to graze.

Lacking a permanent home, these **nomads,** or wanderers, called themselves Arabs. But some nomads eventually settled down in the oases to live as farmers.

The oases also served as trading centers. Among items traded were dates from trees, which also provided shade for oasis dwellers. Nomads brought camel products such as meat and milk. Traders came from long distances to tempt the people of the oases with luxuries such as perfume and jewelry. For A Closer Look at camels and their role in trading, see page 54.

Families of Nomads

In order to survive in their desert environment, nomads lived together in close family groups. Each family could trace its descent from a common ancestor.

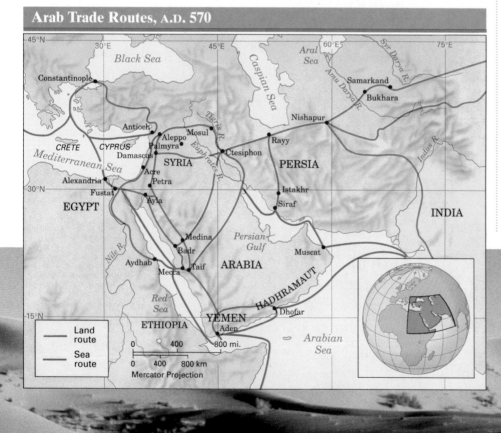

Arab Trade Routes, A.D. 570

◄ Early trade routes connected Arabia to Europe and Asia by both land and sea. What were the advantages of traveling by sea? What were the advantages of land travel?

A Caravan Camel

4:21 A.M., June 11, A.D. 516
Desert just north of Mecca

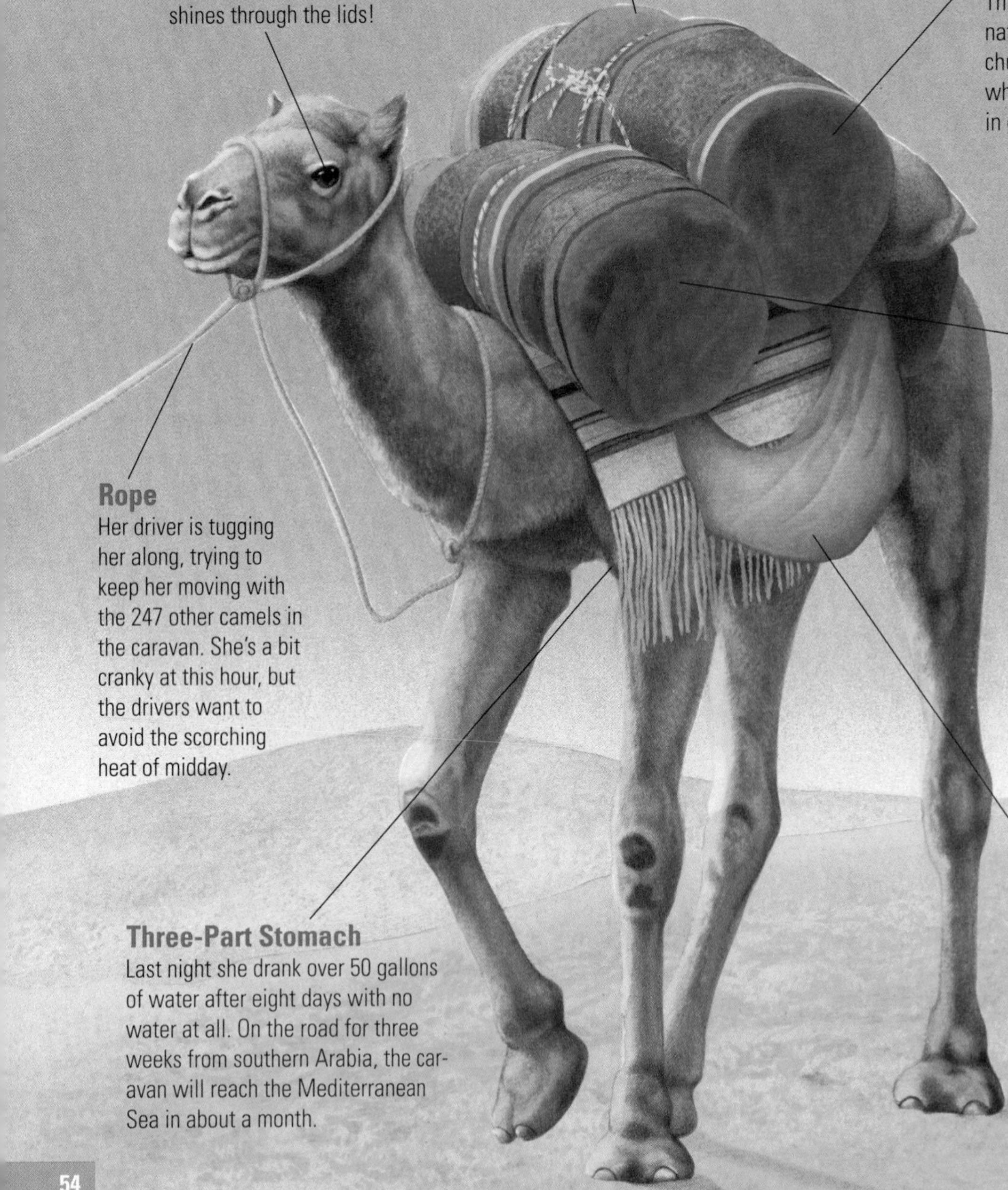

Hump
Her hump stores fat, not water. By the time she returns from this long journey, it will be almost gone. Her arched back carries a tremendous load, making desert trade possible.

Eyelids
During a sandstorm, she can close her eyes and still see, because light shines through the lids!

Frankincense
This sticky sap from a bush native to Arabia is headed for churches in Constantinople, where its strong fragrance is in great demand.

Rope
Her driver is tugging her along, trying to keep her moving with the 247 other camels in the caravan. She's a bit cranky at this hour, but the drivers want to avoid the scorching heat of midday.

Gems
Blood-red rubies and glistening pearls from India will fetch a good price in the market. The trader in charge of the caravan will spend some of his gold on a bolt of shimmering Chinese silk.

Three-Part Stomach
Last night she drank over 50 gallons of water after eight days with no water at all. On the road for three weeks from southern Arabia, the caravan will reach the Mediterranean Sea in about a month.

Salt
Almost as valuable as gold, it's given to tribes along the way to ensure safe passage.

The women prepared the meals and cared for the children. The men tended the animals and guarded against raiders. Because many vital resources were so scarce, families sometimes raided trade caravans or other camps.

To protect themselves from raiders, many families joined together to form **tribes.** Each tribe was headed by a respected member called a sheik. With the help of family leaders, he settled family and tribal disputes.

Each tribe worshiped its own gods, such as a moon or star god. Tribes would carry special **idols,** or sacred images of their gods. The nomads believed that most natural objects, such as the sands, were moved by spirits.

Among the people of the desert in A.D. 500 were settlements of both Jews and Christians. Jews were numerous in the oases of the northwest. Christians lived in the north, east, and south of Arabia.

Because water and grazing land were so scarce, occasionally feuds would break out between nomad tribes over grazing or water rights. Larger tribes sometimes forced smaller tribes to pay to use the oases. For a price, they also protected traders' caravans from raids by hostile nomads.

The families and tribes learned to work out agreements and expand their exchange of goods and information at these watering holes. This increase in trade allowed more people to settle permanently in mud huts near the oases. These permanent dwellings in the desert became the first Arabian towns. ■

■ *Describe the lifestyle of the camel-traveling nomads and how it developed.*

Towns in the Desert

Caravan trade routes, shown in the map on page 53, stretched from one shore to the other of the Arabian peninsula. Traders on these routes carried goods to and from other parts of the world. Ancient trade routes through Arabia linked the Mediterranean world with the East.

As early as 300 B.C., Arabian towns along these caravan routes bloomed into major trading centers. Eventually, trade extended into Persia, Syria, Egypt, and even India and China.

Petra

Petra, in the northwest corner of the peninsula, was a typical caravan trading city. As early as 300 B.C., travelers went to Petra for its abundant spring water.

Petra became the marketplace where wheat, olive oil, wine, hides, slaves, precious stones, and spices

◄ *The treasury building of Petra is built in the mountainside. Arabs once shot at the urn at the top of the treasury. Legend says that one shot in the right location would spill forth all the gold that an Egyptian pharaoh stored there years before.*

The Roots of Islam

➤ *Many shops line the walkway through this modern-day bazaar in Palmyra. This covered bazaar is much like those that existed 1,500 years ago in Arabia.*

■ *How did large trading centers develop in the desert?*

could be found. Petra, which means "rock" in Greek, had many buildings carved out of rock.

The Bazaar

Next to a well, perhaps the most important part of an Arabian city was its **bazaar,** a large open-air market. In hundreds of small shops and stalls, merchants sold local products such as hides, as well as goods from faraway lands.

The bazaar was stocked with brass bowls, finely woven rugs and clothing, gold and silver jewelry, and medical potions. The air of the bazaar was filled with the odors of spices, fish, and incense. There were shouts of shopkeepers trying to attract customers to their stalls. ■

The Holy City of Mecca

By A.D. 500, the city of Mecca was one of the most important stops along the Arabian caravan routes. Mecca lay in the central western section of Arabia in a desert valley surrounded by mountains. A fresh water well there had attracted desert dwellers to Mecca since before A.D. 100.

A Bustling Trade Center

Mecca grew up at the crossroads of two heavily traveled long-distance trade routes. Locate it on the trade routes map, page 53.

In the A.D. 400s, the Quraysh (*KUH rysh*), a local tribe, was eager to increase Mecca's trade traffic. The Quraysh made treaties with people in neighboring areas to ensure the safe passage of the trade caravans through the robber-infested desert. The Quraysh also sponsored their own trade caravans. By the late 500s, Mecca had become the most prosperous trade center in Arabia.

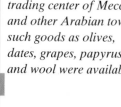

➤ *At bazaars in the trading center of Mecca and other Arabian towns, such goods as olives, dates, grapes, papyrus, and wool were available.*

A Sacred Meeting Place

Mecca was also an important religious center. Arabs from all corners of the peninsula came to Mecca to worship their gods.

Centuries before the Quraysh settled in Mecca, local tribes came to Mecca to worship. For safekeeping, some tribes enclosed idols of their gods in a cube-shaped shrine. They called the shrine the *Kaaba (KAH buh),* which means cube in Arabic. Legends from Mecca indicate that the prophet Abraham built the Kaaba about 2000 B.C.

Worshipers honored the Kaaba and the gods in it by performing religious rituals. For example, they walked around the Kaaba seven times and kissed a black stone embedded in its corner. The stone was said to have been a gift to the prophet Abraham from the angel Gabriel, in recognition of Abraham's belief in only one god. However, inside the Kaaba were stones, statues, and even some Christian pictures, for both Christians and Jews also visited Mecca. By A.D. 500, more than 360 idols of the gods of various tribes were housed within the Kaaba.

The Quraysh encouraged more tribes to deposit their idols there and promised to protect them for a fee. They also prohibited fighting in Mecca near the Kaaba.

During four months of each year, the Quraysh forbade fighting and raiding along the trade routes. With the threat of attack gone, merchants and others could peacefully make their **pilgrimages,** or journeys to sacred places. More and more pilgrims flocked to Mecca. The Quraysh demanded payment from the travelers for the right to worship and trade there.

As the Quraysh in Mecca grew richer from both trade and pilgrimages, their personal values began to change. In the search for greater wealth, many of the Quraysh began to break the tradition of favoring their own kinsmen. They formed business partnerships with members of other families and tribes. This caused hostility and led to feuds between families. ■

⬆ *The city of Mecca was a prosperous trade center and an excellent source for fresh well water. Most important, it was the location of the Kaaba, which for centuries had held religious symbols of different tribes.*

■ *How was Mecca different from other Arab trading cities?*

R E V I E W

1. **FOCUS** What was life in Arabia like in A.D. 500?
2. **CONNECT** What contact did the Arabs make with peoples beyond Arabia?
3. **GEOGRAPHY** Why did families and tribes living in the Arabian desert in the A.D. 500s often fight each other?
4. **BELIEF SYSTEMS** Describe the religious beliefs of the camel-herding nomads.
5. **CRITICAL THINKING** Do you think Arabian trade would have been possible without the camel? Why?
6. **ACTIVITY** Use a modern map of the Arabian Peninsula to list the countries now within this region.

The Roots of Islam

500 540 580 610 650 660 700

L E S S O N 2

Muhammad and Islam

THINKING FOCUS

Find details to support the statement, "Islam is not only a system of beliefs but also a way of life."

Key Terms

- Koran
- monotheism
- Islam
- Muslim
- mosque
- Sunna

Each year, a Meccan trader named Muhammad would spend a month in quiet thought while inside a desert cave. In the year A.D. 610, something extraordinary occurred. The **Koran,** believed by Muhammad's followers to be the written record of God's words, retells that event.

Muhammad was awakened one night by a thunderous voice that seemed to come from everywhere, saying:

> *Recite: In the Name of thy Lord who created, created Man of a blood-clot.*
> *Recite: And thy Lord is the Most Generous, who taught by the Pen, taught man that he knew not.*
>
> Koran, 96:1

Dazed, Muhammad walked to the entrance of the cave. Where was the voice coming from? Suddenly, he thought he heard the voice again: "You are the Messenger of God, and I am the angel Gabriel."

Muhammad looked up. On the horizon he believed he saw an enormous ghostly figure fading away. Muhammad thought he was possessed by a demon. He rushed home to tell his wife Khadija *(kah DEE juh)* what had happened. Alarmed, Khadija consulted a neighbor known for his holiness. He concluded that Muhammad's being chosen as a prophet by Allah was similar to the experiences of the prophets Abraham and Moses.

This news filled Muhammad with awe and fear. At first he did not believe it. But he continued to have similar experiences. Many people would come to believe that Muhammad was a "Messenger of God."

➤ The words beneath this image say, "And among them [was] Gabriel." In Judaism, Christianity, and Islam, Gabriel was thought to be God's messenger to people on earth.

The Life of the Prophet

Muhammad was born into the Quraysh tribe around A.D. 570. Orphaned at an early age, he found work in the caravan trade. At 25, he married a wealthy widow in the trading business. This wealth gave him the freedom to visit Mount Hira each year to think.

On one of these visits in 610, Muhammad is believed by his followers to have had a vision of Gabriel. The angel told him to recite in the name of God. Followers of Muhammad believe the angel then told Muhammad the first of many messages from God.

Muhammad's followers believe that in another vision, the angel Gabriel took Muhammad to meet Abraham, Moses, and Jesus in Jerusalem. From Jerusalem, both Muhammad and Gabriel ascended into heaven, where Muhammad spoke to God.

Inspired by these visions, Muhammad came to believe in **monotheism,** the belief in only one God. The God he believed in was the same God of other monotheistic religions of his time—Judaism and Christianity. Muhammad called his god *Allah,* Arabic for The God.

Spreading the Word

Muhammad, convinced that he was Allah's messenger, began to preach in Mecca. He told people there was only one God. He stressed that all believers were equal in the eyes of Allah. He urged the rich to share with the poor. By 620, Muhammad only had about 100 followers.

Other Meccans resented Muhammad's message. They did not like the way he spoke against the local gods and idols. Muhammad criticized the way the wealthy merchants took advantage of the poor. When Muhammad began to convert some powerful families, many Meccans became hostile.

▲ *On his night journeys to visit Allah, Muhammad was believed to have ascended into heaven. He rode a fabulous creature named Buraq that had a woman's face, a mule's body, and a peacock's tail.*

▼ *This monumental building, the Dome of the Rock, was completed by the Muslims in 691. The rock is believed to be the place from which Muhammad ascended into heaven on his night flights.*

➤ *This sentence in calligraphy states the following message from the Koran: "The Holy Prophet has said, 'The quest of knowledge is obligatory for every Muslim.'" The calligraphy below spells out* Allah *in Arabic.*

How Do We Know?

HISTORY *Many details about Muhammad's early life are uncertain and are known only through stories or legends that have grown about him.*

Family leaders refused to trade with Muhammad's followers. Some Meccans even plotted to kill them.

In 622, fearing for their lives, Muhammad and his followers fled to Medina, an oasis city about 200 miles north of Mecca. This flight to Medina, known as the Hegira *(hih JY ruh)*, marks the beginning of the religion of Muhammad and his followers. Muhammad called the new faith **Islam,** which means "submission" to Allah. Believers in Islam are called **Muslims—** "those who submit to Allah's will."

Returning to Mecca

The Jews and Arabs of Medina welcomed Muhammad and his followers. Their city was on the verge of civil war, and they hoped that Muhammad could unite them. Muhammad hoped that Islam would be accepted by all the people of Medina. Muhammad tried to appeal to the Jews. He first chose their holy city of Jerusalem as the direction that all Muslims should face when praying. Muhammad accepted Abraham, Moses, and Jesus as prophets of God. However, some Jewish leaders would not accept Muhammad as God's latest prophet. Unable to unite the people of Medina, Muhammad expelled from the city the Jews who opposed him. From that day on, Muhammad commanded Muslims to face the Kaaba in Mecca rather than Jerusalem when praying.

With Medina now under Muslim control, Muhammad set about conquering his enemies at Mecca. For eight years, Muhammad's small forces fought the larger Meccan forces. Eventually, many Arab nomadic tribes and leading Meccans joined the Muslim cause. With their support, Muhammad was able to put together an army of more than 10,000. In 630, Muhammad and this army took over Mecca.

One of the first things Muhammad did after his conquest of Mecca was to destroy the tribal idols inside the Kaaba. From that time on, the Kaaba would be empty of all idols. Instead, the Kaaba was dedicated to the one God and became the central shrine of Islam. The black stone, believed to be a gift from God to Abraham, remained embedded in the corner of the Kaaba. The area around the Kaaba became the first **mosque,** or Muslim house of worship.

After destroying the idols, Muhammad ordered one of his men to climb to the top of the Kaaba. He called all of the faithful to come pray to the one true God.

Muhammad appointed a Muslim governor in Mecca, and then returned to his stronghold in Medina to plan his next battle against tribal groups elsewhere in Arabia. By the time of his death in 632, Muhammad's powerful armies had conquered the central and west coastal regions of Arabia. ■

■ How was the religion of Islam founded, and how did it spread?

The Teachings of Islam

Muslims believe that Allah's will is expressed in the Koran. After Muhammad took over the city of Medina, he began to establish an Islamic community with unique customs. When he died, his companions compiled the **Sunna,** or customs and traditions, for Islam.

The Koran

Muhammad's revelations occurred from 610 until his death in 632. Although he left no written record of his experiences, his followers remembered his words. In 633, Muhammad's chief clerk began to gather the revelations into one collection, the Koran.

For the followers of Islam, the Koran completes the earlier revelations of Old Testament prophets and Jesus. The Koran is the final revelation, just as Muhammad is the final prophet.

Islam has close ties to Judaism and Christianity. Many prophets and holy people who are important figures in the

Across Time & Space

Muslims believe the Koran is best read in Arabic, the language in which it was given to Muhammad. Muslims believe that much of the meaning of Allah's words is lost in translation.

▼ *Called to prayer from the minaret (1), Muslims enter the doorway (2), and wash in the ablution fountain (3). They pray under the portico (4), while facing the mihrab prayer niche (5), and listen to an address from the pulpit (6). The minaret and the pulpit are shown in the photograph at the left.*

The Roots of Islam

Bible are also described in the Koran. For example, Abraham is thought to be the father of Jews through his son Isaac. Abraham is also considered to be the father of Arabs through his other son Ishmael.

According to Muslim belief, Jews and Christians are "people of the book." Their holy book, the Bible, is considered by Muslims to be an earlier and incomplete version of God's words. Because of this, Muslims believed that it was wrong to compel Jews and Christians to convert to Islam. But Muslims considered these other religions to be less correct.

The Arabic word *Koran* can be loosely translated as "recitation." In fact, the very first word the angel Gabriel spoke to Muhammad was "Recite." By reciting aloud, many Muslims memorize as much of the Koran as they can.

▼ *All Muslims in good health and with enough money must make a pilgrimage to Mecca once in their lifetime. The people camp outside the Great Mosque in tent cities that protect them from the burning sun.*

The Sunna

The Sunna were the guiding rules for Islam and were based on the way the prophet Muhammad lived his own life. The most basic of these rules were the Five Pillars of Islam. The ideas behind these five duties came from the Koran, but it was in the Sunna that the leaders of Islam set them down.

The first of these pillars is the profession of faith. To express their acceptance of Islam, Muslims repeat the phrase, "There is no god but Allah, and Muhammad is his prophet."

The second pillar is prayer. Muslims must pray five times a day. Prayers follow special rituals, including washing before praying, bowing, and then kneeling while praying. Muslims must always face Mecca when praying. Every Friday at noon, Muslims assemble for public prayer in a mosque.

The third pillar is giving alms, or showing charity to the poor. Muslims must also contribute to public charities, such as the building of mosques and hospitals.

The fourth pillar is the ritual fast during Ramadan, the ninth month of the Muslim year. Ramadan is a holy time, because in this month Muhammad received

his first message from Allah. During Ramadan, Muslims must not eat or drink from the break of dawn until the setting of the sun. Muslims believe that this rigorous fast brings them closer to Allah.

The fifth pillar of Islam is Haji—the pilgrimage to Mecca. All Muslims must make the pilgrimage at least once in their lifetime. The pilgrimage involves elaborate rites that take place over many days. Before arriving at Mecca, the pilgrims bathe, cut their hair and nails, and take off jewelry. They then put on a white seamless garment, symbolizing a state of purity. Because Muslims from all over the world go on these pilgrimages, Haji is a symbol of Muslim unity. ■

Pilgrims circle the Kaaba in the Great Mosque in Mecca. The heavy black covering that protects the shrine is replaced each year. The cloth covers a single doorway that leads into a room inside the Kaaba, believed to hold Allah's spirit.

■ *Why are the Koran and Sunna important to Muslims?*

Islam as a Way of Life

The Five Pillars tell Muslims the specific rituals they must follow in order to be good Muslims. But the Koran and the Sunna cover many additional moral standards that a Muslim must live by in his or her everyday life. The Koran and the Sunna cover diet, marriage, divorce, business contracts, and even the proper way to clean one's teeth. Muslims are forbidden to eat certain foods such as pork, to drink alcohol, to smoke cigarettes, or to gamble. As in most religions, murder and theft are prohibited.

One of the acts the Sunna calls for is jihad. This term itself means "struggle," to do one's best to resist temptation and overcome evil.

63

In some especially religious villages in Islamic countries, women still wear the veil and carry prayer beads. However, in large cities it is not unusual to see women with their faces uncovered.

■ *How does Islam affect many aspects of daily life for Muslims?*

In time, that personal internal struggle also became an external struggle, as Islam expanded its territories and converted many nonbelievers. Islamic wars against those nonbelievers were often called jihad.

The Sunna also sets guidelines for the treatment of women. In pre-Islamic Arabia, women had very few individual rights and freedoms. The Sunna, which was a written record of the traditions and customs that were followed by Muhammad, stressed that women should be considered individuals with rights of their own. Women were granted the right to hold property in their own name and to inherit part of their father's estate, which they had not been able to do before Muhammad.

In many countries where the population is mostly Islamic, women are taking a greater role for themselves outside of the home. They are becoming involved in their societies. Today, Muslims live in many different parts of the world. The role a Muslim woman fills is more a reflection of the customs of the individual country in which she lives than an indication of how all of Islam treats women.

Islam does influence the everyday lives of Muslims, from birth to death. Parents chant the profession of faith over each newborn baby. Children use the Koran to learn to read and write.

Many Muslims carry prayer beads that they use during free moments of the day as they think of Allah. There are as many as 99 names for Allah, all of which describe what God is like. These include such words as *creator* and *protector.* Islamic prayer beads have either 99 or 33 beads, so that Muslims can count off God's names in order to enter paradise. When someone is about to die, the Koran is recited at the person's bedside. Islam is not just a religion—it is a way of life. ■

R E V I E W

1. **FOCUS** Find details to support the statement, "Islam is not only a system of beliefs but also a way of life."
2. **CONNECT** In what ways is Islam similar to Judaism and Christianity?
3. **SOCIAL SYSTEMS** How did Islam affect the rights and status of women?
4. **CRITICAL THINKING** Why do you think Christians and Jews did not accept Muhammad as a prophet of God, even though Muhammad accepted the Christian and Jewish prophets?
5. **ACTIVITY** Interview your classmates or use the encyclopedia to find out what these rituals have in common: Yom Kippur (among Jews), Lent (among Christians), and Ramadan (among Muslims).

During this period, Muslims converted the Berbers of North Africa to Islam. In Morocco, Berbers lived in walled villages called casbahs (below). These Berber women (left) are dressed for a market day.

1492 Sultan Muhammad XI surrenders, ending Muslim rule in Spain. His gold ceremonial sword is shown to the right.

1200

1400

1600

c. 1277 Invaders from central Asia conquer China.

1453 The Byzantine Empire falls to the Ottoman Turks.

1492

The Voyage of Sinbad the Sailor

Retold by Geraldine McCaughrean

This tale is from a collection of stories called One Thousand and One Arabian Nights. *The storyteller is a queen who tells her husband a different story every night. As you read, think about her purpose. Does she want to teach, or just to entertain? What do you think her next story will be about?*

From early, pre-Islamic trading days to this period of conquest and rapid expansion, Arabian storytellers wove tales of imaginative adventures. Here is one of them.

A story is carried from Baghdad—though who can tell if it is true?—of a young man called Sinbad the Porter. Sinbad was known at all the local inns for his beautiful singing voice, and he would often sing in return for a coin or a bite to eat. He was summoned one day to a great house built of white and wine-coloured marble on the skirts of the city. An old man was sitting on the vine-covered terrace, and asked him to sing—which he willingly did:

> *Oh I have carried golden treasure*
> *Half across Arabia's sands,*
> *And I have seen the cost of pleasure*
> *Pouring out of rich men's hands.*
> *But do not think of me as rich, sir,*
> *Because I carry treasure chests,*
> *For I count myself much richer*
> *when I lay them down and rest.*
> *I am just a poor young porter—*
> *All my meat is caught from rivers,*
> *All the wines I drink are water—*
> *All I carry, I deliver.*

The song pleased the old man, and he took a great liking to the Porter.

"The pleasure a good song gives can't be paid for with money alone," said the old man. "Let me give you something of mine. I shall give you the story of my life, which is moderately interesting. My name is Sinbad too. But I am Sinbad the Sailor."

I was born the son of a rich father who died and left me a lot of money. Being a particularly clever boy, I made the sensible decision to invest the money. I invested it in drink and expensive food and stylish clothes and in buying myself a lot of friends at the local inn. Before long I found that my investment had left me with hardly a penny. To tell you the truth, I did not want to be poor in my old age.

So I sold everything I owned and bought instead a silk-sailed ship and cargo. I employed a captain, and we set sail for the rest of the world, turning a furrow through the sea as straight and certain as an arrow through a blue sky. I was confident of making my fortune as a merchant.

One day a solitary island came into view from the mast top—two or three trees and a smooth, grey beach the colour of the atolls in the great Western Ocean.

Some of the sailors were tired of the blood swilling in their veins with the motion of the ship, and we took it into our heads to draw alongside the island and walk about on dry land. The captain was sleeping below decks. We did not trouble to wake him: a friendly fire, a baked fish, a short walk, and we would be ready to set off again. Two of the men even brought a laundry barrel from the ship to do their washing in.

Ali lit a fire, and I made a tour of the island, but there was not a lot to recommend it. We were just deciding that no one could live there, without fresh water, when suddenly Abdul caught sight of a fountain—a geyser, rather—at a great distance from us. Its water gushed higher and higher, seemingly to the height of a castle tower, then dropped out of sight.

"I have been aboard ships for too long—the ground still seems to be moving," I said, embarrassed by losing my balance and falling over. Then the captain's voice drifted to us on the wind.

"Aboard! Aboard! Or you are all dead men!"

"The island is sinking!" someone cried.

"The island is moving!" shouted another.

A deep roaring beneath us was followed by a second eruption of water from the geyser. It spouted so high that the spray reached us on the wind and soaked us to the skin in a second.

Amidst the spray, I could just see the captain giving orders for the ship to pull away. The space of water opened between our landing party and the vessel. Some men ran to the water and leapt in. Others shouted at the captain, calling him names or begging him to pull ashore again. Only one or two of his words reached us across the opening gap.

"Whale! . . . Fire has woken the whale . . ."

Well may you hold your head in wonder, friend. We had indeed moored alongside a giant whale, and the fire we had lit on its back had disturbed it out of a sleep centuries long. The sandy

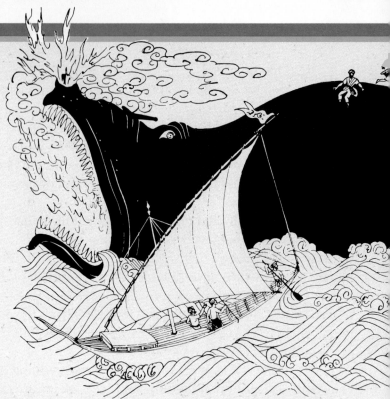

silt of the ocean had washed over the whale, and the winds had
brought seeds and spores and planted its sparse vegetation. But
as it rolled in pain, our fire beginning to burn through its hide
(and making an awful stench), the shallow-rooted trees were
washed away like toothpicks, and the sand swirled round our
knees as we stumbled to and fro. The whale dived.

One sailor was thrown high out of the water by the massive
tail—believe me, friend, those tail-flukes were larger than galleon
sails—and the tail fell on us like the greatest tree in all the gum
forests of Arabia.

To the end of my days I shall weary Allah with my thanks.
The barrel full of my fellow sailors' washing rolled towards me
across the water. I pulled myself across it and floated away, while
my sailor friends swam down with the whale to the kingdom
where only the fish can breathe. Friend, friend, it makes me sweat
salt-water only to think about it.

The ship had long since gone. I was alone on the ocean with
the smell of scorched whale in my nostrils. I began to paddle with
my feet, and my lonely voyage, as you can imagine, was so long
and tiring that I do not remember reaching land.

I woke up beside my barrel on a white beach to find, to my
great surprise, that I was alive. I also found that the fish had eaten
many holes in my feet, and only with pain and difficulty did I
climb the beach and explore.

I saw no one, friend, and nothing. Under the trees the undergrowth was thick—a perfect home for wild animals. Why else
did I climb that tree? But from the topmost branches I could see a
long, long way.

I saw no one, friend, and nothing. In another direction,
however, I glimpsed a shining white dome. Surely it was a fine

mosque at the heart of a spendid city. Its white curve seemed so massive that I was almost afraid to approach.

When I finally reached it, I walked around it five times before I gave up hope of finding a door. Its whiteness was dazzling in the sun. I tried to climb up it, but the white surface was so polished and smooth that I slithered down to the ground again every time. I exhausted myself in the mid-day heat, and that is why I was sitting on the ground in the shade of the white dome when the sun went dark.

I have seen tropical suns set like a single clap of hands. I have seen the moon forget its rightful place and push in front of the sun. But this was no eclipse or sunset.

Looking up, I saw that the sun had been blotted out by the shape of a gigantic bird. Its claws were as large as the tusks of elephants, one toe the thickness of a tree-trunk. Its wings were as huge as my terror, and its feathers as black as my miserable fate. For now I realized that the white dome I was sitting under was nothing other than the bird's unhatched egg. And as slowly and certainly as a ship on a whirlpool is sucked circling down, the huge bird was wheeling down towards me.

Further Reading

Casilda of the Rising Sun. Elizabeth B. deTrevino. Set in 11th-century Spain, this is a romantic story about the daughter of a Moorish king.

The Legend of the Cid. Robert Goldston. The Cid, Rodrigo de Vivar, fought both Moors and Christians in 11th-century Spain.

One Thousand and One Arabian Nights. Retold by Geraldine McCaughrean. More tales of adventure, including several about Sinbad.

LESSON 1

A Century of Expansion

THINKING
FOCUS

How did the Umayyads unite the many lands and peoples of the Islamic Empire?

Key Terms

- empire
- bureaucracy
- emir
- dissent

➤ *The siege, or surrounding of a town, was a major strategy in Islamic warfare. Control of cities was the key to victory. Here Muslims attack mud brick walls with the aid of a catapult.*

M uslim soldiers from Arabia attacked Damascus, Syria, in A.D. 635. Their swords and lances were raised high as they rode their camels through a cloud of dust to the walls of the Byzantine city.

Some soldiers, with their lances, flung small pots of burning oil over the wall, creating smoke and flames that could not be extinguished. Others loaded catapults with rocks to rain down on the Byzantines. By nightfall the battle was won. Damascus was the Muslims'.

Expansion Under Umayyad Rule

The Muslim soldiers who fought the Byzantines at Damascus helped to create an **empire,** a number of countries or territories ruled by one central authority. After capturing Syria, the victorious Muslim armies went on to conquer Mesopotamia in 637.

By the middle of the 600s, Persia fell to the Muslims. The Islamic Empire then expanded farther to the east by securing the lands that

are today known as Afghanistan and Pakistan.

The Umayyads

The Umayyads *(oo MAY yahds)* fought for Islam in these eastern conquests. The Umayyad leader, Muawiya *(mu AH wih ya)*, was one of the soldiers who had helped capture Damascus in 635. He had served for 25 years as the Muslim governor of Syria. During that time, Muawiya had built up a devoted army of followers. After the assassination of the fourth caliph, Muawiya had enough support to take control of the empire in 661.

Umayyad Changes

When Muawiya became caliph, he moved the capital from Muhammad's home, Medina in Arabia, to his own, more central city of Damascus in Syria. From this source of political and military power, Muawiya could better control the growing Umayyad Empire.

While he was caliph, Muawiya began the practice of appointing a son as the next caliph. Thus, Muawiya founded a tradition of a continuous rule by one family. The Umayyads ruled for 90 years.

Westward Expansion

The Umayyads were talented military leaders, and during their years in power, 661 to 750, the Islamic Empire expanded. Their armies advanced west into Africa, converting the Berbers, who lived along the northern coast and the Sahara, to Islam.

In 711, with the help of the Berbers, the Muslims moved northward across the Strait of Gibraltar (juh BRAWL tur). They then began the conquest of present-day Spain and Portugal.

The Muslims were so determined to conquer this new territory that upon landing at Gibraltar, they burned all of their boats. Retreat was not possible. Now they could only march forward. Over the next seven years, the Muslims drove out the Visigoths, who were Christians. Almost the entire peninsula had become Umayyad territory.

From their bases in Spain, Muslim armies repeatedly crossed the Pyrenees (PIHR uh neez) and ventured into France on raids. In 732, the Muslims confronted Charles Martel and his army of Franks. Martel, whose name means "the Hammer," was called that because of his repeated attacks against the Muslims.

Martel's troops stopped the Muslim invasion at the Battle of Tours in 732. This battle was one of the most decisive in history. In effect, the battle determined that Europe would be Christian and not Muslim. Trace the Umayyad conquests and their expansion of the Islamic Empire on the map on page 80. ■

■ *What changes did the Umayyads bring to the Islamic Empire?*

▼ *Buildings in Morocco were often made of dried mud bricks. The same material was used to build walls around Moroccan cities to protect them from enemy attack.*

➤ *Use the map to compare the amount of land Muslims conquered during Muhammad's life and under the first four caliphs with that conquered under the Umayyads. During which time period did the greatest expansion occur?*

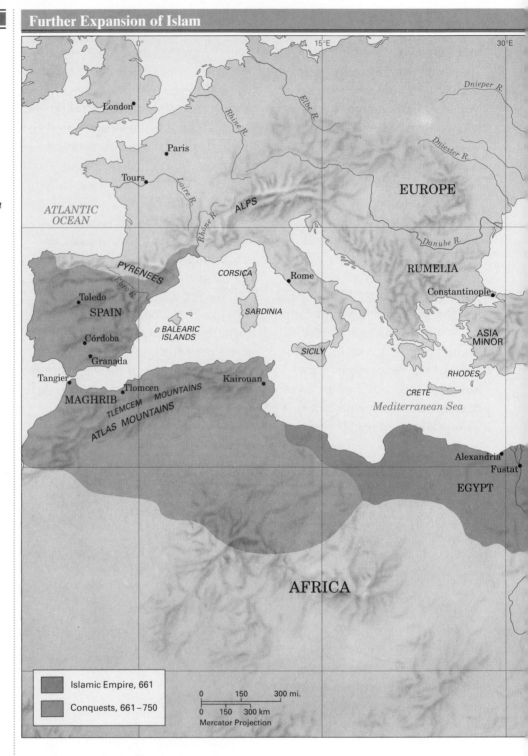

Islamic Empire, 661

Conquests, 661–750

0   150   300 mi.

0   150   300 km

Mercator Projection

An Empire of Many Peoples

As the Muslims conquered new lands, the borders of the Islamic Empire expanded far beyond Arabia. Among the peoples conquered by the Arabs were Christians and Jews. The Arabs also conquered people who had no religion as well as pagans who believed in many different gods.

Treatment of Non-Muslims

The Muslims forced the pagan people to convert to Islam. When these non-Arabs began to convert

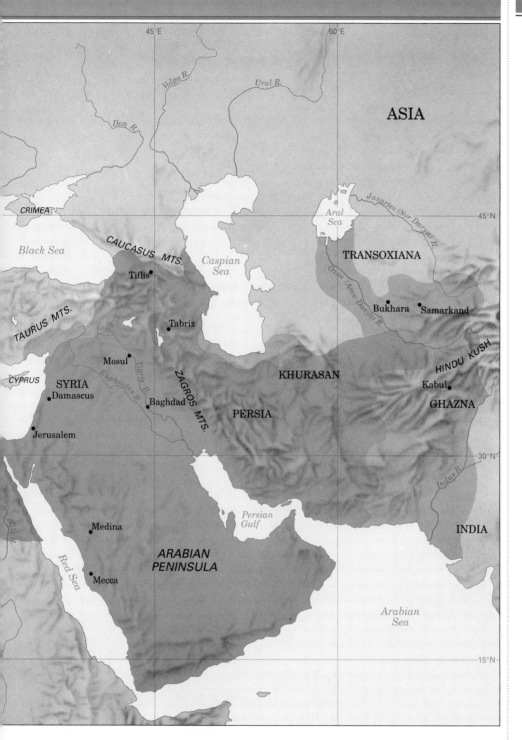

to Islam, they were sometimes not accepted socially by the Arab community. Some Arabs wanted to keep their culture free of outside influences. In time this changed, and an Islamic culture developed that included the customs and traditions of non-Arabs.

The Umayyad Muslims were generally tolerant of people, such as Christians and Jews, who believed in a single God. Muslims considered Jews and Christians to be "people of the book," as they were themselves.

In spite of their general tolerance, the Umayyads established a different system of taxation for non-Muslims. The Christians and the Jews, who did not accept

The Empire of Islam

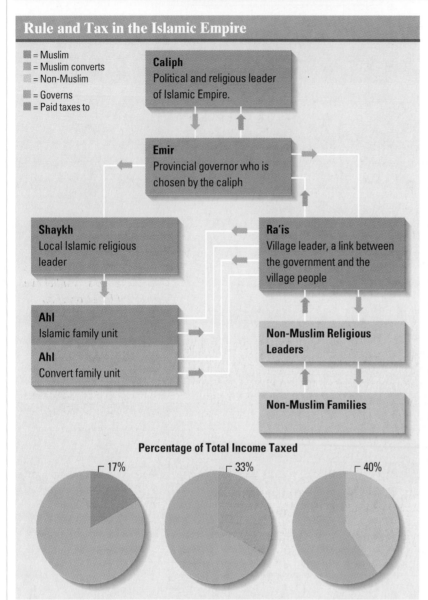

Rule and Tax in the Islamic Empire

- = Muslim
- = Muslim converts
- = Non-Muslim
- = Governs
- = Paid taxes to

Caliph
Political and religious leader of Islamic Empire.

Emir
Provincial governor who is chosen by the caliph

Shaykh
Local Islamic religious leader

Ra'is
Village leader, a link between the government and the village people

Ahl
Islamic family unit

Ahl
Convert family unit

Non-Muslim Religious Leaders

Non-Muslim Families

Percentage of Total Income Taxed

17%   33%   40%

▲ Muslims, converts to Islam, and non-Muslims paid different amounts of taxes and were governed differently in the Islamic villages that made up the empire. Find the different tax rate for each group and decide if the difference is significant.

Muhammad as a prophet of God, had to pay a higher tax. Converts to Islam paid a tax lower than Jews and Christians but higher than those who were Muslims at birth would pay.

The higher tax paid by Christians and Jews was used to help finance the operation of the Muslim army. All Muslim men were required to serve in the army, but non-Muslims did not have to serve. The lower chart above compares the tax paid by Muslims with the taxes paid by converts and "people of the book."

Government

The Umayyad caliph Muawiya successfully ruled over a very diverse empire. He patterned his highly organized government on the Byzantine model that he had first seen when he captured Damascus. He even kept some of the Christians in the same government posts they held in the Byzantine government. This system of rule and order was a **bureaucracy,** consisting of many different departments managed by workers who had been appointed by the caliph or one of his representatives.

Under Muawiya, the provinces were ruled by **emirs,** or governors, appointed directly by the caliph. The caliph was the central authority to whom the emirs reported. Use the upper chart on the left to trace the line of authority that extended from the caliph to the people.

One new emir of Mesopotamia angrily greeted his subjects with this stern warning:

> *I demand obedience from you, and you can demand uprightness from me. . . . Do not be carried away by your hatred and anger against me, it would go ill with you. I see many heads rolling; let each man see that his own head stays upon his shoulders!*
>
> Ziyad Ibn Abihi, c. 670
> (zih YAHD IHBN ah BEE hih)

Muawiya encouraged the emirs to rule this strictly in order to stamp out any **dissent,** or disagreement, among their conquered subjects. ∎

■ How did Muslims treat people of different beliefs?

Umayyad Unity

Under the Umayyad dynasty, there was a succession of one caliph after another. There also developed a new Islamic culture for the Islamic Empire. Abd al Malik (ahb dul mah LIHK), caliph from 685 to 705, was influential in shaping this culture.

A Common Language

Abd al Malik declared Arabic to be the official language of the empire. This enabled the Umayyads to bring the diverse cultures of their empire under control. Until Abd al Malik adopted Arabic as the official language, local government workers had been mostly non-Arabic. They had spoken the languages of their local communities. Now all government business and religious affairs were conducted in Arabic. Anyone who wished to participate fully in the culture had to speak Arabic.

A Common Coinage

Not only was the language the same throughout the empire, but the coins the people used were the same too. Muslims borrowed the idea of coinage from the Persians and the Byzantines. The government began minting Islamic coins around 640.

Abd al Malik was responsible, around 700, for the first pure Islamic coins. They had no images but were inscribed in Arabic with important quotations from the Koran. The coins gave Muslims a symbol of the power of their empire. Having a common coinage also made commerce between parts of the empire easier.

Religious Architecture

One of the first things the Arabs did when they took over a new land was to build a mosque, so they could give thanks to Allah. Muslims throughout the Islamic Empire could always find a mosque. The mosque would be built from materials that were common to the area.

In 688, during the caliphate of Abd al Malik, North Africa was conquered. In North Africa, mosques were made of mud and sticks, because that is what was available for construction. A mosque of this type can be seen on page 116. But the same features that were important to the Islamic religion would be present in every mosque: a minaret, a mihrab, and an ablution fountain. ■

on page 116.

HISTORY *The Koran contains many codes of proper behavior for Muslims: "It belongs not to a believer to slay a believer, except by error. If any slays a believer by error, then let him set free a believing slave, and blood-wit [a fine] is to be paid to his family. . . ." Living by such codes also helped unify the peoples of the empire.*

■ *How did Abd al Malik unify the Umayyad Empire?*

◄ *Islamic coins were inscribed with sayings from the Koran.*

The Empire of Islam

The Umayyad Downfall

The Umayyads conquered many new lands and peoples for Islam. However, by 750, after 90 years of continuous rule, they faced serious economic and political problems.

Many non-Muslim subjects had by this time converted to Islam. After they converted, they paid fewer taxes than they did before they converted. Consequently, as the number of conversions to Islam increased, the amount of tax money available for the empire to spend decreased.

By 732, the Islamic armies were making fewer new conquests. This stopped the flow of captured wealth that had enriched the empire's economy. The decline in tax revenues and the decrease in captured wealth helped contribute to the money shortage the Umayyads experienced. Examine the chart at the left to find how the percentage of the population paying full taxes varied in 727 and 738.

In addition, the Umayyad Empire had gained the reputation of being too much of a worldly kingdom and not interested enough in the religious ideals of the prophet Muhammad. In the last years of the dynasty, the Umayyads' opponents formed secret societies that were devoted to bringing about the downfall of the Umayyads.

One such group, the Abbasids *(AB uh sihdz),* was named after a family headed by al Abbas. Some historians say that al Abbas was an uncle of Muhammad. The Abbasids started a successful rebellion against the Umayyad rulers from their Abbasid stronghold in Persia.

One of the Abbasid generals, Abdullah *(ahb du LAH),* invited 80 Umayyad leaders to a banquet. While his Umayyad guests were eating, Abdullah ordered his men to kill them. By 750, the Abbasid family was able to gain complete control of the Islamic Empire in the East.

Only one of the Umayyads, whose name was Abd al Rahman *(ahb al ra MAHN),* escaped from the Abbasids. He leaped out of a window at Abdullah's deadly dinner, swam across the Euphrates River, and fled in disguise. He wandered all the way across Arabia and Africa and then crossed the Mediterranean Sea into Spain. Once in Spain, Abd al Rahman began to unite the warring Muslim groups there and to build a new Umayyad government.

Now the Islamic Empire was split into two empires. In western Europe the Umayyads held power in Spain, while the Abbasids ruled Arabia and the eastern empire. ■

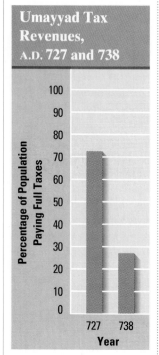

▲ *By approximately what percent did the population that paid full taxes decline between the years 727 and 738?*

■ *What political problems led to the downfall of the Umayyad Empire?*

R E V I E W

1. **FOCUS** How did the Umayyads unite the many lands and peoples of the Islamic Empire?

2. **CONNECT** In what ways did the Umayyads carry out the ideals of Muhammad?

3. **ECONOMICS** What economic problems contributed to the collapse of the Umayyads?

4. **CRITICAL THINKING** Since the Muslims did not necessarily encourage people to convert to Islam, why did they bother expanding their empire?

5. **ACTIVITY** Examine some of the coins of your country. What do the images and inscriptions on the coins tell you about your country?

LESSON 2

The Golden Age

T his island between the Tigris in the east and the Euphrates in the west is a marketplace for the world. All the ships that come up the Tigris will go up and anchor here; wares brought on ships . . . will be . . . unloaded here. It will be the highway for the people. . . .

Praise be to God who preserved it for me and caused all those who came before me to neglect it. . . .

It will surely be the most flourishing city in the world.

Abu Jafur al Mansur, 752

THINKING FOCUS

How did the same wealth that brought the Abbasids power lead to their downfall?

With these words the second Abbasid caliph described his reasons for choosing Baghdad as the new capital of the Islamic Empire. He had made a very wise choice for his capital city.

Baghdad, in Mesopotamia, was ideally located to become a world marketplace. It was situated along ancient trade routes serving both the East and the West. Soon Baghdad, somewhat like an island between the Tigris and Euphrates rivers, grew into a huge city that was the center of trade, learning, and government.

Key Terms

- calligraphy
- faction

Baghdad: A City in the Round

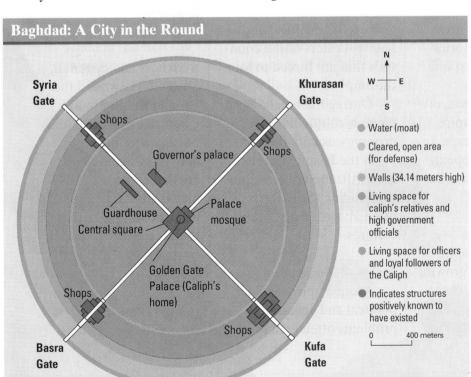

Syria Gate

Khurasan Gate

Shops

Governor's palace

Shops

Guardhouse

Central square

Palace mosque

Golden Gate Palace (Caliph's home)

Shops

Shops

Basra Gate

Kufa Gate

N
W — E
S

- Water (moat)
- Cleared, open area (for defense)
- Walls (34.14 meters high)
- Living space for caliph's relatives and high government officials
- Living space for officers and loyal followers of the Caliph
- Indicates structures positively known to have existed

0   400 meters

◄ *Baghdad was a planned city famous for its beauty and luxury. The caliph's palace was at the center of the city, which was surrounded by three circular walls. Each wall held four gates through which passed roads leading to the four corners of the empire.*

85

The Empire of Islam

To handle this great volume of business, the Muslims developed something very similar to a banking system throughout their empire. There were no bank buildings yet, but business people engaged in giving loans on credit.

Islamic rule unified most of the eastern world. Boundaries were no longer an obstacle. The Muslims introduced a uniform coinage system, which made commerce even easier. Soon brisk international trade brought great wealth to the whole Abbasid Empire and to its rulers.

➤ *This ivory chess piece was presented to Charlemagne, king of the Franks from 768 to 814, by Harum al Rashid, fifth caliph of the Abbasid Empire.*

■ *Why did Baghdad become such an important center of world trade?*

The caliphs and the upper classes grew rich, and they enjoyed spending their money on lavish homes, fine clothing, and elaborate amusements. Horse racing and polo playing were popular activities. People with leisure time could engage in the sport of falconry—training falcons to hunt other birds which the trainer might eat. Wealthy families invited each other to elegant banquets with entertainment by dancers and poets. Many passed their leisure time playing chess and backgammon or gambling by throwing dice. ■

Abbasid Culture

Their great wealth enabled the Abbasids to support the arts and learning. The years from about 800 to around 1000 were a period of high achievement in the areas of art and literature.

➤ *Plaster moldings laced with an intricate leaf design cover the walls and ceilings of this Islamic palace.*

Art and Design

The unique style of Islamic art is unmistakable, because it so often uses Arabic script as its inspiration. Arabic lettering had a special significance for Muslims, because it was used to write down God's words as they had been given to Muhammad. **Calligraphy,** which means beautiful handwriting, flourished under the Abbasids. When used as decoration, the letters were often so fancy that they were almost unreadable. Examples on this and the next page show some of these designs.

Calligraphy and geometric designs, rather than the human form, were common decorations in mosques. The reason Muslims did this was because they were concerned that human images

would distract worshipers from praying to Allah. Some Muslims feared that if they drew images of humans or animals, they would be accused of playing God by trying to create a living thing.

Muslim artists often turned to decorative designs made up of plant patterns. The most common of these floral designs was the arabesque, a winding stem, leaves, and flowers, that formed a spiraling design.

Bookmaking and Literature

In 751, during a raid into central Asia, Abbasids captured some Chinese artisans skilled in paper making. These Chinese prisoners taught their captors the secrets of paper making. In time the skill of paper making spread throughout the Islamic world, making books more available.

The availability of books contributed to the general interest in all types of learning. Caliph al Ma'mum, who ruled from 813 to 833, founded a school in Baghdad called the House of Wisdom. In the school, scholars translated Greek classics in philosophy into Arabic.

The Abbasids later shared these translations with the Umayyads in Spain, who in turn shared them with the Christians in Europe. The Abbasid scholars of Baghdad helped preserve Greek classics that might otherwise have been lost or destroyed.

The Abbasids also became famous for their sensitive poetry:

> *You departed*
> *from my sight*
> *and entered my thoughts,*
> *travelled from my eyes*
> *to my heart.*
>
> Al Abbas Ibn al Ahnaf,
> c. 800

Many poets and writers from far-away flocked to Baghdad, where the caliph welcomed them to his court. ■

Across Time & Space

The craft of paper making was developed in China around 150 B.C. Paper was made by soaking flattened plant fibers and then allowing them to dry on a screen. The first paper making factory in the Islamic Empire was built in Baghdad in A.D. 792.

■ *What achievements in culture led to this period being known as the Golden Age?*

Abbasid Achievements in Learning

The interest in reading also extended to learning about science, mathematics, and medicine. The excellent reputation of Islamic scholars spread across the Islamic Empire into Europe.

Science and Mathematics

Islamic scholars of the Abbasid period were interested in further developing the findings of the ancient Greeks in science, mathematics, and medicine. For example, Islamic astronomers mapped the solar system and believed, long before Columbus's time, that the earth was round.

Modern algebra is based on explorations in mathematics in the early 800s by one of the most famous Abbasid mathematicians, al Khwarizmi *(al KWAH rihz mee)*. Today, we call this type of mathematics *algebra* after the title of one of al Khwarizmi's books, *al jabr*, meaning "the addition of one thing to another."

Medicine

Muslim doctors, who lived during the Abbasid reign, became skilled at diagnosis and treatment of disease. One doctor, ar-Razi, a Persian-born physician of the 900s, wrote the first accurate description of the diseases that we know today as measles and smallpox. Other doctors performed surgery on patients in clean hospitals that were free to the public. At this time, Muslims were also experimenting with the treatment of disease

A window (below) at Princeton University honors Abbasid doctor ar-Razi. Muslims also honored the Greek Aristotle, painted as a Muslim (bottom), for his study of plants, such as coriander, shown at top.

through herbal medicines. Plants, such as coriander, were used for their medicinal powers. One of the leading Abbasid figures of medicine was Ibn Sina, known in Europe as Avicenna *(av ih SEHN uh)*. In his autobiography Avicenna wrote:

> **M**edicine is not one of the difficult sciences, and therefore I excelled in it in a very short time, to the point that distinguished physicians began to read medicine with me. I cared for the sick, and there opened up to me indescribable possibilities of therapy which can only be acquired through experience. At the same time, I was also occupied with jurisprudence and would engage in legal disputations, being now sixteen years of age.
>
> Ibn Sina, c. 1000

In addition to law and medicine, Avicenna had a number of other interests—philosophy, mathematics, and astronomy. He also wrote a vast medical encyclopedia called *Canon of Medicine*. It summed up the medical knowledge of the time and accurately described diseases and treatments.

Interest in treating illness went back to the earliest days of Islamic history. It was the prophet Muhammad himself who stated that Allah had provided a cure for every illness. ■

■ *How was Islamic Baghdad famous as a center of scientific, mathematical, and medical achievements?*

A Divided Empire

The years 800 to 1000 were a golden cultural period for the Abbasid Empire. The end of this period was also a financially difficult time for the government. Tax money was increasingly important to the caliphs because the Abbasids had lost control of several important trade routes. This hurt Baghdad's economy and led the caliphs to increase taxes to support their costly style of living.

Factions and Revolt

During the same period, several **factions,** or opposing groups, began either to leave the empire for other lands or to take control of distant parts of the empire away from the Abbasids. For example, the Fatimids, who were descendants of the Prophet's daughter Fatima, were unhappy about the costly lifestyle of the Abbasids. The Fatimids felt this lifestyle was corrupt compared to the simple lifestyle of Muhammad.

The Fatimids broke away from the Abbasids by the 900s and then migrated into North Africa. By 969, they had conquered most of North Africa and claimed the city of Cairo as their capital.

Seljuk Turks

As groups continued to break away from the weakened Abbasid Empire, it was open to invasion from outside forces. In 1055, Baghdad was conquered by nomadic Turks from Central Asia, who were descended from a warrior named Seljuk.

These Seljuk Turks captured the weak Abbasid caliph, plundered his palace, and took over the government. The Turks allowed the caliph and those who followed him to remain in Baghdad, but only as religious leaders of Islam. Once in control of the government, the Seljuk Turks took their responsibilities as rulers seriously. They began to govern the empire in the tradition of Islamic law.

The Abbasid-Seljuk Empire continued for 200 years but received its death blow when Baghdad fell to Mongol invaders from central Asia in 1258. Thus ended the Abbasid Empire, which had itself begun with the violent assassination of nearly 80 Umayyad leaders in 750. Only one Umayyad leader had survived, and that was Prince Abd al Rahman, who had escaped to Spain. ■

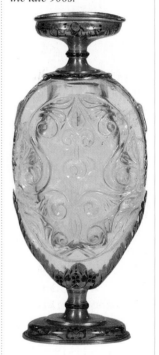

▼ *This delicate crystal vase, decorated with an arabesque floral design, is from the early Fatimid period in Egypt during the late 900s.*

■ *What led to the division of the Abbasid Empire?*

R E V I E W

1. **FOCUS** How did the same wealth that brought the Abbasids power lead to their downfall?
2. **CONNECT** In what ways did the Abbasids further develop the Islamic culture?
3. **POLITICAL SYSTEMS** How were non-Arabs treated by the Abbasids?

4. **CRITICAL THINKING** How were the Islamic trade routes important in spreading new ideas and knowledge?
5. **ACTIVITY** Write your first name in the center of a sheet of paper. Then work the letters into a design in the way that Moslems make Arabic letters become part of an intricate design.

91

The Empire of Islam

Origins of Sports and Games

T hroughout time people around the world have invented ways to relax and play. Abbasid rulers enjoyed recreations like falconry and backgammon. Find out about these and other games and sports that people have devised to fill their leisure hours.

Cricket and baseball are similar types of games that involve using a bat. How does the cricket bat differ from the baseball bat?

➤ *Skimming over the snow on a frosty morning, this man enjoys one of Alaska's most popular sports, dogsledding.*

Get Ready

Collect a pen, pencil, and notebook. Look for reference books, magazines, or local experts to help you explore the origins of a particular sport or game. You need information about the game's equipment and rules. Also, find out where and how the game originated.

Football, for instance, is one outgrowth of games that go back

centuries. All the related games involved kicking a ball, but the ball's shape and the rules of the game varied.

Find Out

Use your books, magazines, and other sources to find the origins of the game you chose. You may want to find the beginnings of a modern game (baseball, charades) and show how it has changed. You might want to follow a game to its origins: Did baseball come from cricket? When was pantomime invented? What about games that began as work? The Abbasids, for example, made a sport of hunting with a trained falcon. Hunting began, though, as a practical

◀ Chess has challenged intellectuals around the globe for centuries. This Spanish engraving, dating from the late 1500s, shows Arabs playing chess.

activity—a way for humans to acquire food.

Move Ahead

Tape a large sheet of paper to the classroom wall. As you and your classmates share your information, each of you should draw a timeline on this sheet. Each timeline should show the origins of a game and how its rules and equipment changed over time.

Make two lists, one of games that began as recreations, the other of games that grew out of some necessary activity such as work or self-defense.

Explore Some More

The horse-loving Abbasid rulers enjoyed polo and horse racing. Level ground and fast-moving Arabian horses created the opportunity for these amusements. Climate, animals, and terrain often affect the development of games. Where did ice hockey develop? Why? Can you think of another sport or game affected by such conditions?

▼ Although board games such as checkers and pachisi have been played since ancient times, some games remain popular for only a few years. For example, have you ever played Admiral Byrd's game?

93

The Empire of Islam

Identifying Main Ideas

Here's Why

When you read, you need to determine what the writer wants you to understand. Identifying the main idea is the key to getting the most from anything you read. For example, if you were asked to tell someone what you read in Lesson 1 about how the Umayyads united the Islamic Empire, you would need to use this skill.

Here's How

The main idea of a paragraph is often stated in a topic sentence. This sentence, which is usually the first or last sentence, tells what the paragraph is about. The other sentences of the paragraph provide facts and details that support the main idea.

In a large section of text, you may find a topic paragraph. Like a topic sentence, a topic paragraph tells you the main idea of the section. The other paragraphs in the section build on and support the topic paragraph.

Look at the summary of Lesson 1 (to the right). In this case, a topic paragraph begins the passage. As you can see from the green highlighting, the passage is about how the Umayyads expanded and unified the Islamic Empire. Supporting details, highlighted in blue, explain how the Umayyads accomplished this.

The main idea of a passage is not always stated in a topic paragraph. For example, if the passage below did not include the first paragraph, you would need to look in the rest of the passage for a common idea or ideas. You would study the supporting details to determine the unstated main idea.

Look back at the passage. The blue highlights the part of each sentence that tells something about how the Umayyads expanded or unified their empire. When you determine what these sentences have in common, you can come up with the main idea of the section.

Try It

Turn to page 83 and reread "A Common Coinage." Write the main idea of that section on your paper. Now list several supporting facts or details that reinforce the main idea.

Apply It

Find a magazine article about a topic that interests you. Identify the topic sentence or topic paragraph of the article. Describe how the other sentences or paragraphs in the article support the main idea.

The Umayyad Empire

In 661, the Umayyads began a 90-year period of rule. During their years in power, from 661 to 750, the Umayyads expanded and unified the Islamic Empire.

Muawiya, the first Umayyad caliph, moved the capital from Medina, in Arabia, to Damascus, in Syria. Muawiya also started the practice of appointing a son as the next caliph. Thus began a tradition of continuous rule by one family.

During their years in power, the Islamic Empire expanded into Africa and present-day Spain and Portugal. In conquered territories, Umayyad Muslims tolerated other religions but gave special privileges to Muslims.

Abd al Malik, caliph from 685 to 705, took other steps to unify the empire. He made Arabic the language of the empire and instituted a common coinage. Mosques built in conquered lands shared a common religious architecture that also provided unity to the empire.

LESSON 3

Islamic Spain

R egularly perform thy prayer at the declension [descent] of the sun, at the first darkness of the night, and the prayer of daybreak; for the prayer of daybreak is borne witness unto by the angels.

Koran, 17:80

According to the Koran, faithful Muslims are directed to pray at not only these three times of day but also in the afternoon and evening. Mosques were built by the Islamic rulers so that the faithful could answer the Koran's call to face Mecca and pray five times every day.

The Great Mosque of Cordoba, Spain, described in A Closer Look on page 97, was begun in 786 by Abd al Rahman. The mosque, completed nearly 200 years later in 976, was a religious, social, and educational center.

THINKING FOCUS

How did Islamic culture influence Spain?

Key Term

- legacy

The Return of the Umayyads

When Abd al Rahman fled to Spain in 750, he discovered that since the time the Arabs and Berbers had invaded Spain from North Africa in 711, rival tribes had been competing for control. No group had succeeded for long. Although there were many Muslims in Spain, there was no unified Islamic government.

Uniting Islamic Spain

By 756, the Umayyad forces in Spain, who did not support the new Abbasid caliphate back in Baghdad, accepted Abd al Rahman as their leader. With this Umayyad help, Abd al Rahman was able to establish an independent Islamic kingdom. He made the ancient Roman city of Cordoba his new capital.

◄ *The arches of the Great Mosque of Cordoba are supported by more than 1,000 pillars of marble, jasper and alabaster.*

95

Abd al Rahman's goals were to unify Spain under a central government, and to protect his realm from Islamic invaders to the south and Christian forces to the north. He succeeded so well that until 1000, there were few invasions.

■ How did the Umayyads unify and protect Spain?

Strengthening Cordoba

The high point for Umayyad power in Spain came about 200 years after the first Abd al Rahman, during the 49-year reign of Abd al Rahman III, which was from 912 to 961. He was the first Umayyad ruler of Spain to adopt the title of caliph, rather than simply governor. He patterned his government after the Abbasids' strong, centralized caliphate in the east, in Baghdad.

During his reign, Abd al Rahman III increased the strength of the army. The caliph bought Scandinavian, African, and German slaves to serve in his forces. This vast army protected his kingdom from the same two forces that had threatened the first Abd al Rahman: Christians in the north and Muslim rivals to the south, especially the Fatimids who had started an empire in Africa. ■

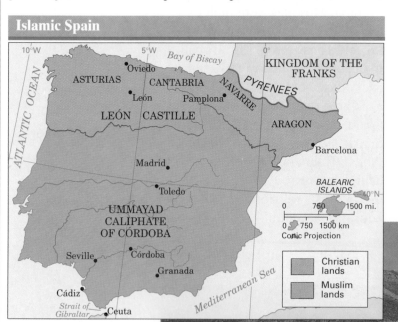

Islamic Spain

Bay of Biscay
ATLANTIC OCEAN
Oviedo
ASTURIAS
CANTABRIA
PYRENEES
NAVARRE
KINGDOM OF THE FRANKS
León
Pamplona
LEÓN
CASTILLE
ARAGON
Barcelona
Madrid
Toledo
BALEARIC ISLANDS
40°N
0   750   1500 mi.
0   750   1500 km
Conic Projection
UMMAYAD CALIPHATE OF CÓRDOBA
Seville
Córdoba
Granada
Mediterranean Sea
Cádiz
Strait of Gibraltar
Ceuta

Christian lands
Muslim lands

➤ Orchards of figs, almonds, and sweet cherries covered the countryside of the Islamic Empire of Spain. What Spanish cities were part of the Islamic Empire of Spain? What area of Spain was still controlled by the Christians?

Glory of Cordoba

With his borders well protected, Abd al Rahman III turned his energies toward making Cordoba a thriving cultural center. Prosperous and well run, the city attracted scholars and artists. Many had come from the Abbasid cultural center of Baghdad. The city's most famous attraction was the Great Mosque, the largest of the city's 3,000 mosques. For A Closer Look at the mosque, see page 97.

In the 900s, Cordoba was western Europe's largest city with a population of 200,000 people.

The Great Mosque at Cordoba

The great city of Cordoba demanded a great mosque. The building begun by Abd al Rahman I in A.D. 785 eventually became the third largest mosque in the world. Twice the wall facing Mecca was pushed outward. With the third addition, the wall and its jewellike mihrab had almost reached the river, so the fourth extension had to be added onto one side.

Did you notice that the pillars don't match? The marble and alabaster pillars under the candy-striped arches came from many different Roman buildings. Above this "forest" sparkled a turquoise- and gold-enameled "sky."

Outside, through open arches, rows of fragrant orange trees repeated the rows of pillars inside. The courtyard and mosque, open to each other, allowed Muslims to feel Allah's invisible presence whether they were inside or outside the mosque.

Orange branches

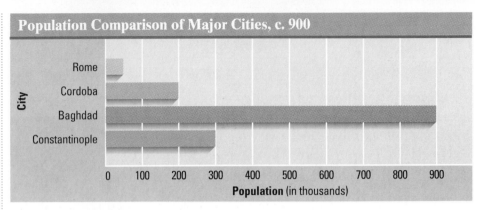

Population Comparison of Major Cities, c. 900

City:
- Rome
- Cordoba
- Baghdad
- Constantinople

Population (in thousands): 0, 100, 200, 300, 400, 500, 600, 700, 800, 900

> In the 900s, there were two Islamic Empires, the Umayyads in the west and the Abbasids in the east. There were also two Christian empires, the Roman Catholics in the west and the Eastern Orthodox Church in the east.

The size and splendor of Cordoba, with its paved and lighted streets and public plumbing in 300 bathhouses, was truly remarkable for a European city of the Middle Ages. Over 100,000 shops and houses filled the city. But it was the 60,000 richly decorated palaces with gardens and fountains, public courtyards, and broad avenues that made Cordoba an urban jewel in Islamic Spain's crown.

A Center of Learning

Poetry and music thrived in Cordoba. Poets and musicians were regarded as important figures in the court of the caliphs, for they produced poems and songs to glorify the empire and its rulers. Cordoba was the cultural and intellectual center of western Islam. The Muslims' interest in Greek learning ignited, and busy translators and copyists produced many volumes of Greek literature, philosophy, and science in Arabic. In the late 900s, the largest of the 70 libraries in Cordoba contained 500,000 volumes. This was at a time when a Christian monastery would have been proud to house several hundred books. A host of clerks, many of them women, carefully hand-copied 70,000 books a year to satisfy the citizens' literary appetites.

Thousands of men and women attended the university and the law school at Cordoba. Scholars from Baghdad traveled to Spain, bringing knowledge and seeking new ideas. Much of this learning was then shared with western Europe by visiting scholars, merchants, and pilgrims who came to Cordoba. This love of learning was Cordoba's greatest **legacy**, or gift, to cultures and civilizations of the future.

> The short-necked lute and the drum were two of the most popular instruments of Islamic music. They were often used to demonstrate and explain musical theory to young students.

The Intellectual Community

Cordoba was an open center of learning in which non-Muslims and Muslims from other lands were welcome to share in the intellectual community. One of the first of the visiting scholars was Abbas Ibn Firnas. He came to Cordoba from Baghdad in the early 900s to teach music at the court of Abd al Rahman III. His interests were diverse, however, and Ibn Firnas soon began to explore the mechanics of flight. He constructed a pair of wings out of feathers on a wooden frame and made an attempt at flight. Ibn Firnas survived his flight experiment with only a back injury. Later, he went on to build a famous planetarium in Cordoba that was complete with revolving planets.

Also playing an important part in the intellectual community at Cordoba were many non-Muslims. For example, Hasdai ben-Sharput was a Jew who served as court physician, treasurer, and diplomat to the caliph, Abd al Rahman III. In fact, the Muslims treated Christians and Jews with such tolerance that some converted to Islam or at least adopted many of its customs.

A City of Merchants

If Cordoba was a center of culture and learning, it was also a city of merchants. Cordoba supported a great many workshops for the production of its famous leatherwork, prayer carpets, ivory boxes, and other handicrafts. Spanish leather goods and textiles were in great demand throughout Europe because of the craftsmanship with which they were made. The art of papermaking, brought from Baghdad, was practiced here also.

Agriculture also flourished under Abd al Rahman III. He encouraged the use of irrigation, which enabled farmers to grow new and exotic crops such as figs, almonds, cherries, bananas, and cotton. Over 4,000 thriving markets sold these agricultural and manufactured products. ■

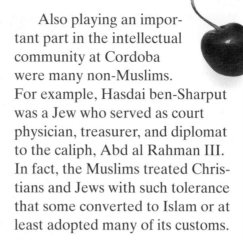

◄ *An artist carved this ivory box in Spain around 1000. The box is intricately decorated with animals, script, and foliage. The inscription around the lid wishes its owner peace and good luck. Craft items like this box, as well as farm products such as cherries and almonds, were all sold in the bazaars of Cordoba.*

■ *What were the greatest achievements of Cordoba?*

The Loss of Spain

By the 1000s, however, a small pocket of Christian resistance had begun to grow larger. Christian forces from the north of Spain began to move southward. The map on page 96 shows the strip of northern territory that remained Christian throughout the first 250 years of Umayyad reign.

The Reconquest

The late 1000s mark the beginning of a period that Christians call the Reconquest. Knights and

➤ *In 1492, King Ferdinand of Aragon and Queen Isabella of Castile are on their way to the city of Granada to welcome it as part of their united kingdom.*

adventurers from all over Europe journeyed to Spain to fight the Muslims. In 1085, the Spanish Christian ruler Alfonso VI seized the Muslim city of Toledo, whose king was friendly to the Christians. The loss of Toledo marked the point of no return in the battle for Spain.

An Empire Lost

After the attack on Toledo, the rest of Islamic Spain gradually fell to Christian soldiers. The Muslim government dissolved into quarreling factions. Just as the Abbasid Empire had begun to collapse when it could no longer unite its parts, the Umayyad Empire in Spain began to die. The Muslims retreated farther and farther to the south as Christian forces invaded from the north.

Cordoba fell to the Christian forces in 1236, almost 500 years after Abd al Rahman had established it as the capital of his empire. In 1236, the last Islamic kingdom in Spain was that of the Berbers in Granada.

The Catholic kingdoms of Aragon and Castile ruled northern and central Spain. When King Ferdinand of Aragon married Queen Isabella of Castile, their combined kingdoms had enough power to expel the Muslims from Spain entirely. In 1492, the forces of Ferdinand and Isabella of Spain drove out the last Berbers.

Most refugees settled in North Africa, particularly in Morocco where the Berbers had originally come from in 711. Today, 98 percent of the Moroccans are Muslim. The official language is Arabic, but many people speak Spanish. ■

■ *What were the threats to the Islamic Empire in Spain?*

R E V I E W

1. **FOCUS** How did Islamic culture influence Spain?
2. **CONNECT** How did the Abbasid Empire influence the start and the development of the Umayyad government in Cordoba?
3. **POLITICAL SYSTEMS** What problems led to the fall of central Islamic governments?
4. **CRITICAL THINKING** How was Cordoba able to become the center of culture for western Europe in the 800s and 900s?
5. **ACTIVITY** Muslims translated many important books of Greek knowledge into Arabic. What English books would you suggest be translated into Arabic? Make a list of books that should be available in Arabic. Tell why each book is significant.

Using the *Readers' Guide*

Here's Why

To find current information about a topic, you need to use reference resources other than encyclopedias and books. Magazines, or periodicals, can provide recently written information about events. Suppose you want to find information about Islam today. How would you find the periodicals you need?

Here's How

The *Readers' Guide to Periodical Literature* is a set of reference books that lists magazine articles by topic. The box below contains two pages from the *Readers' Guide* for the year 1989.

To find an article about Islam, look under the topic **Islam.** There you find a cross reference: *See also* **Muslims.** This reference tells you that more articles about Islam are listed under the heading **Muslims.**

As you can see, there are three other subject headings with *Islam* in the title. These headings also refer you to different subject listings. Where should you look for an article on Islam and Christianity?

If the listings under **Islam** do not have what you want, then look up the heading **Muslims.** There are several subheadings under the subject **Muslims.** One or more articles are listed under each subheading. Each article is a separate entry. An entry includes the name of the article, the magazine that published it, and the date. Then look for that issue of the magazine in the periodicals section of the library.

Try It

Look again at the *Readers' Guide* entries on this page. In what magazines can you find articles about Muslims in the Soviet Union? Who wrote each article? What is the title of the most recent article about Muslims in the Soviet Union?

Apply It

Think about a special holiday or tradition associated with your ethnic background. Use the *Readers' Guide* to make a list of articles about this topic.

1. Title
2. Joint author
3. Subject heading
4. Author
5. Illustrations, portraits, maps
6. Periodical, volume, page numbers, date

ISENBERG, DAVID
1 Reforming the Joint Chiefs of Staff: a timid first step. il *USA Today (Periodical)* 117:12-15 Ja '89
ISIKOFF, MICHAEL
2 (jt. auth) See Hosenball, Mark, and Isikoff, Michael
ISLAM
See also
Muslims
ISLAM AND CHRISTIANITY
See Christianity and other religions
ISLAMIC PAINTING *See* Painting, Islamic
ISLANDS
See also
Barrier islands

MUSLIMS 3
Afghanistan
Afghanistan: Soviet occupation and withdrawal. il maps *Department of State Bulletin* 89:72-90 Mr '89
Afghanistan's uncertain fate. B.R. Rubin. 4 il *The Nation* 248:264-7+ F 27 '89
Target: Kabul. D. Lorch. il pors map *The* 5 *New York Times Magazine* p32-5+ F 12 '89
Egypt
See Also Muslim Brotherhood [Egypt]
Soviet Union
Central Asia: the rise of the Moslems. D. Doder. il map *U.S. News &* 6 *World Report* 106:48+ Ap 3 '89
Islam regains its voice. R.N. Ostling. il *Time* 133:98-9 Ap 10 '89

The Empire of Islam

Chapter Review

Reviewing Key Terms

bureaucracy (p. 82)   empire (p. 78)
calligraphy (p. 88)   faction (p. 91)
dissent (p. 82)   legacy (p. 98)
emir (p. 82)

On your own paper, write the key term hinted at by each sentence below. Write a different sentence that contains the key term.

1. Opposing groups broke away from the empire and left it weak.
2. Many pieces of Islamic artwork are adorned with beautiful writing.
3. Emirs ruled strictly so that they could prevent disagreement among their people.
4. Scientific discoveries were one of the gifts that the Islamic Empire passed on to other cultures.
5. A ruling governor reported to the caliph.
6. The Islamic Empire government had different divisions that were managed by workers appointed by the caliph.
7. Syria, North Africa, Spain, Persia, and parts of India were among the group of countries ruled by the Muslims.

Exploring Concepts

A. Copy and complete the following outline using information from the chapter.

I. A century of expansion
  A. Expansion under Umayyad rule
  B. _____
  C. Umayyad unity
  D. The Umayyad downfall
    1. _____
    2. _____
II. The golden age
  A. Islam under Abbasid rule
    1. _____
    2. _____
    3. _____
  B. The new capital of Baghdad
    1. _____
    2. _____
  C. Abbasid culture
  D. _____
  E. A divided empire
III. Islamic Spain
  A. The return of the Umayyads
  B. _____
  C. The loss of Spain

B. Decide whether each statement below is true or false. Support your decision in writing, using facts and details from the chapter.

1. The Umayyad rulers made changes that both expanded and unified the Islamic Empire.
2. The rulers of the Umayyad Empire were tolerant and did not discriminate against non-Muslims.
3. A political split outside Islam helped bring about the downfall of the Umayyads.
4. Under the Abbasids, culture and learning flourished.
5. The way the Abbasid used their great wealth contributed to the downfall of their empire.
6. Because of their different locations, Baghdad and Cordoba had almost nothing in common.
7. The Islamic people did not share their culture or knowledge with any other peoples.
8. Both the Abbasid Empire and Islamic Spain declined and were conquered when their rulers could no longer maintain unity among the people.

Reviewing Skills

1. Read the section headed Art and Design on page 88 of Lesson 2. Where in the section does the main idea appear? Write down this main idea. Then list three details or facts that support the main idea.
2. Reread the section headed Strengthening Cordoba on page 96 of Lesson 3. What is the main idea of the section? How can you identify the main idea in this section?
3. Use the *Readers' Guide* excerpt on page 101 to answer the following questions:
   a. In what magazine would you look to find an article describing the Soviet involvement in Afghanistan? What are the title and the date of publication for the article?
   b. Under what entry would you find information about Muslims in Egypt?
4. Use the information in Lesson 2 to make a timeline showing events of the Abbasid Empire. Can you make your timeline into a parallel timeline using events of the Umayyad Empire for the same time period?
5. Taking notes and outlining are two ways of studying. If you were outlining or taking notes on the contents of Chapter 4, what two kinds of information would you be writing down?

Using Critical Thinking

1. An empire is formed when one central authority takes control of several other countries. Being ruled by another country affects the government and way of life of the conquered people. The conquered people also affect the ruling country and the empire. What effects did the Byzantines, Persians, and others have on Islam and its empire? What positive effects can empires have on progress and on society in general?
2. Baghdad and Cordoba were prosperous, well-run centers of commerce that also became centers of great art and learning. Judging from the example of these two cities, what are two or three comments you can make about places in which art and learning flourish?
3. Arabic was declared the official language of the Islamic Empire. What were the positive effects of this policy? What negative effects can you think of? Keeping both types of effects in mind, do you think English should be declared the official language of this country? Defend your position.

Preparing for Citizenship

1. COLLECTING INFORMATION Persian and Byzantine coins bore pictures of emperors. Islamic money bore quotations from the Koran. Do research to find out what images and words are used on the currency of the United States. Make a scrapbook of the decorations on the money, including drawings and explanations.
2. COLLABORATIVE ACTIVITY Although mosques do not all look alike, certain features are the same. This is also true for churches and synagogues and other temples. Working in groups of four, prepare an illustrated report on the architecture of these religious buildings. Decide among yourselves who will research each kind of building. One person can find out more about Muslim mosques. Another person can find out about Christian church architecture, the third person should find out about Jewish synagogues, and the other person should find out about Buddhist temples. The group can choose two members to compile the information and write a description of each kind of building. The other two people can illustrate the descriptions. The whole class should decide whether to use the reports in a scrapbook or bulletin board display.

Unit 3

Sub-Saharan Africa

Traders from faraway Europe, Asia, and the Middle East journeyed to the ancient trading empires of Africa seeking gold, ivory, and other exotic goods. Later, they came to conquer and to take away Africans as slaves. The empires fell, but the traditions of the past live on in Africa today. This cavalry brigade, dressed in ceremonial battle gear, parades through Niger just as ancient cavalrymen marched down the trade routes of the early African empires.

500 B.C.

Niger cavalry procession. Agence Hoa-Qui, Paris

A.D. 1700

Chapter 5
West Africa

Would you trade a pound of gold for a pound of salt? West Africans did. Salt was scarce, and they needed it to survive. Africans also exchanged other goods as they built trade networks from about 250 B.C. through the A.D. 1500s. Across the Sahara and along the Niger River, traders carried ivory, cloth, baskets, iron tools, jewelry, and much more. While most of West Africa stayed a land of small villages, trade empires grew around splendid cities.

Throughout this period, West Africans carved brightly colored figures like this one to represent gods, spirits, and ancestors. Such figures were often used in religious ceremonies.

A.D. 500–600 The rulers of Ghana store grain in mud huts like these. Built on high, steep land, the huts keep the grain dry and safe from animals.

500		B.C.	A.D.		500

c. 570 Muhammad, founder of the Islamic faith, is born in the Arabian city of Mecca.

500 B.C.

Throughout this period, religion, dance, and music played an important part in West African village life. Even today villagers like these Dogon people perform religious dances in traditional clothing.

c. 800–1050 Ghana controls West Africa's rich trade, yet villagers continue to use cowry shells for money.

c. 1580 The Songhai control West Africa's wealthiest empire, trading for valuable goods like the Ashanti gold badge above.

| 1000 | 1500 | Today |

1429 Joan of Arc leads French troops to victory over the English at Orleans during the Hundred Years' War.

A.D. 1590

LESSON 1

The Roots of Mighty Empires

THINKING FOCUS

What are some of the ways the early West Africans developed prosperous cities in a landscape with such a varying climate?

Key Terms

- savanna
- sahel
- delta

▼ *Although it is as large as the United States, the Sahara has fewer than two million inhabitants.*

Imagine being on a trip by van across the Sahara in North Africa. After hours of travel, your guide sets up camp in an oasis. Its palm trees offer a refuge of shade from the sun-baked sand of the desert.

While you're relaxing by a stream, your guide proposes a hike. To those hardy enough for the walk, she promises scenes of lush plant life and full rivers.

You decide to go. The sun-baked sand burns through your sneakers, and rocks cut your hands as you scramble over a hill. Finally your guide leads you into a cave. Here, she says, are the scenes promised.

Paintings cover the cave walls. Images of wide rivers teeming with fish, vast plains of tall grasses, thick forests, and people herding cattle. The guide explains that these scenes were painted thousands of years ago—and that they represent the ancient Sahara. Could that barren desert really have been such a paradise? Were the paintings of real life?

A Land of Many Climates

Dried-up riverbeds as well as cave paintings indicate that in 5000 B.C., the Sahara was indeed a land of flowing rivers, lush green pastures, and forests. However, over time, its climate began to change. By about 4000 B.C., rain fell less often, and average temperatures had risen. As a result, the

rivers dried up, and fertile pasture land became bare and bleak. By 2500 B.C., the desert looked much as it does today.

As the desert became drier, many people moved to search for more fertile land. Many Africans journeyed south to West Africa.

Some of those who migrated to West Africa settled on oases located along a strip of grasslands, or **savanna,** on the Sahara's southern border. This region is known as the **sahel** *(suh HAYL),* or "shore of the desert." Its landscape ranges from desert in the north to scattered vegetation in the south. On the sahel, scant rainfall and occasional oases make some farming possible. There are eight climate zones in Africa. Use the map below to determine the sahel's climate region.

Other Africans went farther south of the sahel to settle in the

Africa's climate ranges from heavy rainfall in central and parts of southern Africa to scant rainfall in the north.

Africa: Climate Regions

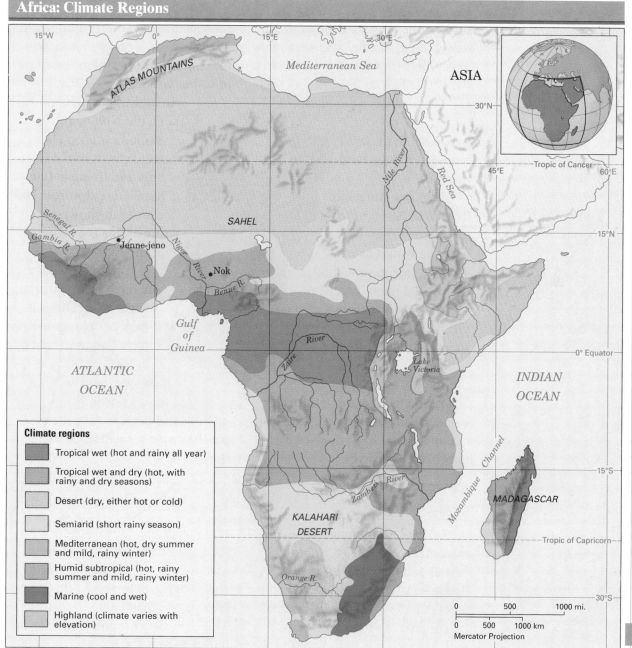

Climate regions

- Tropical wet (hot and rainy all year)
- Tropical wet and dry (hot, with rainy and dry seasons)
- Desert (dry, either hot or cold)
- Semiarid (short rainy season)
- Mediterranean (hot, dry summer and mild, rainy winter)
- Humid subtropical (hot, rainy summer and mild, rainy winter)
- Marine (cool and wet)
- Highland (climate varies with elevation)

West Africa

savannas and rain forests of a more fertile area along the Niger River. There they found relief from the barren Sahara. And along the banks of the Niger, they built some of Africa's greatest empires. ■

A New Technology

Although the vast, scorching Sahara made travel difficult, it did not cut West Africa off from traders to the north. Camel caravans regularly traveled across the desert from North Africa to exchange goods and ideas.

From these North African traders, the West Africans learned iron-making technology. Archaeologists have found iron tools near the city of Nok in present-day Nigeria. The artifacts were made by the Nok people, who lived in the area between 500 B.C. and A.D. 200.

The Nok were the first West Africans to make iron. They began working with it as early as 450 B.C. and, in time, had discovered many practical uses for it. For example, by fitting their spears with iron points instead of stone ones, the spears lasted longer. Also, iron tools were better than stone ones for farming. Using iron-making technology, the Nok vastly improved their lives.

To make iron, the Nok placed rocks rich in iron ore in a clay furnace with charcoal. They then heated the mixture to a high enough temperature to liquefy it.

After the wastes were poured off, a chunk of molten iron remained. A Nok iron maker would then shape that soft, red-hot iron into a tool or weapon. This iron-making process is still used today in some parts of West Africa.

In addition to being iron makers, the Nok were also skilled potters. They used clay to build their huts and to make finely detailed sculptures. The clay head shown here illustrates the artistry of the Nok.

Little is known about why the Nok civilization came to an end. The Nok people seem to have begun to move at least by 300 B.C. However, because they shared their knowledge of iron making and pottery with the people they met, we can trace the path they took. ■

➤ The Nok sculpted humans, animals, and religious figures. Many such sculptures were discovered by tin miners in the 1930s.

■ What aspect of Nok culture demonstrates that trade had a major impact on Nok life?

An Ancient Trade Center

In 1977, the remains of an ancient city were discovered on the inland delta of the Niger River. A **delta** is a triangular-shaped landform made by mud and silt deposited at a river's mouth. The iron and clay artifacts found among the remains of the city closely resembled the articles made by Nok craftspeople to the east. Thus, archaeologists determined that some Nok people had come to this site. The city, called Jenne-jeno, was inhabited from 250 B.C. to A.D. 1400.

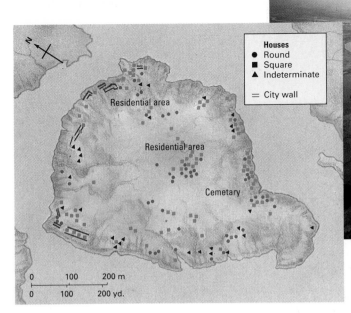

Houses
● Round
■ Square
▲ Indeterminate
═ City wall

Residential area

Residential area

Cemetary

0   100   200 m
0   100   200 yd.

It lies about two miles from the modern city of Jenne in the Republic of Mali.

As you can see in the photo above, the city was built on a flood plain on the river's inland delta. The Niger flooded this plain yearly, and when the waters fell back, they left behind rich, moist soil ideal for farming rice. Indeed, the first people to settle there were rice farmers, who also raised cattle and fished in the Niger.

In addition, the Niger acted as a natural highway for trade. People carried rice, fish, baskets, and pottery to river cities in the north and brought back salt, copper, and stone. Traders went south on the river to bring back gold.

Traders also traveled over land. In fact, camel caravans eventually linked Jenne-jeno with North Africa. By 800, Jenne-jeno had grown from a small settlement into a bustling trade center of about 10,000 people.

Because the people of Jenne-jeno had such an abundant supply of food and other products, many were free to do other things besides farm. Iron tools, copper and gold jewelry, and clay animals have been unearthed in the city. From these finds, archaeologists have determined that well-trained craftspeople lived there.

Despite its flourishing culture and fine location, by 1400, Jenne-jeno was completely abandoned. Archaeologists do not know why this happened. However, at about this time, the nearby city of Jenne was founded. Perhaps many of the people of Jenne-jeno settled in Jenne, which would make them the ancestors of the people who live there today. ■

▲ *This photograph shows the modern city of Jenne on the left and the ancient city of Jenne-jeno in the upper right-hand box. The illustration on the far left is of ancient Jenne-jeno and is based on the research of archaeologists who uncovered artifacts there.*

■ *How did the people of Jenne-jeno obtain the resources they could not produce?*

R E V I E W

1. **FOCUS** What are some of the ways the early West Africans developed prosperous cities in a landscape with such a varying climate?

2. **CONNECT** What things other than goods were exchanged between North African traders and West African traders?

3. **ECONOMICS** In what ways did the inhabitants of Nok benefit from learning the technique of iron making?

4. **GEOGRAPHY** How did the people of Jenne-jeno adapt to the geography south of the Sahara?

5. **CRITICAL THINKING** What would have been the impact on West Africa if the Sahara's climate had not changed so dramatically?

6. **ACTIVITY** Use the clay head pictured on page 110 to make your own Nok-style sculpture of a human or animal head.

111

West Africa

LESSON 2

The Empire of Ghana

What effect did trade have on the people of Ghana?

Key Terms

- matrilineal
- patrilineal

What is it really like to cross the Sahara in a camel caravan? In 1352, Ibn Battuta, a renowned world traveler and writer from northern Africa, decided to cross the Sahara and experience it himself.

The caravan started in North Africa and traveled for 25 days through the northern part of the Sahara to the ancient salt-mining town of Taghaza. Battuta was amazed by Taghaza's unusual dwellings built of blocks of salt.

In Taghaza the caravan traders exchanged dates and gold dust for water to drink and for salt, which they could trade once they crossed the Sahara. Then camels and people headed out into the driest, hottest part of the desert.

That's when their difficulties began. To avoid the worst heat, the caravan traveled from late afternoon to sunrise. One traveler separated from the others to graze his camel and never returned. "After that," wrote Battuta, "I neither went ahead [nor] lagged behind."

Further danger and hardship lay in a stretch with no water at all. Camels had to be killed for food and the water in their stomachs. Finally the exhausted travelers rode into the West African town of Walata. Two months after setting out from the northern rim of the Sahara, they completed the 1,200-mile journey.

► *Caravans of camels, the "ships of the desert," still cross the Sahara today.*

A New Trade Center

Ibn Battuta traveled with traders who were used to making this rough crossing. As a result of these trade caravans, between the 700s and 1500s, large trading empires developed in West Africa.

Ghana was the first of the trading empires. Historians are not certain how and when the empire began. However, they think that around A.D. 300, Berbers from North Africa established the first kingdom north of the upper Niger River in Ghana. The Berbers were originally nomads whose ancestors had migrated from the Middle East. They ruled Ghana for about 400 years until a group of West Africans called the Soninke *(suhn IHN kay)* took control in 780.

Under the Soninke kings, Ghana became a wealthy trading empire. The Soninke easily conquered neighboring peoples because their iron weapons were far superior to the stone ones of their opponents. By the late 900s, Ghana controlled more than 100,000 square miles of land and hundreds of thousands of people. Ghana's location—between the northern Saharan salt mines and the gold fields of Wangara to the south—helped it become a major trade center. Traders from both areas had to pass through Ghana to exchange goods. And the empire acquired much wealth from the taxes collected on the goods.

West Africans used salt to pre-serve and flavor food. They also needed to include a lot of salt in their diet to replace that lost from the body through perspiration.

Salt was scarce in southern

Ghana, but gold was not. West African gold became important to Europe, the Middle East, and North Africa, for use as money and in jewelry. Since the supply from the few gold mines in Europe and Asia had been exhausted, gold had to be found elsewhere.

Fortunately, people in Wangara were glad to trade some of their gold for salt from the north. Gold had limited value for them. Tools, for example, could not be made out of the soft metal. But salt was vital to good health. To the people of southern Ghana, salt and gold were of equal value. And so they made the trade in equal amounts —a pound of gold for a pound of salt. You can learn more about the gold and salt trade in A Closer Look on page 114. ■

▼ *In parts of central Africa, salt is still considered to be as valuable as gold.*

Across Time & Space

Salt was also valued in ancient Rome. In A.D. 500, soldiers transported salt on a highway called Via Salaria, or Salt Road. The term salary comes from the Latin salarium, *which means money paid to soldiers to buy salt. Soldiers "worth their salt" were paid a salary.*

■ *What combination of geographic and economic factors made Ghana an ideal trade center?*

113

Trading Gold and Salt

Trading gold and salt was not an easy way to make a living. Merchants risked dying of thirst almost every time they made the 1,200-mile journey across the Sahara. But those who overcame the hardships got rich and brought great wealth to the south Sahara kingdoms.

Gold masks could hide more than faces. Sometimes the gold in molded objects—like masks, jewelry, or coins—was mixed with cheaper metals. To avoid being cheated, merchants liked to trade their salt for pure gold dust.

Gold pendant, Baule tribe, Ivory Coast

The Muslim people kept the Saharan trade routes safe. They considered stealing a terrible sin and punished thieves severely. "Neither the man who travels nor he who stays at home has anything to fear from robbers or men of violence," wrote traveler Ibn Battuta.

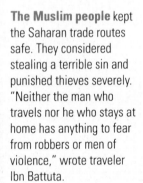

Pass the salt! For centuries, North Africans have been getting their salt from the Atlantic Ocean, just like the person in this picture. First, they filled shallow pools with salt water. Then they let it evaporate. The piles of moist sea salt dried quickly under the blazing African sun.

Salt

114

A Divided Capital

From about 800 to 1050, the gold and salt trade made Koumbi, Ghana's capital, the busiest and wealthiest marketplace in West Africa. Gold and salt were the most sought-after items, but in Koumbi's market people also bought and sold cattle, honey, dates, cloth, ivory, and ebony. In other shops at the market, local farmers sold their produce and craftspeople sold their wares.

Most of the traders in Ghana were Muslims who practiced the religion of Islam. Although Ghana's Soninke kings weren't Muslims, they were tolerant of Islam. Still, they tried to keep Islam separate from the traditional Soninke religion. So they divided many of Ghana's trading towns, including Koumbi, into two sections. One section housed the Muslims, and the other section housed the local people.

A six-mile-long boulevard linked the two sections of Koumbi. The Muslim side had 12 mosques and the homes of Muslim traders. Many of the buildings there were constructed of stone, and some had two stories. This section was also home to the huge Koumbi market.

The Soninke section of the capital looked very different. It was a walled city, and most of its one-story houses were made of wood or clay, with straw roofs. The king lived in this section in a large wood and stone palace.

The king was Ghana's religious and military leader and highest judge. The Ghanaian people came to him to settle their disputes.

> When the king gives [an] audience, . . . he sits in a domed pavilion around which stand 10 horses covered with gold-embroidered cloths. Behind the king stand 10 pages holding shields and swords decorated with gold. . . . At the door of the pavilion are dogs of an excellent breed. . . . Round their necks they wear collars of gold and silver.
>
> al-Bakri, historian, from
> Book of the Roads and Kingdoms, 1068

Thus, while administering justice, the king could also demonstrate his great wealth and power. ∎

▲ Most modern markets in West Africa are operated entirely by women. The woman in the main picture is selling yams. The baskets below the yam seller were woven by West African women. Why do you suppose they designed them to fit snugly into one another?

■ How did the two sections of Koumbi differ from each other?

A New Religion

In the 900s, as trade in West Africa grew more profitable, many Arab merchants came to live in Ghana. With the trading of goods came the trading of ideas. Arab traders brought the first system of

115

West Africa

This mud mosque in Mali is called the Great Mosque. Muslims must pray at a mosque once a week on Fridays. At other times Muslims even pray in the street but always remove their shoes first. Men and women pray separately.

writing and numbers to West Africa. The Ghanaian kings adopted the Arab writing system and even hired Arabs as government officials to help them take care of trade matters.

By 750, Muslim Arabs had created a huge Islamic Empire in the Middle East. And, as the Arabs gained more influence in West Africa, they taught the people of Ghana about their religion. However, reactions to these teachings were mixed. Although Ghana's Soninke rulers held tightly to their traditional religion, many other government officials and merchants eventually converted to Islam, some spending large sums to build expensive mosques for Muslim worship.

Conversion to Islam

Among the first of the converts to Islam were the Mandinke *(man DIHN kuh)* people from the southern Sahara, who served as middlemen in trade between Arab caravans and Wangara gold miners. The Mandinke formed small trade companies that made contact with many different people. They spread Islamic ideas throughout West Africa.

Many West Africans converted to Islam because it stressed belief in the "brotherhood of all believers." This sense of brotherhood encouraged trust and peaceful trade between people of different nationalities. Muslim traders often extended credit to each other simply because they practiced the same faith.

Traditional Practices

Other Islamic practices were harder for the Ghanaians to accept. Muslims, for example, had their own idea about the succession of kings. In Ghana when a king died, he was not succeeded by his own son but by the son of his sister. This system of tracing succession through the females of the family is known as **matrilineal** succession. Muslims, on the other hand, practiced **patrilineal** succession, in which the throne passes from father to son.

The people of Ghana continued to practice matrilineal succession to determine who inherited family property. This practice was too well established to abandon. Still, many Ghanaians considered themselves Muslims. They were just selective about the ideas they would adopt. ■

■ *In what ways did Ghanaians benefit from their contact with Arab traders?*

A Fallen Empire

Though Ghana benefited in many ways from Islamic influence, it was an Islamic sect that eventually brought down the Soninke empire. The Muslims who lived within Ghana's border were peaceful and helped Ghana maintain its trading empire. But the Al Moravids, a group of Muslim warriors who lived in the Sahara, set out to conquer Ghana in the middle 1000s.

The Al Moravids were strict Muslims who believed that they should conquer land in the name of Islam. When a drought drove them from their homelands, they raided settlements on the fringes of the Sahara and eventually Ghana. Their army captured Koumbi in 1076. But they could not keep their hold for long.

In 1087, the Soninke regained control from the Al Moravids. However, when they tried to re-establish their empire, they many problems. Some of the states they once ruled had firmly adopted Islam and supported the Al Moravids. Other states broke away to form separate kingdoms.

King Sumanguru, who wanted to rebuild Ghana's empire, ruled one of these kingdoms. In 1203, he overthrew the Soninke king and took over Koumbi. Meanwhile, a new kingdom to the east called Mali, ruled by the Mandinke, was steadily gaining power. In 1235, the king of Mali defeated Sumanguru at the Battle of Kirina. Thereafter, Mali replaced Ghana as the major power in West Africa. ■

■ *How did the brief takeover by the Al Moravids lead to Ghana's downfall?*

R E V I E W

1. **FOCUS** What effect did trade have on the people of Ghana?
2. **CONNECT** How did the Nok culture help the Soninke defeat neighboring peoples?
3. **GEOGRAPHY** How did the location of the West African gold and salt mines benefit Ghana?
4. **BELIEF SYSTEMS** What Islamic practice was particularly difficult for the Ghanaians to accept? Why?
5. **CRITICAL THINKING** The Arabs who practiced Islam were tolerant of the West Africans who held onto their traditional beliefs. How might Ghana's empire have differed if they had not been tolerant?
6. **WRITING ACTIVITY** Imagine that you are visiting Koumbi in the 1100s. This is your first trip to this part of the world, and you don't speak the language. In your journal, record what you see in each section of the city. What does the marketplace look like? Why do you think the city is divided as it is?

L E S S O N   3

The Empires of Mali and Songhai

THINKING FOCUS

What events led to the development of the great trade empires of Mali and Songhai?

Key Term

• griot

▼ *Trade still thrives in Mali on the shores of the Niger River.*

In 1235, the Battle of Kirina marked the fall of Ghana and the end of King Sumanguru's reign. But it also meant the rise of the kingdom of Mali and the beginning of King Sundiata's reign. The battle is rich in legends that are retold today.

According to legend, Sumanguru and Sundiata were magicians. Their magic would decide the battle's victor. In the heat of the match, King Sundiata furiously roared at the warriors of King Sumanguru, and they scurried for cover. When Sumanguru bellowed in return, the heads of eight spirits magically appeared above his head.

However, Sundiata's magic was more powerful, and he defeated the spirits. Then Sundiata fixed Sumanguru with his gaze and aimed an arrow at him. The arrow only grazed Sumanguru's shoulder, but it drained him of all his magical powers.

A present-day Mandinke **griot,** or storyteller, finishes the tale:

> The vanquished Sumanguru looked up towards the sun. A great black bird flew over above the fray. . . . "The bird of Kirina," [the king] muttered. Sumanguru let out a great cry and, turning his horse's head, he took to flight.
>
> Recorded by D.T. Niane of Mali, from a griot in Guinea, Africa

To the griot who described this battle, Sundiata was a hero.

Mali Develops a Prosperous Trade

Sundiata became king of the new empire of Mali, which had once been a part of Ghana. And he established its capital at Niani, on the upper Niger.

Sundiata never fought again after Kirina. He relied on his army to extend Mali's boundaries. The king focused on restoring prosperity to his kingdom.

Sundiata first concentrated on improving agriculture. His soldiers cleared land for farming, and they planted rice, yams, onions, beans, grains, and cotton. In a few years, Mali became a productive farming region.

However, as in Ghana, Mali's economy was based on trade. The many years of fighting in Ghana had interrupted trans-Saharan trade—trade that crossed the Sahara. So, once Mali controlled Ghana's gold mines, Sundiata set about restoring the salt and gold exchange with Niani as the kingdom's new trade center.

Sundiata and his successors expanded Mali's trade routes north and east across the Sahara to Cairo, Egypt, and to Tunis in Tunisia. You can locate these cities in the Atlas on the map on page 527. Mali controlled salt mines in the north at Taghaza and copper mines in the east at Takedda.

In addition to the gold mines at Wangara, the people of Mali had discovered a new source of gold at Bure, not far from the new capital on the Niger River. From Bure they easily shipped gold along the Niger to interested traders. The Niger became a busy highway for trading gold and other goods.

Less than 100 years after the victory at Kirina, Mali had become the most powerful kingdom in Africa. By the late 1300s, Mali was three times as large as Ghana had ever been. ■

▲ *Onions may have been such an important crop because their strong flavor can be used to season other foods.*

■ *How did Sundiata and his armies extend Mali's trade empire?*

Mansa Musa Enriches the Empire

Mali's greatest ruler, Mansa Musa, succeeded to the throne in 1307. Mansa Musa was a devout Muslim, but he respected all his subjects' beliefs. He allowed those who desired it to worship their traditional gods. However, many of the people who lived in trade centers had been influenced by the Arab traders and had already converted to Islam. Under Musa's rule, conversions greatly increased, mainly due to Mali's expanding trade.

The North African writer, Ibn Battuta, praised the newly converted Muslims for faithfully "observing the hours of prayers, studying books of law, and memorizing the Koran." However, as a traditional Muslim, Battuta was shocked by some West African customs that survived despite Islamic influence. For example, West African women were quite independent. He also found that people still scarred their faces to show their clan affiliations.

Nevertheless, in accordance with Islamic teachings, many of Mali's rulers made pilgrimages to the holy city of Mecca in the Middle East. Mansa Musa made the 3,500-mile journey in 1324.

According to some accounts, which may have become exaggerated over time, Mansa Musa was accompanied on this journey by as many as 50,000 people—friends, family members, doctors, advisers, and five hundred slaves carrying golden staffs. In addition, 80 to 100 camels, each

▲ *Arab historians reported that Mansa Musa's glittering procession to Mecca almost put Africa's sun to shame.*

Detail from a map of Mali, c. 1375, when Mali was said to be "four or more months' journey in length, and as much in width."

■ *What effect did West African rulers' conversion to Islam have on the empire?*

Under Mansa Musa, culture and learning flourished in Niani and other trade centers such as Timbuktu. When Musa returned from Mecca, he brought Arab scholars back with him. Mansa Musa invited these scholars to teach in Mali's learning centers. As Muslims, they welcomed the opportunity to instruct their brothers in scholarship and religion.

Likewise, Muslim traders welcomed the opportunity to trade with fellow Muslims in different states. Thus, they helped to increase Mali's trade empire as well as their own profits.

loaded with 100 pounds of gold dust, are said to have traveled with him to Mecca. Hundreds of other camels carried food, clothing, and supplies.

Mansa Musa's pilgrimage helped put Mali on the map. For when word of his wealth spread to Europe, European mapmakers began to include Mali on maps of Africa.

Even Mali's borders expanded under Mansa Musa's rule. New land was acquired both peacefully and as the result of war. Most of Mali was divided into states, which were under Musa's control. Some regions were allowed to remain independent as long as their rulers pledged their loyalty and a portion of their wealth to Mali. ■

Power Shifts to Songhai

After Mansa Musa died in 1332, Mali was ruled by a series of kings who were unable to protect its vast territory. Berber nomads attacked caravan routes in the desert and threatened to take Timbuktu. People from the southern rain forests raided Mali's southern border. And in the west, the Songhai on the middle Niger River began to revolt.

The Songhai were a mixture of farmers, traders, fishermen, and warriors who lived along the Niger near the city of Gao. For hundreds of years, the Songhai had fought off Mali's control. Sometimes they succeeded; sometimes they failed.

Under Mansa Musa, Mali ruled Gao and most of the Songhai kingdom for about 50 years. However, when he died, the Songhai stopped

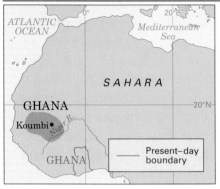

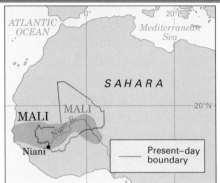

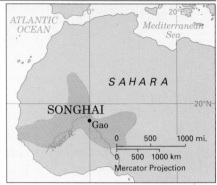

paying taxes to Mali. In 1435, a Songhai prince named Sunni Ali declared Gao's independence. Aided by the Songhai warriors, he successfully fought off Mali's attempts to regain the city.

Under attack on all sides after 1400, Mali gradually weakened. Mali's rulers were unable to drive off the invaders. Berbers took over the trade and learning centers of Timbuktu and Walata in the mid-1400s. In 1464, under the guidance of Sunni Ali, the Songhai began conquering their neighbors and expanding their kingdom.

A new Songhai empire thus grew out of a region that had once been part of Mali, just as Mali had grown out of a state in the empire of Ghana. Gao became Songhai's capital and Sunni Ali its king.

Sunni Ali was a Muslim, but he was not a devoted believer. After he died, his son, a non-Muslim, took over the throne. The new ruler was intolerant of Muslims, so many Muslims joined forces to overthrow him. The Muslims wanted a ruler who shared their beliefs. The ruler they supported was Askia Muhammad. In the 1490s, Askia overthrew Ali's son and declared Islam the state religion.

Askia's armies expanded the borders of Songhai and encouraged many non-Muslims to convert. The new king invited Muslim scholars to his empire, and its cities became great centers of culture and learning once again. At the height of its power in the late 1500s, the Songhai empire was larger and wealthier than Mali had ever been. In time, as the number of Muslims and Muslim traders increased, Songhai would become the greatest trade empire of West Africa. ■

▲ *Compare the growth of ancient Ghana, Mali, and Songhai. Note that although a present-day Ghana and Mali exist, there is no longer a Songhai.*

■ *How did Askia Muhammad's strong rule help Songhai become such a great trade empire?*

▼ *Under the leadership of Askia Muhammad, Timbuktu flourished, attracting scholars, traders, and craftspeople from all over the Muslim world.*

Songhai Collapses

Askia's heirs succeeded him to the throne. Over time, however, these rulers created a small but powerful Islamic group at the top of the ruling society. This group distanced itself from people who were not Muslims. As a result, certain states broke away from the empire, resentful of the Muslim kings.

But the major threat to Songhai came from Morocco in North Africa. In 1585, Morocco's ruler

Timbuktu's location at the edge of the Sahara Desert and only eight miles from the Niger River led to the popular saying of the day "Timbuktu, meeting point of the camel and canoe."

captured Songhai's salt mines in Taghaza. The Moroccan ruler also wanted to control Songhai's source of gold in West Africa. Ownership of both these two important resources would ensure a control of trade. The ruler of Morocco

■ *Why did the ruler of Morocco fight for control of Songhai?*

decided that this was worth fighting for.

In 1590, he sent 4,000 soldiers under Muslim Spaniard Judar Pasha to conquer Songhai. After a five-month-long journey across the Sahara, Pasha arrived in Songhai with only 1,000 men. But his soldiers carried something new to the region, something they had acquired in the Middle East—guns.

Songhai's soldiers outnumbered Pasha's by at least 25,000 men. But swords and arrows were no match for guns. Gao fell, and then Timbuktu, and finally most of Songhai.

Pasha never found the gold mines. So, gradually the North Africans lost interest in making Songhai a colony, although they stayed there another 150 years. What had once been a peaceful, well-organized empire became a series of military camps.

Songhai was the last great trading empire of West Africa. No other West African kingdom ever rivaled its power or strong hold on trade. But many people, especially rural villagers, relied little on this or any other trading empire. The villagers stayed faithful to a way of life that was based on traditional religion and customs. ■

R E V I E W

1. **FOCUS** What events led to the development of the great trade empires of Mali and Songhai?

2. **CONNECT** What are some of the things the empires of Ghana, Mali, and Songhai had in common?

3. **ECONOMIC GEOGRAPHY** Why do you suppose all the capitals of the great West African trade empires were located on the Niger River?

4. **CRITICAL THINKING** In what ways were Mansa Musa

and Askia Muhammad alike? In what ways were they different?

5. **CRITICAL THINKING** What might the North Africans have done if they had found Songhai's gold mines?

6. **WRITING ACTIVITY** Write a poem about King Sundiata's victory over King Sumanguru at the Battle of Kirina. If you like, you can enrich the legend told in this lesson by including some "magical" touches of your own.

Reviewing Skills

1. Give one interpretation of the following West African proverb: "When you are carrying beef on your head, you do not use your feet to catch grasshoppers." What does it tell you about West African culture?

2. Give one interpretation of this West African proverb: "You change your steps according to the change in the rhythm of the drum." Can you think of a proverb with a similar meaning? An opposite meaning?

3. Review Understanding Kinship at the bottom of page 126. What is the main idea of this section? What supporting details do you find in the Family Units section? What supporting details do you find in The Family in Society?

4. Suppose you wanted to read an article about the West African trade empires. Where would you look to find the names of magazines that cover that subject?

Using Critical Thinking

1. Ideas are carried along trade routes together with goods and products. Therefore, the direction of trade routes can affect the course of history in very important ways. Suppose trade caravans had been unable, or traders unwilling, to cross the Sahara. How might African society be different today? What effect might such isolation have had on the spread of religions?

2. Suppose a young person harms another young person. How would the punishment in American society in the 1990s differ from that in a West African village in the year 1000? Which punishment do you think would be more effective? Why? Which would be more fair?

3. How did the Nok people make iron, and how did this skill benefit their culture? Do you think the culture you live in would be very different if we did not have metalworking skills? If the world ran out of metal ores completely and our supply of new metal were cut off, how do you think society would be affected? What kinds of adjustments would you have to make in your own life?

Preparing for Citizenship

1. **WRITING ACTIVITY** In Lesson 3 you read part of the story of the battle between Sumanguru and Sundiata, as told by a modern-day Mandinke griot, or storyteller. The language was colorful and the facts were somewhat exaggerated. Choose a recent event of importance in your life or in the world at large and retell it in the style of a modern-day American storyteller. After you write your story, practice reading it and then telling it aloud.

2. **GROUP ACTIVITY** Suppose you lived in West Africa in the time of one of the great trade empires, shown on page 121 of this chapter. Would you prefer to live in the exciting capital city of one of the empires, with its great culture, its exchange of people and ideas, and its many goods and services? Or would you prefer the security and warmth of life in a small, rural village? Organize a debate on the question and prepare arguments for your side.

3. **COLLABORATIVE LEARNING** In all the West African cultures this chapter talked about, the importance of cultivating enough food to survive and to trade was stressed. Read through the chapter and list all the foods that were mentioned. Then divide into groups of three or four students. Have each group choose a food (two examples are rice and yams) and find a recipe for it in a cookbook. Then meet with the members of your group to prepare the dish and bring it to school for a potluck lunch.

Chapter 6

Central and Southern Africa

They called themselves Bantu, which means "the people." They spread out from West Africa over 2000 years ago, settling in the grassy savannas and the steamy rain forests of central and southern Africa. Some traveled to the coasts, where they built trading empires. But European traders plundered these empires and took many people away as slaves. Nevertheless, the heritage of "the people" continues. Most central and southern Africans today still think of themselves as Bantu.

During this period, a Bantu group called the Kikuyu became cattle raisers. They used shields like this one to defend their grazing land.

c. A.D. 200 Bantu migrate southward and begin farming and herding. Zulu people living in South Africa today, like this boy, trace their heritage to the early settlers.

B.C. A.D.

500 B.C.

A.D. 476 A barbarian general overthrows the last emperor of the Western Roman Empire.

Centuries-old traditions continue today. This young Kenyan woman, adorned with gold, bronze, and beads, participates in a ritual celebrating her coming of age.

A.D. 1000–1300 Bantu people called the Shona build the Great Zimbabwe, which means "Houses of Stone" (above). This grand city becomes Zimbabwe's capital and trade center.

1000

1500

Today

A.D. 786 Islamic ruler Abd al Rahman III begins building the Great Mosque in Cordoba, Spain.

A.D. 1300 Mali becomes the largest West African trading empire.

A.D. 1700

L E S S O N   1

The Bantu Migration

How did the Bantu migration affect the peoples of central and southern Africa?

Key Terms

- migrate
- age set

➤ *Bantu-speaking peoples, such as these Kikuyu women, now live in much of central and southern Africa.*

Canoe, people, rain, head, brother. Such words are ordinary enough, but 100 years ago scholars studying Africa's history were quite puzzled by them. The scholars wondered why people from a variety of central and southern African cultures used similar words for these items.

More than 300 distinct languages are spoken in central and southern Africa. Yet all of them have certain words in common and possess similar structures. How could so many peoples have developed such similar languages? Could they have been in contact with each other? Or did their languages all originate from a single parent language?

Words like these—canoe, people, rain, head, and brother—provided the key to the puzzle. They all seem to have originated from one language, now called

Bantu. Scholars think that this language was first spoken by a people who lived in the Nok region of West Africa between 500 B.C. and A.D. 200. These people are believed to be the ancestors of diverse peoples in modern central and southern Africa.

Geography

Sometime between 500 and 300 B.C., small groups of Nok people began to search for new land to settle. Some went to the south and some to the east. At different times over the next 2,000 years, descendants of these people settled across central and southern Africa.

They found grassy savannas, wide valleys, and steamy rain forests. Look at the map on page 137 to see where the migrants traveled.

Vast savannas and dry grasslands cover much of central and southern Africa. These serve as convenient travel corridors as well as grazing ranges for both wild and domesticated herds. Wherever the migrants went, they avoided areas infested with tsetse flies. The bite of these insects spreads a disease called sleeping sickness that is fatal to humans and cattle.

In the east lies a string of lakes and valleys some 4,000 miles long and 20 to 30 miles wide called the Rift Valley. This valley was formed in prehistoric times by a crack, or rift, in the earth's surface. It snakes along the continent from Mozambique to just south of Sudan, as the map on page 525 shows. The Rift Valley has dry grasslands, but has a good water supply, and few, if any, disease-carrying insects. So it is an ideal place to graze cattle and the perfect avenue along which to herd them north or south.

In the rain forest of the Congo Basin, along the equator, dense jungle supports a large population of animals and people. But the thick undergrowth makes travel by foot difficult. So people who live there primarily use the network of rivers for transportation. ■

■ *Describe three geographic regions in central and southern Africa.*

Origins of the Bantu

In about 450 B.C., the Nok people began to work with iron. They created iron hoes, spears, axes, and fishhooks. Iron tools proved to be much stronger and longer lasting than those made from stone, wood, or bone. With better tools, the Nok could clear more land and grow more crops such as sorghum, yams, and millet. They also could catch more fish and game than ever before.

These improved tools gave the Nok a more regular and plentiful food supply. Having more food meant that more people could be fed. So the Nok population grew. Families had more children, and as those children grew up, they needed farmland of their own.

Finding New Fields

Faced with the need for more land, young Nok farmers had to **migrate,** or move to resettle. They set out to find new land that they could clear and cultivate. Some of them moved east across the savanna, while others moved south into the rain forest.

But the Nok still needed fresh farmland, and so they spread farther south through Africa. By A.D. 280, descendants of the Nok

▼ *Compare this map to the one on page 525 of the Atlas. Which present-day countries have Bantu-speaking people?*

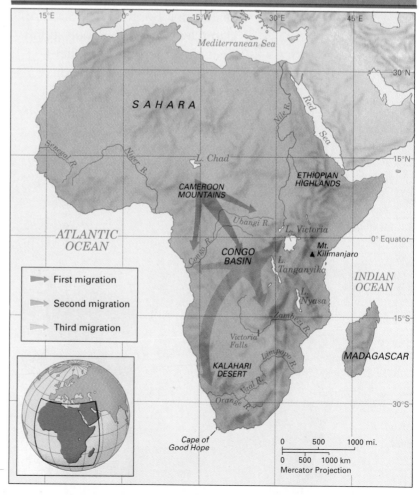

Bantu Migration in Africa, 500 B.C.–A.D. 1500

Insects continue to pose a problem in Africa today. The anopheles (uh NAHF uh leez) mosquito, which causes malaria, breeds in areas with standing water. The tsetse fly spreads sleeping sickness, and locusts can destroy a field of crops in minutes.

▲ Tsetse flies are shown here at twice their actual size.

■ Why did Bantu groups continue to migrate across Africa?

➤ Bantu migrants learned new skills from the peoples they encountered. Some became cattle raisers, like these modern herders in Kenya. Others learned to weave cloth with intricate patterns.

were farming near the southeastern coast of Africa, on the fertile slopes of Kilimanjaro and Mt. Kenya, and also in the highlands around Lake Victoria. And all of these people called themselves Bantu, meaning "the people" in the language they shared.

Making New Contacts

As the Bantu migrated across central and southern Africa, they came into contact with native groups of hunter-gatherers and herders. But they existed peacefully with these people because no group desired to live on the other's land. For example, Bantu farmers did not want the hunter-gatherers' forest land, because their crops could not grow in the forest.

Gradually, though, the Bantu and local cultures influenced each other. The local people began to realize that Bantu agriculture produced a more reliable food supply than either herding or gathering. So they too became farmers and adopted the Bantu's iron technology and language. Others gave up their native lifestyle when they married into the Bantu culture.

The Bantu fitted into their new environments by adopting the lifestyles of the native people. For example, the Bantu who settled in the Rift Valley turned to raising cattle like the local herders. In the Congo Basin rain forest, heavy rains and dense vegetation prevented Bantu farmers from raising crops, so many turned to fishing. The Bantu there also learned crafts such as basket making, weaving, woodcarving, and boat building.

As groups of Bantu settled in different areas, their common language developed into many different languages. Nevertheless, all Bantu languages have kept some of the characteristics of early Bantu. Thus, despite the cultural variety in central and southern Africa today, most of the people there speak a Bantu language and think of themselves as Bantu people. ■

Bantu Society

The basic political and social unit among most Bantu groups was the village. Bantu villages were commonly ruled by a chief and a council of elders. In densely populated areas, some Bantu groups formed kingdoms and empires, such as Kongo and Zimbabwe.

Other groups, like the Kikuyu, did not live in villages or kingdoms. The Kikuyu are Bantu farmers who at one time lived in scattered clans around Mt. Kenya. They were organized on the basis of kinship, with the father as the head of the family.

But in times of crisis or special need, the Kikuyu relied upon a social structure based on age sets. An **age set** is a group of people of the same age. Age sets performed specific functions according to the members' age. Children were placed in an age set based on the year of their birth. All members of an age set advanced through the stages of life, or age grades, together. Each age grade met certain needs of the society as a whole. Look at the diagram to the right. What were the responsibilities of people in your present age group?

Strong loyalties developed within an age set. Much as you feel loyalty to classmates or other children in your grade, the Kikuyu developed ties to their age-set comrades. Age-set ties, however, lasted for life. Although the members of Kikuyu society lived independently in scattered clans, they were unified by the age-set system all their lives. ■

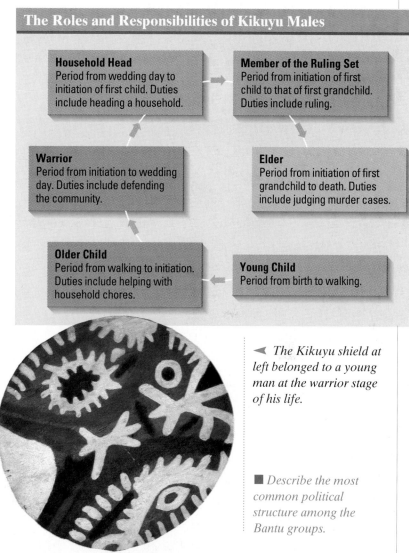

The Roles and Responsibilities of Kikuyu Males

Household Head
Period from wedding day to initiation of first child. Duties include heading a household.

Member of the Ruling Set
Period from initiation of first child to that of first grandchild. Duties include ruling.

Warrior
Period from initiation to wedding day. Duties include defending the community.

Elder
Period from initiation of first grandchild to death. Duties include judging murder cases.

Older Child
Period from walking to initiation. Duties include helping with household chores.

Young Child
Period from birth to walking.

◄ *The Kikuyu shield at left belonged to a young man at the warrior stage of his life.*

■ *Describe the most common political structure among the Bantu groups.*

R E V I E W

1. **FOCUS** How did the Bantu migration affect the peoples of central and southern Africa?
2. **CONNECT** Why do scholars think the Nok people may have actually been the Bantu?
3. **CULTURE** Why do you think the original language of Bantu groups might have changed after they settled in a new territory?
4. **CRITICAL THINKING** In the Indian language Sanskrit, the word for mother is *matar*. In Latin it's *mater*, and in German it's *mutter*. What conclusions might you draw from these similarities?
5. **ACTIVITY** Make a list of your duties and responsibilities at home or at school. How do they compare with those of Kikuyu people of the same age?

Central and Southern Africa

Making a Vertical Profile

Here's Why

Relief maps use color to show the elevations of landforms. A vertical profile gives a graphic view of the same information. Suppose you wanted to study the early people of Africa. Having a vivid picture of the lands on which these people lived could help you understand them. Could you construct a vertical profile to get this picture?

Here's How

Look at the map on this page. A line has been drawn at 3°S. Use the key to see how the elevation changes along this line. Then look at the vertical profile below the map. It shows the elevations along the 3°S line.

To construct a vertical profile first choose a line along which to draw it— in this case, 3°S. Draw a horizontal line on your paper to represent the profile line. Use the same scale as the map scale. Next look at the map key to see what elevations are represented on the map. Draw a vertical line at one end of your horizontal line. Use the elevation key as the vertical scale along this line. Then use the map to note elevation changes along the profile line. Do this by placing points on the profile to show where and to what degree the elevation changes. Finally, connect the points to complete the profile.

Try It

Construct a vertical profile of the African continent at 15°S. Use graph paper to help you mark elevation segments and place the points of elevation. What is the highest elevation? The lowest?

Apply It

Construct a vertical profile of a location in your state. Use your town as the place to locate your profile line. What is the highest elevation along your line? The lowest?

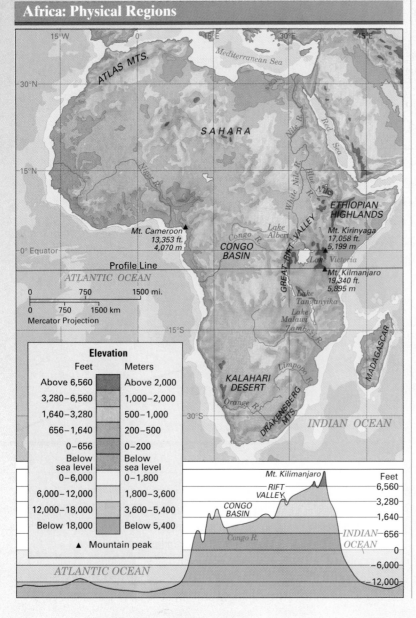

Africa: Physical Regions

Elevation	
Feet	**Meters**
Above 6,560	Above 2,000
3,280–6,560	1,000–2,000
1,640–3,280	500–1,000
656–1,640	200–500
0–656	0–200
Below sea level	Below sea level
0–6,000	0–1,800
6,000–12,000	1,800–3,600
12,000–18,000	3,600–5,400
Below 18,000	Below 5,400

▲ Mountain peak

L E S S O N   2

The Rise of Coastal Trading States

The last mainland market-town . . . is called Rhapta, a name derived from the small sewn boats. Here there is much ivory and tortoise shell. . . . The people of Mouza . . . send their small ships, mostly with Arab captains and crews who trade and intermarry with the mainlanders of all the places and know their language.

Into these market-towns are imported lances made especially for them at Mouza, hatchets, swords, awls, and many kinds of small glass vessels; and at some places wine and not a little wheat, not for trade but to gain the goodwill of the barbarians. Much ivory is taken away from these places . . . and also rhinoceros horn and tortoise-shell, different from that of India, and a little coconut oil.

This passage, taken from *The Periplus of the Erythraean Sea,* describes trade between the Arab city of Mouza and Rhapta, an East African port. It was written in about A.D. 100 by a Greek merchant. He had been sent by the Romans occupying Egypt to investigate rumors of a booming trade between Indian Ocean ports.

THINKING FOCUS

How did East Africa become part of an international trade network?

Key Terms

- monsoon
- city-state

Sailing with the Winds

This Greek merchant was writing about the Indian Ocean trade network between East Africa, Arabia, India, Ceylon, and the East Indies. Although trading between Arabs and East Africans probably began in about 900 B.C., the Indian Ocean trade network wasn't really established until about 200 B.C. For it wasn't until then that the Arabs learned to use the seasonal winds known as **monsoons** to sail across the Indian Ocean.

Every year without fail the monsoon blows from the northeast between November and March

▼ *Sailors on the Indian Ocean still sail dhows much like those that Arab traders once used.*

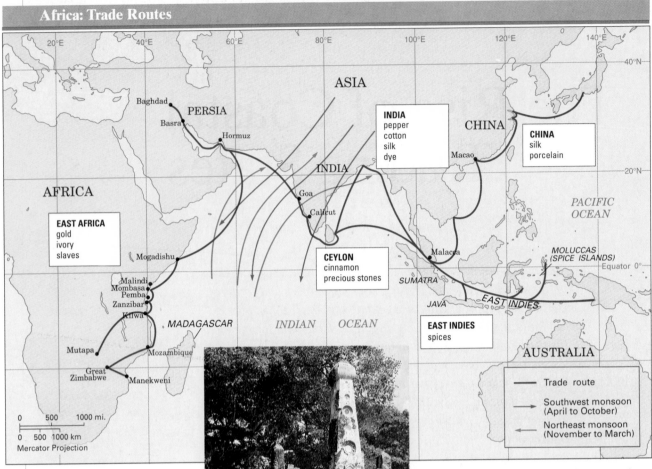

and from the southwest between April and October. So Arab merchants used these winds to propel their ships, called dhows (*dowz*), from Arabia down the African coast. They could reach Kilwa before the winds died down in March. Then the winds carried them from Kilwa back home again in April. With proper planning,

Arabian ships could sail to nearly any Indian Ocean port. But they had to sail back when the winds changed—or wait a year for the next monsoon blowing homeward.

While trade between the East Africans and the Arabs was growing, Bantu migrants were settling in East Africa. Scholars do not know exactly when the first Bantu arrived on the coast. But in the A.D. 700s, Arab travelers recorded Bantu words being used in East Africa. And Bantu language and culture became dominant among the original coastal people. ■

➤ *Chinese porcelain plates are embedded in this pillar-tomb from the 1700s, which stands in the ancient trading settlement of Kunduchi in present-day Tanzania. The plates are reminders of the vast trade network that once crisscrossed the Indian Ocean.*

■ *Describe the monsoons and explain why they were so important to the Indian Ocean trade network.*

The Rise of City-States

Beginning in about A.D. 900, a new immigration of people began to affect the character of the coastal cities. Arab, Persian, and Indian traders came to share in the profits from preparing goods for sale to incoming ships. And, although the Bantu outnumbered them, they nevertheless had an impact on Bantu culture and language. Many of the coastal Bantu adopted Islam as their religion, as the West Africans were doing at this time. They also added foreign words, particularly from Arabic, to the Bantu language. In fact, to refer to themselves, these coastal Africans eventually adopted the Arabic word *swahili (swah HEE lee),* meaning "people of the shore."

The Swahili served as the link between foreign traders and inland Africans. One such group of inland Africans was the Bantu who had migrated to southeastern Africa. These Bantu had found large deposits of gold and other minerals there. By 1100, they were shipping these precious metals from Sofala, a southern port city,

to Kilwa and other Swahili ports to be exchanged for foreign goods. Other inland Africans brought ivory, grain, and sometimes slaves to the coastal cities to trade for foreign spices, fabrics, and porcelain *(PAWR suh lihn).*

Soon the merchants of one port city were in competition with those of another. There were great riches to be made in import-export trade, and each group of coastal merchants tried to attract a larger share of the business.

At this time, too, many ports became **city-states,** or independent states made up of a city and its surrounding territory. The rulers of the city-states grew rich from trade and from taxes they required merchants to pay on the goods that passed through their port. ■

■ *Describe a typical East African trading town of the 1300s.*

From Riches to Ruin

The most prosperous city-state was Kilwa, the southernmost port on the Indian Ocean trade route. By 1100, traders in Kilwa controlled the export of gold and ivory from southern kingdoms. The local rulers and merchants became very wealthy from this trade.

The North African traveler Ibn Battuta

visited Kilwa in 1331. He described it as "one of the most beautiful and well-constructed towns in the world." He claimed, "The whole of it is elegantly built." In addition to the mosque shown below, Kilwa had a huge

▼ *The Great Mosque at Kilwa was built in the mid-1400s. Although most of it is now in ruins, the domes and cloister recall how glorious the East African city-states once were.*

143

Central and Southern Africa

palace, vast irrigated gardens, and houses many stories high that were built of stone.

Gedi, a trading town built in the 1300s, also had a mosque, a palace, and large houses built of stone. These houses had bathrooms with drains and overhead basins to flush toilets. In addition, the city was obviously well planned. The streets were not only laid out at right angles, but they had drainage gutters as well.

Then, in 1498, the first Portuguese explorer arrived. His name was Vasco da Gama. The Portuguese government had commissioned da Gama to find a way to sail from Portugal around southern Africa, into the Indian Ocean. They hoped that by developing such a trade route they would seize control of the Far East spice trade. But as Vasco da Gama piloted his ship northward along the East African coast, he realized that controlling East African trade would be quite profitable, too.

In 1505, a well-armed Portuguese fleet attacked Kilwa and then Mombasa. Neither city was able to defend itself against the Portuguese cannon. An observer aboard one of the ships that attacked Mombasa recorded the event. He described how the admiral ordered his men to destroy the city and carry off whatever they wanted. As a result, the observer says, " . . . everyone started to plunder the town and search the houses, forcing doors with axes and bars."

After conquering Kilwa, Mombasa, and other city-states, the Portuguese tried to monopolize trade in East African ports. But they did not have enough ships and men to maintain control over the entire Indian Ocean trade network. And by the late 1500s, Swahili groups had regained control of several ports from the Portuguese.

▲ *The carvings on this doorway from Lamu, near Kilwa, speak of the rich Swahili culture that dominated the coastal city-states of East Africa.*

■ *Who caused the destruction of many East African trading centers, and why?*

He who wants to string pearls
must be an excellent diver;
he who manages to succeed
is a [pearl] diver, a fisherman;
the soul is a vast ocean;
in it there is the treasure-trove of mother-of-pearl;
he that is afraid of drowning,
[for him] the oyster shells produce no pearls.

Swahili poem, 1700s

The cities never again saw the prosperity of earlier times. But the unique Swahili culture and language are still a vital part of the African tradition. ■

REVIEW

1. **FOCUS** How did East Africa become part of an international trade network?
2. **CONNECT** How was the growth of trade in East Africa similar to the growth of trade in West Africa?
3. **CULTURE** Who were the Swahili, and how did their culture develop?
4. **CRITICAL THINKING** How was life in inland Bantu villages different from life in coastal trading towns?
5. **ACTIVITY** Imagine you are a sailor on a merchant ship sailing from India to East African ports in the 1100s. Describe, or map out, the voyage you might make. Include the dates for your voyage, names and descriptions of African ports at which you would stop, and a list of the cargo your ship would carry back to India.

144

L E S S O N   3

The Rise of the Zimbabwe State

Until the 1800s, few non-Africans had seen the interior of south-central Africa. The wild terrain made traveling there almost impossible. And foreigners who had been there spoke mainly about the tropical diseases.

But in 1867, an American hunter brought startling news from south-central Africa. He claimed that hundreds of miles into the interior lay the ruins of an ancient kingdom. In 1888, a hunter and trader, Willi Posselt, reported on his search for the treasure:

The main gate was in a state of decay, a portion having fallen in. We climbed on to the wall and walked along this until we reached the conical tower. The interior was covered with dense bush; tall trees towered above the undergrowth, and suspended from them were masses of "monkey rope," by means of which we lowered ourselves and entered the ruins. I could not find any trace of human remains or of any implements, nor was the hope of discovering any treasure rewarded with success.

THINKING FOCUS

Describe some of the ways the Shona benefited from their decision to settle on the site now known as the Zimbabwe Plateau.

Key Terms

- plateau
- oral tradition
- malaria

◄ *This view of Great Zimbabwe shows the outside wall that surrounded the king's court and measured more than 820 feet long. The cone-shaped tower rises above the wall.*

The Builders of Great Zimbabwe

The Zimbabwe Kingdom

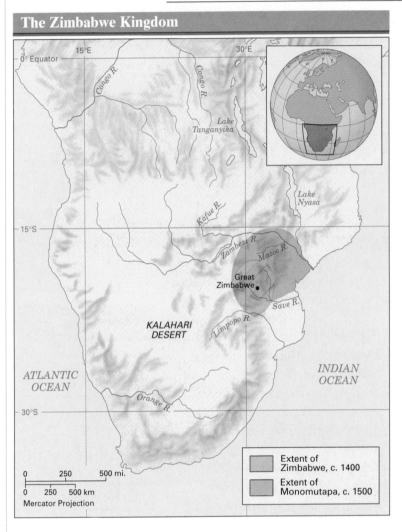

Extent of Zimbabwe, c. 1400

Extent of Monomutapa, c. 1500

0   250   500 mi.
0   250   500 km
Mercator Projection

▲ *How do the sizes of the empires of Zimbabwe and Monomutapa compare with those of modern African nations?*

■ *How did archaeologists learn about the founders of Great Zimbabwe?*

they refused to believe that Africans could have developed the technology needed to build such impressive structures. Instead, scholars preferred to think that these ruins were from an ancient society of white people who had come there from another continent.

Actually, the Africans had a rich history and technology. But in the 1800s, many Europeans mistakenly believed that the people of Africa were inferior to white people, because they lived differently than Europeans did.

In the early 1900s, archaeologists began studying the ruins of Great Zimbabwe to learn more about its founders. They examined artifacts—objects made by humans—such as iron tools, copper jewelry, and beads. They also studied the documents of early explorers and listened to the accounts of modern Shona. Finally they concluded that Africans, not white people, were the founders of this once prosperous kingdom.

Historians now know that Great Zimbabwe was built by the Shona sometime between A.D. 1000 and 1300. The Shona were Bantu farmers and cattle raisers who had come to this area in about A.D. 300 during the Bantu migration.

The Shona chose to settle in this area for a number of reasons. It had abundant rainfall for growing crops and plenty of trees for building material and firewood. Also, the plateau was free from disease-carrying tsetse flies. And the earth there was rich in granite, iron, copper, and gold. ■

The ruins that Posselt wrote about are those of Great Zimbabwe. They are scattered over 100 acres of a high **plateau,** or raised, flat surface of land, in modern Zimbabwe. The people who live there today are called Shona. Historians believe they are the descendants of the builders of Great Zimbabwe, which in their language means "Houses of Stone."

When the ruins were first discovered, European scholars marveled at the elaborate curved steps, walkways, and hidden passages. They were particularly impressed with the 30-foot-high walls made from 900,000 stones. However,

A Kongo King

11:47 A.M., May 15, 1544
Mbanza, capital of the Kongo kingdom

Salt

The heavy block, worth its weight in gold, was just presented to him by the governor of one part of the kingdom. The gift proves the governor is still loyal to the king.

Collar

He's wearing his finest African gold for today's tribute ceremony. He wants to show everyone—his subjects and the Portuguese traders— his power and authority. He has to be clever to balance the demands made on him from all sides.

Zebra Skin

The king is pleased that this gift is wrapped in a valuable skin. At the feast after this ceremony, the king will strengthen his ties to the governor by giving him an elegant drinking glass from Venice. The king trades for jewelry with the Portuguese.

Throne

Gleaming with ivory and inlaid gold, his chair is the only seat in the room. The king's men-at-arms stand at attention with their spears. The governors cluster in small groups, waiting for their chance to kneel before the king.

Boots

Of all the European goods the king gets from the Portuguese, these are his favorites. He paid for them with beautiful African cloth he received at last year's tribute ceremony.

151

The Portuguese in Kongo

Portuguese traders developed a prosperous and friendly relationship with the Kongo people. In 1490, the Portuguese king sent teachers and missionaries to educate the Mani-Kongo and members of his court. A **missionary** is someone who goes to a foreign place to teach religion.

Under the missionaries' guidance, the Mani-Kongo converted to Christianity and even sent his son to a missionary school. Later, his son became king and was baptized with the Christian name of Affonso I.

Affonso continued his father's contact with the Portuguese. He adopted many Portuguese customs and encouraged members of his court to attend school. Some even began to wear European clothes and to import European furniture.

➤ *An African artisan carved these Portuguese explorers in ivory. Look at the faces on the carving. How do you think the carver felt about the Portuguese?*

However, some people resented the Portuguese influence. They wanted their king to adhere to local traditions.

Nevertheless, the alliance between the Kongo and King John remained strong until the early 1500s. By then Portugal had begun settling the island of São Tomé, 250 miles off the Kongo coast. Most of the settlers were criminals being deported from Portugal. They had little regard for the African people and a great desire to improve their own lives.

■ *How did the slave trade become established in Kongo?*

When the Portuguese governor of São Tomé discovered that sugar grew well there, he immediately began looking for workers for the large farms, or **plantations.** He knew slave labor would cost the least and thereby leave more money as profit. So the governor turned to nearby Africa to find slaves.

At first, Affonso supplied him with slaves, not realizing that the Portuguese had a different notion of slavery than he did. Enslaving war prisoners was an accepted practice in Africa. But Africans did not mistreat their slaves or separate them from their families, and slaves could eventually earn their freedom. The Portuguese, however, treated slaves like beasts of burden, working them so hard that many died. When this occurred, they simply bought more. ■

Slaves, Guns, and Civil War

The merchants of São Tomé were not satisfied with the limited number of slaves they could obtain from the Kongo. The buying and selling of slaves had become quite a profitable business. And with a new Portuguese colony in South America, called Brazil, the demand for slaves was greater than ever.

The Portuguese merchants stopped at nothing to get slaves. Since Africans customarily enslaved prisoners they took in war, the merchants tried to get village chiefs to declare war on each other. And since native criminals were punished with slavery, they encouraged crime among the people. The Portuguese also supplied rival villages with guns and even bribed officials to encourage revolts against the Mani-Kongo. They offered European goods and guns to any chief who would supply them with slaves. Some missionaries even became slave traders.

The Kongo rulers were trapped in a tangled web. A chief needed guns for protection from slave raiders. But the only way to get guns was to trade slaves for them.

Desperate to put an end to this problem, Affonso wrote a series of letters to King John. In one, written in 1526, he pleaded:

Merchants are taking every day our natives, sons of the land and sons of our noblemen. . . . So great is the corruption and licentiousness [immorality] that our country is becoming completely depopulated.

In letter after letter, Affonso asked the Portuguese king to ban slave trade in Kongo. But King John did nothing. And, by 1540, King Affonso had even decided to support the slave trade in order to increase his own wealth and power.

By the 1600s, the Kongo kingdom was breaking apart. The Portuguese pressured Kongo chiefs in the provinces to rebel against the Mani-Kongo. As a result, the chiefs of some provinces declared their independence from the kingdom. Civil wars erupted as villages staged raids against each other to capture slaves and sell them to the Portuguese.

Thus, contact with the Portuguese had a severe and long-lasting effect on the people of Kongo and all of Africa. The Portuguese destroyed Kongo's trade in goods and replaced it with trade in human beings. Kongo lost many strong and able people to slavery. Finally, civil wars sparked by the Portuguese brought an end to the Kongo kingdom. ■

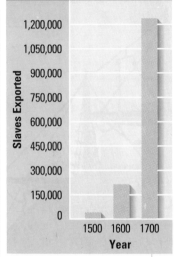

Kongo Slave Trade

Slaves Exported / Year

1,200,000	
1,050,000	
900,000	
750,000	
600,000	
450,000	
300,000	
150,000	
0	1500 1600 1700

▲ *In 1622, Queen Nzinga of Matamba visited a Portuguese official to plead for peace. He refused to give her a chair, so she sat on one of her servants instead. Look at the graph of the slave trade to see if the queen's pleas were answered.*

■ *Why did civil war erupt in Kongo?*

R E V I E W

1. **FOCUS** How did Kongo change after the arrival of the Portuguese?
2. **CONNECT** Compare the relationship of Portugal and Kongo with that of Portugal and Monomutapa.
3. **HISTORY** Describe the differences between the Portuguese and the Kongo people in their attitudes toward slaves.

4. **CRITICAL THINKING** Why do you think King John ignored Affonso's plea for help?
5. **WRITING ACTIVITY** Write a letter from King Affonso of Kongo to King John of Portugal in which King Affonso describes the effects of the slave trade in Kongo and asks King John to put a stop to it.

Chapter Review

Reviewing Key Terms

age set (p. 139)
city-state (p. 143)
currency (p. 150)
malaria (p. 148)
migrate (p. 137)

missionary (p. 152)
monsoon (p. 141)
oral tradition (p. 148)
plantation (p. 152)
plateau (p. 146)

A. For each sentence below write whether it is an example of a city-state, an oral tradition, or a currency. Explain your answer.
1. A mother sings songs to her children that she learned as a child.
2. At the restaurant the man pays for his dinner with a gold coin.
3. In addition to a mosque, Kilwa had a huge palace and houses of many stories.

B. Write whether each statement below is true or false. Then rewrite the false statements to make them true.
1. The Nok people migrated because the climate grew cold.
2. To sail by the monsoons, Arabs left for West Africa between April and October.
3. The Portuguese treated slaves harshly.
4. Christian missionaries taught African natives about Islam.
5. Many of the people in Africa suffered from malaria.
6. The Kikuyu used age-set groups during times of crisis.
7. Zimbabwe is located on a low plateau.

Exploring Concepts

A. In this chapter, you read about several groups of African people. The chart below compares four of the groups. Copy the chart on your own paper. Then complete the chart using information from the chapter. The first section has been done for you.

Peoples of Central and Southern Africa

	Occupations	Additional Information
Kikuyu	Farming	They relied upon age set groups in times of crisis.
Swahili		
Shona		
People of Kongo		

B. Answer each question with information from the chapter.
1. What are three kinds of terrain in central and southern Africa?
2. Why do most people of central and southern Africa speak a Bantu language and think of themselves as Bantu?
3. What products did the city of Rhapta import around A.D. 100? What did Mouza import from Rhapta?
4. How did the Indian Ocean trade between 1100–1500 affect the town of Kilwa?
5. What do we know about the people who founded Zimbabwe?
6. How did the Shona use the gold of Zimbabwe? How did they mine the gold in the 1100s?
7. What products did the people of the Kongo trade with the people around them before the Portuguese arrived?
8. What were the long-term effects of the Portuguese on Monomutapa and Kongo?

Reviewing Skills

1. Look at the map on this page. Construct a vertical profile of the land at 20° S. What is the highest elevation shown on your vertical profile? The lowest?
2. Use the following entry from the *Readers' Guide* to answer the questions.
   Monsoons
   Seasonal winds: a blessing or a curse?
   R. A. Borthwick. il maps *Journal of Economic Development* 129:21–7+ Ap '89
   a. What is the title of the article?
   b. Who is the author?
   c. What is the title of the periodical?
   d. On what pages does the article appear?
3. Imagine that African villagers are explaining a truth about life to their children. How might the villagers communicate this truth?

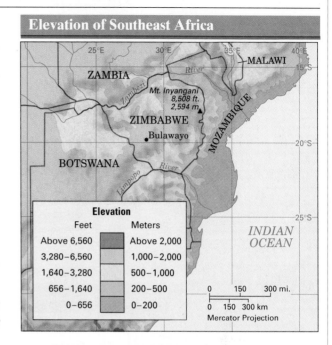

Elevation of Southeast Africa

Elevation		
Feet		**Meters**
Above 6,560		Above 2,000
3,280–6,560		1,000–2,000
1,640–3,280		500–1,000
656–1,640		200–500
0–656		0–200

Mercator Projection

Using Critical Thinking

1. If you wanted to know whether early African people suffered from sleeping sickness, what information in the chapter might help you to determine this?
2. What were the trading practices of the Arabs of Mouza around A.D. 100? What values of the Arab people do these trading practices reveal? Do you think these values are still important today? Explain your answer.
3. Reread Willi Posselt's report about the ruins of Great Zimbabwe. Imagine that you are one of the discoverers of the ruins of Great Zimbabwe. You come upon the city on a high plateau. You see a tower and a 30-foot wall around the city. Inside the buildings, you eventually discover hidden passages. What would you determine about the Shona's relationships with other groups from these observations?

Preparing for Citizenship

1. COLLECTING INFORMATION Alex Haley was the first black American to trace his family's history back to a village in West Africa. Look in Haley's book, *Roots, the Saga of an American Family* to find out how he used oral tradition to trace his family's roots.
2. INTERVIEWING Bantu villages were commonly ruled by a chief and a council of elders. Interview an official in your city or town. Find out how your town's government is organized. Is there anyone who functions like a chief? Is there any group that acts like a council of elders? If there are, what are their titles and responsibilities?
3. COLLABORATIVE LEARNING Work in committees to research one or two cities in your state or region that were founded as centers of trade. Locate the cities on a map. Find out what products were exported and imported by these cities, and whether this trade is the basis of their economy today. If not, find out how the economy of the city has changed. Each committee should decide what information is important and report it to the class.

Unit 4
Asian Civilizations

Reflect for a moment on this Chinese landscape—the grassy bluffs, the lush trees, the peaceful river, the family quietly taking its leave. For centuries, Asian artists, thinkers, and priests have been fascinated by such moments of calm natural beauty. Yet not all has been peace and beauty in China, Japan, India, and central Asia. Over the past 2,000 years, there have been times of chaos and fighting, even centuries when powerful rulers dominated vast empires.

220

Saying Farewell at Hsün Yang *by Qiu Ying, c. 1495*

1923

Chapter 7

Three Empires

This ceremonial sword belonged to an Ottoman sultan.

The conquerors came from homelands in central Asia. The Mongols swept down and captured lands from China to the Middle East. The Ottoman Turks migrated to Asia Minor and then set their sights on new frontiers. The Mughals trekked over the steep passes of the Himalayas and invaded India. Through strong leadership and tolerance toward the people they conquered, the Mongols, Ottomans, and Mughals built great empires.

1260–1294 Led by Kublai Khan, the Mongol Empire reaches its height. Mongol warriors (left) take control of the Middle East from Egypt.

950	1100	1250	1400

1235 Mali defeats Ghana to become the major power in West Africa.

1096–1291 European Christians fight Arab Muslims for control of Jerusalem and the Holy Land.

997

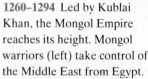

During the 1400s and 1500s, the Ottomans built a powerful and wealthy empire. Sultan Sulieman wore the jewels at the right on his turban. Sultan Bayezid wore the silk caftan at left as he sat on his throne.

1556–1605 The Mughal Empire prospers under Akbar. In the painting at the right, Akbar directs the building of a fort in his capital.

| 1550 | 1700 | 1850 | Today |

c. 1600 The Kongo kingdom breaks apart due to civil wars sparked by the Portuguese.

1923

■ *What effect did the environment of the steppes have on the Mongol people?*

allegiance to him. They would then become the new leader's *nöker,* or followers. Their allegiance to him outweighed any allegiance to clan or tribe.

For all Mongol groups, the need to protect themselves and compete for grazing lands was crucial. To do so, the Mongols developed incredible skill on horseback.

Mongols had such control over their mounts that they could ride long distances using only their feet. Their hands, then, were free to wield weapons in battle. Their exceptional riding skill and their great ability in using weapons while on horseback gave the Mongols a distinct advantage over their less-skilled enemies. ■

Mongol Leadership

Horses also helped the Mongols in another way. Each soldier had at least three or four extra horses carrying food and water. Because he didn't have to stop for fresh food, water, or horses, the Mongol soldier could travel vast distances quickly.

A Mongol soldier carried an array of weapons into battle: two or three bows; three quivers of arrows; and an ax, rope, and sword. His bow was short enough to be used while riding, yet it was strong enough to launch an arrow into a target 350 yards away.

Although clans and tribes often fought with each other, once in a while a strong leader could unite them all against a common enemy. The founder of the Mongol Empire was such a leader.

The Great Khan

Temujin (*TEHM yoo jihn*), known today as Genghis Khan, was born in 1167. When Temujin was 12 years old, his father, a tribal chief, was murdered by a rival chief. Fearing that he would be killed next, Temujin fled with his mother and four brothers. Although it was nearly impossible for very small groups to survive the environment of the steppe, Temujin, with the help of his mother,

Across Time & Space

The modern country of Mongolia, which lies between China and the Soviet Union, is officially known as the Mongolian People's Republic. Nearly all the people of Mongolia are the descendants of the Mongols, who built an empire in the 1200s.

➤ *The energy of Mongols in battle is shown in this painting from a manuscript page. Notice how the artist has used swirling figures to give a feeling of movement to the scene.*

kept the family alive. Thus began his reputation as an intelligent and resourceful leader.

Temujin's reputation continued to grow, and in 1206, an assembly of tribal chiefs elected him the great **khan,** or leader, of the Mongols. They gave Temujin the name Genghis Khan, which means "ruler of all within the seas." He was 39 years old.

Genghis Khan the Warrior

Genghis Khan shaped the powerful Mongol warriors into a tightly structured army. He grouped soldiers into units of 10,000 troops. These units were subdivided into smaller groups of 1,000, 100, and 10. The smaller groups had individual leaders who reported to the group leader above them. This type of military leadership created a clear chain of command within the larger army and helped create order on the battlefield. Genghis further strengthened the Mongol army by incorporating defeated enemy troops who would swear allegiance to the Mongol ruler.

Genghis Khan also devised elaborate signals to be used as communication amid the noise and confusion of battle. Soldiers used drums, horns, shouts, and even bird calls to communicate with each other. Mongol leaders could then direct and organize their troops as situations developed on the battlefield.

Using this highly skilled and structured army, Genghis Khan added vast areas to his empire. The Mongols conquered all the lands between Beijing and the Caspian Sea.

Genghis Khan the Ruler

Although Genghis Khan knew the strength of his warriors, he realized that there were areas where the Mongols were weak. The Mongols lacked a written language. So Genghis used a captured scribe to create a written language for them. He also used the skills of foreign craftspersons and specialists

▲ *The great Mongol ruler Genghis Khan is pictured in this portrait from a Turkish manuscript. Most representations of Mongol rulers come from other cultures.*

Three Empires

to improve his army. From them he learned how to use catapults and gunpowder bombs. These weapons helped the Mongols besiege enemy fortresses.

Genghis respected the knowledge and beliefs of others. During his rule, Genghis Khan opened his empire to foreign travelers.

Missionaries and merchants were allowed to journey through Mongol lands. He also made a series of laws forbidding fighting among tribes. Despite the fact that Genghis Khan introduced several reforms, he is said to have admitted that "man's highest joy is in victory: to conquer one's enemies." ■

■ *What qualities did Genghis Khan possess that made him a successful ruler?*

The Later Khans

Genghis Khan died in 1227. In 1229, the empire was divided into four sections, called khanates. His four sons were each assigned a khanate. His third son, Ogadei *(ahg ah DY),* was elected the Great Khan, the overall ruler of the Mongol Empire. One khanate included part of present-day China and present-day Russia. Another occupied most of southern Russia. The third was in Persia, and the

khanate of the Great Khan was in what is now western Mongolia.

The growth of the Mongol Empire continued after Genghis's death. China was conquered in 1234. In 1237, Ogadei sent Mongol horsemen to conquer the rest of southern Russia, as well as Poland and Hungary. Upon Ogadei's death in 1241, the Mongol leaders ended their attacks in Hungary and returned to Mongolia to elect

▼ *The Mongol Empire grew rapidly and eventually covered much of Asia. Name the four sections that the Mongol Empire was divided into after the death of Genghis Khan.*

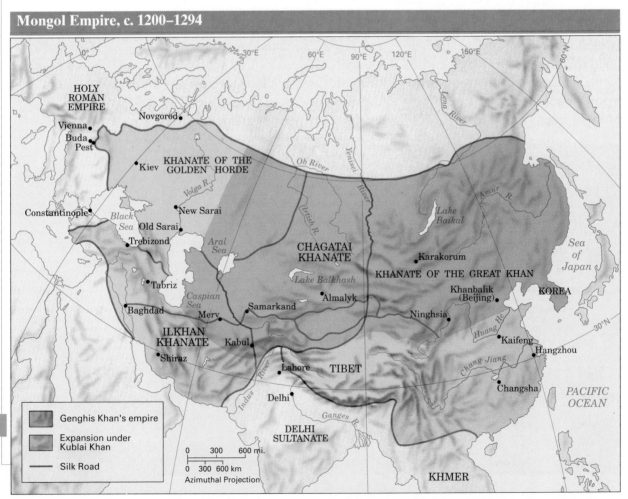

Mongol Empire, c. 1200–1294

HOLY ROMAN EMPIRE
Vienna
Buda
Pest
Novgorod
Kiev
KHANATE OF THE GOLDEN HORDE
Volga R.
Ob River
Yenisei River
Lena River
Constantinople
Black Sea
New Sarai
Old Sarai
Trebizond
Aral Sea
Irtish R.
CHAGATAI KHANATE
Lake Baikal
Amur R.
Sea of Japan
Tabriz
Caspian Sea
Lake Balkhash
Karakorum
KHANATE OF THE GREAT KHAN
Baghdad
Merv
Samarkand
Almalyk
Khanbalik (Beijing)
KOREA
ILKHAN KHANATE
Kabul
Ninghsia
Huang He
Kaifeng
Shiraz
Indus River
Lahore
TIBET
Chang Jiang
Hangzhou
Delhi
Ganges R.
Changsha
PACIFIC OCEAN
DELHI SULTANATE
KHMER

Genghis Khan's empire
Expansion under Kublai Khan
— Silk Road

0   300   600 mi.
0   300   600 km
Azimuthal Projection

a new Great Khan. This halted the Mongol expansion into Europe.

Kublai Khan

Twenty years later, Genghis Khan's grandson, Kublai Khan, was elected Great Khan. Under Kublai's reign from 1260 to 1294, the Mongol Empire reached its height. The Mongols extended their borders to include eastern Europe, most of the Middle East, China, and the intervening territory. The map on page 166 shows the lands controlled by the Mongol Empire at its height.

Although the Mongol Empire grew, not all Mongol attempts to conquer other lands were successful. Under Kublai Khan, the Mongols tried to invade Japan in 1274 and 1281. Both invasion attempts were stopped by a typhoon, or hurricane, which destroyed most of the Mongol ships.

Like his grandfather Genghis, Kublai developed many programs to help stabilize the empire. Unlike the Chinese, Kublai respected merchants, and under his rule both internal and foreign trade flourished. He also established a postal system with riders covering up to 250 miles a day. Postal stations also served as inns for traveling merchants. Thus, the postal service helped communication and trade.

Breakdown of the Empire

Ultimately, however, the Mongols were better conquerors than rulers. They simply were not able to control the vast area they had won in battle. Communication among the four khanates became increasingly difficult.

How Do We Know?

HISTORY *Much of what we know about the history of the Mongols comes from legend and from their appearance in the histories of other peoples. These peoples were generally enemies of the Mongols. How might this lack of primary-source material from the Mongol viewpoint affect our view of the Mongols today?*

UNDERSTANDING CONQUEST

The Romans in the 2nd century. The Mongols in the 12th century. The British in the 19th century. Each group was famous for conquering vast territories and diverse peoples.

Reasons for Conquest

What motivates one group to conquer another? There are probably as many reasons as there are human needs—security, food, land, wealth, beliefs, and power. The Mongols, for example, originally conquered to gain grazing land. But, over time, they conquered to expand their empire's wealth and power base.

The power that accompanies control of territories and people also motivated many Roman conquests. But the desire for security pushed conquest. The Romans fought three wars over Sicily, an island in the Mediterranean Sea. Rome eventually won control of Sicily in 149 B.C.

In the 1700s and 1800s, the British launched a series of conquests to satisfy a need for resources and markets. The British built an empire that ranged around the world to Africa, Asia, North America, and Australia.

Conquest and Empire

Few great empires exist today. The Mongol Empire broke up because of rebellions by conquered peoples and problems in adminis-tering such a large area. Throughout history, successful conquests have not guaranteed successful empires.

Three Empires

Moreover, the Mongols were no longer the fierce warriors who had swept down from the steppes. Some began to adopt the social customs, languages, and religions of the people they had conquered. Ghazan Khan, who ruled in Persia, made Islam the state religion and adopted much of the Persian culture. In China, the Mongols accepted Tibetan Buddhism, but they were also influenced by the culture of the Chinese.

By 1300, the unity of the Mongol Empire had disappeared. It was then easy for the conquered peoples of the empire to overthrow their invaders. The Persians drove out the Mongols in 1335, and the Chinese followed suit in 1368.

In 1370, Timur the Lame, or Tamerlane as he is known to Europeans, made a final attempt to build a lasting empire. Timur was a Muslim Turk of Mongol descent. He ruled from Samarkand in what is now Soviet Central Asia. Timur led successful raids throughout central Asia to Persia and Mesopotamia, Asia Minor, southern Russia, and India.

Timur's empire lasted for 45 years. When he died in 1405, his empire was divided among his sons, as Genghis Khan's had been. His heirs fought among themselves for control, and Timur's fourth son, Shahrukh *(shah ROOK),* won control. After his death in 1447, the empire gradually lost its power. ■

The Impact of the Mongols

Although the Mongols were fearsome warriors who conquered vast territories, that was not their only memorable accomplishment. The Mongols also showed tolerance, or respect, for different religions. They believed that there was truth in each religion. Thus, many religions existed in their empire, including Christianity, Daoism, Buddhism, and Islam.

The Mongols also promoted trade and travel throughout their empire. The Silk Road, which had run from China through central Asia to Mesopotamia and Syria during the Roman Empire, became active again under Mongol protection.

Travelers from both Europe and the Arab world visited the Mongol Empire. The Italian Marco Polo visited the court of Kublai Khan in the late 13th century. He later wrote a book describing his visit, which was the first accurate record of China by a European.

The 14th-century Moroccan writer Ibn Battuta also described the world of the Mongols in a book

about his travels through Africa, Asia, and Europe. The records that Ibn Battuta kept of his many experiences throughout Asia served to open up the Mongol world to other people of the time.

In addition to impressing travelers, the Mongol Empire fostered the spread of ideas from Asia to Europe. Also benefiting Europe was the spread of such Chinese inventions as the compass and gunpowder. The compass would make possible Europe's golden age of discovery, and gunpowder would alter the rules of European warfare. ■

▲ *This painting shows travelers on the well-protected Silk Road during the Mongol reign.*

◄ *This statue of a Chinese goddess was made during the Yuan, or Mongol, Dynasty.*

■ *What were the positive effects of Mongol rule?*

REVIEW

1. **FOCUS** How did the Mongols affect Europe and Asia?
2. **CONNECT** Compare social bonds among the Mongols to social bonds among the Kikuyu.
3. **CULTURE** What Mongol qualities contributed to their success as conquerors?
4. **CRITICAL THINKING** Ibn Battuta and Marco Polo traveled freely throughout the Mongol Empire. What does this indicate about Mongol rule?

5. **CRITICAL THINKING** Both Genghis Khan and Kublai Khan made significant contributions to the Mongol Empire. Which of the two was the greatest Mongol leader? Why?
6. **ACTIVITY** Read the poem "Kubla Khan," written in 1798, by the English poet, Samuel Taylor Coleridge. What does the poem tell you about the late 18th-century view of the Mongol Empire?

Three Empires

LESSON 2

The Ottoman Empire

The year was 1257. The Mongols had decided to conquer Baghdad, the capital of the eastern Islamic Empire and home of the Abbasid Caliphate. Hulagu, the Mongol khan, sent the following message to the caliph:

You have learned the fate brought upon the world since Genghis Khan by the Mongol armies. . . . How then should entry into this city be refused to us, who possess such strength and power? Beware of taking arms against the Standard!

The Abbasid caliph refused to surrender to Hulagu and replied:

O young man, . . . do you not know that . . . all the worshipers of Allah . . . are slaves to this court of mine, and that I can command them to muster?

Unfortunately, the caliph could not raise enough support. Mongol armies attacked Baghdad in January 1258. One month later, the city fell. The Mongols killed about 200,000 citizens and burned most of the city. Both the Abbasid Caliphate and the Golden Age of Islam were destroyed.

➤ *This manuscript page from the* History of the World *by Jami Al-Tawarikh records the destruction of Baghdad in 1258 by the Mongols.*

170

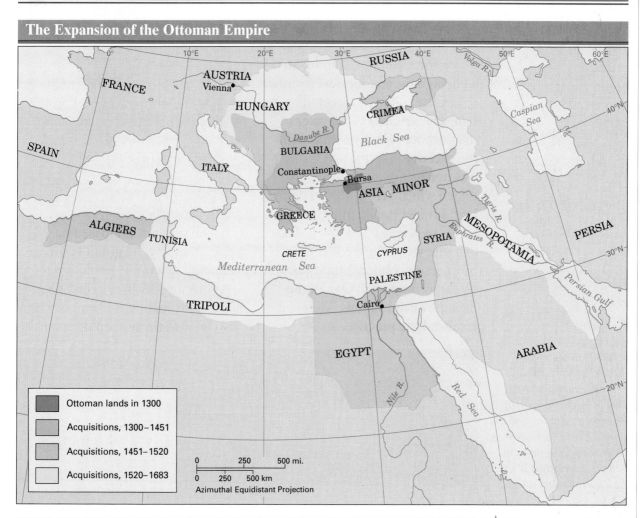

Ottoman lands in 1300

Acquisitions, 1300–1451

Acquisitions, 1451–1520

Acquisitions, 1520–1683

0   250   500 mi.

0 250 500 km

Azimuthal Equidistant Projection

The Early Ottoman Empire

As a result of the westward movement of the Mongols, many Turkish tribes were driven from their homelands in central Asia. Some of these tribes, who had converted to Islam, settled in Asia Minor and established small states.

Around 1300, one Muslim state was governed by a chief named Osman. Osman and his followers, who became known in the West as Ottomans, were ghazis. **Ghazis** were warriors who fought to expand the frontiers of Islam. As Osman won victories over Christian Byzantine armies, he attracted new followers to his armies.

Osman's armies conquered and united various lands in Asia Minor previously controlled by Byzantium. These conquests formed the core of the Ottoman Empire. Under Osman and his successors, the Ottoman state grew. One of their greatest successes was the capture in 1326 of the Byzantine city of Bursa, which they made the Ottoman capital.

Muslim Ottoman expansion alarmed Christian Europeans, who assembled an army to stop them. But the Ottomans destroyed the European forces in 1389 at Kossovo, in present-day Yugoslavia, and emerged as the most powerful state in the region. In the map above, find this early range of the Ottoman Empire. ∎

▲ *The Ottoman Empire expanded steadily for four centuries. Use the scale to determine the greatest extent of the empire from east to west.*

■ *How did the Ottoman Empire begin and expand?*

171

Three Empires

Rulers and Subjects

In the Ottoman Empire, all campaigns of conquest were either led by the sultan or directed by him. The **sultan** was the ruler of the Ottoman Empire. Although the succession to the sultanship was hereditary, no rules determined which prince should be the heir. Princes fought among themselves to become the sultan. In fact, the winner often killed his brothers to eliminate their possible threat to his power. One of the most powerful sultans, Mehmed, legalized the practice.

To whichever of my sons the Sultanate may be vouchsafed [granted], it is proper for him to put his brothers to death, to preserve the order of the world.

Ottoman legal code, about 1460

State Organization

The sultan was advised on state affairs by the **grand vizier,** or prime minister. The grand vizier oversaw a political system that extended throughout the empire. He also headed the governing council

➤ *The Selim Mosque symbolized the majesty of the Ottoman Empire. It is also known as the Blue Mosque because of the color of its tiles and stained glass. As you can see in the photograph on the left, the mosque is still used for religious services today.*

The world around 1550 seemed to belong to the Ottomans. But events after the death of Suleiman in 1566 sent the Ottoman Empire into a long, gradual decline from which it never fully recovered. ■

■ *What were Suleiman's accomplishments?*

Decline of the Ottoman Empire

After the reign of Suleiman, the Ottoman Empire slowly began to lose both its territories and its military superiority. Although the empire lasted until the 20th century, it never again reached the prominence it had enjoyed under Suleiman.

Several factors contributed to the empire's decline. First, much of the empire's monetary strength depended on constant expansion. When the conquests slowed down after 1571, revenues from conquered lands declined. In addition, a new trade route to India was found. The old trade route through Ottoman territory became less important. Thus, trade revenues declined drastically. The empire underwent considerable financial hardships.

Second, the janissaries began to play a more active and often disruptive role in the government of the empire. Eventually, the sultans lost control over the powerful janissaries. This lack of a strong, central leadership had a disastrous effect on the empire. The sultans who followed Suleiman were incapable of directing the elaborate political system that the Ottoman Empire depended on to survive.

The combination of these factors led to a decline that continued over the next 350 years. By the 1800s, the Ottoman Empire was known as The Sick Man of Europe. In 1923, a large part of the empire was reorganized into independent nations. The lands that remained became the country of Turkey. All members of the Ottoman Dynasty were expelled from Turkey. The Ottoman Empire had come to an end. ■

◄ *Mehmed VI, the last Ottoman sultan, was removed from power in 1922. Over 600 years of uninterrupted Ottoman rule had come to an end.*

■ *Why did the Ottoman Empire decline?*

REVIEW

1. **FOCUS** How important a factor was leadership in the rise and fall of the Ottoman Empire?

2. **CONNECT** How did the Mongol Empire and Ottoman Empire compare in their treatment of religious groups?

3. **HISTORY** Why did westerners call Suleiman The Magnificent, while his own people called him The Lawgiver?

4. **CRITICAL THINKING** How did Istanbul represent the best qualities of the empire?

5. **WRITING ACTIVITY** Write a poem or passage praising a former United States leader, as Baki did for Suleiman.

LESSON 3

The Mughal Empire

THINKING FOCUS

What factors contributed to the rise and fall of the Mughal Empire?

Key Term

- salary

➤ *When invaders such as Mahmud crossed into northern India, they were startled by its lush beauty, as in this countryside near Rawalpinda on the Pakistan-India border.*

> *T*he whole country of India is full of gold and jewels, and of the plants which grow there are those fit for making apparel, and aromatic plants and the sugar-cane, and the whole aspect of the country is pleasant and delightful. Now, since the inhabitants are chiefly infidels and idolaters, by the order of God [Allah] and his Prophet it is right for us to conquer them.

These are the reasons that the Turkish Sultan Mahmud of Ghazna gave for his invasions of India. Between 997 and 1030, Mahmud invaded northern India 17 times.

Mahmud had long heard tales about the riches of India from Muslim scholars and merchants who had traveled there. The scholars went to India to study astronomy, medicine, and mathematics. The merchants brought back Indian gold, jewels, and silks. Eventually, soldiers and conquerors traveled to India for less peaceful purposes.

As Muslims spreading the word of Muhammad to unbelievers, the sultan and his followers felt that their invasion of India was both just and holy. A famous Persian epic poet named Firdausi (the pen name of Abul Kasim Mansur)

lived in Ghazna during the time of the Turkish invasions of India. He had a rather different explanation of the sultan's motive, and it wasn't positive:

> *T*o plunder their neighbors and gain all themselves
> Is what men desire,
>   using God as excuse.

On the Eve of the Empire

India's geography—with its forbidding mountain ranges and inviting valleys—both discouraged and attracted invaders. The land falls into three distinct geographic regions. Curving across the far north of India from east to west are the Himalayas, the highest mountains in the world. The Himalayas, 200 miles wide in some places, seem to be perfect natural barriers to foreign invasion. Nevertheless, invaders penetrated the mountains through steep passes, such as the 33-mile-long Khyber Pass, located in the northwest.

South of the Himalayas lie the fertile plains of northern India. Many invaders were attracted to the valleys of the Brahmaputra, Ganges, and Indus rivers, which include some of the richest farmland in the world.

Farther south is the Deccan, or southern plateau. The Deccan forms most of the southern peninsula. It is separated from the north by the Vindhya mountains and a series of other low mountain ranges. This rugged southern region with its mountainous terrain and numerous rivers presented an awesome challenge that few invaders chose to take.

The geographic regions of India helped lead to political divisions, especially between the south and north. Hindu states in the south suffered few foreign invasions. However, in the north, Hindu kingdoms had to compete for power with a succession of invaders. The map below shows the side-by-side existence of regional Muslim and Hindu states by the early 1500s. Muslims, such as

▼ *Look at the physical map of India. Using the elevation legend, describe northern and southern India. Had you been a Muslim invader, where in India would you have settled? Why?*

India's Physical Regions and the Kingdom of Northern India

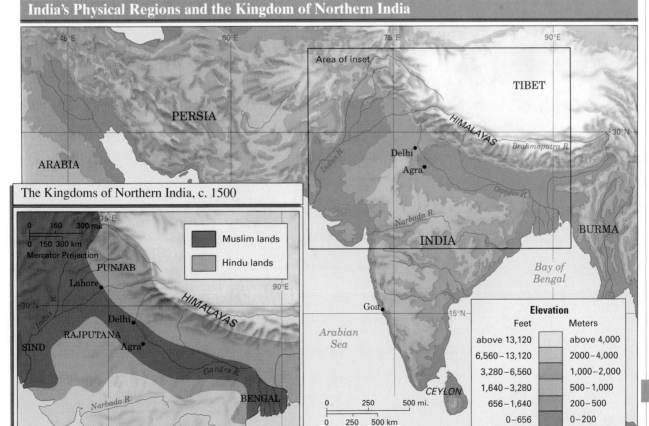

The Kingdoms of Northern India, c. 1500

Muslim lands

Hindu lands

Elevation	
Feet	Meters
above 13,120	above 4,000
6,560–13,120	2000–4,000
3,280–6,560	1,000–2,000
1,640–3,280	500–1,000
656–1,640	200–500
0–656	0–200

179

■ In what ways was northern India a divided country during the 1500s?

Sultan Mahmud, captured several Indian cities and set up their own governments. In other cities, power remained in the hands of native Hindu princes.

These states often reflected the different world views of Muslim and Hindu cultures. The Muslim faith in one God and a strong desire to spread that faith contrasted sharply with the more tolerant Hindu belief in various forms of god. Also, the Hindus lived in a caste system—a strict social order in which a person's position was fixed by birth and was unchangeable. Muslims, however, had a less rigid social structure—individuals could change their social status with hard work and luck. These basic differences in religion and social structure led to constant tension and open conflict between the neighboring states. ■

Founders of the Empire

The greatest of the Muslim states was the Sultanate of Delhi in north central India. In 1517, a Muslim Turk from central Asia named Babur invaded India. He conquered the Delhi Sultanate in 1526 and went on to found the Mughal Empire.

Babur's Arrival

Related to Timur on his father's side and Genghis Khan on his mother's side, Babur seemed a fitting conqueror and founder of a world empire. Babur had dreamed of reestablishing a great empire in the Mongol tradition. In 1527, he defeated the Rajputs, the strongest Hindu state in India. During Babur's reign, which lasted until his death in 1530, the empire covered most of northern India. His empire was called the Mughal, from the Persian-Indian word for Mongol.

Babur was a wise and kind leader. Like many Mughal emperors who followed him, Babur was

➤ This painting, on the right, honors the founders of the Mughal dynasty— Timur, Babur, and his son Humayun. Timur wears a turban jewel, like the one above, a symbol of high rank.

well educated. Throughout his life Babur wrote about the Indian world that he had conquered—its people, animals, landscapes, and customs. But he also seemed genuinely homesick for items from his homeland in central Asia such as good horses, grapes, muskmelons, ice, cold water, good bread and hot baths. Babur wrote in his memoirs, the *Babar-nama*, that "the chief excellency of Hindustan [India] is, that it is a large country, and has abundance of gold and silver."

Akbar the Ruler

Despite his longings for his homeland, Babur remained in India. His grandson, Akbar, who reigned for 49 years (1556–1605) would be remembered as the greatest Mughal emperor.

Akbar's rule began when he was only 13 years old. During his reign the empire expanded to cover most of north and central India and Afghanistan. Look at the map on page 183. Estimate how many miles the empire covered under Akbar.

We know many details about Akbar's life and personality from his biographer, Abul Fazl. For example, we know that "Akbar ate one meal a day— of 40 dishes—and enjoyed ice brought from the mountains." Abul Fazl also tells us that Akbar took great interest in good craftsmanship. He wrote that Akbar often visited the more than 100 workshops around the palace where crafts and weapons were made.

Akbar's Requirements for a Short Journey	
500 Camels	50 Torch bearers
100 Elephants	500 Pioneers
100 Bearers	150 Sweepers
50 Tent makers	30 Leather workers
400 Carts	50 Carpenters
100 Water carriers	500 Troopers

Perhaps Akbar's greatest accomplishment was the integration of Hindus into the empire. Akbar divided the empire into provinces and set up a civil service system to manage its lands. Each job had a **salary,** or fixed payment, and jobs were given only to qualified people, without regard to religion. Thus, many non-Muslims were able to enter government service.

In addition, Akbar reformed the unfair tax system of the empire. He

◄ *This finely crafted spoon was created in one of Akbar's palace workshops in the late 1500s.*

◄ *The Mughal court used huge numbers of people and animals. This chart shows what Akbar needed to go on a short journey.*

▼ *Babur's Mughal army crossed these Himalayas to invade and conquer northern India.*

reclassified the value of land according to its ability to produce crops. Taxes were lower for those with less productive land. This was fairer than the old system, which made every farmer pay the same rate.

Earlier Muslim sultans had tried to force the Hindus to convert to Islam and often destroyed Hindu temples. Akbar showed great respect for religious differences. He stopped the practice of enslaving prisoners of war and converting them to Islam. A tax on

mother was a Rajput princess, wrote, "My father always associated with the learned of every creed and religion."

Akbar the Art Patron

During Akbar's reign, the Mughal court became a center of culture. Akbar invited artists, poets, and musicians to his court and encouraged them to produce works for the court.

Miniature painting reached great heights under the Mughals. Often the subject of the painting was the emperor himself engaged in some pursuit, such as hunting, receiving guests, or laying out a new garden. ■

Akbar had his new capital city, Fatehpur Sikri, built in 1570. In the painting on the right, Akbar is being welcomed back to Fatehpur Sikri by his sons in 1584. Fatehpur Sikri was abandoned after being inhabited for only 14 years, but the city still stands.

■ *Evaluate this statement: Akbar was a just and tolerant Mughal emperor.*

Hindu pilgrims and the *jizya* tax, which was imposed on all non-Muslims, were both abolished. Even Akbar's personal life reflected this religious tolerance. He married women of different religions, including several Rajput princesses. He invited scholars of different faiths to his court and sponsored debates on religion. Akbar's son Jahangir, whose

Inheritors of the Empire

The Mughal Empire continued to grow in size and splendor as Akbar's successors followed his policies. In 1605, Akbar's eldest son Jahangir *(juh hahn GEER)* inherited the throne.

Jahangir was less interested in the day-to-day administration of the empire than his father had been. Fortunately, the government was so stable that it did not really need much of Jahangir's attention. Jahangir has a strong interest in nature. He kept a pair of cranes with him in his tent when travelling. He also had his court painters record detailed images of birds, plants, and animals.

Jahangir's son, Shah Jahan (*SHAH juh HAHN*), ruled from 1628 to 1658. Jahan is renowned as the largest Mughal spender and builder. He poured huge amounts of money into construction projects in Delhi, which he made the capital in 1648. The projects included palaces with walls of marble inlaid with precious stones and ceilings of gold and silver.

Without doubt, Shah Jahan's most famous architectural undertaking was the Taj Mahal. With its inlaid white marble, pointed arches, and domes, the Taj reflects the Mughal style of architecture.

Twenty-two thousand laborers built the Taj Mahal over a 22-year period. A Catholic priest witnessed the difficult construction process.

Blocks [of white marble] had been brought there from over forty leagues away [about 120 miles] for the erection of these edifices. Some of these blocks. . . . were of such unusual size and length that they drew the sweat of many powerful teams of oxen and . . . buffaloes, which were dragging enormous, strongly-made wagons, in teams of twenty or thirty animals.

Sebastien Manrique, *Travels,* 1650

To learn more about the splendor of the Taj Mahal, see A Closer Look on page 184.

Only a very wealthy nation could afford such massive building efforts. At one point in the reign of Shah Jahan, "750 pounds of pearls, 275 pounds of emeralds, 5,000 gems from Cathay, corals, topazes, and . . . tubs of uncut diamonds" formed only a part of the Mughal treasury.

But, as time went on, Shah Jahan's spending took its toll on the empire. Shah Jahan added some of the Deccan Hindu states to the Mughal lands. But the cost of military campaigns, combined with huge building projects, seriously drained the treasury. ■

■ *How did the rule of Jahangir and Shah Jahan affect the empire?*

▼ *The Mughal Empire expanded greatly in a relatively short period of time. How much larger was the empire after the death of Akbar?*

The Expansion of the Mughal Empire

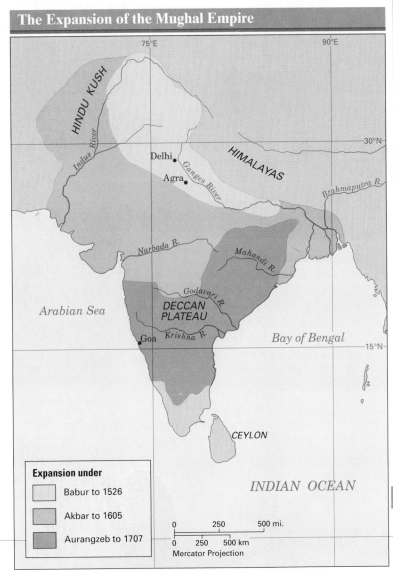

Expansion under

- Babur to 1526
- Akbar to 1605
- Aurangzeb to 1707

0   250   500 mi.

0   250   500 km

Mercator Projection

183

The Taj Mahal

Mumtaz Mahal was the beloved wife of Shah Jahan. When she died in childbirth in 1631, her heartbroken husband built for her the most glorious tomb in the world—the Taj Mahal.

The rose was her favorite flower. Some say it was a model for the floor plan of the building. Can you see a rose in the design?

Courtesy
Archeological Survey of India
Government of India.

Mumtaz Mahal

Shah Jahan

From the white marble dome to the precise gardens, every part of the Taj Mahal fits together. Caravans brought rare, colorful jewels from around the world so that the flower designs inside would be the right colors. Craftspeople and architects came from Turkey, Persia, and even Venice, Italy, to work on the tomb.

Mumtaz Mahal and the Shah were constant companions, even on his military campaigns. He trusted her opinion on everything from art to politics, and showered her with gifts of roses and diamonds. He was so crushed by her death that his beard turned white overnight.

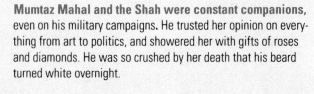

End of the Empire

He reinstated the *jizya,* the tax on non-Muslims. He prohibited the building of new Hindu temples, and he tried to force Hindus to convert to Islam. These policies caused many Hindu rebellions, especially in the Deccan. Aurangzeb spent the last 25 years of his reign fighting a rebellious group of Hindus known as the Marathas. The cost of 25 years of war greatly strained the Mughal economy.

◄ Aurangzeb, the last great ruler of the Mughal Empire, is shown in this painting from a Mughal miniature album.

The empire weakened further under Aurangzeb *(AWR ung zehb),* Shah Jahan's son. Aurangzeb, who ruled from 1658 to 1707, also fought in the Deccan. He captured several more Hindu states, but the cost of the wars drained an already low treasury.

Policy Changes

Although Aurangzeb continued his family's military activities, he made important policy changes.

Foreign Invaders

Aurangzeb was the last Mughal ruler to reign over a great empire. After his death in 1707, successive rulers continued to lose land to various rebelling factions, especially the Marathas. Although the Mughals still ruled a small kingdom at Delhi, their empire no longer existed.

The final blow to the Mughals would come not from neighboring invaders but from Europeans. As stories of Mughal splendor and growing weakness spread, European nations began to invade by sea. In 1818, Great Britain took control of India. The last Mughal ruler formally gave up the throne in 1858. ■

■ *Why did the Mughal Empire decline?*

R E V I E W

1. **FOCUS** What factors contributed to the rise and fall of the Mughal Empire?
2. **CONNECT** How were the early invaders of India similar to the early Ottomans?
3. **GEOGRAPHY** How did India's geography affect invasion attempts?
4. **CULTURE** How does the Taj Mahal represent the height of Mughal architecture?
5. **CRITICAL THINKING** Compare and contrast the rule of Akbar to that of other Mughal rulers. Defend the statement that Akbar was the greatest Mughal ruler.
6. **CRITICAL THINKING** Babur, Akbar, Jahangir, Shah Jahan, Aurangzeb—during whose reign would you have liked to live? Why?
7. **WRITING ACTIVITY** You have now read about the rise and fall of three great empires: the Mongol, the Ottoman, and the Mughal. Write an imaginary conversation between the three great emperors: Genghis Khan, Suleiman, and Akbar. Have them discuss what an empire should be like.

Three Empires

Reading Mughal Paintings

Here's Why

By studying art from the past, you can learn about the beliefs, actions, values and customs of people who lived long ago. Art flourished under the patronage of the Mughal emperors. Mughal paintings are rich in information. But first, you must learn how to "read" paintings.

Here's How

Like books, paintings often tell a story. When you study a painting, look for the main idea and identify the major characters. Examine how the painter sets the scene and determine what action is taking place. Then look for cultural details and clues to the emotions of the characters.

Study the painting on the opposite page. This scene by Nar Singh was painted to il-illustrate Abul Fazl's *Akbar-nama,* or history of Akbar.

Akbar's religious and cultural tolerance is the main theme of the painting. The central figure is Akbar, who sits enthroned under a bright red canopy. You may recognize him: on page 182, you saw a painting of his return to Fatehpur Sikri. The key on this page identifies Akbar with the numeral one (1).

The figures who form a circle in front of Akbar are all religious scholars. Find the figures labeled in the key by the numeral two (2). These men are two of the three Jesuit priests whom Akbar had invited to teach about Christianity in 1580. One is Rudolpho Aquaviva, the head of the mission. The other is either the translator Francisco Henriques or the Jesuit priest Antonio Monserrate. The rest of the figures in the circle are thought to be Muslims and Hindus. Outside the courtyard, in the painting's second level, two guards stand watch (3). The bottom level shows horses and passersby (4).

The painting's setting is the Ibadat-Khanah, or House of Worship, located within Akbar's palace at Fatehpur Sikri. Akbar encouraged scholars of diverse faiths to engage in religious discussions at the Ibadat-Khanah. Muslims, Hindus, Christians, Parsees, Zoroastrians, and Jews were all made welcome by Akbar.

This scene shows an evening session at the House of Worship. A heated debate is underway, with participants vigorously discussing the merits and flaws of Christianity and Islam.

In the *Akbar-nama,* Abul Fazl gives a version of what took place that evening. Fazl claims that Father Aquaviva challenged a Muslim

religious scholar to a trial by fire. Fazl says Aquaviva offered to enter a fire holding the Bible if a Muslim scholar would do the same, holding the Koran. Other accounts say that it was actually Akbar or the Muslims who challenged the Jesuits. Although the versions differ, it seems clear that a trial by fire was discussed but rejected.

Now look for important details in the painting. Notice that many of the men hold books, and that books lie scattered on the floor. In this respect, the scene is typical: Akbar enjoyed religious and philosophical debate, and he surrounded himself with learned men.

اثرای بوی یا دری ، دلف از و نشوران نصاری بنهم وفطرت نشان کتابهی داست دران بزم اکهی کهه طرا

Note how the painter conveys the emotions of the religious scholars and the vigor of the debate. You can see that many of the men are gesturing. This suggests that the scholars were speaking emphatically, and that several conversations were taking place at once.

You have seen how to "read" paintings. Now try to use what you have learned and interpret a painting on your own.

Try It

Look again at the painting of Akbar being welcomed to Fatehpur Sikri, on page 182. What is the painting's main idea, or theme? Who are the major characters? Where does the scene take place, and what is happening in this scene? What cultural information can you gain from examining the painting's details? How does the painter suggest the characters' emotions?

Apply It

Find books that include paintings by American artists of the 1900s, such as Grant Wood, Andrew Wyeth, or John Sloan. Choose a painting that shows an aspect of life in the United States. "Read" the painting, using the approach taught in Here's How.

The fact that Akbar sits above the others symbolizes the power of the emperor. The architecture, decorations, and beautiful floor coverings show the splendor of the royal court. The absence of women in the painting is significant. Women were excluded from the business of the Mughal court, except as entertainers.

Three Empires

Chapter Review

Reviewing Key Terms

clan (p. 163)
divan (p. 173)
ghazi (p. 171)
grand vizier (p. 172)
janissary (p. 173)

khan (p. 165)
millet (p.174)
salary (p. 181)
steppe (p. 162)
sultan (p. 172)

4. janissary, Ottoman
5. khan, Mongol
6. millet, Ottoman
7. sultan, Ottoman

A. In the following list, each key term is paired with the name of the empire to which it is related. Write a sentence using each of the pairs, showing how they are related. Use the Glossary on pages 543–549 to check your understanding of the meanings.
1. clan, Mongol
2. divan, Ottoman
3. ghazi, Ottoman

B. Write the key term that is described by each sentence below.
1. Both the winter and summer weather of the vast semiarid plain of central Asia was very uncomfortable.
2. The prime minister had other responsibilities in addition to advising the sultan on state affairs.
3. Workers under Akbar were given a fixed payment for their services.

Exploring Concepts

A. The Mongol, Ottoman, and Mughal empires all had strengths that helped them grow and prosper. They also had weaknesses that caused problems or contributed to their declines. Make a chart like the one below. Use all three lessons in the chapter to complete the chart with important strengths and weaknesses of each empire. If a quality was a strength at one time and a weakness at another, write it in both places on the chart.

Empire	Strengths	Weaknesses
Mongol		
Ottoman		
Mughal		

B. Support each statement with facts and details from the chapter.
1. The structure of Genghis Khan's army showed that one of his strengths was his strong ability to organize.
2. Being the son of a sultan of the Ottoman Empire could be dangerous.
3. Students in the Palace School received an excellent education to prepare them for positions in the Ottoman Empire.
4. Mongol and Ottoman rulers usually practiced a kind of religious tolerance in their empires.
5. Suleiman was known both as The Magnificent in other lands and as The Lawgiver to his own people.
6. Modern leaders could learn many lessons about fair and efficient ways to govern their countries from Akbar.
7. Money played an important role in the decline of both the Ottoman and the Mughal empires.

Reviewing Skills

1. This painting shows Akbar crossing the Ganges in 1567 on his prized elephant Uduja. He is pursuing Ali Tuli Khan and Bahadur Khan, two brothers with whom treaties had failed. What does the painting tell about ways of war?
2. What do the painting's details tell about the Ganges? Discuss the river, ways of river travel, the natural setting, and its plants and animals.
3. Akbar agreed with this Sufi proverb: "Religious rituals and prayer are good but the dwelling of the Beloved is not in the mosque, temple, or church; it is in a pure heart." Explain this proverb in your own words.
4. If Mongol rulers had had one modern type of map, they would have known the time in all parts of their empire. What kind of map is that?

Using Critical Thinking

1. Many Mongol, Ottoman, and Mughal leaders encouraged religious freedom. Some did not. How did religious freedom benefit the empires? What happened when it was denied? How is it guaranteed in the United States? How does it benefit us?
2. The Mughal emperor Shah Jahan had a budget deficit because he spent more than his country produced. Compare his budget problem and our own. Who decided what was spent in the Mughal Empire? Who had responsibility to cut back? Who decides and has responsibility in the United States? Could we face the Mughals' fate if we let our deficit go on? Give reasons for your answer.
3. Compare the Ottoman education system with ours. What did they accomplish? What do we accomplish? What could happen without our education system?

Preparing for Citizenship

1. **COLLECTING INFORMATION** In small groups, study modern maps of areas once held by Mongols, Ottomans, and Mughals. List the names of the modern countries. Collect news articles about them and discuss together the nature of life in these areas today.
2. **COLLABORATIVE LEARNING** Help your class elect members for a Hall of Fame of Mongol, Ottoman, and Mughal leaders. As a class, make a list of leaders. Working in small groups, choose a candidate for each group to promote. Decide how to present your candidate's qualities. For example, let one member make a poster, one a brochure, one a press release, and so on. Carry out a written and illustrated campaign for a class presentation and election. Post the winning candidates' portraits in a Hall of Fame exhibit.

Chapter 8
China

Throughout this period, scholars wrote using artistic characters. Each character in Chinese represents a word. This character, known as *yong,* means "eternity."

All was chaos and confusion after the Han Dynasty fell in A.D. 220. For 360 years, groups battled for power. Still, scholarship survived, and so did beliefs like Daoism and Confucianism. When the Sui Dynasty reunited China in 589, leaders built on such traditions and beliefs to bring the country together. Later dynasties continued to inspire great advances—beautiful works of art, a strong economy, and marvelous new inventions.

617 Taizong (above) begins the Tang Dynasty, a time when art and poetry flower in China. Beautiful ceramic figures like the one at the left are often buried with emperors and nobles.

200

550

900

220

476 The Western Roman Empire collapses.

1066 Normans from northern France conquer England.

During this period, guard towers along the Great Wall of China (below) and geographical barriers helped keep invaders out of China.

1368 Emperor Taizu founds the Ming Dynasty. This Ming dragon, crafted of gold thread on silk later in this period, was a symbol of imperial power. Many even believed that such dragons protected the emperor.

1250

1600

1950

1450s Johann Gutenberg and other Europeans begin using movable type to print books.

1912

L E S S O N   1

An Emerging Empire

THINKING FOCUS

What were some of the obstacles to unity in China, and how did Emperor Wen overcome them?

Key Terms

- Confucianism
- Buddhism
- Daoism

▼ *Han Dynasty ministers used stamps like the one above to seal documents.*

Silk robes flowing, an aged man hurries through the dark streets of Luoyang, capital of the Chinese Empire during the late Han Dynasty. It is a crisp autumn morning in A.D. 220.

He moves swiftly along the broad boulevard, over the marble bridge, through the gardens, into the Outer Court. There he will meet Emperor Xian Di *(shehn tee)*. Emperor Xian Di, whom Heaven chose to rule China. Emperor Xian Di, whom he must inform of the latest attacks by the nomadic horsemen to the north!

In the Outer Court, other silk-robed officials also have grim news. In the countryside, landowners refuse to pay tax to the court. Some are even assembling private armies to fight against the empire. The few peasants who have survived the floods, famine, and plagues of recent years have no money for food, nor can they buy new seed. Many must now work for low wages on the estates of the wealthy.

In the capital, the wealthy compete to win court positions for their children. The emperor cannot possibly please them all. In the provinces, army generals fight each other for power. The troops are loyal to the generals instead of to the emperor.

The honor guard approaches. The smell of incense fills the air. Attendants in splendid robes carry the emperor's silk-draped platform to the marble terrace high above the courtyard. The curtains part. The Son of Heaven, the emperor, emerges to take his place on the throne. How can he solve the problems that plague the empire?

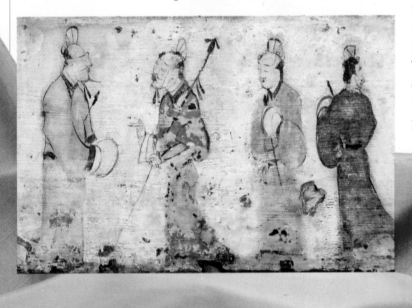

Years of Disorder

Emperor Xian Di, the last of the Han emperors, could not solve the many problems of the empire. In A.D. 220, China's first great empire broke apart. China was fragmented into small, competing kingdoms.

Geography Creates Regions

The Han Empire included the area of China shown in orange on the map below. Though the area makes up only one-third of modern China, it was here that most important events in Chinese history took place.

The eastern third of China, the area around the modern cities of Nanjing, Luoyang, and Changsha, has been the center of China's population throughout history. What natural features shown on the map explain why people settled here? The Qing Ling *(chihng lihng)* Mountains divide this fertile area into two regions, northern and southern China.

Before the unification of China under the Han Dynasty in 221 B.C., people living in northern and southern China had almost no contact with each other. Even during the Han Dynasty, only traders, soldiers, or government officials were likely to travel from one region to another.

Barriers Protect the Empire

Geography not only divided China but also protected it from the outside world. In ancient times, the Himalayas to the southwest and the Taklimakan Desert to the west limited Chinese contact with

Across Time & Space

Don't be confused if you see the Chang Jiang written as the Yangtze River on older maps. Chang Jiang is spelled according to the Pinyin system for writing Chinese in our Roman alphabet. In 1958, the Chinese officially adopted Pinyin, replacing older systems.

▼ *The earliest civilizations in China developed along a river, the Huang He. Find the Huang He and the Chang Jiang on the map.*

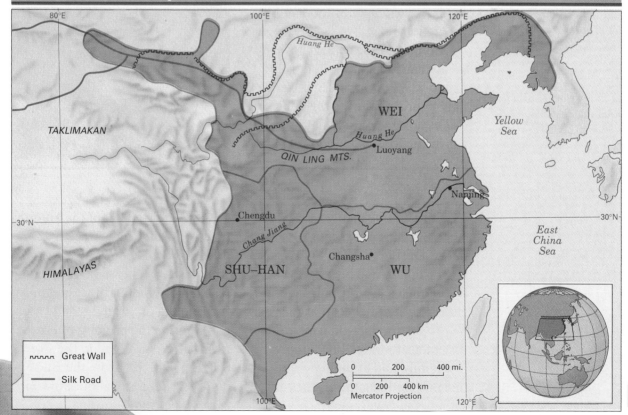

Division of the Han Empire, A.D. 220–264

80°E — 100°E — 120°E

Huang He

TAKLIMAKAN

WEI

Yellow Sea

Huang He

QIN LING MTS.

Luoyang

Nanjing

30°N — 30°N

Chengdu

East China Sea

Chang Jiang

Changsha

SHU–HAN

WU

HIMALAYAS

Great Wall

Silk Road

0   200   400 mi.

0   200   400 km
Mercator Projection

100°E — 120°E

193

China

The Romans saw Chinese silk for the first time in 53 B.C., when they were fighting the Parthians. The Parthians had traded with the Chinese for over 200 years and used the colorful silk in their battle pennants. Within 25 years, silk made up over 90 percent of Rome's imports from China.

➤ *The woman charged with teaching manners to the ladies of the emperor's court writes out some of her rules of conduct. This is an illustration for the scroll* The Admonitions of the Instructress of Court Ladies, *a work from the 200s.*

■ *Find evidence to support this statement: Geographic features made China difficult to unify.*

the civilizations of India, Persia, and other areas. Another natural barrier protected China to the east. What was it? China was vulnerable in the north, however. There, a huge open steppe, or grassy plain, left China open to attack by invaders.

Chaos Reigns

Barbarian invasions and other problems finally brought an end to the Han dynasty. Then tribal invaders, Chinese army generals, and aristocratic families were left to struggle for control of various regions. For about 360 years after the Han Dynasty ended, China was in a state of political chaos.

In the south, large landowners controlled local affairs in most areas. They kept private armies to defend their lands, and they fortified their homes. Many small farmers were forced to give up their land and work the landowners' fields in exchange for food and protection.

Control of the central government changed hands often from 220 to 589. Southern China's economy improved during this time of chaos, however. Good harvests and a growing foreign market for silk

helped the capital city, Nanjing, become a center of commerce. By the 500s, merchants from Southeast Asia, India, and Persia traded in the city.

In the north, various groups of nomads from the steppes invaded China and set up a series of short-lived kingdoms. As these nomadic peoples became accustomed to settled life, they willingly adopted the language, traditions, and government structure of the native Chinese. By 589, descendants of the invaders were fully integrated into northern Chinese culture and society. ■

The Spread of Buddhism

For Chinese in all classes, the years of chaos were years of uncertainty. During the Han Dynasty, most Chinese had been followers of Confucius. **Confucianism** included a set of beliefs that focused on proper conduct—having respect for elders, fulfilling one's duties in a family, and attaining virtue through studying the classics or serving the government.

But after the fall of the empire, much of Confucianism seemed useless. People began to turn to **Buddhism,** a religion based on the teachings of Siddhartha Gautama, the Buddha or "Enlightened One," and offering the promise of escape from suffering. What do the selections on page 195 from the Buddha's teachings say about how one can escape from suffering?

*L*ike a spider caught in its own web is a person driven by fierce cravings. Break out of the web, and turn away from the world of sensory pleasure and sorrow.

If you want to reach the other shore of existence, give up what is before, behind, and in between. Set your mind free, and go beyond birth and death.

Our life is shaped by our mind; we become what we think. Suffering follows an evil thought as the wheels of a cart follow the oxen that draw it.

Our life is shaped by our mind; we become what we think. Joy follows a pure thought like a shadow that never leaves.

From the *Dhammapada*, translated by Eknath Easwaran

Buddhism originated in India around 530 B.C. Traders and missionaries traveling along the Silk Road introduced the religion to China during the Han Dynasty. However, it attracted few followers then, mostly because it was foreign. Now, in the troubled times at the end of the Han Dynasty, the new religion became attractive.

The Buddha taught that life is a cycle of pleasure and sorrow, of death and rebirth. Suffering, he taught, was a basic part of life. It was caused by paying too much attention to material things in life— to what the Buddha referred to "the world of sensory pleasure."

But a person could escape from suffering, according to the Buddha. Through meditation, he taught, one could achieve enlightenment—a state of complete freedom and peace.

The idea of freedom from the chaos of the earthly world appealed to Chinese people of all classes. It appealed to regional rulers living in constant fear of attack, to landowners worried about crop failure, and to peasants longing for their own plots of land. By the 400s, most regional kings supported Buddhism. Buddhist temples and monasteries thrived throughout China. The Buddhists accumulated much valuable land. They also owned grain mills, and operated hospitals, schools, and inns. ∎

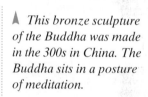

▲ *This bronze sculpture of the Buddha was made in the 300s in China. The Buddha sits in a posture of meditation.*

■ *Why did the Chinese find Buddhism more appealing than Confucianism after the fall of the Han Dynasty?*

The Reunification of China

More than 300 years after the Han Dynasty ended, a northern official named Yang Jian reunited the Chinese Empire. He seized power and declared himself emperor of northern China in 581 and then conquered the south by 589. Yang Jian's title was Emperor Wen, and the dynasty he founded is known as the Sui *(sway)* Dynasty.

A National Identity

Emperor Wen's greatest challenge was to reverse the forces that divided China. He used several techniques to do this.

195

China

For one thing, he followed ancient Chinese political practices. For example, when his supporters proclaimed him emperor, he accepted the traditional imperial gifts, including red doors for his house and a robe with a red sash—but only after he had refused them three times, as tradition demanded. By following such ancient traditions, the emperor reminded his people of their common history.

Like emperors of the Han dynasty, Emperor Wen organized public works projects. These projects focused people's attention on the common goals of the empire. Using forced labor crews, the emperor built a grand capital city at Changan. Find this city on the map on page 205. He also oversaw the rebuilding of the Great Wall, which had been built after 214 B.C., to protect China from the central Asian nomads who continued to attack the north.

During Emperor Wen's reign, workers began work on the Grand Canal between the Huang He, formerly called the Yellow River, and the Chang Jiang. After the Grand Canal opened in 605, it transported government officials, grain, and silk. Find the Grand Canal on the map on page 205.

Scholarship had been important in earlier Chinese society. Emperor Wen renewed this tradition by founding colleges for the study of the classics. He also set up schools for learning calligraphy, or the writing of Chinese characters, and for accounting and law. Since many ancient manuscripts had been lost after the fall of the Han Dynasty, Emperor Wen collected books from throughout the empire. Scholars organized and classified the texts; then clerks copied them by hand. In this way,

The Great Wall of China extends 4,000 miles from Inner Mongolia to the sea. If a similar wall was built along the border between the United States and Canada, about how far would it extend from the Atlantic to the Pacific Ocean?

Emperor Wen ensured the preservation of the Chinese classics.

The Administrative System

Emperor Wen set up a new system of administration to govern his huge empire efficiently. He created several departments for different government functions. Each department was divided into several smaller offices that performed specific duties. For example, within the Department of State Affairs were six offices. They were responsible for the army, finance, punishments, public works, rites, and civil office.

Officials were classified into nine ranks, or levels. Rank determined salary. Officials of the first rank earned 900 bushels of grain per year, while eighth-ranked officials earned 50.

Emperor Wen ordered local governments to send three worthy men to the capital each year. There they were tested in three areas: general literary ability, mastery of a single classic literary work, and the ability to take action in response to certain situations. Those who performed well on the exams were appointed to one of the lower ranks of government.

To prevent officials from showing favoritism or gaining influence in local affairs, Emperor Wen declared that officials could not serve in their home areas. Traveling inspectors, and often even the emperor himself, visited the provinces to check on local officials.

Three Belief Systems

Emperor Wen was a Buddhist. He founded many temples and monasteries, and he encouraged other Buddhists to support them. But he recognized that the other Chinese belief systems could help to strengthen his dynasty.

The emperor knew that Confucianism was an important tradition in Chinese government. So he emphasized the Confucian ideas of good conduct, scholarship, and public service.

Emperor Wen also encouraged **Daoism** *(DOW ihz uhm),* a belief system based on the teachings of Laozi, a Chinese philosopher who lived from 606 to 530 B.C. Daoists emphasized living in harmony with nature and being content with one's life.

By encouraging followers of all three belief systems, Emperor Wen promoted Chinese unity rather than divisiveness. The unified empire that he created continued under the Tang Dynasty, which followed the Sui Dynasty. ■

▲ *This painting of Emperor Wen is a detail from the scroll* Portraits of the Emperors, *completed during the 600s.*

■ *What steps did Emperor Wen take to reunify China?*

R E V I E W

1. **FOCUS** What were some of the obstacles to unity in China, and how did Emperor Wen overcome them?
2. **CONNECT** How does the fall of the Han Empire compare with the fall of the Roman Empire?
3. **GEOGRAPHY** What were the natural barriers that protected China on the east, west, and southwest?
4. **BELIEF SYSTEMS** Why was Emperor Wen wise to allow the practice of Buddhism, Confucianism, and Daoism in his empire?
5. **CRITICAL THINKING** Why might a country benefit by having a strong national identity?
6. **ACTIVITY** You are a public relations expert working for Emperor Wen. You have been asked to promote his campaign to unite north and south China. Design a poster that shows some of the factors that have kept northern and southern China separated. The poster should also explain or illustrate the advantages of unity.

Heaven My Blanket, Earth My Pillow

Poems by Yang Wan-Li

In the next lesson, you will read about a period of great achievement in Chinese government, trade, science, and art. The poet Yang Wan-Li in many ways symbolized that achievement.

Today our political leaders are usually not poets or artists. In the Song period of Chinese history, which you will study in the next lesson, government officials were also judged on their accomplishments in literature or art. Yang Wan-Li, a respected finance administrator, was also a well-known poet. His poems, like others of the period, express feelings of calm and harmony with nature. As you read, look for examples of these feelings.

Written on a Cold Evening

The poet must work with brush and paper,
but this is not what makes the poem.
A man doesn't go in search of a poem—
the poem comes in search of him.

Evening Lake Scenes

1
The lake seems glued to the sky—
   no banks are visible.
In the middle of the lake, water plants float.
It is evening—geese are forming V's,
   crows are forming flocks;
they land, then fly up again,
   taking a long time to settle for the night.

2
I sit watching the sun set over the lake.
The sun is not swallowed by mountains or clouds:
it descends inch by inch, then disappears completely,
leaving no trace where it sinks into the water.

In the Gorge: We Encounter Wind

Our boat is becalmed in the middle of the river—
the mountains are silent and gloomy at sunset.
Suddenly a clap of thunder sounds in the darkening sky
and the trees along the shore begin to sway.
A powerful wind blows in from the southern sea
and sweeps angrily through the gorge.
The sailors cheer;
    the great drum is beaten.
One man flies to the top of the mainmast.
As a sail unfurls I pull my hands into my sleeves
and watch ripples like goose feathers
    swirl by in the water.

Rain and Cold

I comb my hair and sleep overcomes me:
I dream that all my white hairs are being cut.
I wake up: the wind is leaking through a crack in the window
swinging a spider's web back and forth.

Night Rain at Kuang-k

The river is clear and calm;
    a fast rain falls in the gorge.
At midnight the cold, splashing sound begins,
like thousands of pearls spilling onto a glass plate,
each drop penetrating the bone.

In my dream I scratch my head and get up to listen.
I listen and listen, until the dawn.
All my life I have heard rain,
    and I am an old man;
but now for the first time I understand
    the sound of spring rain
        on the river at night.

Further Reading

Heaven's Reward: Fairy Tales from China. Catherine Edwards Sadler. These stories have been retold for thousands of years in China.

Treasure Mountain: Folktales from Southern China. Catherine Edwards Sadler. These stories tell of greedy officials and noble peasants.

L E S S O N   2

The Flowering of Chinese Culture

Key Terms

- aristocrat
- meritocracy
- mandate
- currency
- money economy

➤ *Here is a part of the Chinese text of the poem by Li Bo. This landscape is painted in ink on silk in the manner of one of the greatest artists of the Song Dynasty, Guo Xi. In an essay on painting, Guo Xi said that enjoying a landscape painting could be a substitute for wandering through the mountains.*

*B eside my bed the bright moonbeams bound
Almost as if there were frost on the ground.
Raising up, I gaze at the mountain moon;
Lying back, I think of my old home town.*

Li Bo, "Quiet Night Thoughts,"
701–702

If you were to write a poem about a nature scene near your home, how might your poem be like this one? How would it be different? Before you read on, study the painting and reread the poem.

李　白
望月怀远
窗前明月光
疑是地上霜
举头望明月
低头思故乡

The poem was written by Li Bo, the most beloved poet in China's history. He lived during the Tang Dynasty. The dynasty began when Li Yuan, a rebellious lord who had taken power from the Sui emperor, proclaimed himself emperor in 618. The Tang Dynasty was followed by the Song Dynasty, which lasted until 1279. Together, these two dynasties ruled over the most artistically brilliant era in Chinese civilization.

Poetry and painting are two areas in which Tang and Song artists excelled. A favorite theme of both poets and painters was the harmony they saw in the natural world. In the poem you read, Li Bo remembers the place where he grew up. He notes that the moon that he sees in the poem is the same mountain moon that shines on his home town. Nature unites two different times and places in the poem.

Do you think that the painting shown on page 202 expresses the same mood as the poem? The painting shows a mountainous landscape. But notice the person in the foreground. The size of the figure in relation to the landscape seems to

suggest that people, or human activities, are not very important when compared with the beauty of the natural world. Nevertheless, the painter chose to place a human figure in the scene. Perhaps the painter is implying that people can live in harmony with nature, provided they recognize their small place in it.

Chinese painters did not simply draw what they saw. They tried to represent the spirit, or essence, of the subject. This feeling of harmony with their subject helped them to create a sense of life in their work. The Chinese landscape painter and poet Wang Wei explained Chinese painting this way:

Such paintings cannot be achieved by the physical movements of the fingers and the hand, but only by the spirit entering into them. This is the nature of painting.

Wang Wei, from *Introduction to Painting*, 699–759

◄ *During the Tang Dynasty, pottery figures such as this fashionable lady were made in molds and painted. A pale, round face was thought to be most beautiful.*

▼ *Chinese civil service examinations were stamped with seals such as this.*

The Civil Service System

Painting and poetry were not the only things the Chinese achieved during the Tang and Song dynasties. They also developed a fair and efficient system of administration.

More Schools for More People

The Sui and early Tang rulers used examinations to find good candidates for public office. But only an **aristocrat,** a member of

a wealthy and influential family, could afford to study for the civil service exams. Preparing for the tests took years and meant traveling to special schools in the capital. As a result, aristocrats held most government jobs.

Later Tang and then Song governments recruited civil servants from other classes. It was still difficult for peasants to spend years studying, but during the Song Dynasty nearly half the civil servants came from classes other than the aristocracy.

A System Based on Merit

Officials appointed under earlier dynasties often held their positions for life, even if they were not very good at their jobs. Under the Tang and Song dynasties, civil servants who did their jobs well were promoted. Those who did poorly were demoted or even fired. Such a system, in which people are chosen and promoted on the basis of their performance, or merit, is called a **meritocracy.** The Chinese were the first people to establish a meritocracy. Other countries, such as the United States and France, set up similar administrative systems about a thousand years later.

Power to the Emperor

The Chinese had long believed that each emperor received from heaven a **mandate,** or order to govern. This is why one of the emperor's titles was "Son of Heaven." In theory, the emperor had absolute power. In practice, he had always shared his power with wealthy, landowning families.

Under the meritocracy, aristocrats had less power. They held fewer government positions and risked losing their positions if they did not perform well. Officials who were not from the aristocratic class were grateful for their positions and thus more loyal to the emperor. The emperor trusted them to enforce his laws, even in regions far from the capital. ■

▲ *This character used by an emperor of the Song Dynasty means "by order of the emperor." Calligraphy was a subject on the civil service examination.*

■ *Why did the aristocracy find it more difficult to gain influence under the civil service system?*

The Birth of a New Economy

To manage government business efficiently, official inspectors, tax collectors, and messengers needed to travel throughout the empire. To make this possible, the Tang and Song governments built an extensive system of roads and waterways. These, in turn, spurred trade and encouraged the spread of ideas within China.

Better Roads and Waterways

By the late 700s, relay hostels, or inns, with horses and food for traveling bureaucrats were in use along all main roads. Mounted messengers and foot runners carried government mail. One observer of the day wrote, "It took only a few days for all the news from distant places to reach the authorities." The roads also made it possible to move grain, tea, and other goods. Some 9,600 runners regularly supplied fresh seafood to the Tang capital of Changan from coastal cities about 800 miles away.

The government also improved canals and waterways for the growing numbers of sailboats, hand-driven paddle-wheel boats, and rowing ships that used them. The

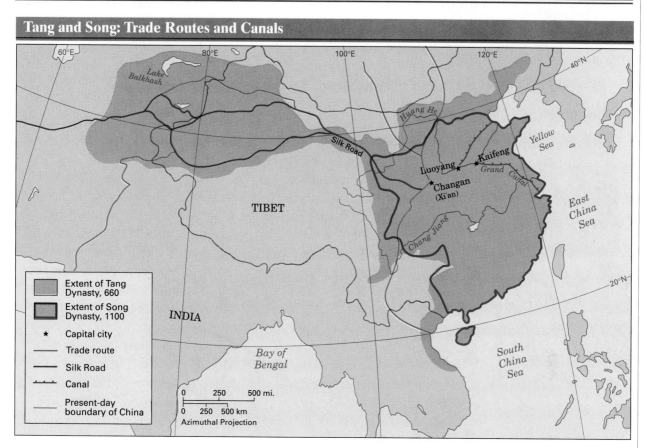

government sponsored hostels along the rivers and extended the canal system. By 850, the rivers and canals formed a vast network of about 1,200 miles extending to much of eastern China.

New Crops and Farming Methods

Though built for government use, roads and waterways promoted trade throughout China. At about the same time, Chinese farming became more productive. Around the year 1000, travelers introduced a new, fast-ripening rice from the area that is now Cambodia. Farmers could plant two or sometimes even three crops of this rice each year instead of just one.

Under both the Tang and Song dynasties, the government assigned plots of land to free peasants. Government officials taught farmers to build irrigation ditches and dams with pumps driven by human, water, or wind power. Farmers could then turn dry land into paddies, or wet fields, to grow more rice.

A population shift resulted from this boom in agriculture. Southern China was better suited for growing rice than northern China. As more and more land was turned into rice paddies, more and more people could live on what the land produced. The population of southern China grew steadily. Also, Mongol invasions in the north forced many to flee to the south. Many became tenants on large southern farms. The graph above shows this growth in population.

Farmers soon produced more food than they needed. So they sold the extra food, or surplus, to

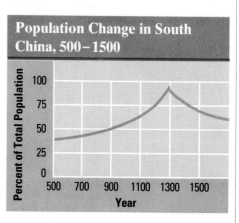

How did the Grand Canal help to unite northern and southern China? What percentage of the total population of China lived in the south around 620? What percentage lived in the south around 1280?

205

China

▲ *This copper plate was used for printing money during the Song Dynasty.*

■ *What factors led to a money economy in China?*

people in other regions, using the new roads and waterways to send crops to market. Market towns grew larger in rural areas.

A Thriving Merchant Class

Using this network of waterways, merchants transported products inexpensively in Chinese sailing ships called junks. Junks also carried goods along the coast, as seen from this description of a Song coastal city:

> M*erchants from [southern and central provinces] come to this town in seagoing junks to sell such dutiable goods as spices. . . . [Northern] merchants come bringing copper cash, silk thread, silk floss, silk gauze and thin silk, and do an extremely thriving trade with them.*
>
> From *The Continuation of the Comprehensive Mirror for Aiding Government,* 1088

Merchants made copper coins with holes in the center and strung on a string called a *cash.* Usually there were a thousand coins in a cash. In earlier times, bartered goods, such as lengths of silk, had also been used in trading. As trade increased, merchants found it easier to trade in cash.

But cash was heavy. Imagine carrying 50 dollars in coins in your pocket! In 1024, the Song government used an engraved metal plate like the one shown to the left to print the world's first paper **currency.** As cash and paper currency became the most common items exchanged for goods, a **money economy** developed. Money was now the standard by which people judged the value of a bushel of rice or a length of silk.

The business of trade required more shopkeepers, bankers, inspectors, tax collectors, storehouse workers, and others. As a result, the merchant class grew.

Merchants tended to live in cities and towns, where trading activity was greatest. Cities grew in size as rural workers flocked to the cities to fill jobs related to trade. ■

A Continuing Heritage

Although the Chinese prospered through their thriving new trade network, they continued to value their ancient traditions.

The civil service exams, for example, required candidates to study the Confucian classics. The classics became available after the invention of printing in the late 700s,

Inventions in China and Europe

100, Use of writing paper
(*European writing paper–900, from Cairo*)

577, Matches invented
(*European matches–1500s*)

100	200	300	400	500	600

200, Fishing reel developed
(*European fishing reel–1650*)

400, Rudder developed
(*European rudder – c.1300*)

about 700 years before the development of printing in Europe.

Historians call this renewed emphasis on Confucian ideas Neo-Confucianism. Writers began to find new meanings in Confucian texts and to relate them to problems of the time.

Respect for the past, however, did not keep the Chinese from moving forward. Between 200 and 1200, new inventions improved life in China. Look at the timeline below. Notice that many Chinese discoveries took centuries to reach the West. Chain drives of the type that were later used in bicycles, for example, were in use in China in 976 in silk-making machinery. When was this invention first used in the West?

Printing

Of all the inventions made during the Tang and Song periods, printing was probably the most significant. By making books, calendars, and government pamphlets available to many more people, printing hastened the spread of knowledge throughout China.

Woodblock printing was the earliest form of printing. The Chinese began to use this method in the late 700s, about 600 years before Europeans learned about it. To make a woodblock print, skilled craftspeople carved raised Chinese characters on a wooden "page." They brushed ink onto this page

and laid a piece of paper over it to make a print. The entire process was done by hand.

How long do you think it would take you to carve the words in this sentence onto a block of wood? Chinese scholars spent 21 years carving and printing all 130 volumes of the Confucian classics.

Around 1045, a Chinese commoner named Pi Sheng invented a less time-consuming method of printing using movable type. He cut ideograms, the Chinese characters, out of sticky clay and baked them until they were hard. Then he made each page by placing the necessary characters into an iron frame. This method of printing was very quick and efficient for printing many pages of a work.

By 1100, Chinese scholars used books on law, medicine, mathematics, and science to learn from both the past and the present. New techniques for treating disease or planting crops, for example, spread much more quickly in print than by word of mouth. An observer named Fang Tazong wrote the

How Do We Know?

HISTORY *The oldest surviving printed book in the world is the* Diamond Sutra, *one of the sacred books of Buddhism. It was made in China in 868.*

▼ *About how long after the Chinese first used matches did Europeans make matches?*

c.8th century, Paper money developed
(*European bank note issued–1658*)

1041–1048, Movable type developed
(*European movable type–1450*)

700	800	900	1000	1100	1200

976, Bicycle chain drive developed
(*European bicycle chain drive–1770*)

207

China

The Chinese first used gunpowder for fireworks during the Tang Dynasty. A Chinese book published in 1044 gives a precise formula for making gunpowder.

➤ *This compass was made by using a magnetic rock called a lodestone. The compass maker cut a thin sheet of metal into the shape of a fish and rubbed it with the lodestone to make it magnetic.*

■ *Find evidence to support this statement: Chinese inventions showed a respect for the past as well as a desire to improve on it.*

following about education in the province of Fujian during Song times:

Every peasant, artisan and merchant teaches his sons how to read books. Even herdsmen, and wives who bring their husbands food at their work in the fields, can recite the poems of the men of ancient times.

Other Inventions

Another important invention was gunpowder, which may have been discovered as early as the 600s. However, the Chinese did not invent guns to explode the gunpowder, as Europeans did almost as soon as they learned about it. Nevertheless, by the 1200s, the Chinese made and used gunpowder in large quantities. A document written in 1221 states: "On the same day were produced 7,000 gunpowder crossbow arrows, 10,000 gunpowder ordinary arrows, 3,000 barbed gunpowder packages and 20,000 ordinary gunpowder packages."

Another invention made traveling easier. For travel by sea, the Chinese used charts of the stars and a compass they called a "fish."

Chinese astronomers began mapping the stars as early as 300 B.C. Star charts dating from about 940 show many familiar constellations. The "fish" was a piece of metal shaped like a fish that pointed south when floated in water. This description of how sailors used the magnetic fish was written in 1119:

The sailors are sure of their bearings. At night they judge by the stars. In daytime they tell by the sun. When it is cloudy, they rely on the south-pointing needle.

Europeans learned about these inventions during the years that followed the Song Dynasty. These years were a period of Mongol domination in China. ■

REVIEW

1. **FOCUS** What were the most significant achievements of the Tang and Song dynasties?
2. **CONNECT** How did the civil service system in the later Tang and Song dynasties differ from that of the Sui Dynasty?
3. **CULTURE** What common theme runs through many poems and paintings of the Tang and Song dynasties? How is this theme related to the religious beliefs of the period?
4. **ECONOMICS** How did Chinese agricultural growth

make necessary the development of a money economy?

5. **CRITICAL THINKING** Would you describe your school as a meritocracy? Explain.
6. **ACTIVITY** Assume that you are the inventor of one of the items pictured in the timeline on pages 206 and 207. Describe your invention and explain its purpose to your classmates, who have never heard of such a device. Be sure to point out how your device could improve their lives.

LESSON 3

China and the Larger World

On this [New Year's] day all the rulers, and all the provinces and regions and realms where men hold land or lordship under [the Great Khan's] sway, bring him costly gifts of gold and silver and pearls and precious stones and abundance of fine white cloth, so that throughout the year their lord may have no lack of treasure and may live in joy and gladness. . . . I can also assure you for a fact that on this day the Great Khan receives gifts of more than 100,000 white horses, of great beauty and price. And on this day also there is a procession of his elephants, fully 5,000 in number, all draped in fine cloths embroidered with beasts and birds. . . . Let me conclude with one more fact, a very remarkable one well worthy of mention in our book. You must know that a great lion is led into the Great Khan's presence; and as soon as it sees him it flings itself down prostrate before him with every appearance of deep humility and seems to acknowledge him as lord. There it stays without a chain, and is indeed a thing to marvel at.

Marco Polo, from *Travels*

THINKING FOCUS

What factors caused China to open trade at some times and remain isolated at others?

Key Term

• despot

◄ *In this portrait of Kublai Khan, he is dressed in the traditional clothing of a Chinese emperor.*

This detailed account of a day at the Great Khan's court at Beijing was written by Marco Polo, a traveler from Venice, Italy. Polo lived in China from 1275 until 1292. The Great Khan in this report was Kublai Khan, a grandson of Genghis Khan.

Although only 17 years old when he arrived in China, Polo served Kublai as an ambassador and in other ways. At the time of his visit, all of China, as well as much of the rest of the world, was under Mongol rule.

209

China

The Mongols in China

While southern China prospered under the Song Dynasty, Genghis Khan made life very difficult for people in northern China. His well-organized and skillful

Mongol horsemen traveled for weeks at a time, making surprise attacks along the Chinese frontier. They learned to use catapults and gunpowder bombs to break through city walls. With few horses and inferior riding skills, Chinese armies were rarely able to defeat the Mongols. In 1234, a few years after Genghis Khan's death, the Mongols completed the conquest of northern China.

Mongol warriors, like the one in the upper picture, shot arrows from large bows with force enough to pierce armor. They rode small, sturdy horses like the one shown in the ceramic model above. This ceramic horse was found in a tomb from the Tang Dynasty.

A Mongol Dynasty

Kublai Khan was chosen *khan,* or ruler, in 1260. In 1267, Kublai moved his capital from Mongolia to Beijing *(bay JIHNG)* in northern China in order to be closer to his subjects.

Kublai adopted certain Chinese traditions of government to make it easier for him to rule and be accepted by the Chinese. For example, he rebuilt the capital in the traditional Chinese style and declared himself emperor and Son of Heaven. He even founded his own dynasty, called the Yuan *(yu AHN),* which lasted until 1368.

However, unlike many northern barbarians before them, Kublai Kahn and the Mongols did not try to change Mongol culture so that it became more like Chinese culture. They used some Chinese systems of government, but only to strengthen Mongol rule. The most important government positions were held by Mongols or by other non-Chinese, including Marco Polo. The Chinese themselves were given the least important jobs. Government documents were usually written in Mongolian and then translated into Chinese.

Kublai Khan staged many attacks on the Song Dynasty in southern China. His forces finally overpowered the last group of Song defenders in 1279. Kublai thus became the first ruler to control all of China in over 300 years.

An Interruption in Progress

Although the Mongols maintained the basic Chinese government structure, their occupation of China disrupted economic and social development. It also slowed the remarkable progress of Chinese civilization under the Tang and Song dynasties. Millions of Chinese died during the decades of the Mongol invasions, including about half the population of the North. Some were killed by the Mongol attacks while many more died from outbreaks of disease that often followed the attacks. Once highly populated areas, such as the eastern province of Anhui, were almost empty of people by the time the attacks ended.

Much of the wealth of the Tang and Song dynasties was lost as the Mongols burned cities and used vast areas of fertile farmland as pastures for their horses. They neglected canals and irrigation systems, and fertile fields soon became parched and barren. Many farmers lost their land to the Mongols, and many civil servants lost their jobs.

In the south, the Mongols hoped to win support from the wealthy landowners by letting them keep their lands. However, the Mongols seized land from the peasants, forcing them to seek work as hired hands on large estates. Thus the rich remained rich, while the poor became even poorer.

A Direct Link to the West

The Mongols disrupted Chinese life and culture. However, they strengthened China's links to the rest of the world. Camel caravans traveled throughout the vast Mongol Empire, from Beijing to central Asia to the Black Sea, carrying silks and ceramics for the Western market. The Mongols expanded the Chinese system of postal relays, establishing stations with supplies and horses for travelers who crossed the Asian steppe.

Travelers who crossed the Indian Ocean to China found thriving port cities, such as Guangzhou (GWAHNG joh), sometimes known as Canton, and Fujien (FOO jihn). Merchants, missionaries, and diplomats from the Arab world gathered in southern China's seaports. Through Arab merchants, many goods from the West and from southeastern Asia were traded in Chinese ports.

Increased contacts with the world not only expanded trade in China but also aided the spread of ideas in the West. For example, knowledge of printing and gunpowder probably spread from China to western Asia and then to Europe during the Mongol period. ■

■ In what ways did the Mongol conquest of China affect the livelihood of most Chinese people?

The Ming Dynasty

Merchants prospered under Mongol rule. But most Chinese were eager to expel the foreigners who did not appreciate China's traditions. The Chinese rebelled against the Mongol rulers and founded a new dynasty in 1368. The rebel leader and founder of the Ming Dynasty was Emperor Taizu (ty TSOO). The Ming Dynasty continued to rule China until as late as 1644.

Familiar Traditions

Emperor Taizu turned to familiar traditions for help in restoring the empire. He reestablished the civil service examination system and encouraged promising scholars. He undertook public works projects: repairing irrigation systems, building reservoirs, and extensively rebuilding the Great Wall. He helped homeless people by

◄ Blue and white ceramics such as this Ming vase became the most popular kind of ceramics for trade. Cobalt, used to make the blue color on this vase, was first imported during the Mongol period.

211

China

giving them land in regions left devastated by the Mongols. Unlike earlier emperors, Taizu also seized large estates, abolished slavery, and raised the taxes of the rich. Such measures narrowed the gap between rich and poor.

More Power to the Emperor

Ming rulers made themselves extremely powerful. For example, Emperor Taizu abolished the position of prime minister and controlled all departments of government directly.

While earlier emperors had welcomed open discussion of issues, Ming emperors made decisions in secret councils. Emperor Taizu even created a secret police force to spy on officials. Historians estimate that he accused at least 100,000 people of corruption or treason and then executed them. Such a ruler, who holds absolute power and uses it abusively, is called a **despot.**

The Forbidden City was the innermost square of the Imperial City. It was surrounded by a moat and a high wall. The Forbidden City contained palaces for members of the imperial family, and the Hall of Supreme Harmony, shown below, where the emperor held court. Why do you think that this part of Beijing was called the Forbidden City?

The Ming emperors ordered a splendid new capital built on the site of the old Mongol capital of Beijing. During the early 1400s, about one million workers labored to complete the new city. Great walls, 40 feet high, surrounded a central area known as the Imperial City. Here grand halls, courtyards, and gardens provided a costly and lavish setting for the business of government.

A Superior Naval Power

At first, the emperors wanted to show the world the power of the Ming Dynasty. Between 1403 and 1433, court official Zheng Ho gathered a fleet of ships and made seven voyages to the Middle East and to the east coast of Africa. You can read more about Zheng Ho in A Closer Look on page 213.

But the Ming emperors soon decided that the rest of the world had little of value to offer China. They forbade further explorations and ended the costly voyages after 1433. They even made it a crime for any Chinese subjects to leave the country by sea.

The Voyages of Zheng Ho

Fifty years before Europeans began searching for a sea route to the East, Chinese ambassador Zheng Ho explored the West. His emperor sent Zheng Ho to collect presents and to display the splendor and power of China. Under these orders, Zheng Ho sailed to southeastern Asia, India, Arabia, and Africa in the early 1400s.

Zheng Ho, detail from a woodcut by Lo Mou-teng, 1597

Chinese pearls

Everywhere he went Zheng Ho brought pearls and Ming vases to show off China's wealth. Most foreigners had never seen pottery so delicate and beautiful.

Ten times larger than European ships of the period, the junks Zheng Ho sailed had room for 500 people.

Ming vase

Zheng Ho brought back giraffes, zebras, tigers, and ostriches. When they saw the giraffe, people told the emperor Zheng Ho had brought back a *Chin Lin,* a mythical creature that appeared when the wisest emperor ruled. The emperor is said to have replied, "That is no *Chin Lin,* and I am no wise man."

213

The Tribute Giraffe with Attendant, *by artist Shen Tu,* A.D. *1414*

China

Contact with the West

Ming emperors discouraged Chinese merchants from trading with foreign countries. They wanted to prevent Chinese contact with people they regarded as inferior.

Despite trade restrictions, the world discovered China. The first Portuguese ship reached China in 1514, and by 1557, the Portuguese had established a settlement on the coast of China at Macao, near Guangzhou. Jesuit missionaries opened missions and worked at converting some Chinese to Christianity.

These missionaries, who were well educated in mathematics, astronomy, and the arts, carried knowledge and inventions between East and West. For example, the Chinese learned about European astronomy and mathematics.

European traders seeking Chinese tea, silk, and porcelain brought with them sweet potatoes and corn from the Americas. They introduced beef and dairy cattle, which the Chinese then raised in the fertile pastures of the south. Increased trade also brought more gold and silver to China.

Throughout the Ming Dynasty, despotic rulers tried to restrict trade. They also wasted money on lavish court life and withdrew from day-to-day affairs within China. Eventually, the people grew tired of heavy taxation and careless government. In the early 1600s, peasants in the southern regions rebelled against the despots. ■

■ *In what ways did the Ming dynasty affect trade and other contacts with the West?*

The Qing Dynasty

▼ *Notice the similarity between the imperial headpiece of this Qing Dynasty empress and that of Kublai Kahn, on page 209.*

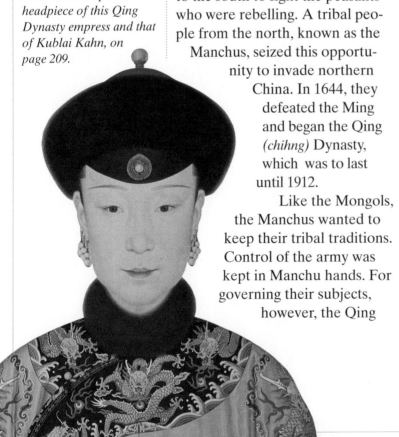

The Ming ruler sent armies to the south to fight the peasants who were rebelling. A tribal people from the north, known as the Manchus, seized this opportunity to invade northern China. In 1644, they defeated the Ming and began the Qing *(chihng)* Dynasty, which was to last until 1912.

Like the Mongols, the Manchus wanted to keep their tribal traditions. Control of the army was kept in Manchu hands. For governing their subjects, however, the Qing adopted Chinese traditions. The Manchus continued the Ming government structure and civil service system. They even allowed many Ming officials to remain in office. Positions in the local government positions were filled mostly by Chinese rather than Manchu officials.

Culture and Population

The Qing rulers also assigned scholars to edit Chinese literary and historical works, including the Confucian classics. The large-scale shift from woodblock printing to movable type in the 1500s triggered a boom in publishing and a rising literacy rate. In 1726, a famous encyclopedia of 5,020 volumes was completed. Of course, a volume of entries written in Chinese characters takes up far more pages than the same entries written in English.

The population of China was about 60 million in 1400. By 1580, it had more than tripled, and it continued to increase rapidly during the Qing Dynasty. By 1850, the population was about 430 million. This population growth was partly due to the nutritious foods introduced during the Ming Dynasty. As population grew, China's territory also increased. During the Qing Dynasty, China doubled in size, expanding north into Manchuria and Mongolia, west into Tibet, and south into what is now Burma and Vietnam. Compare the map on page 533 with the map on pages 522 and 523 of the Atlas to see how China grew.

Cities and Trade

As China's population grew, the cities also expanded. Farmers sold their crops locally to merchants, who transported them to the cities. Peasants found work in small handicraft industries, such as weaving.

The Qing emperors allowed a limited amount of trade between China and other nations through the port at Guangzhou. For the most part, however, the Chinese believed that there was little to be gained by contact with other peoples. They preferred to follow the traditional patterns of Chinese life that had been outlined centuries before by Confucius. ■

▲ *What flags can you see over Guangzhou's harbor in this 1847 painting?*

■ *What aspects of traditional Chinese government did the Qing retain?*

R E V I E W

1. **FOCUS** What factors caused China to open trade at some times and remain isolated at others?
2. **CONNECT** What impact did Mongol rule have on the economic progress of the Tang and Song dynasties?
3. **ECONOMICS** How did the Ming attitude toward foreigners affect trade?
4. **POLITICAL SYSTEMS** Compare and contrast Mongol rule and the Qing Dynasty.
5. **CRITICAL THINKING** Why did invaders from the North not try to replace the Chinese culture with their own culture?
6. **WRITING ACTIVITY** You are a Portuguese trader who has just returned from Macao, China, in 1500, with a shipload of goods. Write a paragraph in which you describe your purchases and explain why you think Europeans will buy them.

215

China

Comparing Two Maps of China

Here's Why

No single map can show you everything about a region. Maps have many purposes. Often you learn more by comparing maps than by examining them individually.

For example, you can compare topographic and land-use maps of China. Using the two maps together will help you see how China's physical features affect how people use land in China.

Here's How

Look at the topographic map on this page. It shows physical features such as mountains, deserts, lakes, and rivers. A key explains how colors on the map show elevations.

Study the land-use map of China on the facing page. This map helps you see what types of economic activities are most dominant in different areas of China.

Compare the two maps to see how geographical factors have influenced land use in Beijing. Find Beijing on the topographic map. You can see that a river and a connecting canal link Beijing with both the Yellow Sea and the Grand Canal.

Beijing's elevation is fairly low. Notice that deserts lie to the west and northwest of Beijing and that the land rises to the west and north. Beijing itself lies on the northern edge of the North China Plain. The map shows

that Beijing is approximately 40°N. Its latitude and elevation are much like that of central Illinois.

From the topographic map, you have learned that Beijing has water resources, which could be useful for farming, industry, and trade. Because of its latitude and elevation, you can infer that Beijing is in an area that would be a good place to live, work, and farm.

Now look at the land-use map to see what economic activities are important to Beijing. The map's color coding tells you that Beijing is in an urban and industrial area. Most of the surrounding land is used for farming. Find the city of Tianjin, southeast of

People's Republic of China: Physical Regions

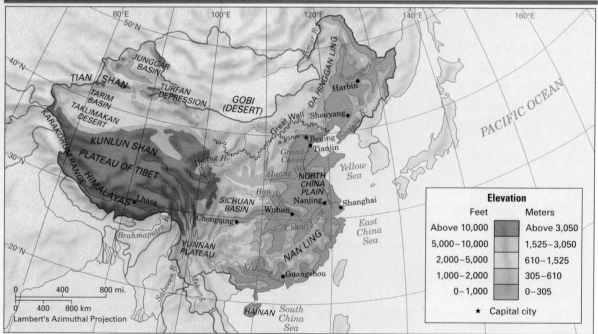

Beijing. Goods manufactured in Beijing are shipped from port facilities near Tianjin. The photograph to the right helps illustrate the importance of the Grand Canal to these two cities. Beijing's industries clearly benefit from the water transportation routes that link the city to markets in China and abroad.

Try It

Look at the western area of China on the topographic map. Find the Himalayas, the Karakorum Shan (Range), and the Kunlun Shan. These mountains are located in the most rugged area of China.

Now locate China's cities. What areas have few cities?

What geographical features might account for this?

Study the land-use map. What is the main land use in the western half of China? What is the main land use in China's eastern half? What aspects of China's geography explain these differences?

Finally, locate China's urban and industrial areas on the land-use map. What information from the topographic map might help

explain why these urban and industrial areas are located here?

Apply It

Find topographic and land-use maps of your state in an encyclopedia or atlas. Compare the maps. Then write a short report about how information from the topographic map helps explain the locations of cities and land use.

People's Republic of China: Land Use and Resources

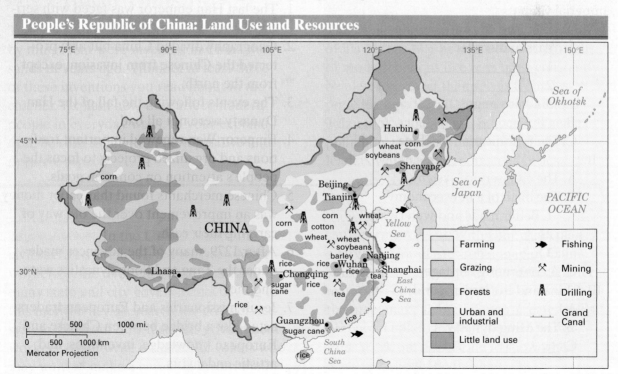

China

Chapter 9

Japan

A Buddhist monk tends a simple garden of rocks and sand. A beautiful woman warrior knocks her foe from his horse. A poet writes three lines about a frog in a pond. What can these brief moments tell us about Japan since the 500s? The monk shows religious simplicity. The woman warrior symbolizes both a love of beauty and a respect for combat. And the poet reflects a quiet reverence for nature. Each quality has played an important role in the unfolding of Japan's unique history and way of life.

Throughout this period, Buddhism influenced life in Japan. The bowl and whisk are part of the Zen Buddhist tea ceremony. With the whisk, the drinker stirs and froths the tea.

794 Japan's emperor makes Kyoto the capital. One of the city's loveliest sights is the Golden Pavilion, built 600 years later as a mountain villa for Japan's rulers.

500	700	900	1100

632 Muslim armies begin building a great empire. By 750, they control lands from Spain in the West to India in the East.

552

Since the 1300s, the Japanese have enjoyed *Noh* drama, featuring a masked dancer on a darkened stage. This wooden *Noh* mask is more than 500 years old.

Toyotomi Hideyoshi, left, becomes Japan's military ruler in 1585. Probably the most admired Japanese hero, he rises from a peasant background to become a powerful leader.

1800s Ando Hiroshige creates prints like the one above showing a warrior approaching a village in a beautiful setting.

1300	1500	1700	1900

1638–1715 King Louis XIV rules France and drains the treasury with his luxurious lifestyle and many wars.

1854

L E S S O N   1

Land of the Rising Sun

How did the geography of Japan influence its development?

Key Terms

- isolation
- Shinto

➤ *Izanagi and Izanami stood together on the Floating Bridge of Heaven and held council. "Is there not a country beneath?" they asked. Then they decided to create the islands of Japan.*

In the beginning, there was chaos. Then Heaven and Earth began to separate, and gods came to life. In the seventh generation, two gods—Izanagi and Izanami—decided to create a drifting land on the oceans. Izanagi reached down from heaven and thrust a jeweled spear into the ocean. When he withdrew the spear, drops fell from its point, forming the islands of Japan.

This is how the world began, according to Japanese mythology. The myths go on to tell how the next generation of gods struggled for power. The Sun Goddess gave life to everything around her. But her brother, the Storm God, was wild and fierce. He ruined his sister's rice crop and so upset her that she hid in a cave. Without her, heaven and earth went dark.

Other gods brought the Sun Goddess a beautiful bronze mirror and a sparkling jewel to coax her out of the cave. When she came out and told of the Storm God's mischief, the other gods banished him to the earth. His descendants lived on the Japanese islands.

After many years, the Sun Goddess sent her grandson, Ninigi (*nee NEE gee*) to take control of the island of Honshu. As symbols of his divine power, she sent with him her bronze mirror, her jewel, and a

great iron sword. Two generations later, according to legend, Ninigi's grandson Jimmu conquered the Storm God's descendants and in

660 B.C. became the first emperor of Japan. Today, the divine objects described in the legend—the mirror, the jewel, and the sword—are the symbols of the emperor's heaven-sent power.

The Islands of Japan

Millions of years ago, volcanic mountains pushed up out of the Pacific Ocean. The tops of these mountains are the islands of Japan. As you can see from the map on page 224, Japan consists mainly of four large islands—Hokkaido *(hah KYD oh),* Honshu, Shikoku, and Kyushu *(kee OO shoo).* Japan also includes many smaller islands.

Together, the major Japanese islands total about 146,000 square miles, about the size of Montana. However, the four main islands are so spread out that their north-south curve covers about 1,200 miles. If the main islands were placed next to the eastern coast of the United States, they would reach from Maine to Georgia.

The Japanese islands lie on a very unstable part of the earth's surface. Each year Japan has more than 1,500 earthquakes, though most are mild. And 60 of its 150 major volcanoes are still active. Typhoons are also frequent in Japan. The heavy winds and rains batter its coasts, flood its valleys, and uproot its trees.

Mountains and hills cover most of Japan, leaving less than 20 percent of it for farming. Japan has few natural resources such as coal, iron, or other minerals. The sea has always been Japan's greatest resource. It provides food for the Japanese as well as transportation routes. Japan's seas have also acted as a natural barrier, keeping Japan in **isolation,** or setting it apart, from much of the world. The seas often shielded Japan from invasion by northern Asian tribes.

Because they live on islands, the Japanese were able to control the flow of people and ideas into their country. As a result, Japanese culture developed with few influences from other countries, except China. ■

Across Time & Space

Although Japan has few natural resources, its economy today is the third largest in the world. To keep its factories humming, Japan must import 99.8 percent of its oil, 90.7 percent of its natural gas, and 81.8 percent of its coal. It is no longer an isolated nation.

■ *Why is the sea Japan's greatest natural resource?*

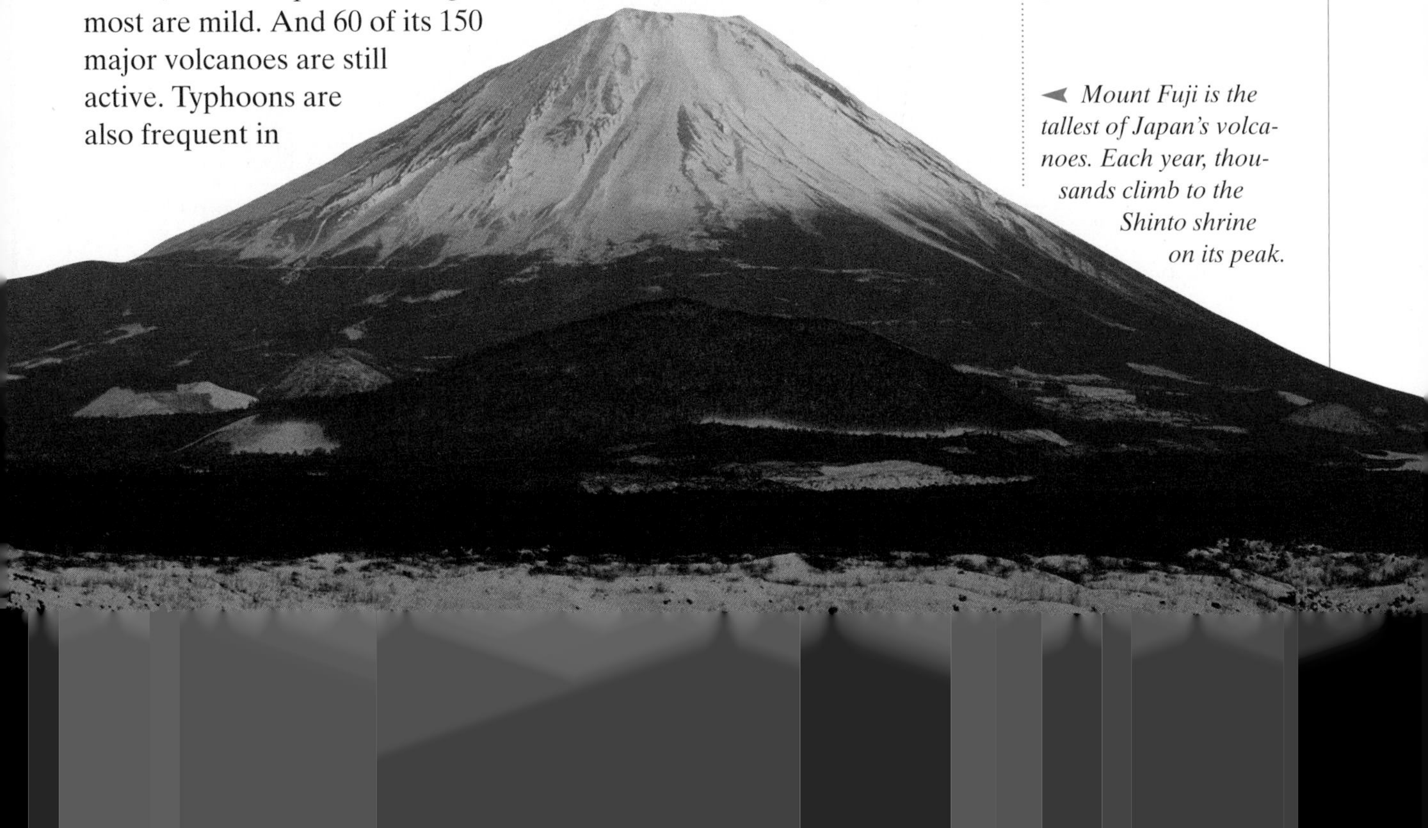

◄ *Mount Fuji is the tallest of Japan's volcanoes. Each year, thousands climb to the Shinto shrine on its peak.*

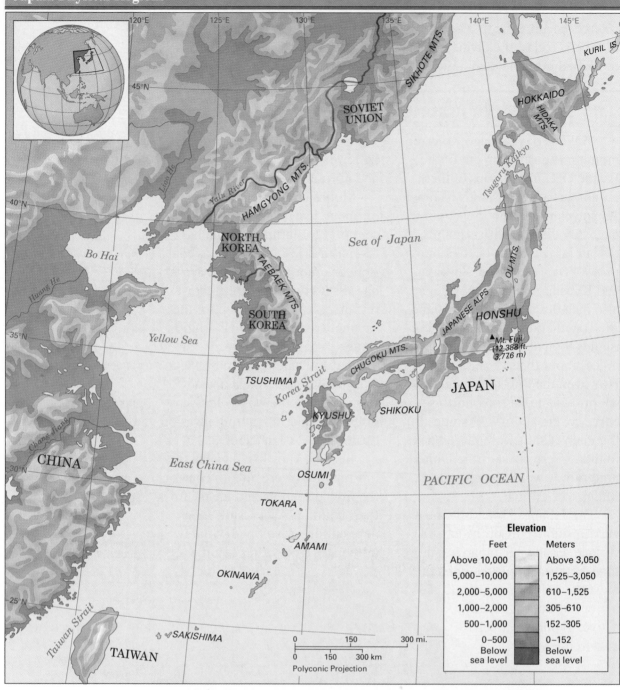

Japan: Physical Regions

Elevation

Feet	Meters
Above 10,000	Above 3,050
5,000–10,000	1,525–3,050
2,000–5,000	610–1,525
1,000–2,000	305–610
500–1,000	152–305
0–500	0–152
Below sea level	Below sea level

0   150   300 mi.
0   150   300 km
Polyconic Projection

▲ *On which island is Mount Fuji?*

➤ *Stone spearheads such as this show where and how people of the Jomon culture lived.*

The Early People of Japan

Despite its isolation, many peoples migrated to Japan. Stone tools and weapons found in Japan show that it has been inhabited for thousands of years.

Among the first people were hunter-gatherers who lived over 10,000 years ago. Other immigrants pushed them north about 200 to 100 B.C. The Ainu *(EYE noo)*, who live on Hokkaido, may be descendants of these hunter-gatherers.

Early Cultures

In about 8000 B.C., people of the Jomon *(JOH mahn)* culture, who probably came from Korea

224

and northern Asia, first appeared in Japan. Ancient accumulations of shells, fishhooks, and harpoon points show that the Jomon were fishers and hunter-gatherers.

About 200 B.C., the Jomon culture was gradually replaced by a new, settled society known as Yayoi *(yah YOY)*. The Yayoi settled in the fertile Yamato plain on the largest island, Honshu.

The Yayoi introduced the cultivation of rice in water, after which rice became Japan's most important crop. Rice needs a lot of water, and the islands' summer rains make them ideally suited to rice growing.

The Yayoi used metal tools to irrigate and level the land. This development changed the Japanese from hunter-gatherers to farmers.

Between A.D. 200 and 300, an even more complex culture began to replace the Yayoi. Archaeologists call this the "tomb culture." The people of this culture left huge graves filled with such things as bronze mirrors, crowns, and clay figurines of armor-clad warriors and horses. These objects suggest that rulers of this culture were from a respected warrior class.

Early Religion

The religion of early Japan, **Shinto,** revolved around nature. Shinto teaches that the natural

world is filled with divine spirits, or *kami.* Worship of the highest-ranking *kami,* the Sun Goddess, came to be identified with Japan's emperor.

Sometime after 400, one ruling warrior clan from the plains of southeastern Honshu became more powerful than other ruling clans. From this family came Japan's first emperor. He was the first of a line of emperors from one family that continues even today. You have read how this family was said to be descended from the Sun Goddess. The idea of the emperor being divine may have been influenced by ideas from China. ■

▲ These "wedded rocks" are linked by a straw rope. In the Shinto religion, they are associated with the gods who created the islands of Japan.

▼ The Jomon culture takes its name from its pottery, created by pressing cords into the wet clay.

■ How did the lifestyles of the peoples of the Jomon, Yayoi, and "tomb" cultures compare and contrast? How do we know?

Chinese Influence in Japan

In 552, a Korean king sent the emperor a copper and gold image of the Buddha and Buddhist scriptures. He suggested that the emperor make Buddhism, which had come to Korea from China, the religion of Japan.

The emperor consulted his advisers. Leaders of the powerful Soga clan thought that Buddhism would strengthen the government as it had in China. Other clans opposed it and even fought battles with the Soga. The Soga won, and

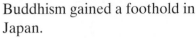

■ *Why did Chinese culture spread throughout Japan?*

▼ *In the painting (top), Prince Shotoku is shown twice as tall as the ladies of his court to indicate his royalty. The Great Buddha Hall (bottom), one of the largest buildings at Nara, was built in 745.*

Buddhism gained a foothold in Japan.

By 593, Prince Shotoku, who was related to the Soga, ruled Japan as the nephew of the empress. He encouraged Buddhism and the spread of Chinese culture.

Prince Shotoku brought Chinese artists, craftspersons, and clerks to Japan. He sent court officials to China to study its culture and government. He welcomed Buddhist priests, who brought Chinese language, arts, mathematics, and agricultural techniques to Japan.

Shinto linked the Japanese to their homeland and their past. But Buddhism was accepted along with Shinto because it met spiritual needs not met by Shinto. Buddhism promised rewards to the faithful and the good.

After Prince Shotoku's death, members of the government imposed a series of Chinese-style changes called the Taika Reforms. Under this plan, the government declared that all farmland in the provinces—areas outside the capital—was the property of the emperor. The land was divided into small plots, and clan leaders were assigned to oversee the land in their territories. In this way the central government gained more control over the clans as well as wealth from taxes on the land.

In 710, the government established a new capital called Nara in the Yamato plain. Religion and art flourished in Nara.

Although the Taika Reforms reduced the power of the clans, they had little effect on the lives of the peasants, or poor farm workers. In a collection of Japanese poems made about 700 and called the *Man'yoshu*, an anonymous poet described the hardships he faced in the countryside:

*H*ere I lie on straw
 Spread on bare earth,
With my parents at my pillow,
My wife and children at my
 feet,
All huddled in grief and tears.
Must it be so hopeless—
The way of this world?

As before, small farmers still gave up part of their harvest. The difference was that after the reforms, they gave it to government officials instead of to clan leaders. ■

R E V I E W

1. **FOCUS** How did the geography of Japan influence its development?
2. **CONNECT** How is the history of Japan's first emperors different from that of China's early emperors?
3. **BELIEF SYSTEMS** Describe the Shinto religion. How is it related to the Japanese emperor?
4. **CULTURE** By what means did Prince Shotoku help spread Chinese culture in Japan?
5. **CRITICAL THINKING** Contrast the effect of the Taika Reforms on the landowners and on the peasants.
6. **ACTIVITY** Find Japan on the maps on pages 530 and 531 of the Atlas. How much of Japan is used for crops? What else do the maps tell you? Organize this information on the chalkboard.

LESSON 2

A Developing National Culture

> *L*ady Dainagon is very small and refined, white, beautiful, and round, though in [behavior] very lofty. Her hair is three inches longer than her height. She uses exquisitely carved hairpins. Her face is lovely, her manners delicate and charming.
>
> Lady Murasaki, *The Diary of Murasaki Shikibu,* c. 980–1015

This portrait tells us a lot about the qualities that were admired at the Japanese court around the year 1000. One important physical characteristic was a woman's hair. People thought the longer her hair, the lovelier the woman.

Because lightness of skin was admired, both women and men covered their faces with white powder. Women even blackened their teeth to heighten the effect. They also shaved their eyebrows and painted false ones high on their foreheads.

Members of the court wore clothing embroidered with gold, silver, and multicolored thread. A woman might wear 12 or more silk robes at one time, all tied with a single sash. The sleeve of each robe would be a different length so that the woman's arm was a rainbow of colors.

THINKING FOCUS

How did moving the capital to Kyoto affect the development of Japanese culture?

Key Terms

- regent
- courtier

◄ *Lady Dainagon might have used hairpins such as these.*

A Court of Refinement

The finely dressed women and men of the court lived in the new capital of Kyoto, then known as Heian. Here they developed a culture of refinement and luxury. The capital that had been established at Nara in 710 was abandoned because the power of the government was overwhelmed by that of the Buddhist clergy. Buddhist temples and monasteries were a center for cultural activity. However, the clergy tried to interfere in politics. After the move to Kyoto in 794, the emperor strictly limited the number of Buddhist temples and monasteries that could be built. In this way he limited Buddhist influences on his government. Moving the capital also had the effect of isolating Kyoto from events in the provinces.

Even before the court moved to Kyoto, nobles of the Fujiwara

227

Japan

▲ *This fragment of a scroll shows a court lady named Kodai no Kimi in her many layers of robes. Their costumes were so heavy that many women found it difficult to move.*

■ *What were some of the activities of the courtiers at Kyoto?*

clan had come to be the most powerful of the emperor's advisers. The Fujiwara were related to the emperor by marriage. To make sure that their power would grow, members of the clan continued to marry into the imperial family. In fact, it became the custom for imperial princes to marry Fujiwara women. Members of the Fujiwara clan served as **regents** for the emperor, exercising power in the emperor's name for most of the time between 858 and 1185. As the Fujiwara clan's power over the imperial family increased, high government offices became increasingly closed to other families. Also, the emperor became much more a religious symbol than a government leader.

During this relatively peaceful period, Japanese culture flourished. Of the 100,000 people in Kyoto, only about 5 percent were **courtiers,** people who took part in the highly refined social life of the court. Nonetheless, it was these courtiers who created the culture of the period. Japanese literature and customs developed, using language and traditions that the courtiers had adopted from China.

The Kyoto court became one of highly refined manners and tastes, a place where delicacy was valued above all. Every action was thought to carry meaning and every event had great potential. Stories from the literature of the age tell of men falling in love with women after just a glimpse of hair from behind a screen.

The Shingon (*SHIHN gahn*) form of Buddhism was popular among courtiers. Shingon Buddhism involved elaborate ceremonies and rituals and stressed the importance of art and learning. Art, especially poetry and literature, became very important at the court of Kyoto. ■

The Literature of the Court

Poetry was the favorite form of writing among Japanese courtiers. They composed short poems for every occasion, and poetry contests were very popular.

The courtiers greatly admired beauty, especially in nature. Their writing expresses a sentimental sadness at the fragile beauty of natural things. This feeling of sadness at the death of beauty is expressed by the Japanese word *aware* (*ah WAH ray*). What does this poem describe that might arouse feelings of *aware?*

*T*his perfectly still
   Spring day bathed in
   the soft light
From the spread-out sky,
Why do the cherry blossoms
So restlessly scatter down?

Ki no Tomonori, *Kokinshu*, c. 905

New Writing Systems

One thing Japan borrowed from China was its writing system. Formal writing was in Chinese, and so was early poetry. But because they wanted to express feelings in their own language, the Japanese developed a set of characters called *hiragana* to represent Japanese. *Hiragana* symbols represent syllables rather than words. Compare Chinese symbols and *hiragana* in the chart on this page. Why do you suppose that writing in *hiragana* allowed the Japanese to be more expressive than writing in Chinese? Women, who were not expected to learn Chinese, used *hiragana* to write some of the greatest literature of the age.

Diaries and Tales

After poetry, diaries were the favorite form of writing. These personal accounts help us understand the values of the times. For example, the diary of Murasaki Shikibu, a lady of the Fujiwaras, tells a great deal about the roles of women. Because she was a girl, she was not taught to read or write Chinese. She tells how she found a way to learn:

Writing Styles of Japan				
Style	**Words**		**Description**	**Origin**
	(shinto)	*(haiku)*		
Kanji	神道	俳句	Pictograms of concepts	Writing system adopted from Chinese characters
Hiragana	しんとう	はいく	Phonetic symbols of one syllable each	Writing system originated and simplified in Japan

> When my elder brother Shikubu no Jo was a boy, he was taught to read the Chinese classics. I listened, sitting beside him, and learned wonderfully fast, though he was sometimes slow and forgot. Father, who was devoted to study, regretted that I had not been a son.
>
> Lady Murasaki, *The Diary of Murasaki Shikibu*, c. 980–1015

The crowning literary achievement of this time was Murasaki's *Tale of Genji*, a long account of the life and loves of a fictional prince. Genji has the virtues valued by the Kyoto court: he is handsome and romantic. But the mood of the tale is often one of sadness. ■

▲ Hiragana *was developed during the 800s. Another style of Japanese writing,* katakana, *was developed later to spell words from foreign languages.*

■ *What kinds of literature developed at the court of Kyoto?*

▼ *Two ladies of the court watch as Prince Genji walks in the garden by moonlight.*

229

Life in the Provinces

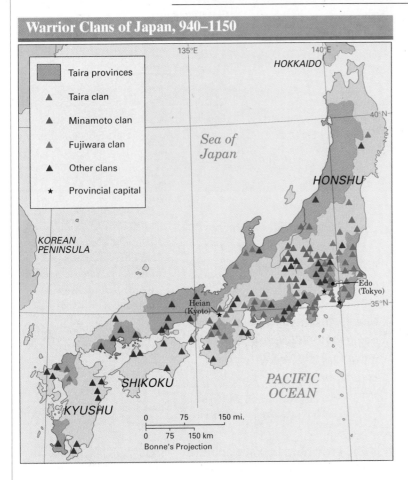

Legend:
- Taira provinces
- ▲ Taira clan
- ▲ Minamoto clan
- ▲ Fujiwara clan
- ▲ Other clans
- ★ Provincial capital

135°E · 140°E
HOKKAIDO
40°N
Sea of Japan
HONSHU
KOREAN PENINSULA
Edo (Tokyo)
35°N
Heian (Kyoto)
SHIKOKU
PACIFIC OCEAN
KYUSHU
0   75   150 mi.
0   75   150 km
Bonne's Projection

▲ *What families were in power in the provinces?*

■ *How did life in the Japanese provinces differ from life at the Kyoto court?*

The courtiers were able to live as they did because they were supported by what was produced in the provinces. Farmers paid part of what they grew to imperial tax collectors. Courtiers also collected part of what was produced on their private estates. But caught up in the life of the court, courtiers preferred to ignore the provinces. The responsibility for what went on there was in the hands of provincial nobles.

Japan had a long tradition of private ownership of land. In the 600s, clans in the provinces had been unhappy with the Taika Reforms, which had broken up their lands and reduced their power. Taking advantage of the imperial government's involvement with court life, provincial nobles took over more and more land. By 1100, some provincial nobles had acquired large estates that were free of government control.

In order to avoid paying taxes and serving as soldiers in the imperial army, many small landowners gave over their land to the nobles. They ended up as tenant farmers, paying rent in crops for the privilege of farming land owned by the nobles. Others became carpenters or menial laborers on the huge private estates. Most peasants remained as poor and as miserable as ever, spending their days at backbreaking work and their nights in crowded huts.

The Kyoto courtiers were out of touch with all of this. They were isolated in a world of luxury and fine culture at Kyoto. The "dwellers among the clouds," as they were called, probably looked upon lowly workers as barely human. ■

R E V I E W

1. **FOCUS** How did moving the capital to Kyoto affect the development of Japanese culture?

2. **CONNECT** Why was Buddhism able to coexist with Shinto in Japan?

3. **HISTORY** How did the central government's involvement with court life affect conditions for Japanese farmers?

4. **CRITICAL THINKING** What do you think might have been the eventual result of the isolation of the ruling class at Kyoto?

5. **WRITING ACTIVITY** Imagine that you are a member of the emperor's court at Kyoto. Write a diary entry that describes either clothing worn by courtiers or your daily life at court.

LESSON 3

The Power of the Shoguns

*J*omyo Meishu of Tsutsui . . . was attired in a dark blue hitatare, a suit of black-laced armor, and a five-plate helmet. At his waist, he wore a sword with a black lacquered hilt and scabbard. . . . He let fly a fast and furious barrage from his twenty-four arrow quiver, . . . He abandoned the weapon and fought with his sword.

Anonymous, from
The Tale of the Heike, 1100s

The passage you just read is from a collection of Japanese tales of war. It tells of a warrior monk. Warrior monks, and many more warriors who were not monks, were common in Japan during the 1100s. It was a time when many swords slashed and many arrows struck their marks.

Life for these warriors was clearly quite different from that of the Kyoto courtiers described in *The Tale of Genji*. How had they come to exist in Japan?

THINKING FOCUS

What impact did samurai values have on Japanese culture and religion?

Key Terms

- shogun
- daimyo
- samurai
- sect

◄ *This print of two warriors fighting with swords is from a famous series titled* One Hundred and Eight Popular Heroes *from Shii-hu Ch'uan.*

231

Japan

A Warrior Government

How Do We Know?

HISTORY *For warriors in medieval Japan, the ritual and ceremony of the battle were as important as the battle itself. Stories describing heroism in battle were popular. The Tale of the Heike, for example, tells about battles between the Taira and the Minamoto in the 1100s.*

▼ *Cherry blossoms were sometimes used as a symbol for samurai in the literature and art of Japan. A samurai knew that his time on earth was likely to be as brief as the flowering of a cherry tree.*

As the Kyoto court maintained its isolation, lawlessness spread in the provinces. Rebellions of nobles and even of Buddhist monks were put down by the government.

The central government had long been dominated by the Fujiwara family. But as its income from taxes and its power over provincial nobles decreased, the government came to depend on warlike provincial nobles for help in putting down rebellions. Also, less powerful nobles came to depend on the most powerful clans for protection. It was a dangerous age, one in which men—and even a few women, as this description shows—won fame as warriors:

*T*omoe was especially beautiful, with white skin, long hair, and charming features. She was also a remarkably strong archer. . . . Tomoe galloped into their midst, rode up alongside Moroshige, seized him in a powerful grip, pulled him down against the pommel of her saddle. . . . She discarded armor and helmet and fled toward the eastern provinces.

Anonymous, from
The Tale of the Heike, 1100s

In the 1100s, nobles of the Taira and Minamoto warrior clans battled for control. By 1185, the Minamoto were victorious. Led by Yoritomo, they set up a warrior government. In 1192, Yoritomo was given the title **shogun,** meaning "great general," by the emperor.

Because Yoritomo didn't want his warriors to be distracted by court life in Kyoto, he made his headquarters at Kamakura, near present-day Tokyo. The emperor continued to live at Kyoto. But the real power resided in the shogun's headquarters at Kamakura.

The Rise of the Samurai

The shogun was supported by the nobles who owned large estates in the provinces. These nobles became known as **daimyo** *(DY mee oh).* Each daimyo relied on warriors to protect his estate. As reward for their service, the warriors themselves won small pieces of land.

The warriors were called **samurai** *(SAM uh ry),* which means "those who serve." The samurai became a new class in society— mounted, armored warriors who often held positions as officials in the provinces. You can read more about a samurai warrior in A Moment in Time on page 233.

The Impact of Foreign Invasion

Under the Kamakura shoguns, Japan enjoyed stable rule and trade with China flourished. In the late 1200s, however, Japan was threatened by the Mongols under Kublai Khan. In 1274, when Mongol forces launched an attack from Korea across the Sea of Japan, they had to turn back because of a storm. But in 1281, Mongol forces numbering as many as 150,000 landed on Kyushu.

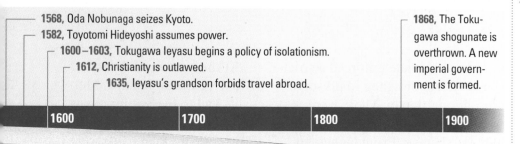

1568, Oda Nobunaga seizes Kyoto.
1582, Toyotomi Hideyoshi assumes power.
1600–1603, Tokugawa Ieyasu begins a policy of isolationism.
1612, Christianity is outlawed.
1635, Ieyasu's grandson forbids travel abroad.

1868, The Tokugawa shogunate is overthrown. A new imperial government is formed.

1600   1700   1800   1900

Under the Tokugawa each daimyo was required to swear an oath of loyalty to the shogun and to give military aid when called upon. In addition, each daimyo had to spend part of every other year in Edo, serving the shogun. The daimyo were forced to leave their wives and eldest sons in Edo when they returned to the provinces.

Foreigners in Japan

When Portuguese traders reached Japan in 1542, they also brought Catholic missionaries.

By the early 1600s, the shogunate saw these foreigners as a threat. The Tokugawa knew of Europe's religious and political wars. They feared the turmoil might spread to Japan. Also, they feared that if the daimyo became rich from foreign trade, they might rebel.

Between 1612 and 1635, therefore, the shogunate issued decrees that outlawed Christianity, restricted travel, and banned virtually all European trade. In effect, Japan was set on a policy of strict isolation from western influences. ■

■ *What steps did the Tokugawa shoguns take to unify Japan?*

UNDERSTANDING ISOLATION

The islands of Japan were cut off, or isolated, from other countries. Even so, in the 1630s, Japan's government felt the need to adopt a policy of political and economic isolation. How were these kinds of isolation different?

Kinds of Isolation

Mountains, jungles, or seas can isolate a culture. This is geographic isolation. For example, the Hawaiian islands were unknown to the rest of the world until Captain James Cook landed there in 1778.

Japan's isolation in the 1630s was deliberate. In America today, the Amish deliberately isolate themselves from the culture that surrounds them. Living in farming communities in Pennsylvania and the Midwest, they practice simplicity as a religiously dictated way of life and do not use modern inventions such as electricity or telephones.

Results of Isolation

Geographic, or deliberate, isolation limits the influences of other cultures and often strengthens the unique qualities of a culture.

Also, isolation limits technological and commercial growth. An isolated culture cannot borrow or adapt the ideas of other cultures. For Japan of the 1800s, the lure of increased trade and new knowledge was to make isolation less attractive than it had been.

239

Control of the Classes

The shogunate enforced a strict social system designed to preserve a traditional Japan. There were four official classes below the shogun and daimyo. From highest to lowest they were samurai warriors, artisans, peasants, and merchants.

Restrictions on Each Class

To keep the daimyo in line, the shogun made them swear an oath of allegiance. The shogun took away the warriors' lands and instead paid them salaries for their services. The once-illiterate samurai learned to read and write and became educated administrators.

Since artisans didn't threaten the shogun's control, few restrictions were placed on them. They thrived in towns, selling their wares to samurai and merchants.

Peasants made up the bulk of the population. Because they were so numerous, the government placed many restrictions on them. Peasants were forbidden to travel beyond the land on which they worked. Also, tax collectors took about half of their crops, leaving them with just enough to survive.

At the bottom of the social scale were the merchants. Merchants had to live within towns and were excluded from political affairs. Finally, merchants were not allowed to dress lavishly or to live in luxury.

The Rise of the Merchant Class

Despite government regulations, the merchant class prospered. More and more merchants were needed to bring food, cloth, and other goods to Edo. They also traded in other cities where the daimyo and their followers might stop to rest.

Before the Tokugawa era, money was not much used in Japan. But merchants found money much less bulky to carry than the bushels of rice traditionally used for trade. By 1600, gold and silver coins were in use, and by 1700, Japan's economy was based largely on money. Merchants controlled the flow of money by setting prices and charging interest on loans. They grew rich from their trade and their power grew with their wealth. ∎

Across Time & Space

Today the tiny, mineral-poor islands of Japan account for a full 10 percent of the world's economic output, and Japan ranks third in the world in production of manufactured goods. Japan's brand names are known all over the world, on everything from cameras to cars to grand pianos. Virtually all of the VCRs sold in the United States are made by Japanese companies.

■ *How did Japan's economy change during the Tokugawa era?*

➤ *A daimyo and his samurai warriors make their way to Edo. Daimyo were required to spend part of each year at the shogun's court.*

A New and Different Culture

The merchants had leisure time and money. They spent it on new forms of entertainment that be-

came available in cities. In the late 1600s, areas of cities were set aside as pleasure quarters. There city dwellers could find theaters, tea-houses, gambling houses, wrestling, and public baths.

The upper classes officially scorned these amusements as lower-class entertainment. They clung to the traditional arts such as Noh theater and the tea ceremony. Still, they allowed the pleasure centers to prosper and gradually were attracted there themselves.

Some of the new cultural forms, such as Kabuki theater, were long lasting. Kabuki theater had its origins in performances of wandering ballad singers and dancers, who acted out stories by dancing and gesturing. Kabuki, which is still popular today, was a rich blend of music, dance, and mime and involved spectacular staging and costumes. The plays' subjects ranged from adventures of brave samurai to tales of romance and broken hearts.

Besides plays for the Kabuki theater, new forms of literature also included epic novels about samurai exploits and short poems called **haiku.** A haiku is a poem of three lines that is intended to create a mood or bring about a sudden insight into human existence. A haiku has 17 syllables. The first line has five syllables, the second seven, and the third five. Matsuo Basho, one of Japan's greatest poets, wrote hundreds of haiku, including the following:

O ld pond:
　　Frog jump-in
Water-sound.

Matsuo Basho, Untitled, 1686

During the 1500s and 1600s, education spread to all classes, and the economy boomed. When Japan emerged from its self-imposed isolation and reopened its doors in 1854, the West saw a unique and successful civilization. ■

◄ *Small bunraku puppets, like the one at left, were often used in plays performed in the cities. Entertainment and everyday scenes were common subjects of colorful prints such as the one below showing a Kabuki performance from the 1700s. These prints, made from wood blocks, were popular with the merchant class.*

■ *What role did the new merchant class play in the development of a new popular culture?*

R E V I E W

1. **FOCUS** Why did the Tokugawa shoguns want to keep Japan isolated?
2. **CONNECT** How did the Tokugawa shogunate go about creating stability that had been lacking in medieval Japan?
3. **ECONOMICS** What was the role of the merchants within Japan's early economy?
4. **CULTURE** What forms of popular entertainment emerged in Japan in the late 1600s? Why did the samurai scorn these forms?
5. **CRITICAL THINKING** How does the phrase "It takes money to make money" apply to the merchant class under the Tokugawa shogunate?
6. **WRITING ACTIVITY** Write a haiku of your own, following the form explained on this page. Use a single image from nature as the subject of your haiku.

241

Japan

Recognizing Assumptions

Here's Why

Suppose you are in charge of planning the refreshments for a meeting. You choose pizza as the food to be served. In planning the menu, you made an assumption: that most people at the meeting would like pizza. You were probably so sure of this that you accepted it as a fact. You didn't feel the need to ask if your friends would like to eat pizza.

An assumption is an idea that is accepted as fact without proof or demonstration. Often the assumption is so deeply rooted in a culture or in an individual's beliefs that it is not even stated.

For example, look at the picture of court women on the next page. From this illustration of *The Tale of Genji,* you might make an assumption that women played a very subordinate role in Japan in the 900s. You may also feel that the decorative

box and makeup shown below seem to reinforce your assumption. However, you learned in Lesson 2 that Lady Murasaki contributed greatly to Japanese culture. In fact, Lady Murasaki wrote *The Tale of Genji,* which some authorities consider to be the world's first novel.

Most assumptions can be proven to be either true or false, depending on the actual facts. In either case, you need to be aware of your unstated assumptions in order to correctly evaluate your conclusions.

Here's How

Assumptions that are correct can help you make sound decisions quickly even when you don't have all the facts. Incorrect assumptions, on the other hand, can cause you to make poor and even harmful decisions. Use the following steps to help you identify and evaluate your assumptions.

First, put your assumptions into words. Suppose you were to read that marriages were often arranged in medieval Japan. Perhaps you might feel sorry for the people who were forced into these arranged marriages. Try to express in words exactly what ideas you accept as facts that influenced your decision or your feelings. In

this case, you make two assumptions: First, you assume that the men and women in medieval Japan were not allowed to take part in the choosing of their mates. Your second assumption is that in cultures where people who do not make this choice independently, the men and women involved are not happy.

Second, identify the basis of your assumptions. Think about why you hold certain assumptions. Many useful assumptions are based on experience. Others are an unquestioned part of a culture or of certain religious beliefs. Your assumption that your classmates would like to eat pizza was probably based either on your own experience or on the experience of others. Your assumption that people do not want arranged marriages is probably so much a part of your culture that you have never even heard it stated.

Remember that people in different cultures have different values. Your assumptions about arranged marriages are based on life in your culture. Therefore, these assumptions cannot be accurately applied to events that happened in medieval Japanese culture or to other cultures different from yours. Be careful not to apply your assumptions to cultures where they are not appropriate.

Third, check your assumptions for accuracy. Be sure you have enough accurate information to test your assumptions. In medieval Japan, for example, young men and women were not denied totally the right to choose partners. In fact, it was the custom for young girls to write the names of their choices for husbands on papers, which were then attached to a sacred tree so that the local god would know their wishes. Also, among farming families, if the parents did not approve of their daughter's choice, the young man could arrange for "the theft of the bride," a custom that provided a way for the couple to marry without the parents' approval. When you test your assumptions against more accurate or more complete information, you may find that they are incorrect.

Try It

Reread The Impact of Foreign Invasion on pages 232 and 233 in Lesson 3. Note the size of the forces and the firepower and weapons of the Mongols and the samurai. Think about what assumptions you might make about the intensity and outcome of the battle. Then follow the three steps listed in Here's How. How well did the facts bear out your assumptions? On what factors were your assumptions based? What factors did your assumptions leave out?

Apply It

Write a sentence or two identifying the assumptions that might have led to each of these actions. Explain on what the assumptions might have been based.

1. You expect a homework assignment in social studies. However, you make plans to go to your sister's high school volleyball game that evening.
2. You go with friends to a local park and they suggest swimming in a lake you've never been in before. You dive into the water.

Chapter Review

Reviewing Key Terms

courtier (p. 228)   samurai (p. 232)
daimyo (p. 232)   sect (p. 234)
haiku (p. 241)   Shinto (p. 225)
isolation (p. 223)   shogun (p.232)
regent (p. 228)   succession (p. 238)

A. Be sure you understand the meanings of the key terms. Then answer each question by writing one or more sentences.
   1. How did courtiers influence the culture of Japan between 858 and 1185?
   2. What title means "great general"?
   3. Which Japanese religion had many sects?
   4. How was a line of succession to the title "shogun" established?

B. Write whether each statement below is *true* or *false*. Then rewrite the false statements to make them true.
   1. Japan's seas have kept Japan in isolation from much of the world.
   2. The religion of early Japan, Shinto, revolved around ancient feudal rites.
   3. The nobles who owned large estates became known as daimyo.
   4. In the 1600s, poets in Japan often wrote haiku, poems with exactly 17 lines.
   5. Japanese warriors were called samurai, which means "those who rule."
   6. From 858–1185, members of the Fujiwara clan were often regents for the emperor.

Exploring Concepts

A. Copy the timeline below on your own paper. After each date, write the importance of the date in the history of Japan. The first entry is done for you.

B. Answer each question with information from the chapter.
   1. How did Shinto lead to a political tradition for the emperors of Japan?
   2. How did Prince Shotoku encourage Buddhism and the spread of Chinese culture in Japan in the late 500s?
   3. What changes were made by the Taika Reforms? What were the results?
   4. What values characterized the court at Kyoto?
   5. What task were the clan leaders given under the Taika Reforms? Instead of performing this task, what did they do while the courtiers were preoccupied?
   6. How were the Mongols defeated in 1281? What effect did the Mongol invasion have on the Japanese government?
   7. What decrees did the Tokugawa shogunate issue in 1633? What was the effect of these decrees?
   8. When Japan reopened its doors to foreigners in 1854, how had it changed?

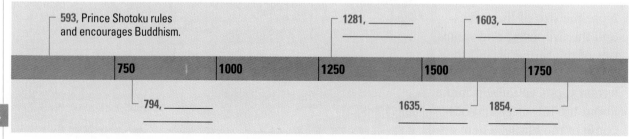

593, Prince Shotoku rules and encourages Buddhism.

750   1000   1250   1500   1750

1281, _____

1603, _____

794, _____

1635, _____

1854, _____

244

Chapter 9

Reviewing Skills

1. Turn to page 225 and read the paragraphs in the first column that describe the Yayoi culture. The last sentence of this section is, "These objects suggest that rulers of this culture were from a respected warrior class." What assumption does the author make in this sentence?

2. Read the first paragraph on page 239. The Tokugawa shoguns forced the daimyo to leave their wives and eldest sons at the shogun's court in Edo when the daimyo returned to the provinces they governed. What assumptions did the shogun make about the daimyo?

3. Look at the map on page 528 of the Atlas. What areas of Japan have few cities? Look at the topographical map of Japan on page 224. What geographical features might account for the lack of cities in certain areas?

4. You want to summarize the history of Japan on a poster that shows the most important historic events. What graphic device would you use to give visual impact to written facts and dates?

Using Critical Thinking

1. The men and women of the Kyoto court lived very different lives from the rest of the Japanese people. What were the positive effects of their lifestyles at court? What were the negative effects?

2. During the late 1500s, General Oda Nobunaga began to unify Japan. He destroyed a Buddhist monastery and its 20,000 residents because the monks inside had dared to help an enemy army. Do you think his actions were justified? Why or why not?

3. Why did Yoritomo want his warriors to live in Kamakura instead of Kyoto? What do you think he feared might happen if they went to Kyoto?

4. In the early 1600s, the shogunate issued decrees that set Japan on a policy of isolation. When Japan emerged from its isolation in 1854, the West saw a unique and successful civilization. What do you think would happen if the United States began a policy of isolation, including an end to foreign trade, today?

Preparing for Citizenship

1. COLLECTING INFORMATION Japan experiences more than 15,000 earthquakes a year, though most are mild. Find out what causes earthquakes and where the world's major earthquakes occur. To what extent can they be predicted? How do people try to control earthquake damage, especially in cities?

2. WRITING ACTIVITY Japan, an isolated nation, developed a unique and successful civilization. Locate other island nations on a globe. Choose one to study. Find out for how long, and to what extent, this nation was isolated. How much, in spite of isolation, was it influenced by other nations? Write a brief report describing the nation you chose.

3. GROUP ACTIVITY Today most Japanese people live in urban areas. Find out which of the cities mentioned in this chapter are major cities of Japan today. What are Japanese cities like? How are they similar to cities in Western countries? How are they different?

4. COLLABORATIVE LEARNING Work in committees to study different kinds of Japanese arts, such as haiku poetry, the tea ceremony, and Kabuki theater. Using information you find, create a sample of the art form you study. One committee might recite a poem and another perform a skit for the class. As a class, discuss how the art forms of a country help its people take pride in their nation.

Medieval Societies

Today is tournament day, and the squires display the helmets of their knights for all to see. The nobles of the castle gather with the peasants of the countryside to watch the bold warriors. Soon the knights will mount their horses, grab their lances, and demonstrate their battle skills. These are the men who defend the European castles and set out on holy crusades for the glory of their kings and their God.

330

The Showing of the Helms Before the Tournament, from Livre des Tournois du Roi Rene. *Bibliotheque Nationale, Paris*

1450

Chapter 10
Feudal Europe and Japan

A castle rises high on a rocky mount, defended by massive stone walls. Such fortresses protected people in both Europe and Japan from invaders about 1,000 years ago. The sturdy stone walls, three feet thick, shielded peasants from attack. The peasants paid for their safety by serving the lord of the castle or giving him land. This arrangement, called the feudal system, ruled life in Europe and Japan for centuries.

Viking chieftains who invaded Europe in the 800s wore helmets like this.

c. 900–1100 To protect their castles, European landowners build walls with rounded turrets that are difficult to attack. This castle was built along the border of present-day France and Spain.

400	700	1000

c. 700 Ghana becomes the first large West African trading empire.

c. 900 Cordoba, Spain, is the cultural and intellectual center of western Islam.

476

never go to the King, nor seek his favor, nor in any way reveal thyself to him."

And Roland's face had grown as red as fire, and his eyes blazed with anger, and his hands were clenched until the knuckles whitened. And Bertha, ending her story, wept, not for herself, but for her husband, who was dead and for their son, who must endure this poverty. But Roland said, between his teeth, "The King is feasting even now off yonder with the Governor, while thou, his sister, scarcely hast a crust. But trust me, thou shalt share this feast, my mother"; and he made as if to leave the cave. But Bertha caught him by the sleeve and cried, "What wouldst thou do, my son?"

Roland made answer, "Naught that I should not do," and freed himself, but gently, and went forth, and made his way to the Governor's castle. There he entered in, and came on to the hall where Charlemagne feasted. And many a noble knight was there, and ladies, richly dressed.

But Roland took no heed of them. He came on through the hall and to the King, and said to him, "My mother is hungry, and it is not meet that she should fast while ye have plenty here, and still to spare." And he took up the dish of food that had been set before the King, also his goblet filled with wine, and turned to leave the hall.

But those about cried out and rose and would have caught hold of Roland; but Charlemagne hindered them. "Let the boy go," he said, for suddenly he remembered a dream that he had had not long before.

In his dream he had heard his sister Bertha calling him, and she was in deep distress. Then in his dream the love he once had felt for her returned, and he sought everywhere to find her, but he found her not. Then a lad like to the one who had but now gone from the hall, came to him and took him by the hand and said, "Come now with me, and I will take thee to thy sister Bertha, for she is my mother."

Charlemagne went with him in his dream, and so came to a cave and found his sister there, and she was weeping. Then it seemed to him his heart would break with pity for her grief, and he had cried, "Bertha!" and with that cry had wakened, and it was all a dream.

But it was because of that he had let the lad go free, and now he bade the attendants follow him secretly and see which way he went. If it was to his mother, and the food and wine were indeed for her, then they were to bring both son and mother back with them, not with roughness but as though they honored them.

As they were bidden so the attendants did. They followed Roland but so stealthily that he did not know of it, and so came

meet   proper

to a cave, and saw him enter there, and afterward they heard him speak and someone answer him. Then they, too, made their way into the cave and saw the Lady Bertha there (but guessed not who she was) and Roland had set the food before her and was urging her to eat; but she would not, and only wept.

When Roland saw the men he thought they had come there for harm, and ran and fetched a staff and made ready to defend his mother. Then the attendants told him that they meant no ill; they had but come to bring him and his mother to the King and that the King intended only good toward them.

Then Roland's heart was lightened, but his mother feared. She feared what Charlemagne might do to them when he discovered she was Bertha. But she rose, and prepared herself as best she could to come before him.

So the attendants brought them back to Charlemagne; and when the King saw that it was indeed his sister Bertha they had brought, he cried aloud, and went and took her in his arms, and there were tears upon his cheeks. And Bertha wept again, but now with joy, and all was forgiven between them.

After that she and Roland were arrayed in garments fitted to their rank, and went with Charlemagne to Rome, and saw him crowned as Emperor. Oliver went with them, riding at Roland's side, and joying in his good fortune.

When Charlemagne returned to France again he brought Bertha and Roland with him, and Roland was trained in all things fitting one of high degree, and he was dear to Charlemagne; so dear, indeed, that none was dearer, not even Charlot the Emperor's own son and heir to France. And Bertha dwelt in the palace, and in time was married to Count Ganelon, the Emperor's counselor and friend.

As for her son, as years went on he came to be the most famous Paladin in all of France, and was beloved alike by high and low; but this was not until years afterward, when Roland had learned the duties of a page, a squire, and then a bachelor, and last of all a knight. And through all this his cousin Oliver was ever his dearest friend, so that a saying rose, "As dear to each other as are Roland and Oliver."

Further Reading

Adam of the Road. Elizabeth Gray Vining. Searching for his minstrel father and his dog, Adam wanders 13th-century England. He meets jugglers, minstrels, pilgrims, and nobles in a journey that shows you the life and customs of the time.

Charlemagne and His Knights. Katharine Pyle. Additional stories about the adventures of Roland and other knights.

Knights in Armor. Shirley Glubok. This art book is based on the collection of armor in New York's Metropolitan Museum of Art. Here you can see exactly what the knights wore.

The Master Puppeteer. Katharine Patterson. A 13-year-old boy in feudal Japan tells his story of everyday existence and life in the theater. The ancient art of Japanese puppetry provides the backdrop for this adventure story.

The Merry Adventures of Robin Hood. Howard Pyle. The book retells the legend of a man who robs from the rich king and gives to the poor peasants.

LESSON 1

Europe After the Roman Empire

Key Terms

- monastery
- feudalism
- hierarchy
- fief
- vassal
- oath of fealty
- knight

➤ *This Anglo-Saxon box lid from the 700s was carved from whalebone. It shows warriors attacking a fortress. What kinds of weapons can you see in the carving?*

W hen the barbarian Odoacer took command of Rome in A.D. 476, he removed the powerless emperor Romulus Augustulus. The Western Roman Empire lay like a skeleton fallen in its own useless armor.

To Romans, it must have seemed the end of the world. All along the 10,000-mile border of the empire, there was war. Orientus, a Roman poet in the 400s, wrote:

S ee how swiftly death comes upon the world, and how many people the violence of war has stricken. Some lay as food for dogs; others were killed by the flames that licked their homes. In the villages and country houses, in the fields and in the countryside, on every road—death, sorrow, slaughter, fires, and lamentation.

Rise of the Germanic Kingdoms

The fall of Rome marked both the end of the ancient world and the beginning of a new era. Historians call this period, which lasted until about 1450, the Middle Ages, or the Medieval Period. Some have called the early part of this period the "Dark Ages" because little that was written at that time has come down to us. Historians do know, however, that important changes took place in Europe.

New kingdoms were set up in the lands the Germanic invaders had conquered. The map below shows the barbarians' division of rule in Europe. One Germanic group called themselves the Franks, or "the bold." Find the part of Europe where the Franks settled.

A Conquering People

In 481, the 15-year-old warrior Clovis became king of the Franks. He led them for 30 years in wars that widened the boundaries of the Frankish kingdom. Eventually, it included most of what are now France and Germany. Clovis also led the Franks into Christianity.

After the collapse of the Western Roman Empire, the only tie with the stability of earlier times was provided by the church of Rome. It continued such traditions of the empire as using Latin and making its center in Rome.

Elsewhere in Europe, monks formed religious communities known as **monasteries.** There they devoted themselves to preserving the ideas of ancient Rome and Greece as well as church writings.

The church supported Clovis because it wanted to continue to serve Christians in the area ruled by the Franks. In order to do that, the church had

◄ *This Roman eagle of gold and precious stones was made by an Ostrogoth goldsmith.*

▼ *Find present-day France and England on the map of Europe on page 524 of the Atlas. Which Germanic tribes settled in the areas that became France and England?*

Barbarian Kingdoms

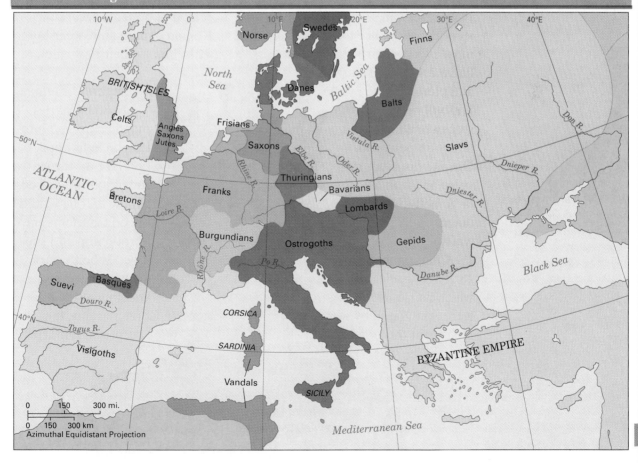

Feudal Europe and Japan

to cooperate with the king. Once Clovis had been baptized and had accepted the support of the church, the leaders of the church encouraged him to spread Christianity. "Every battle you fight is a victory for us," a bishop wrote to Clovis.

A New Royal Family

The sons and grandsons of Clovis were more interested in squabbling among themselves than in ruling the kingdom. A new family rose to power from within the king's household. The Mayors of the Palace, officials of the king, were the kingdom's real rulers.

■ *What important changes took place in Europe after the fall of Rome?*

It was a Mayor of the Palace, Charles Martel, or Charles the Hammer, who defeated Muslim invaders from Spain at Tours, France. Martel's victory against the Islamic armies in 732 made him a hero. It was said that he saved northern Europe for Christianity.

In 751, Martel's son, Pepin, asked the head of the church, Pope Zacharias, to recognize him as king. Pepin was the first king to rule with the blessings of the church. King Pepin's son Charles, who was called Charlemagne, would also rule with the church's support. ■

Charlemagne's Empire

Charlemagne was to become more than the king of the Franks. He would become emperor, the ruler of the former Western Roman Empire. Charlemagne stood a head taller than almost everyone around him. He had a drooping moustache and piercing blue eyes. His bull neck and stocky build made him look powerful. Despite his squeaky voice and rather large belly, Charlemagne looked like a warrior.

Charlemagne's 48 years of rule, which began in 768, were dominated by war. He fought the Lombards

This gold likeness of Charlemagne at the cathedral of Aachen was made to hold his bones.

in Italy, the Saxons to the north, the Avars and Slavs to the east, and others, 60 campaigns in all.

Charlemagne made his defeated opponents accept the Roman church and swear loyalty to him as their new ruler.

An Emperor Crowned

In 800, Charlemagne marched into Italy to help Pope Leo III put down a rebellion there. Leo knew that he would need Charlemagne's protection and support. When Charlemagne rose from kneeling at the altar on Christmas day, the pope surprised him. He placed a crown on Charlemagne's head and declared him emperor.

Charlemagne and the pope both knew that only the head of the Eastern Roman Empire at Constantinople could legally claim the title of emperor. But the title fit Charlemagne well. As emperor, Charlemagne dedicated himself to strengthening the church and bringing learning to his empire.

An Age of Learning

Although unable to read or write, Charlemagne liked to have men of letters around him. His greatest scholar was a religious man from England named Alcuin.

By Charlemagne's time, most of Europe's libraries had been destroyed during periods of war. Very few people knew how to read the few books that were left. Led by Alcuin, Charlemagne's scholars copied by hand these manuscripts to keep them for future ages.

Charlemagne himself longed to learn to write. He kept a writing tablet under his pillow while he tried to learn. But he eventually decided he was too old to master the written word.

Charlemagne also made sure that religious services were performed the same way throughout Europe. He forced illiterate clergy to become educated, and tried to rid the church of corruption.

As Charlemagne grew old, his empire began to unravel. Enemies were hammering away at its borders. From the east came a people called the Magyars. From North Africa and Spain, Muslims attacked. And from Scandinavia came a group of fearless warriors

known as Vikings. The map on page 260 shows these invasions.

But all of this was to be someone else's problem. In 814, at the age of 72, Charlemagne died.

Europe After Charlemagne

Charlemagne's son, Charles the Pious, lacked his father's shrewdness and strength. Long before he died in 840, his sons, Lothair, Charles, and Louis, were fighting for control of the empire. For a while, the empire was divided among them, as you can see on the map on page 260. Their kingdoms came apart as landowners became more independent.

As Europe broke up into smaller kingdoms, people looked to local lords to defend them. With the Magyars, Muslims, and Vikings at their borders, the people had much need for protection.

After Charlemagne's death, the Vikings found Europe falling apart, and ready for the taking. The

A stained-glass window in the cathedral at Chartres, France, tells the stories of Charlemagne and of his loyal knight and nephew, Roland. This section shows Charlemagne and two of his warriors.

How Do We Know?

HISTORY *Historians know quite a bit about what Alcuin did and thought while he worked at Charlemagne's court. Many of Alcuin's letters to other churchmen can still be read today.*

259

Feudal Europe and Japan

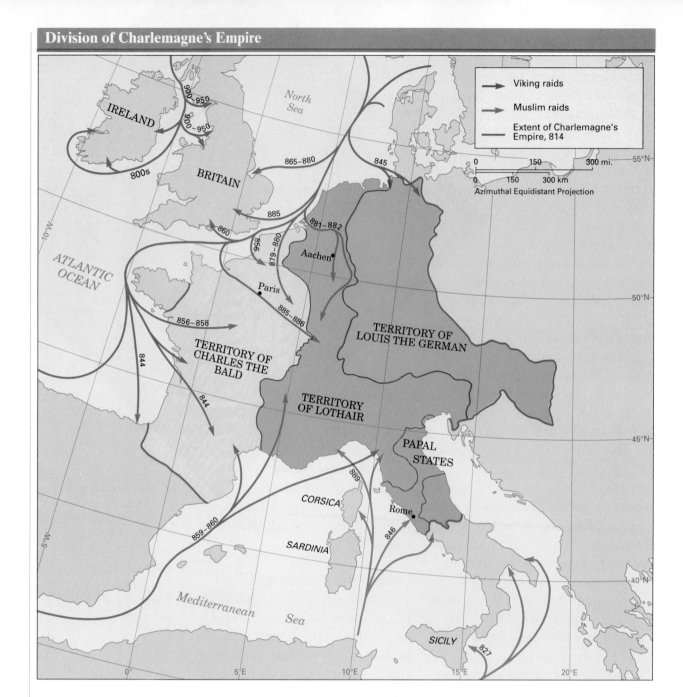

Division of Charlemagne's Empire

▲ *Where in Europe did Vikings attack?*

■ *How did Charlemagne improve learning and the quality of the church in medieval Europe?*

Vikings sailed out of Scandinavia into coastal villages throughout Europe, plundering, killing, burning, and taking prisoners. By the time a local army arrived, the Vikings were gone. In time, they grew bolder, establishing camps from which they raided the countryside. ■

Medieval England

During the 800s, England suffered most at the hands of the Vikings, who launched attacks along the coast. England was saved only by the tough resistance of the Anglo-Saxon king, Alfred the Great. From his base in Wessex, Alfred fought the Vikings for three decades until his death in 899.

A New Ruler

When King Edward, a descendent of Alfred, died childless, the right to the English throne came into question. An English assembly chose Edward's brother-in-law Harold as king. But Edward's cousin William, Duke of Normandy in France, felt his right to the throne was stronger. He said that Edward had promised him the kingdom. He also argued that Harold had sworn to support his claim.

William and his Norman army invaded England. On October 14, 1066, at the Battle of Hastings, William's Norman forces defeated Harold's Saxon infantry.

King William the Conqueror, as he came to be called, was a descendent of Vikings who had settled in France. He had ruled his territories in France with a firm hand and also took firm control of England. He took the land from Harold's followers and, using a system called feudalism, divided it among his own followers.

A New Order

Feudalism was a social and political system that developed in Europe after the fall of the Roman Empire and lasted until about 1200. It was rooted in the people's need for protection against invaders and in landowners' needs for defense. Without Roman administrators or soldiers, small farmers turned to powerful landowners for protection. People received protection in return for service as soldiers or for turning over title and ownership of their land to the larger landowners. With feudalism came new relationships among people. **Hierarchies** developed; they were orders of rank and authority within different classes of people or organizations.

Under the feudal system he established in England, King William ruled all of England. He gave large estates, called **fiefs,** to the warriors who had served him. The new landowners became his subjects, or **vassals.** In exchange for the land awarded to him, each vassal swore an **oath of fealty** to the king. That is, the vassal promised to remain loyal to his lord. He also promised to provide his lord with armed, mounted soldiers, or **knights,** for military duty.

William's vassals, in turn, granted parts of their fiefs to other people. The king's vassals became lords with vassals of their own. These vassals became lords to individual knights. Each vassal swore an oath of fealty to his lord. All levels of society were bound, by loyalty and by need, to their king. ■

▲ *A flag with this design was carried by William the Conqueror's troops at the Battle of Hastings.*

■ *Describe the condition of Europe after Charlemagne's death.*

R E V I E W

1. **FOCUS** What conditions after the fall of Rome led to the rise of feudalism?
2. **CONNECT** Compare and contrast the rule of Charlemagne in western Europe with that of Prince Shotoku in Japan.
3. **CITIZENSHIP** What similarities and differences do you see between the feudal system of governing and our government today?
4. **CRITICAL THINKING** Do you think a law of succession would have prevented the Battle of Hastings? Why?
5. **WRITING ACTIVITY** In the early days of the Middle Ages, Romans and Germanic people lived side by side and influenced each other. In the United States, also, different ethnic groups live side by side. Choose one ethnic group. Describe some of the ways that group has influenced American culture.

LESSON 2

Daily Life in Feudal Europe

How did the feudal system affect the everyday lives of people in Europe?

Key Terms

- homage
- manor
- serf
- guild

➤ *This cutaway view shows the home of a peasant family and their animals. What would you find most uncomfortable about living in this home?*

*H*is hood full of holes with the hair sticking through,
His clumsy knobbed shoes cobbled over so thickly,
Though his toes started out as he trod on the ground . . .
Two miserable mittens made out of old rags, . . .
He wading in mud almost up to his ankles,
And before him four oxen, so weary and feeble
One could reckon their ribs, so rueful were they.

This description of a medieval peasant is from the poem *Piers the Plowman*, which was written in the late 1300s in England by William Langland. The harsh conditions endured by peasants like the one Langland described in his poem had not improved at all for hundreds of years.

In 1066, the rulers of England changed, but the lives of English peasants remained the same. In the hierarchy of the feudal system that William the Conqueror established in England, peasants were at the bottom.

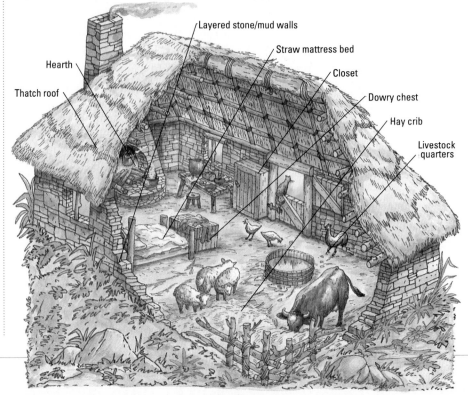

Layered stone/mud walls

Straw mattress bed

Closet

Hearth

Dowry chest

Thatch roof

Hay crib

Livestock quarters

The Feudal System

After the victory at the blood-soaked field of Hastings went to William the Conqueror, life in England changed for many. William planned to rule in peace, using the system of feudalism that was already in place in France.

If you think of feudal society as a house with many rooms, then loyalty was the set of beams that held it up. Vassals paid **homage,** or showed honor, to their lords. The word homage comes from the French word for "man." The vassal was to be the lord's man in body, mind, and spirit.

When an oath of fealty was sworn between a king and a lord or between a lord and a knight, the bond of loyalty was formalized in a ceremony. The vassal knelt before his lord. Placing his hands between the lord's hands, he swore to serve his lord in loyalty and love. Then the vassal and his lord kissed, and the lord gave his vassal a clod of earth symbolizing the fief that the vassal would use. When a vassal died, a lord went through the ceremony with the vassal's oldest son.

In 1066, feudalism was not fully developed in England. William and his Norman lords set about to change all that. William ordered a survey to be taken of the ownership of every bit of land in England. The results of the survey were written in *The Great Domesday Book,* which became a valuable source of information for the king's tax agents. Then William distributed the land as fiefs to his Norman followers. ■

■ *Why was loyalty important in the feudal system?*

▼ *These ivory chess pieces from the 1100s show three different classes of medieval society: a king, a knight, and a member of the clergy—a bishop.*

Life in the Country

William and his Norman lords built fortified castles on their fiefs all over the island kingdom of England. By 1100, several hundred castles had been built throughout the countryside. These Norman fortresses helped to shape the lives of the kings, lords, and knights who made up English nobility.

Nobles

For the lord of a fief, a castle might be home. For others who lived on his land, it was both a

> ➤ *This painting from* Les Tres Riches Heures du Duc du Berry *shows a rich feast held inside a castle. A lord and his guests, who are other nobles and clergy, are in the foreground. What can you see in the far background?*

center for feudal life and a place of safety during battle. Castle walls were three feet thick. They were built to withstand blows from battering rams and flaming missiles launched from enemy catapults. Windows were mere slits through which the archers could shoot their arrows. A Norman castle was usually a tower built at the top of a hill and surrounded by a deep trench, or moat.

The Norman castle was built for

UNDERSTANDING HIERARCHY

The knight made an oath of fealty to the lord of the manor. In turn, the lord swore to be faithful to the more important lord who had granted him his fief. The feudal hierarchy to which knights and lords belonged extended from the humblest peasant all the way up to the king.

Hierarchy as Ranking

A hierarchy is a system by which persons or things are ranked one above another. A group of equals, such as the members of a sports team, cannot be considered a hierarchy.

The meritocracy that Emperor Wen developed in China was a hierarchy with the emperor at the top. Beneath him stood courtiers, administrators, and clerks. Each group, from the administrators up through the emperor, had greater powers than the group below it.

Other Hierarchies

Hierarchies make it clear where people stand in relationship to each other and define their various responsibilities. Most workplaces such as offices and factories are hierarchies, with a boss or president

over several rankings of supervisors and workers.

In the Middle Ages, city dwellers did not participate in the feudal hierarchy, which involved lords, vassals, and peasants. However, some professions in the towns did have organizations that were hierarchies. You will read about these trade organizations, or guilds, later in the lesson. Unlike the peasant who could never become a lord, a worker in a guild could advance. He could "climb" the hierarchy ladder, from the lowest trainee to the highest rank of trade or craft master.

264

Becoming a Medieval Knight

Page	Squire	Knight
• Serving in household • Learning swordplay • Playing chess and other strategy games • Hunting with hawks and falcons • Learning code of courtesy expected of knight	• Acting as personal servant to knight • Learning jousting • Assisting knight in battle • Taking charge of prisoners captured in battle	• Serving lords as warriors • Overseeing land as vassals • Taking part in tournaments
Age 7	**Age 13–14**	**Age 18–22**

security, not for comfort. The lord and lady of the castle usually slept behind a curtain in the main dining hall. Also sleeping in the hall might be a small mob of knights, guests, servants, and dogs. The floor was covered with herbs to keep down the smell of bones and other refuse. On a winter morning, inhabitants would wash by plunging their arms through ice-crusted water in a bucket.

Life in a castle was far from glamorous, and few who lived there were the courteous knights and ladies of legend. A knight was often the landless younger son of a lord's vassal. The lord provided the knight with food, lodging, armor, and a horse in exchange for his services. But between wars the castle's knights fought among themselves or bullied the servants unless the lord of the castle kept an eye on them.

The lady of the castle had very little power, except over female servants. Medieval women were supposed to be subject to their husbands and fathers, just as vassals were subject to their lords. However, most of the daily life of the castle was within women's domain. Besides cooking and cleaning, women also managed the

▲ The chart shows the stages that a young man went through before he became a knight. Why do you think it was such a long and rigorous process?

◄ This woman of the 1300s wears clothing such as that worn by ladies of English or French castles.

265

Feudal Europe and Japan

with a straw roof. Although the animals may have stayed on the other side of a partition, they helped to heat the home in winter.

In the early Middle Ages, farming methods improved in Northern Europe and England. See A Closer look on page 267 for additional information on advances in medieval farming. But farming was still hard, and peasants were bound to the plots of land that they tilled for their lords. Some were so poor that they would not even have owned the scrawny oxen described by William Langland. Instead, they would borrow oxen from their lord or a neighbor.

The peasant woman produced food and clothing for her own household and also took care of her children. William Langland wrote of peasant women's work in *Piers the Plowman:*

In this miniature painting, peasants are shearing sheep and harvesting grain in fields surrounding a castle. Does this picture of peasant life differ from the images conveyed in Piers the Plowman *on this page and on page 262?*

making of clothing and medical care for everyone in the castle. When their husbands were at war, women took over the **manor,** the castle and entire estate.

Peasants

The lord's castle might be a cold, drafty fortress. But the peasants, or **serfs,** who lived in the village on the lord's estate, had even less comfortable homes.

As you can see in the picture on page 262, a typical peasant family lived with its animals in a hut

*W*hat they save from
  their spinning they
spend on house rent,
on milk and oatmeal to make
  porridge
to fill their children when they
  cry for food.
They themselves suffer the
  sting of hunger
and of winter misery, rising at
  night
to rock the cradle in its
  cramped corner,
to card and comb wool, to
  mend and wash,
to scrub and wind yarn, to
  weave rushlights.
It's painful to read or to write
  verses
on the hard lives of women
  who live in hovels. . . .

Medieval Farming

The cycle of changing seasons brought an endless round of work to peasant families. But improvements like the wheelbarrow, horseshoes, and new crops slowly began to soften their harsh lives.

Protecting horses' feet from wear and injury, better horseshoes allowed these strong animals to pull metal-tipped plows. Plowing deeper meant farmers could get at the richest soil, grow more crops, and store food for lean times.

Month by month, this page from a 15th-century French "book of hours" shows the activities of the farm year. Read it left to right and top to bottom. In the January snow, peasants cut the winter wheat they had sowed in September. October found the peasant crushing grapes for wine by foot.

Not the same old bean and pea soup!
New plants like cabbage, parsley and leeks added flavor and nutrition to the boring peasant diet.

Leeks

Parsley

Cabbage

Peas

➤ *Here Pope Urban II blesses a church at Cluny in the 1000s. The monastery at Cluny in France was established in 910, and was a leader of the reform movement within the church. By the late 1000s, there were about 200 monasteries administered by the center at Cluny.*

■ *How did each class help to keep a feudal manor running?*

▼ *A monk in his study is shown here on an ivory book cover from the Middle Ages.*

Clergy

Society in the Middle Ages was described by Alfred the Great as consisting of "men of prayer, men of war, and men of work." Perhaps the men and women "of prayer" had the most comfortable lives of any in the Middle Ages.

The influence of the clergy—from pope, archbishops, and bishops to priests, monks, and nuns—extended to every part of medieval life. Most medieval manors included a small church. From baptism to marriage to burial, the ceremonies of the church guided the lives of medieval men and women.

Also, people at this time saw life on earth as a brief preparation for the eternal life to come. They believed only a few would spend eternity in heaven. Many sinners, people believed, would spend eternity in the flames of hell.

The power to condemn or to forgive sinners made the church a considerable force in medieval society. Many people entered the clergy to find refuge from the sinful world around them. Others, however, joined the church to acquire status and influence.

Thousands of monks, nuns, and servants also lived and worked in large stone structures. A monastery was a complex community with many different buildings—granaries, breweries, bakeries with huge ovens, wineries, and the abbey church and library.

Inside the library, monks hunched over tall desks and copied manuscripts in beautiful handwriting, or drew illustrations. With the same devotion and care, monks and nuns of the Middle Ages also taught children, fed the poor, cared for the sick, and provided shelter to travelers. Most of the clergy worked long hours and reaped few earthly rewards. Their devotion to the church mirrored a vassal's dedication to his lord. ■

Move Ahead

Tape a large sheet of paper to the wall of your classroom. Each student should mention a question that he or she asked. Use the questions to create categories on the chart. For instance, some people may have asked about school hours. If so, a student might write on the chart: "Hours in School per Day (or Week)."

Do everyone's answers agree? If not, find out where the information came from. Is one magazine or book more recent than another? Is one author more knowledgeable and respected than another?

When your chart is complete, discuss the information. What Japanese ideas would you like American schools to adopt? Why?

Explore Some More

Choose another area of American life, one you're very familiar with. It might be sports, games, crafts, music, art, or some current concern—animal welfare, the environment, or political campaigns, for instance.

Find out whether the Japanese share this interest of yours. If so, do they pursue it in the same way? If not, can you find out why not?

▲ *May 5, Boys' Day, is a school holiday in Japan. On this day most families fly carp flags outside their homes. The symbol of the carp—a fish that swims against river currents—inspires boys to face life's difficulties with courage.*

◄ *Like Boys' Day, Girls' Day is also a school holiday in Japan. Celebrated on March 3, Girls' Day centers around dolls. Girls display their dolls and hold tea parties where they serve little cakes iced with cherry-blossom frosting.*

Chapter Review

Reviewing Key Terms

bushido (p. 273)
chivalry (p. 273)
feudalism (p. 261)
fief (p. 261)
guild (p. 269)
hierarchy (p. 261)
homage (p. 263)

knight (p. 261)
manor (p. 266)
monastery (p. 257)
oath of fealty (p. 261)
serf (p. 266)
vassal (p. 261)

A. Write whether each of the following statements is true or false. Then rewrite the false statements to make them true.

1. Monasteries were simple town churches in the Middle Ages.
2. Knights were monks and nuns on horseback.
3. Most castles had a hierarchy, or tower.
4. Bushido was the samurai code of loyalty and conduct.
5. A fief was a kind of musical instrument.
6. Feudalism was a religious and economic system of rule in medieval Europe.
7. Knights and their lords sailed to battles on warships called vassals.
8. Serfs were the peasants who lived on a lord's estate.
9. A medieval woman had to take an oath of fealty to her husband at her marriage.
10. A guild was a union of tradespeople.

B. Use each word below in a sentence that shows what the word means.

1. guild
2. manor
3. homage
4. chivalry
5. hierarchy

Exploring Concepts

A. Create an illustrated "people summary" of the chapter by drawing pictures of one person from each lesson as listed below. Write a sentance describing each person you draw.

Lesson 1:	Lesson 2:
barbarian	peasant
Charles Martel	monk
Charlemagne	nun
Pope Leo III	King John
Alcuin	Lesson 3:
Viking	samurai
Alfred the Great	shogun
William the Conqueror	Sir Lancelot

B. Support each of the following statements with facts and details from the chapter.

1. After the fall of Rome, Europe became a place of warfare.
2. Viking conquests in Europe were made easier by the weakness of Charlemagne's heirs.
3. In a way, France was saved from Muslim invasions because of the failures of Clovis's descendants.
4. Under William the Conqueror there developed a highly organized system for ruling England.
5. Loyalty held English feudal society together.
6. Castles in 12th-century England were built for safety but were not very comfortable for those living within.
7. Peasants led difficult lives.
8. The church played a very important role in the lives of most of the people in Europe during the Middle Ages.
9. Japanese feudalism and European feudalism were different but similar.
10. There were several reasons why feudalism endured 400 years longer in Japan than in Europe.

Reviewing Skills

1. Read the group decision below. Then make a chart that gives both the individual and group advantages and disadvantages of the decision.

   Instead of collecting money to donate to a charity, your class decides to spend several Saturdays helping senior citizens in the neighborhood maintain their houses by raking leaves, painting fences, and hauling away rubbish.

2. Review the section called An Age of Learning in Lesson 1 on page 259. What unstated assumption did Charlemagne make about knowledge and learning?

3. Suppose you are outlining a chapter that compares and contrasts the nature of feudalism in Europe with that of feudalism in Japan. What two kinds of information would you need to find and list in your outline?

Using Critical Thinking

1. In this chapter, you learned how the advent of fighting from horseback and using armor changed the nature of warfare. You also learned about the changes in military technology that permitted armies to defeat mounted knights. What were those new inventions of the 1300s and 1400s? Do you think the country with the most sophisticated weapons always wins a war? Explain your answer.

2. "They worked hard, and they were poor. They had almost nothing to their names, and the little they had was not much use in this world." This bleak description, along with the quotes in the chapter from *Piers the Plowman,* might easily describe the peasants of Europe in the Middle Ages. Do the quotations also describe the plight of some people today? If so, who? Where? How are their conditions similar?

3. Craftspeople in medieval Europe began their apprenticeships when they were very young and worked long hours for no pay while they learned the skills they would need for their life's work. Imagine that you are transported back in time to the Middle Ages. What trade would you be interested in learning to master? Which do you think is more important, the kind of vocational training young people received in the Middle Ages or the general education you're getting now? Explain your answer.

Preparing for Citizenship

1. **COLLECTING INFORMATION** Research what happened on that day in June of 1215 when the powerful landowners made King John of England agree to the revolutionary ideas of the Magna Carta. Imagine that you are King John and tell the class about your experience in a way colorful enough to make them feel they are witnessing history.

2. **GROUP ACTIVITY** In two groups, draw hierarchies of your school system and of your town government or a local business. Draw organization charts that show who reports to whom. Your finished products will probably resemble pyramids, with many people at the bottom and fewer on each level as you move toward the top.

3. **COLLABORATIVE LEARNING** In groups of five, plan a five-minute TV documentary on one of these topics: Charlemagne's kingdom, William's conquest and rule of England, life on a medieval manor, or feudalism in Japan. Assign one person to research the subject, one to write the script, one to make simple costumes and scenery, one to prepare ads, and one to direct the documentary. Each student in the group should also play one of the characters. If possible, videotape the documentary.

Chapter 11

Europe: Rule, Religion, and Conflict

Throughout this period, Christians looked toward Jerusalem as their holy city. This map from late in the period depicts the city at the center of the world.

It was the Age of Faith, as the Catholic church dominated much of Europe from 1000 to 1300. As early as the 800s, the church won power from Europe's kings. Then in 1096, the world truly saw the church's might. That year the pope gathered 30,000 knights, archers, and swordsmen in Constantinople. This massive army hoped to drive the Muslims out of the holy city of Jerusalem. Yet battles over the Holy City would go on for almost 200 years.

800s The Catholic church becomes the center of life in Europe. Many visit churches to see holy objects, like this jeweled container holding the remains of St. Stephen.

| 650 | 750 | 850 | 950 |

900 Cordoba, the largest city in Western Europe, is the center of western Islam.

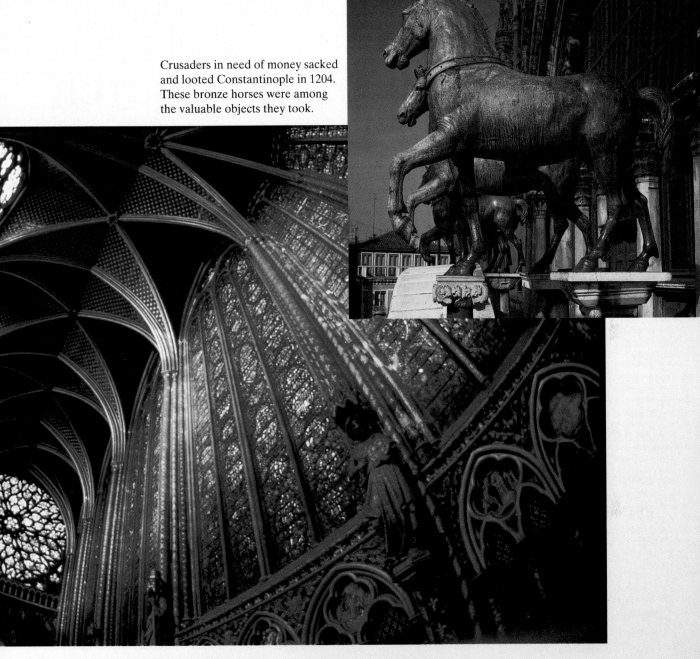

Crusaders in need of money sacked and looted Constantinople in 1204. These bronze horses were among the valuable objects they took.

1240s Parisians build La Sainte Chapelle Cathedral in their city. Such magnificent structures with costly stained-glass windows show the wealth and power of the Catholic church.

1050	1150	1250	1350

1185 The Minamoto family unites Japan under its shogunate rule.

1204

L E S S O N   1

The Power of the Church

➤ *This painting shows the building of Chartres Cathedral. The cathedral was so important to the people that even noblemen and their ladies helped haul stones.*

Many townspeople stood on the church steps awaiting the decision about the new cathedral. This decision would affect their town's future. At last the smiling bishop appeared at the doorway to announce the long awaited answer. Yes, a cathedral would be built in their town to the glory of God!

An architect was selected to design the cathedral and supervise the beginning of its construction. The expense would be great since many workers would be needed: stonecutters, woodworkers,

carpenters, masons, blacksmiths, roofers, glassmakers, sculptors, and more. For hundreds of men in the town this would become their life's work. For a few it would even mean their death, since there was the possibility of falling from the scaffolding on which the workers stood as they built the walls ever higher.

The townspeople knew it could take as many as 100 years to complete the building of the cathedral. However, it was difficult for them to imagine that their great-great-grandchildren would be as old as they were now when the building was finished.

Why would these people, who lived in western Europe in A.D. 1200, spend so much money, time, and labor to begin building something that they would not even live to see completed? Because the cathedral allowed them to celebrate, in stone and glass, the power of the church and of God in their lives.

A Powerful Church in Europe

Between 800 and 1300 almost all the people of Europe were Christians. Only one branch of the faith existed in Europe, and it was headed by the pope in Rome. The Christian religion was organized in such a way that it was the center of spiritual life and an important political force.

The Church Hierarchy

The church was organized in a hierarchy so that each member of the **clergy,** or ordained members of the church, had a specific rank. The priest of the local church, or parish, had a certain group of duties. These included leading religious services, visiting the sick, and conducting ceremonies such as baptisms and weddings. Many parishes together formed one diocese (*DY uh sihs*). Heading each diocese was a bishop, who, in turn, had a different group of responsibilities.

The dioceses were united into provinces, or archdioceses, under the authority of archbishops. Cardinals, who were second in power only to the pope himself, oversaw the archbishops. The cardinals also acted as counselors to the pope and were responsible for electing new popes. Leading the entire church was the pope. *Pope* comes from the Latin word for "father."

The Church's Influence

The church encouraged Christians to help save their souls by giving donations to the churches of Europe. This brought in much money for the churches. In addition, popes, cardinals, and bishops were often nobles with land of their own who left this land to the church when they died. By 1050, the church was the largest landholder in western Europe.

In addition to possessing large amounts of land and wealth, the church had another advantage. The clergy were often the only members of society who could read and write. Even most kings were illiterate, so they needed bishops, abbots, and clerks to write documents and keep records. Thus the clergy also had the opportunity to advise kings on all sorts of matters.

The career of Abbot Suger (*SOO zhair*) is an example of how religion and politics were often intermingled during this time. Suger was born in 1081 into a peasant family living near Paris. As a boy he showed high

Popes wear miters with peaks in front and back. Miters developed from tiaras like the one shown on page 284.

The spires of the famous Chartres Cathedral, built on a hill 50 miles southwest of Paris, are visible for miles around.

intelligence and was selected by his village priest to be educated in a monastery, where his closest friend happened to be the son of the king of France. In 1108, that friend was crowned King Louis VI of France.

Suger became a monk and, in 1122, an abbot, or leader of his monastery. As Louis's friend and adviser, he worked to increase the cooperation between Louis and his nobles by stressing the fact that they shared a common faith. When King Henry of Germany invaded King Louis's lands in 1124, Abbot

■ *Describe the hierarchy of the church.*

Suger loaned the king the sacred banner from the monastery to carry into battle. The banner rallied so many French nobles to the king that Henry retreated before the battle began.

From 1147 to 1149, the new king, the son of Louis VI, left his crown with Abbot Suger and appointed him regent to rule his lands while he, the king, was away at war. During these years, Suger developed fairer methods of taxation and prevented a rebellion from taking away Louis's rule. ■

A Power Struggle Between Kings and Popes

Kings and nobles had gained the power to appoint bishops and other officials of the church during the 800s. They sometimes even sold these positions to the highest

Pope Gregory, wearing a jeweled tiara, is adored by two cherubs, or childlike angels. The jewel-encrusted gold cross reveals the wealth possessed by the church.

bidder. In particular, kings rewarded their allies by appointing them to be bishops of the church. The fact that the kings possessed such great power over the church strengthened their authority. Yet, because these church officials appointed by the kings often behaved immorally and quite selfishly, many people lost respect for the church.

Pope Gregory VII

One monk, named Hildebrand, was part of a reform movement to free the church from the control of kings and nobles. He wanted the church to be free of this control so that the clergy might concentrate on performing its mission of saving Christians. Hildebrand became pope in 1073 and took the name Gregory VII. In 1075, Gregory issued a document stating that the pope was above kings and only the pope could appoint cardinals and bishops. The document warned that government officials who did not obey the pope could be removed from office.

King Henry IV

Henry IV, king of Germany and Italy, considered Gregory's document an attack on his power as king. So, while continuing to appoint bishops in his kingdom, Henry fired back a letter to the pope. In it the king demanded that the pope step down from his office.

But Gregory would do no such thing. Instead, in 1076, he announced the **excommunication** of Henry, thus expelling Henry from the church. Henry was condemned to live as an outcast from the church-oriented society of the 1000s. The excommunication also meant that Henry's subjects were no longer obliged to obey him as their king.

Henry looked for support from his nobles and bishops but found little, because Gregory had also threatened them with excommunication if they supported the king. To save his throne, Henry realized he had to give in to the pope. He then traveled to Italy barefoot during the winter to present himself to the pope as a humble beggar. Gregory kept Henry waiting for three days in the snow outside his castle before finally canceling the excommunication.

The Treaty

Pope Gregory had won this battle, but the struggle between the kings of Germany and the popes continued until 1122. In that year, church leaders, nobles, and representatives of the king and the pope met in Worms, Germany, where they agreed to a treaty called the Concordat (*kuhn KAWR dat*) of Worms. The king agreed to having the pope select church leaders. ■

◄ Henry IV wears a crown and holds the scepter and the orb and cross, symbols of monarchy. The orb and cross theme is repeated on the top of the crown.

■ *Why is the conflict between Henry IV and Pope Gregory significant?*

The Age of Faith

While popes and kings fought for power, the common people of western Europe tried to live their lives according to the principles of the church. The mission of the church was to save the soul of all members so that they would go to heaven after they died rather than hell. This **salvation,** or saving, came through accepting the beliefs of the church, living a moral life, and performing good works.

People also paid one-tenth of the produce from their lands to the church each year. This **tithe** (*tyth*) could be paid in money, produce, or labor. People also had to pay rent to the lord on whose land they farmed.

Daily Life

The church was the center of daily life in every village and town. Church bells announced the time

▲ *People are admitted into the church through baptism.*

➤ *During daily mass, the Last Supper of Jesus and his disciples is remembered.*

▲ *The Catholic church teaches that marriage is the formal union of man and woman as husband and wife in the sight of God. In the 1000s, people married as early as the age of 13.*

➤ *At burial ceremonies a priest offered a blessing for the dead and welcomed the soul into heaven.*

for work, meals, rest, and for mass, the worship service. Churches were also centers of community activity. Often large and sturdily constructed, they served as gathering places for town meetings and as places of refuge during wars or heavy storms. The doorsteps or courtyard of a church might even be where the local farmers' market took place.

Church holidays provided the peasants with relief from their sunup-to-sundown farm labors. On these special days, Christians celebrated events in the life of Jesus and remembered famous saints of the church. After attending mass, the people spent the remainder of the holiday visiting, feasting, and dancing in the church courtyard.

A shared faith gave the church members a sense of community, but it also kept those with different beliefs outside this community. For example, Christians did not accept Jews socially and often even persecuted them. Jews were also generally not allowed to participate in trade. Furthermore, although they received special protection from the pope and the king, Jews were required to pay a tax whenever the king demanded.

Religious Orders

Many people in the church wanted a religious life that was less secluded than that of monks living in a monastery. As a result, during the 1200s, several new orders, or religious communities, were formed. These new orders did not shut themselves off from the world as other monks and nuns did. Instead, they lived in the towns and worked to bring Christianity directly to the people.

One new order was founded in 1209 by Francis of Assisi. Francis was born in Italy in 1182, the son of a wealthy merchant. After a carefree youth, he spent a year battling a serious illness. During that time, he had a vision of Christ that changed him forever.

Francis disowned his father and rejected a large inheritance, making a vow instead to live his life in poverty as Jesus had done. Francis concentrated all his efforts on rebuilding churches and serving the poor. Many people were drawn to follow his simple way of life. A new religious order, now called the Franciscans, formed to follow his example.

Francis was also a talented poet and musician. This is one of his poems.

> *B*e praised, my Lord, for all your creatures.
> In the first place for the blessed Brother Sun, who gives us the day and enlightens us through you.
> He is beautiful and radiant with his great splendor.
>
> St. Francis of Assisi, from "The Canticle of Brother Sun," 1224

Universities

Until the 1100s, education had taken place within monasteries and bishops' cathedrals. There young men planning to enter the clergy were educated. As European towns grew during the 1100s, people began wanting to get better educated—often still at bishops' cathedrals. This enthusiasm for learning was partly sparked by the flow of knowledge from the Muslim world. The Muslims had important schools in cities such as Cordoba and Baghdad. Muslims and Jews had studied and translated writings of Greek philosophers, such as the works of Aristotle, which had been lost to Europe after the fall of Rome. Europeans learned about the Greek philosophers through Islamic writings and translations.

In Europe, groups of students gathered in towns to study philosophy, theology, medicine, and law under their favorite teachers. They began to form **universities,** or guilds of students and teachers. By the 1200s, universities had replaced monasteries and cathedrals as the popular centers of learning.

The peaceful landscape and gentle animals are symbols of Francis of Assisi's love for nature and all living things. The halo around Francis's head identifies him as a saint. Francis was declared a saint in 1228, two years after his death.

Religious Art

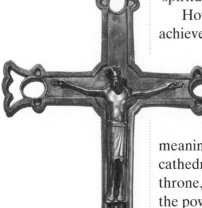

➤ *The floor plan of a Gothic cathedral is laid out in the shape of a cross. At the front of the cathedral is a crucifix. A crucifix is a cross with the figure of Jesus on it. This one is made of bronze.*

■ *How did the church influence European culture between the 1100s and 1300s?*

In the painting and sculpture of this time, artists often vividly portrayed events in the life of Christ, such as the crucifixion. The artists also generally painted Christ in a highly stylized, as opposed to realistic, manner. Artists stylized their paintings to express their own spiritual beliefs.

However, the greatest artistic achievement of the age was the designing and building of Gothic cathedrals. The word *cathedral* comes from the Greek word meaning "chair." It was in the cathedral that the bishop had his throne, which was the symbol of the power of his office.

Gothic architecture dominated Europe for the 400 years from 1140 until the 1500s. One of the innovations introduced by architects of these cathedrals was ribbed arches, which emphasized the shape of the pointed ceilings. Another was flying buttresses, which were used outside the cathedral to support the heavy structure. Look at the drawing of a flying buttress on page 504 in the Minipedia.

Gothic cathedrals were enormous buildings, generally the largest buildings in any community. Their vast interiors were designed to fill onlookers with awe at the power of God. In these masterpieces of design and construction, a variety of artistic elements was combined. Among these were elements such as sculptures of Jesus and the saints; paintings that showed scenes from the life of Christ; and stained-glass windows, which looked like walls of colored light and usually illustrated stories from the Bible.

For believers, the cathedral, which had an interior of immense open spaces, religious images, and colored light, was the closest thing to experiencing heaven on earth. As Abbot Suger, a pioneer in the design of Gothic cathedrals, wrote of the cathedral of St. Denis, "The entire cathedral is pervaded [filled] by a wonderful and continuous light." ■

R E V I E W

1. **FOCUS** What aspects of European society did the church dominate from 1100 to 1300?

2. **CONNECT** How does the hierarchy of the Catholic church compare to the feudal hierarchy of western Europe?

3. **BELIEF SYSTEMS** What is excommunication? What role did it play in the struggle between popes and kings?

4. **CRITICAL THINKING** Was Pope Gregory justified in excommunicating Henry? Explain.

5. **WRITING ACTIVITY** Prepare a news story describing the building of a new Gothic cathedral in the late 1100s. Be sure to include quotations from at least three people who would be involved in building or using the church.

LESSON 2

The Byzantine Empire

You are a young merchant in the year 1000 seeking your fortune in Constantinople *(kahn stan tuh NOH puhl)*, the capital of the Byzantine Empire. You have endured a 1,500-mile sea voyage from your home in Venice, Italy, to reach this city so rich in works of art and architecture and so busy with commerce. Now, at last, you get your first glimpse of it.

Sailing into port, you see on your left the walls that help protect the city from invaders. Ahead is the Sacred Palace, home of the emperor. Behind it is the towering dome of the great Hagia Sophia *(HAY jee uh soh FEE uh)*, a glorious Christian church.

Upon docking, you immediately head up Middle Street, the main street of the capital, which leads right to the palace. This street is crowded with peddlers' canopied stalls. You search the stalls, hurrying past fruit, vegetables, and fish.

Then, quite suddenly, you see what you came for—long rolls of Chinese silk cloth, embroidered in rich threads of gold. You will exchange your gold coins for the cloth. You will then take the cloth back to Venice, where you can sell it for a handsome profit.

THINKING FOCUS

Compare the Eastern Orthodox Church and the Church of Rome.

Key Terms

- literacy
- classic
- patriarch
- icon
- schism

◄ *Constantinople, now called Istanbul, still remains a busy port of trade. The craftsmanship that went into making this silver communion cup was typical of the kind of care artisans took in crafting the goods they sold in Constantinople.*

The Roman Empire in the East

Anyone from the West would have experienced wonder upon arriving at Constantinople. Since Constantine had had Constantinople built to be the eastern capital of the Roman Empire, he also had it modeled after Rome. And, like Rome, it became a magnificent center of the Christian faith.

Two Centers of Christianity

Since the time of Jesus' disciple Peter in A.D. 64, the city of Rome had been the center of the Christian faith. According to Christian tradition, Peter was the first bishop of Rome. Christians regarded the pope as the successor to Peter. The pope was the leader of the Christian faith as well as being the bishop of Rome.

In the late 300s, Emperor Theodosius I went one step further. He made Christianity the official religion of the Roman Empire. In addition, when Theodosius I died in 395, his will formally split the empire, leaving half to each son.

Over the next one hundred years, tribes of barbarian invaders captured most of the lands that were controlled by the Western Roman Empire. In 476, one of these tribes, the Goths, overthrew the last emperor of the Western Empire, bringing it to an end. However, the pope and the Roman church still existed in the West. Furthermore, the Eastern Roman Empire, or Byzantine Empire, continued to thrive.

The Byzantine emperor became the head of both the government and the Christian religion in the East. The people of the Byzantine Empire believed the emperor's authority came from God and extended to all matters of church and state. Constantinople became a second center of Christianity.

A Center of Trade

The emperor of the Byzantine Empire ruled with the help of a complex system of advisers and officials. Specialized departments handled different tasks, such as collecting taxes.

Constantinople became a center of world trade. From the lands around the Black Sea came furs and hides, grain, and wine. From Arabia came spices, gems, and silk. And from Africa came ivory and slaves. On the map at left, locate the trade routes used by merchants from these countries.

The empire generated vast amounts of money from trade. The government taxed everything that came through the city.

The Byzantines—those who lived in the Byzantine Empire—sold many of their own products, too. In the rural areas of the empire, farmers produced grapes,

▼ *Why was Constantinople such an ideal port for trade?*

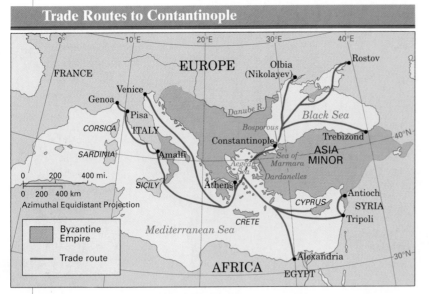

Trade Routes to Contantinople

olives, and wheat for export. In the capital, manufacturers produced glassware, enamel, ivory, and silk.

Attracted by the wealth to be made in trade and industry, people from all over the world came to live in Constantinople. By the year 1000, one million people lived in this thriving city.

Life in the Empire

What was daily life like for the Byzantines? Many of them worked as farmers in rural areas. Craftspersons and traders, who were heavily taxed by the government, lived in the cities. Except for government officials and wealthy merchants, most Byzantines were poor.

Byzantine women had little freedom. They were kept at home, and seldom received any formal education. However, a few women of the wealthy upper classes were educated at home.

The government set up its own schools and libraries, in addition to those run by the church. As a result, there was a higher rate of **literacy**—knowing how to read and write—than in western Europe. At school, the sons of prosperous Byzantine merchants studied the works of famous Greek and Roman writers such as Homer, Virgil, Plato, and Aristotle. These ancient writings were called the **classics.** Even the name of the magnificent church built in 537 during the reign of Emperor Justinian symbolized Byzantine respect for learning. The church was called the Hagia Sophia, which is Greek for "holy wisdom." ■

In this mosaic in the church of Hagia Sophia, Mary and Jesus are receiving a model of the church from Emperor Justinian on the left, and a model of the city from Emperor Constantine.

■ *Why was the Byzantine Empire so powerful?*

Europe: Rule, Religion, and Conflict

This Byzantine church in present-day Bulgaria shows the continued use of the rounded arch in Eastern Orthodox architecture. The interior is rich in icons.

The Eastern Church

As the official state religion, Christianity powerfully influenced the lives of the Byzantines. The bishop of Constantinople—called the **patriarch**—dominated the Byzantine church. However, the emperor, the head of both church and state, held more power and authority than the patriarch.

Contrasts with the West

Although the eastern and western churches were both Christian, they differed in many ways. One of these differences was that the Byzantines tolerated much more discussion and debate about religious matters. In the Byzantine church, services were conducted in Greek, the language of the people. The use of their native language allowed the worshipers to become more involved in the service. In the western church, services were conducted in Latin, a language known only to the priests and the well educated.

The architecture of Byzantine churches was also different from that of western churches. Byzantine churches were plainer on the outside, usually featuring a rounded dome, as you can see in the photograph. Their interiors, however, were richly decorated with carvings, painted tiles, and murals. There were **icons** of Jesus and the saints that were nonrealistic, flat images meant to put the viewer in a spiritual frame of mind. Church leaders hoped the faithful would use the icons to worship or honor those religious figures they represented.

Clashes over Authority

Between the years 700 and 1050, the pope still claimed to have authority over the entire Christian church—not just the Church of Rome. However, serious differences of opinion existed between the members of the eastern and western churches. The controversy over icons is one case in point.

Byzantines used icons in many ways. They prayed or lit candles before them or carried them in religious processions. However, some Byzantines thought this devotion to the icons went too far. They feared that people worshiped the icons themselves as gods. Others disagreed, saying that the icons only helped them to worship God better.

In 726, Byzantine Emperor Leo III, fearing that the icons were being worshiped as gods, ordered them destroyed. Many Byzantines refused to comply with the order. From Rome, Pope Gregory III, who was in favor of icons, condemned the emperor's actions. Gregory thought that icons were important for honoring holy people of the past and providing a way for those who could not read to learn about their faith.

As the argument between Emperor Leo III and Pope Gregory III intensified, Gregory made allies of the Franks. Gregory needed the friendship of these Germanic tribes so that they would support and protect him in any war with the Byzantine Empire. In 800, to solidify this alliance, the pope crowned the leader of the Franks, Charlemagne, the only true and holy Roman emperor. Thus, Charlemagne became the first Holy Roman Emperor. However, this action outraged the Byzantines, because they believed that the Byzantine emperor was the only true and rightful Roman emperor.

A Schism in the Church

In 1054, the basic question of who was supreme, the western pope or the eastern patriarch, was still a big issue. The matter finally reached a climax over the question of who was responsible for the churches of southern Italy. When the eastern patriarch, Patriarch Cerularius (seer u LAIR ih uhs), lost that argument, he retaliated by closing any churches in Constantinople that celebrated the mass in the western style. At this point, Pope Leo IX of the West excommunicated Patriarch Cerularius of the East, who in turn excommunicated the pope. This led to a split, or **schism,** into two separate churches, the Roman Catholic church in the West and the Eastern Orthodox church in the East. ■

Across Time & Space

The mutual excommunication of the leaders of the Eastern and Roman churches lasted until our century. In 1964, the then-current pope and the patriarch met in Jerusalem. The next year, the two leaders made a formal statement that undid the excommunications.

■ *What factors led to the schism between the churches in the East and West?*

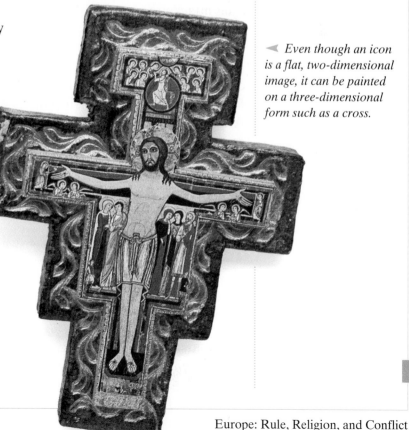

◄ *Even though an icon is a flat, two-dimensional image, it can be painted on a three-dimensional form such as a cross.*

293

Europe: Rule, Religion, and Conflict

The Empire Under Attack

Throughout its long history, the Byzantine Empire endured frequent attacks on its borders. Invaders sought to acquire the empire's great wealth, as well as to acquire the territory itself, because it was so well located for conducting trade with many countries. As a result, emperors had to maintain a powerful military. They also had to build defensive walls around the city of Constantinople.

The Decline of the Empire

The walls protected the city of Constantinople, but they did not protect the empire. After Emperor Justinian extended the empire to its greatest size in the 500s, a period of decline began. In the early 600s, Persians attacked from the east and the south. They took Egypt and marched north, but were unsuccessful in taking Constantinople. Furthermore, in the 630s, Muslim Arabs attacked from the south, capturing the empire's lands in Palestine and Syria.

During the 800s and 900s, the empire again prospered. Trade increased and many of the lost territories were regained by the Byzantines.

An Invasion of Turks

But then in 1071, the invasion of a powerful army of Seljuk Turks threw the Byzantine Empire into decline again. The Seljuk Turks came from Turkestan in central Asia. They were named in honor of Seljuk, their first leader. The Seljuks defeated the Byzantines in 1071 at the battle at Manzikert in present-day Turkey.

The Seljuks continued to capture Byzantine lands, and by 1081 established a new capital in Nicaea (ny SEE uh), only 200 miles southeast of Constantinople. In 1095, the Byzantine emperor sent a desperate message to Pope Urban II. Just 40 years before, the patriarch of the East had excommunicated the pope of the West. Now the Byzantine emperor had no choice but to risk humiliation and plead with the pope for military assistance from the West in order to defend Constantinople against the Turkish invaders. ■

➤ *Seljuk Turks ride camelback on the bottom of this colorful ceramic bowl from Persia.*

■ *Why did the Byzantine Empire decline in power between the early 600s and late 700s?*

REVIEW

1. **FOCUS** Compare the Eastern Orthodox Church and the Church of Rome.
2. **CONNECT** Explain why the Eastern Orthodox Church became a separate church from the Church of Rome.
3. **HISTORY** Explain why it was difficult but necessary for the Byzantine emperor to ask for the pope's help in 1095.
4. **CRITICAL THINKING** Do you think Pope Gregory III was justified in condemning Emperor Leo III for his decision to have all icons destroyed? Why?
5. **WRITING ACTIVITY** Use a dictionary to discover the meaning of the word *iconoclast*. Put yourself in the role of Pope Gregory III and write a letter to Emperor Leo III in which you use the word *iconoclast*.

Recognizing Bias

Here's Why

Different people may view the same event in different ways. This sometimes occurs because people have differing backgrounds and beliefs that influence, or bias, their opinions. Knowing how to recognize bias helps you evaluate what you read or hear.

The descriptions on this page present two very different views of the crusade of Frederick II. Recognizing evidence of bias can help you evaluate these accounts.

Here's How

To evaluate what you read, you often need some background information. Frederick II of the Holy Roman Empire led the Sixth Crusade. Several features of this crusade were unusual.

• Frederick not only captured Jerusalem, but he did so without using force.
• Before the crusade began, Pope Gregory IX had declared Frederick an enemy of the church. Therefore, many people did not understand why Frederick claimed to represent the church.
• Frederick sponsored the Treaty of 1229, which provided religious freedom for Muslims in Jerusalem.

Read Frederick's account of the crusade, on the left below. You can see his bias. He believes he has accomplished a miracle. He appeals to his readers' emotions and religious faith by referring to "the Lord." He credits his own success to God. He groups together all other leaders and says that they failed because they used force.

Try It

The patriarch of Jerusalem wrote the account of the crusade at the right below. Reread the background information in Here's How. Because Frederick had been declared an enemy of the church and had sponsored a treaty with the Muslims, the patriarch of Jerusalem viewed Frederick as an opponent of Christ. Describe the viewpoint of the patriarch. Explain how his bias shows in his description of Frederick's crusade.

Apply It

Bring to class two articles from a magazine or two letters to the editor from a newspaper that show bias. Discuss with your classmates what evidence helps you identify bias in each case.

L et all rejoice and exult in the Lord,... who... does not make boast of horses and chariots, but has now gained glory for Himself, in the scarcity of His soldiers, that all may know and understand that He is glorious in His majesty;... for in these few days, by a miracle rather than by strength, that business has been brought to a conclusion, which for a length of time past many chiefs and rulers of the world... have never been able till now to accomplish by force, however great, nor by fear.

Letter from Frederick II to
Henry III of England

I f it should be fully known how astonishing, nay rather, deplorable, the conduct of the emperor has been in the eastern lands from beginning to end, to the great detriment of the cause of Jesus Christ and to the great injury of the Christian faith, from the sole of his foot to the top of his head no common sense would be found in him. For he came, excommunicated, without money and followed by scarcely forty knights, and hoped to maintain himself by spoiling the habitants of Syria.

Letter from Gerold,
Patriarch of Jerusalem

303

Chapter Review

Reviewing Key Terms

classic (p. 291)
clergy (p. 283)
crusade (p. 296)
excommunication (p. 285)
icon (p. 292)
infidel (p. 296)

literacy (p. 291)
patriarch (p. 292)
salvation (p. 285)
schism (p. 293)
tithe (p. 285)
university (p. 287)

A. The key terms in each group are related in some way. Write a sentence or two showing how the words in each pair or group are related to each other.

1. clergy, salvation
2. excommunication, patriarch, schism
3. crusade, infidel
4. classics, crusade, university
5. icon, schism

B. Each phrase below is related to a key term as it is used in the chapter. Write a sentence that includes each phrase and the key term to which it relates. The first one has been done for you.

1. money, produce, or labor: A tithe, or one-tenth of a person's income, could be paid in money, produce, or labor.
2. paintings and figures
3. Aristotle, Plato, Homer, and Virgil
4. Byzantine schools and churches
5. philosophy, theology, law, and medicine
6. "full of enthusiasm and ardor"
7. worship services, weddings, baptisms
8. belief, moral life, good works

Exploring Concepts

A. On your own paper, copy and complete the timeline using information from the chapter. Then write a summary of the chapter based on the dates and events in this timeline.

B. Write a sentence to answer each question using information from the chapter.

1. How did the crusades help bring about the end of the Byzantine Empire?
2. How did the crusades reflect the power of the church in Europe?
3. What positive effects did the crusades have on trade, learning, and art in western Europe?

4. In what way were the crusades a failure?
5. How did the establishment of religious orders and universities help expand the church and the community?
6. Describe three ways in which the church was the center of community life in Europe around 1000.
7. Why did King Louis the VI appoint Abbot Suger as regent in 1147?
8. How did the architecture of Byzantine churches differ from that of western churches?
9. Summarize the dispute over icons between Leo III and Gregory III.

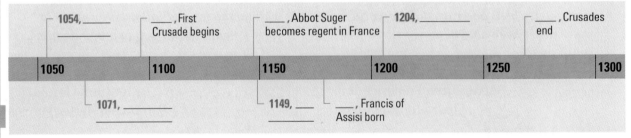

1054, _____ / _____   _____, First Crusade begins   _____, Abbot Suger becomes regent in France   1204, _____ / _____   _____, Crusades end

1050   1100   1150   1200   1250   1300

1071, _____ / _____   1149, _____   _____, Francis of Assisi born

Reviewing Skills

1. Read the excerpt from Pope Urban II's sermon on page 295. What kind of audience does the pope seem to be addressing? How does his sermon show evidence of bias?
2. Read the Chronicle of Nicetas excerpt on page 301. How would you describe the viewpoint of Nicetas? Explain how he uses bias in his description of the crusaders' pillaging.
3. What is the main idea, or theme, of the painting on page 291? Who are its main characters? Describe what you think is happening in the painting.
4. Suppose your teacher has asked your class to divide into groups of four members each. Each group is to think of a way to present village life as it was in Europe during the time period covered by the chapter. After a lengthy discussion, the other three members of your group decide to do a mural, but your preference is to do a dramatic presentation. You have tried to convince the others to do the dramatic presentation, but you are unable to change their minds. What would you do now?

Using Critical Thinking

1. "The cathedral was the model for the Christian universe; for believers it was the closest thing to heaven on earth." Write one or more paragraphs to answer the following questions about the above quotation. Is it a statement of fact, opinion, or reasoned judgment? Why? Given the information in the chapter, what might the statement mean? Is the statement supported by information in the chapter? How?
2. The beginning of Lesson 2 talks about some of the trade that existed between western Europe and the East before the crusades began. The Seljuks invaded the Byzantine Empire in 1071. That same year, they seized Jerusalem and prevented Christians from entering the city. What effect did the actions of the Seljuk Muslims have on the beginning of the crusades? How did they influence trade between East and West? Write a paragraph or two describing the Seljuk influence and the effect of the crusades themselves on international commerce.

Preparing for Citizenship

1. WRITING ACTIVITY Imagine that you work for King Henry IV as a clerk. As such, you are a member of a very special group of people: you are one of the few individuals in western Europe at this time who can read and write. The king has asked you to record the story of his excommunication by Pope Gregory. Write two or three paragraphs describing this event.
2. ARTS ACTIVITY In the library, find books on European, Byzantine, or Muslim arts and crafts from the period between 1000 and 1300. Choose one style and find a picture that represents that style. For example, it could be a picture of enameled jewelry or embroidered cloth, a carving, a mural, a painting, or a sculpture. Draw a picture of your own that is similar in style to the picture you are looking at.
3. COLLABORATIVE LEARNING Divide into groups of three to four people each. As a group, gather and present visually as much information as you can about the people of Europe and the lands around the Mediterranean from 1000 to 1200. Your presentation should consist of a variety of visuals, such as maps, timelines, charts, or graphs, or any combination of those formats. It also can include written notes, but it should not simply be a report. One person from each group should explain the group's project to the class.

305

Europe: Rule, Religion, and Conflict

Unit 6
Europe: 1300-1600

A traveler passing through the city gates of Florence one day in the 1400s remarked that this was a city "in which much money was to be made and many were making it." But something new was happening here as well. Florence, Italy, was a center for a revolution in arts and ideas that swept through Europe. Europeans began to think more about life on earth than about life after death. They found new ways to paint, to look at life, and to worship. Explorers even pushed out the horizons of the known world.

1300

*Map of Florence by Vincenzo Catena, c. 1480.
Museo di Firenze, Florence.*

RVCANO

S.FRANCESC

S MINI
ATO

BELLO
SGVA
RDO

S. FELICE

PORTA
S. PIE
GATT
OLINI

1600

Chapter 12

The Renaissance

From the 1300s to the mid-1600s, Europe went through a renaissance, or "rebirth." People broke from bonds of the church and feudalism. Scholars and artists studied the ideas of classical Greece and Rome. Writers told stories of everyday people. Paintings burst with life. To many, this was the beginning of the modern world

1434 Cosimo de Medici (above left) begins his rule of Florence, Italy. The wealthy Medicis support architects who design the city's impressive buildings (above).

1300	1350	1400	1450

1370 Mongol leader Timur begins a series of raids through central Asia.

1420 The Chinese build the Great Temple of the Dragon in Beijing.

1300

Throughout this period, painters portrayed figures who almost seemed to come alive. This work by Ghirlandaio shows a wealthy young lady of Florence and her attendants.

Traders bring tulips to Europe from Constantinople in the 1500s.

c. 1515 Michelangelo completes the statue *Moses.* This sculpture shows the power and emotion of the aging wise man.

1500   1550   1600   1650

1650

L E S S O N   1

Europe at the End of the Middle Ages

THINKING
F O C U S

How did the problems of the 14th century bring about changes in European society?

Key Terms

- plague
- monarchy
- heretic
- individualism

R ing-a-ring o' roses,
A pocket full of posies,
A-tishoo! A-tishoo!
We all fall down."

The words may be a little different, but you probably still recognize this children's rhyme: "Ring-Around-the-Rosie."

As common as this verse is, few people know that it describes one of the most destructive events of the Middle Ages—the Great Plague. The **plague** was a disease that swept like wildfire through Europe beginning in 1347. People later called the plague the Black Death, because black spots

formed under the skin from internal bleeding.

A rosy rash and sneezing were also symptoms of the disease. People carried bunches of herbs called "posies" in their pockets to try to ward off the illness. They believed herbs could help prevent the disease, but the posies had no effect. Millions of people "fell down" and died as wave after wave of the Black Death washed over Europe.

The plague spread quickly, infecting rich and poor alike. On the next page is an Italian man's description of the helplessness he felt as the disease spread.

► *The plague overwhelmed Europe during the 1300s. In this painting,* The Triumph of Death, *by Francesco Traini, a hunting party comes across the coffins of three plague victims. The monk at the far left reminds the hunters of how fleeting life is.*

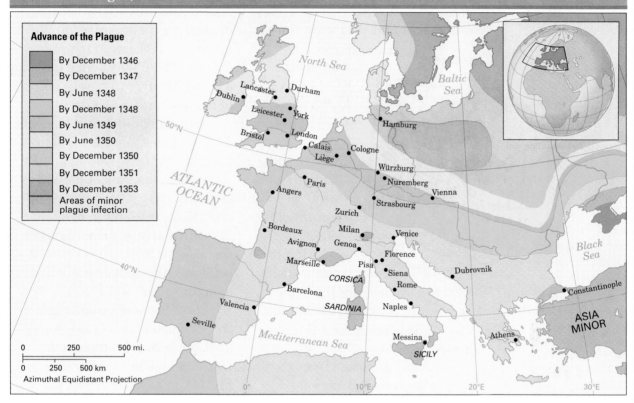

Advance of the Plague

- By December 1346
- By December 1347
- By June 1348
- By December 1348
- By June 1349
- By June 1350
- By December 1350
- By December 1351
- By December 1353
- Areas of minor plague infection

North Sea
Baltic Sea
Dublin
Lancaster
Durham
Leicester
York
Bristol
London
Calais
Liège
Cologne
Hamburg
Würzburg
Nuremberg
Vienna
Paris
Angers
Strasbourg
ATLANTIC OCEAN
Zurich
Bordeaux
Milan
Venice
Avignon
Genoa
Florence
Marseille
Pisa
Dubrovnik
Siena
Rome
Barcelona
CORSICA
Valencia
SARDINIA
Naples
Seville
Constantinople
Black Sea
ASIA MINOR
Mediterranean Sea
Messina
SICILY
Athens

0   250   500 mi.
0   250   500 km
Azimuthal Equidistant Projection

50°N
40°N
0°   10°E   20°E   30°E

I do not know where to begin describing its relentless cruelty; almost everyone who witnessed it seemed stupefied [stunned] by grief. . . . I, Agnolo di Tura, known as the Fat, buried five of my children with my own hands. . . . Nobody wept for the dead, since each was awaiting death; and so many died that everyone thought that the end of the world had come.

Europe in Crisis

During the 350 years before the plague, the population of Europe had more than doubled in size. Because the agricultural techniques of the Middle Ages were fairly crude, farmers had trouble growing enough food for the large population. Then disaster struck. Unusually heavy rains fell during the years from 1315 to 1319, causing the farmers' grain to rot in the fields. Thousands of people starved to death.

When the plague struck in 1347, it devastated many areas already weakened by the famine. Look at the map above, and follow the progress of the plague as it swept across the continent. The

▲ The Great Plague began in Asia and was carried to Europe by the fleas on black rats. These rats lived on trade ships that traveled between Asia and Europe. In Europe the plague moved from south to north, along trade routes.

▼ Many Europeans used "remedies" for the plague. Two popular remedies were pomanders, which were oranges stuck with cloves, and peeled onions. Neither worked, however.

population recovered in most areas from the 1347 outbreak. New outbreaks of the plague hit Europe in 1360 and 1374. By the late 1300s, one-fourth to one-third of the population of Europe had died. In some towns, over 50 percent of the people died.

After the plague, there were too few people. There were not enough people to harvest the crops or produce all the necessary goods.

Because there were fewer people to do work, peasants demanded better wages and lower rents. Landlords resisted peasant demands. Like others before them, many peasants moved to towns or villages. There they hoped to find a better life, free from the control of the landlords.

Some landlords passed laws to force peasants to work for their traditional wages. Throughout Europe, bitter resentment brewed as landlords tried to enforce those laws. Many peasants joined forces to storm and burn manor houses. As peasants broke their ties with landlords, the feudal system began to falter.

These economic and social crises chipped away at the foundations of medieval society in the 1300s and 1400s. Conditions were ripe for great social change. ■

▲ *Neither rich nor poor was spared from the plague. These woodcuts from* The Dance of Death *by Hans Holbein show death visiting a poor farmer and a scholar.*

■ *How did the plague affect the society and economy of western Europe?*

Rise of Central Governments

During the Middle Ages, power rested in the hands of nobles who owned feudal estates. But from the 1100s to the 1300s, the power in Western Europe had begun to shift from the nobles to kings. These kings were attempting to form **monarchies,** or strong central governments ruled by a king or queen. Monarchies in countries like England and France began to gain power and authority. Kings and queens collected taxes, raised armies, and ruled their subjects through central governments.

However, the increasing power of some kings was not well received by everyone. Revolts by many nobles against kings and contests between kings for territory produced war. These wars raged almost constantly in the 1300s and 1400s. The longest war of the later Middle Ages was the Hundred Years' War. This war began in 1337, when the king of England claimed to be the rightful king of France. The French king resisted, and war lasted on and off for another 116 years. Finally in 1453, the French troops defeated the English.

Joan of Arc

At the point during the war when French fortunes had sunk to their lowest, a young woman helped bring about a remarkable reversal. Joan of Arc grew up in the small French village of

▼ *Joan of Arc is still celebrated as a heroine who helped save France from the English, as shown in this French statue.*

Donremy. Like most peasants, she never learned to read or write.

Joan left home in 1429 at the age of 17. She insisted that she had received messages from God telling her to help drive the English out of France. Joan asked one of the French nobles to let her speak to Charles, heir to the throne.

Charles decided to test Joan. He had one of his nobles sit on the throne while he stood with the rest of the court. When Joan entered, she went to Charles, although she had never seen him before. This helped convince Charles that Joan spoke the truth.

Charles gave Joan soldiers and supplies and sent her off to Orleans. At this town in northern France, the English and French had been engaged in a fierce battle for several months. Before she left, Joan dictated a message for the English leaders. She hoped to persuade them to leave France without further bloodshed:

Surrender to the Maid [Joan] sent hither by God the King of Heaven, the keys of all the good towns you have taken and laid waste in France.

The letter did not convince the English to surrender. Instead, the 17-year-old Joan rode off to Orleans to fight bravely alongside her soldiers. Joan defeated the English at Orleans and went on to win four other battles against them.

Joan was captured in May 1430. The English army and the Church tried her as a witch and a **heretic,** or one who speaks beliefs different from the accepted church opinion. Her sentence: to be burned at the stake. Joan was only 19 years old when she died.

New Ways of Fighting

The Hundred Years' War was a turning point in medieval warfare. Before this war, horse-mounted knights, clad in heavy armor, fought other knights using weapons such as shields, axes, and lances.

New weapons made horse-mounted knights more vulnerable in battle. By the 1330s, the English were using longbows, which could be fired more rapidly than could a crossbow. Knights were easy targets for armor-piercing arrows. When knights dismounted, their heavy, clumsy armor made them almost helpless on the ground.

The introduction of guns and gunpowder in the 1320s made the biggest impact on the way wars were fought. Beginning in the 1400s, soldiers carried long handguns known as harquebuses *(HAHR kuh buhs uhs)* into battle.

These new weapons gave foot soldiers such a strong advantage that they made medieval knights obsolete. During the 1300s, rulers began to raise large armies by hiring professional soldiers to protect their own kingdoms. ■

◄ *Warfare changed greatly during the Hundred Years' War. New weapons, such as the longbow and the cannon, made both the knight and the castle obsolete.*

Across Time & Space

Twenty-five years after Joan of Arc was executed, the Catholic Church decided that Joan had not been a witch. Five centuries later, on May 16, 1920, Joan of Arc was declared a saint by the Roman Catholic Church.

■ *Why did the feudal system begin to crumble?*

313

Trade and Commerce

In spite of the famine, plague, and wars of late medieval society, manufacturing and trade flourished. After the horror of the plague began to fade, goods and services were more in demand than ever.

Manufacturing and commercial activity had long been centered in the towns of Europe. Towns, especially those on trade routes, were prosperous, bustling with people buying and selling food and goods.

Town society was made up of merchants, shopkeepers, and artisans who were socially above the laboring class and below the nobility. This commercial class tended not to rely heavily on the church for guidance on how to live their lives. Instead, the members of this class focused on achieving earthly success and wealth.

Because of their shrewd business skills, the Italians dominated European trade. Italian towns like Florence and Milan were some of the most prosperous and powerful in Europe. Italy's location on the Mediterranean Sea made trade with Asia, Africa, and the rest of Europe easy.

Italian traders bought and sold fine woolens, cotton in dozens of colors, and silk woven with gold and silver threads. They also traded wines, furs and leather, jewels, ivory, and metals. They traded spices, too—salt from the coast of France, and cinnamon and peppercorns from the islands of Southeast Asia.

Some of the wealthiest Italian merchants were bankers and moneychangers. Over 500 different currencies were in use in Europe at the time. For a fee, moneychangers would exchange Portuguese coins for French, or Italian coins for English.

▼ *The commercial class became increasingly powerful during the 1300s and 1400s. Members of this class tended to be concerned with making money. They made their money by trading such goods as silk, linen, saffron, and salt.*

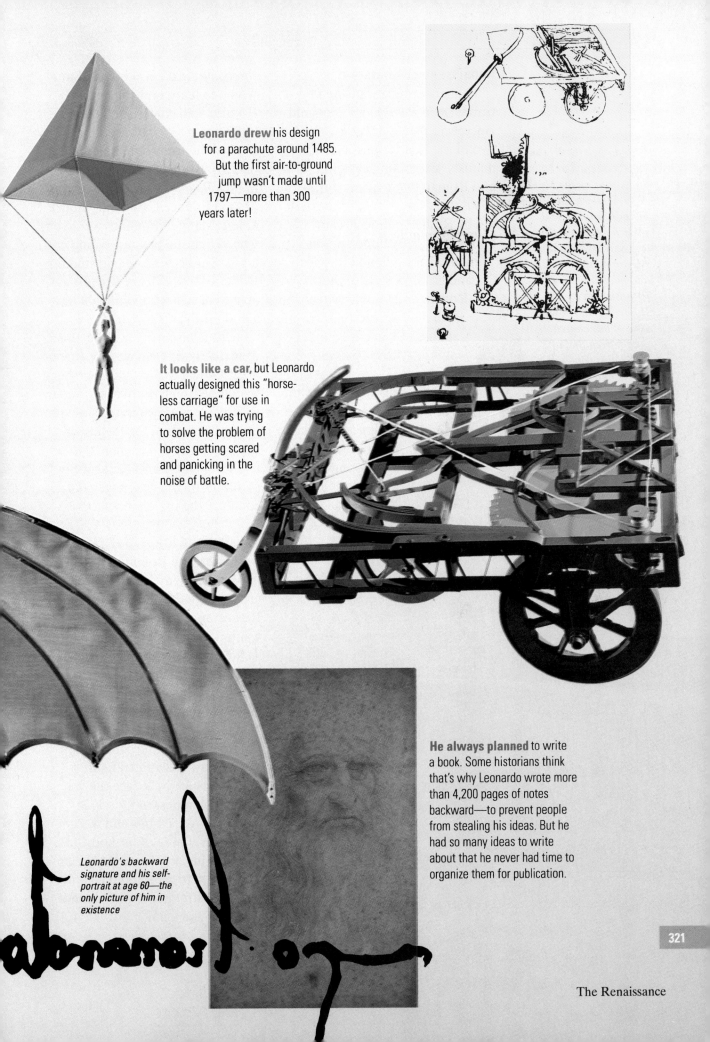

Leonardo drew his design for a parachute around 1485. But the first air-to-ground jump wasn't made until 1797—more than 300 years later!

It looks like a car, but Leonardo actually designed this "horse-less carriage" for use in combat. He was trying to solve the problem of horses getting scared and panicking in the noise of battle.

Leonardo's backward signature and his self-portrait at age 60—the only picture of him in existence

He always planned to write a book. Some historians think that's why Leonardo wrote more than 4,200 pages of notes backward—to prevent people from stealing his ideas. But he had so many ideas to write about that he never had time to organize them for publication.

The Renaissance

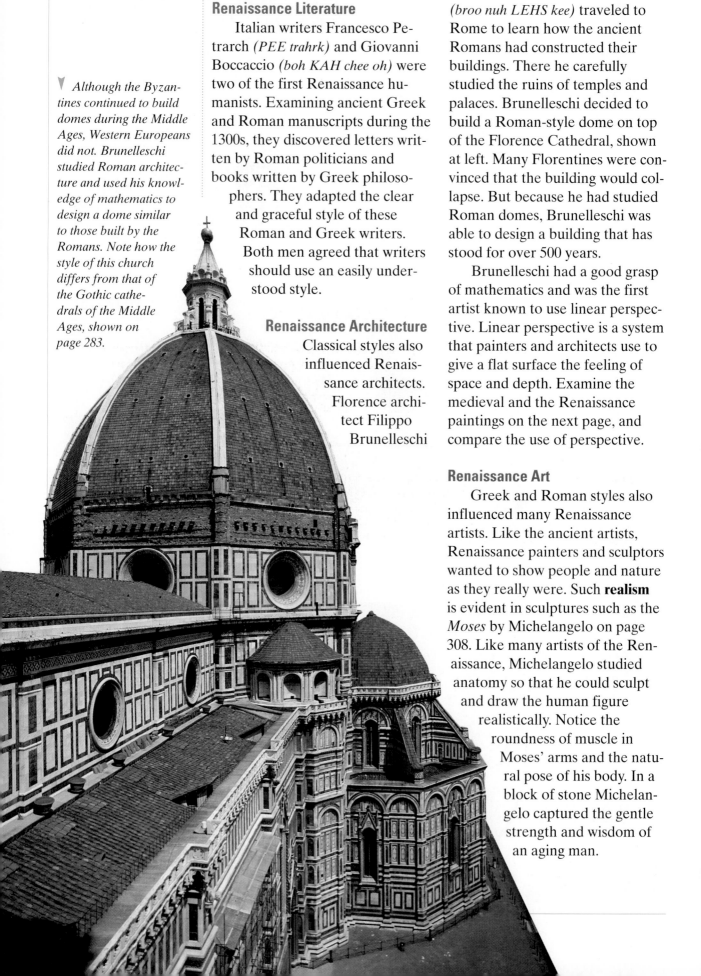

Although the Byzantines continued to build domes during the Middle Ages, Western Europeans did not. Brunelleschi studied Roman architecture and used his knowledge of mathematics to design a dome similar to those built by the Romans. Note how the style of this church differs from that of the Gothic cathedrals of the Middle Ages, shown on page 283.

Renaissance Literature

Italian writers Francesco Petrarch *(PEE trahrk)* and Giovanni Boccaccio *(boh KAH chee oh)* were two of the first Renaissance humanists. Examining ancient Greek and Roman manuscripts during the 1300s, they discovered letters written by Roman politicians and books written by Greek philosophers. They adapted the clear and graceful style of these Roman and Greek writers. Both men agreed that writers should use an easily understood style.

Renaissance Architecture

Classical styles also influenced Renaissance architects. Florence architect Filippo Brunelleschi *(broo nuh LEHS kee)* traveled to Rome to learn how the ancient Romans had constructed their buildings. There he carefully studied the ruins of temples and palaces. Brunelleschi decided to build a Roman-style dome on top of the Florence Cathedral, shown at left. Many Florentines were convinced that the building would collapse. But because he had studied Roman domes, Brunelleschi was able to design a building that has stood for over 500 years.

Brunelleschi had a good grasp of mathematics and was the first artist known to use linear perspective. Linear perspective is a system that painters and architects use to give a flat surface the feeling of space and depth. Examine the medieval and the Renaissance paintings on the next page, and compare the use of perspective.

Renaissance Art

Greek and Roman styles also influenced many Renaissance artists. Like the ancient artists, Renaissance painters and sculptors wanted to show people and nature as they really were. Such **realism** is evident in sculptures such as the *Moses* by Michelangelo on page 308. Like many artists of the Renaissance, Michelangelo studied anatomy so that he could sculpt and draw the human figure realistically. Notice the roundness of muscle in Moses' arms and the natural pose of his body. In a block of stone Michelangelo captured the gentle strength and wisdom of an aging man.

and a friend of Erasmus who lived from 1478 to 1535. Based on the Renaissance concept of the individual worth, More proposed that all men should be treated equally.

In his most famous book, *Utopia*, More described the rules of a society in which all men are equal and everyone works together to achieve happiness:

> *T*he second rule of nature is to lead a life as free of anxiety and as full of joy as possible, and to help all one's fellow men toward that end.
>
> Sir Thomas More, *Utopia*, 1516

Some Renaissance writers tried to entertain as well as educate their audiences. William Shakespeare, born in England in 1564, was a poet, an actor, and a master playwright. Shakespeare's characters are full of life, wit, and passion. They reveal the strengths and weaknesses of people from all walks of life. Many plays are built around historic figures, such as Julius Caesar and the kings of England.

The following passage reflects Shakespeare's attitude toward life and art:

> *A*ll the world's a stage, And all the men and women merely players. They have their exits and their entrances, And one man in his time plays many parts . . .
>
> William Shakespeare, *As You Like It*, 1599

Medicine

The achievements of the northern Renaissance were not limited to the arts. Medicine also made advances. In Switzerland, Paracelsus, a physician and chemist, discovered a new way to treat illness. He treated his patients with tiny doses of poisons to destroy diseased tissue.

The surgeons of the 1500s often had to treat injuries caused by firearms and cannons. Ambroise Paré, a French surgeon, developed bandages to replace the common practice of the time of cauterizing, or burning, the edges of a wound. He also was the first to use thread to close a wound. Paré's attitude toward his medical skills might be described as evidence that he was a humanist in the northern tradition: "I treated him, God cured him." ■

◄ *William Shakespeare, shown at left, wrote many of the most famous works of the Renaissance.*

■ *Describe some of the achievements of the northern Renaissance.*

1. **FOCUS** How was the northern European Renaissance different from the Italian Renaissance?
2. **CONNECT** How did feudalism in northern Europe make the character of the Renaissance different in the north than in Italy?
3. **CULTURE** How did the scholar Erasmus represent northern humanism?
4. **CRITICAL THINKING** Why was the printing press an important part of the Renaissance?
5. **WRITING ACTIVITY** Imagine that you live in Paris in the early 1500s. You have a sister or brother who lives in Florence whom you write to regularly. Write a letter to her or him discussing the changes that the Renaissance has brought to life in your city.

Chapter Review

Reviewing Key Terms

dowry (p. 328)
heretic (p. 313)
humanism (p. 319)
individualism (p. 315)
mercenary (p. 318)
monarchy (p. 312)
patrician (p. 327)

patron (p. 327)
plague (p. 310)
realism (p. 322)
Renaissance (p. 317)
republic (p. 317)
secular (p. 332)

A. Write a sentence or two using each pair of words. The sentences should show how the words are related.
1. mercenary, republic
2. patrician, patron
3. Renaissance, realism

B. Each key term can be used to describe a fact about the time in history covered in the chapter. Use each key term in a sentence that gives a fact about this time.
1. plague
2. monarchy
3. individualism
4. Renaissance
5. secular
6. humanism
7. realism
8. dowry
9. heretic

Exploring Concepts

A. During the Renaissance, the skills and talents of many individuals were encouraged and developed. Copy the chart on your own paper. Notice the titles and the information given. Using information from the chapter, add one contribution for each person.

	Name	Contribution
Leaders	Joan of Arc	
Writers	Petrarch and Boccaccio	
	Erasmus	
	Sir Thomas More	
	Shakespeare	
Artists	Michelangelo	
	Brunelleschi	
	da Vinci	
	Brueghel	
Inventors and Scientists	Gutenberg	
	Paré	
	da Vinci	

B. Support each statement with facts and details from the chapter.
1. One of the major changes brought about by the Renaissance was the development of a new sense of individualism.
2. The plague ravaged Europe and directly affected the state of the feudal system.
3. Greek and Roman art, literature, and philosophy played important roles in the development of Renaissance ideas and ideals.
4. Ruling families were a very important feature of the Italian city-states.
5. During the time of the Renaissance, there were great artistic and intellectual achievements across the European continent.
6. The population of Italian Renaissance cities included three social classes.
7. Life in an Italian Renaissance city had many advantages and disadvantages for all classes of the population.
8. The Renaissance was a time of renewed creativity and new beginnings.
9. The ideas of the Renaissance were spread in a variety of ways.

Reviewing Skills

1. Study the da Vinci drawing of a printing press at the right. The type bed is at the top of the incline. When the press is moved down by turning the operating lever, the type bed is pulled up the incline by a rope tied to the geared axle on the left. Releasing the lever lets the type bed roll down the incline for resetting. Is the press up or down here? What advantages does a wheeled type bed have?

2. Read the section headed Individualism Today on page 315. What evidence of bias do you find in that section? How is the bias expressed?

3. If you wanted to find a recent magazine article about Joan of Arc, Leonardo da Vinci, or the city of Florence, where would you look?

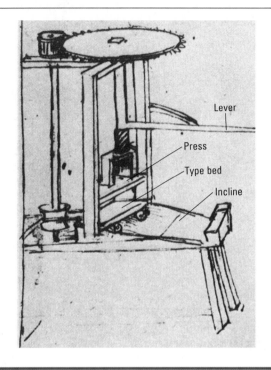

Lever

Press

Type bed

Incline

Using Critical Thinking

1. The invention of a printing press with movable type was a great advancement. What might your classes in school be like if a printing press with movable type had not been invented?

2. Ideas of the Renaissance were spread through travelers on business and by way of the printed word. Review the highlights in the history of communication as shown on pages 507–510 of the Minipedia. Compare and contrast the ways that ideas were communicated in the Renaissance with the ways that new ideas are communicated today.

Preparing for Citizenship

1. **WRITING ACTIVITY** Reread the description of Brueghel's painting *The Peasant Dance* on page 329. Pretend that you are a young peasant living in the 1500s. Write a brief essay about Brueghel's painting expressing your feelings about the way the artist has portrayed the characters.

2. **GROUP ACTIVITY** With three classmates, plan a panel discussion on the topic "Should Artists Be Supported by Patrons?" Two classmates take the position that patrons have always been needed for art to flourish. The other two argue that no other profession is given financial support, so why should artists be supported?

3. **COLLABORATIVE LEARNING** Review the information about the Renaissance cities and the different social classes in Lesson 3. Divide into groups of four to eight students each. Each group will be responsible for dramatizing a scene from everyday life at that time. Assign the following tasks to members of the group:
   (1) write the scene,
   (2) get costumes and act out the scene,
   (3) design and create the scenery,
   (4) gather props and prepare advertisements of the production.
   When all preparations have been completed, present the minidrama.

Chapter 13

Reformation and the Scientific Revolution

Handwritten papers nailed to a church door . . . a telescope aimed at the stars . . . an apple falling from a tree: each played a part in a great era of change that swept across Europe. Christian leaders such as Martin Luther and John Calvin tried to reform the Catholic church. Scientists such as Nicolaus Copernicus and Galileo helped launch a scientific revolution.

1319 *The Madonna and Child with Saints* by the Italian artist Simone Martini shows a scene approved by Catholic leaders. Reformers questioned the power of the Catholic church.

1300

1400

1500

1302

1492 Christian forces drive out the Moors, the last Islamic kingdom in Spain.

ideas also influenced John Hus, an eastern European priest. In fiery sermons, Hus spoke out against the practice of selling indulgences and called for reform.

Spiritual Movements

Spiritual movements also formed in response to the abuses of the church. These groups did not seek to reform the church but rather to express religious feelings in their own way. One such group, the Mystics, believed that a person could experience God through prayer, without the aid of a priest. Since the Mystics believed that both men and women could experience God directly through prayer, many women were drawn to Mysticism. Margery Kempe and Catherine of Siena were two well-known Mystics.

From Philip IV of France to John Wycliffe of London to the Mystics of the 1300s and 1400s, people questioned the church's authority. They paved the way for Martin Luther, whose ideas would change the church forever. ■

▲ Catherine of Siena claimed that she "was chosen and sent on to this earth in order to right a great scandal." That scandal was the Great Schism.

T hen the Archbishop said to [Margery Kempe]: "I have received bad reports about you. They tell me you are a very wicked woman." And she replied: "Sir, they tell me that you are a wicked man. . . ."

Then an important cleric in a furred hood said: "Hold your tongue: talk about yourself, and leave him alone. . . ."

Then the Archbishop said to her: "You will swear that you will neither teach the people in my diocese, nor argue with them."

"No sir, I will not swear that," she said, "because I shall talk about God . . ."

Straight away an important cleric produced a book, and quoted St. Paul against her, saying that no woman ought to preach.

She in reply said: "I am not preaching, sir, I do not get up in a pulpit. I only use conversation and holy talk and I intend to do that as long as I live."

From *The Book of Margery Kempe*, c. 1432

■ What church doctrine did the early reformers oppose?

R E V I E W

1. **FOCUS** What challenges did the Catholic church face between 1300 and 1500? Why?

2. **CONNECT** Why might it be said that the church reformers of the 1300s and 1400s were carrying out the spirit of the Renaissance?

3. **HISTORY** How did corruption within the church contribute to its loss of authority among the people?

4. **BELIEF SYSTEMS** What basic principle did early religious reformers emphasize?

5. **CRITICAL THINKING** Find evidence from the lesson to support this statement: Power corrupts. Do you think this generalization always holds true? Explain.

6. **ACTIVITY** Enact a scene in which people are buying indulgences. Have one or two students pretend to be each of the following: priests, people who want to buy indulgences, reformers, and church officials who condemn the reformers as heretics.

341

LESSON 2

Martin Luther and the Reformation

What was Luther's role in the Reformation?

Key Terms

- Protestant
- Reformation
- pamphlet

➤ *The entrance doors to All Saints Church are now inscribed with Luther's* Ninety-Five Theses.

Martin Luther, a priest and professor at the University of Wittenberg, approached All Saints Church in Wittenberg on October 31, 1517. Quickly he nailed some papers, handwritten in Latin, to the church door.

No crowd gathered to see what Luther was doing. However, on the outskirts of Wittenberg, people were gathering around Johann Tetzel, a Dominican monk. Tetzel had been authorized by the pope to sell indulgences.

It was against such practices that Luther was protesting in the papers he nailed to the church door. In these papers, his *Ninety-Five Theses,* Luther explained his objections. He saw the practices as proof of how greedy and corrupt the Catholic church had become. Luther challenged the church to defend itself—if it could. He read over one of his theses:

Why does not the Pope, whose riches are at this day more ample than those of the wealthiest of the wealthy, build the one Basilica of St. Peter's with his own money, rather than with that of poor believers?

Luther's *Ninety-Five Theses* was really an invitation to scholars to debate certain church issues. He had no idea that his challenge to the church would light a fire of protest and change that would sweep across Europe.

Luther Questions the Church

Martin Luther was born on November 10, 1483, in Eisleben, Germany. Luther's father, a hard-working miner, wanted his son to be a lawyer. So in 1501, Luther began studying law at the University of Erfurt.

A Man of Faith

One day in 1505, Luther was caught in a thunderstorm and thrown to the ground when a bolt of lightning struck nearby. Like most men and women of his time, Luther believed that God could come to the aid of humans. In the storm he cried out, "Help, St. Anne, and I'll become a monk." True to his word, that same year Luther ceased studying law and joined the monastery in Erfurt.

Luther was a model monk, and in 1507, he was ordained a priest. A year later, Luther was selected from among his peers to teach at the University of Wittenberg.

A New Religion

As a monk Luther had struggled to understand the true nature of godliness. The church taught that the performance of religious ritual and good deeds was necessary to ensure the soul's salvation. Luther worked hard to satisfy the church and save his soul. But he worried that his actions might not satisfy God.

◄ At the University of Erfurt, Luther became known for his long and serious talks. His friends nicknamed him "the philosopher." This engraving depicts Luther as he looked at this time.

Across Time & Space

Reform is not restricted to either the Middle Ages or the church. In the 1950s and 1960s, Martin Luther King, Jr., led a social reform movement in the United States seeking racial equality. Under the leadership of this Baptist minister named for Martin Luther, the movement for civil rights gained wide support from blacks and whites. His policy of nonviolent protest helped curb racial injustice in the South.

◄ Johann Tetzel sold so many indulgences that some people made fun of him in a popular rhyme: "As soon as money in the box rings, The soul from Hell's fire springs."

343

Luther's fears vanished, however, when he read St. Paul's letter to the Romans: "He who through faith is righteous shall live" (Romans 1:17). To Luther, Paul's message seemed clear: the path to God is through faith alone. Forgiveness was not something the church could grant, nor was it something individuals could achieve on their own. Instead, it was given by God to each person who accepted Him. This theory became known as justification by faith, meaning that a person could be made just, or good, by his or her faith in God.

Luther's belief in justification by faith led him to question the Catholic church's practice of selling indulgences. He objected not only to the church's greed but to the very idea of indulgences. He did not believe the Catholic church had the power to pardon people's sins. Rather, Luther taught that salvation could be achieved only through God's mercy. No one needed to seek or buy salvation through the church.

By nailing his theses to the church door, Luther was not acting as a heretic. He was simply inviting other scholars to respond to his ideas in a debate, an ordinary method of learning at universities of his day.

At first, no one accepted Luther's invitation. Over the next few years, however, his *Ninety-Five Theses* sparked a religious movement to reform the Catholic church. Because the reformers were protesting against what they felt to be the abuses of the Catholic church, they came to be known as **Protestants.** And because they wanted to reform the Catholic church, that is, improve it by making changes, their movement is known as the **Reformation.** ■

■ *How did Martin Luther's beliefs conflict with church doctrine and practices?*

▼ *Luther claimed that his burning the bull was purely symbolic; in reality he thought it was the pope himself who should have been burned.*

The Reformation Begins

Luther's *Ninety-Five Theses* were soon translated from Latin into German. Within a year, his ideas were known throughout Europe. As one historian put it, they spread "as if angels from heaven themselves had been their messengers." Encouraged by this success, Luther wrote hundreds of essays between 1517 and 1546, in which he stressed justification by faith and criticized church abuses.

Finally, in 1520, Pope Leo X issued a bull—a statement of the pope's authority—condemning Luther and banning his works. Defying the pope, Luther publicly burned the bull. The break with the church was then complete. In January 1521, Pope Leo X excommunicated Luther.

However, Charles V, the Holy Roman Emperor, decided to give

Luther one final chance. In 1521, at a meeting in Worms, Germany, the emperor demanded that Luther recant, or take back, his teachings. Facing church officials and an excited assembly of people, Luther refused. He said in part:

> I do not accept the authority of popes and councils. . . . My conscience is captive to the word of God. I cannot and I will not recant anything. . . . Here I stand, I cannot do otherwise. God help me. Amen.

A near riot broke loose. Luther strode out, his hands raised high in triumph. Yet the emperor later declared him an outlaw whom anyone could kill without punishment.

Fortunately for Luther he had a powerful friend in Frederick the Wise, Prince of Saxony. The prince arranged a pretend kidnapping of Luther and hid him away for about a year in the castle at Wartburg. Here, Luther translated the Bible from Greek into German. His translation allowed the German people to read the word of God without having to rely on the interpretation by the priests.

Luther continued to write works in which he attacked the church or discussed books of the Bible. His teachings eventually inspired a new Protestant religion called Lutheranism. This new religion would continue to oppose the once all-powerful Catholic church. ■

◄ *Turn this woodcut portrait of Luther upside down to see what his opponents thought of him.*

■ *How effective were the church's responses to Luther's teachings?*

▼ *Many people feared that the art of printing, new to Europeans, came from the devil. But by 1500, there were more than 1,000 print shops in Europe.*

Protestantism Spreads

Why did Luther's ideas, which challenged the centuries-old Catholic church, succeed? First, many people recognized the widespread corruption within the church and were eager for reform. Second, Luther wrote and spoke with conviction. His words were immensely appealing to the people.

The printing press, developed in Europe about 1450, also contributed to Luther's success. Printed **pamphlets** containing unbound essays on current topics could spread new ideas quickly to many people. By 1523, about a million copies of Luther's pamphlets were in circulation. The printer in A Moment in Time on page 346 is typical of the craftsmen who worked the early printing presses and published Luther's pamphlets.

As the Reformation spread, it gained the support of European peasants. In 1524 and 1525, arguing that everyone was equal under God, a group of poor German peasants took up arms against their wealthy landowners. Known as the Peasants' War, this revolt was badly organized and lacked strong leadership. Government armies quickly crushed the uprising.

The peasants were surprised and disappointed to discover that Martin Luther did not support them in the Peasants' War.

A Printer

4:29 P.M., August 24, 1620
Great Hall, Northumberland House, London

Eyes
He can read both English and Latin backward and forward. When he started working for the king's printer at age 14, it was hard for him to read the backwards-facing metal type.

Arms
The printer's arms ache from lifting the heavy iron plate of the press hundreds of times since 7:00 this morning.

Beard
He keeps his London-style beard neatly trimmed. After a country childhood, he enjoys city entertainments like seeing plays by Shakespeare.

Woodcut
Pages with pictures, like the one he just took off the press, are still carved in one piece. Most pages are made with movable type that will be taken apart as soon as all the books are printed.

Title Page
The book's title, *Novum Organum,* and its author's name, Francis Bacon, are surrounded by fancy pictures.

Paper
This sheet was thrown away because a young apprentice mixed up a *p* and a *q*. On this page Bacon says printing, gunpowder, and the magnet have changed the world.

Apron
He tries to keep his clothes free of ink, but our printer is called the "dirty-hands" apprentice. His friend, the "clean-hands" apprentice, gets to handle the paper.

In the pamphlet *Against the Robbing and Murdering Hordes of Peasants,* Luther criticized the rebels for seeking economic gain in the name of God. As a result, Luther lost the support of many social reformers.

However, Luther's ideas became popular with the German princes. Luther did not believe that the church should own property. He also thought that rulers should appoint clergy members. Thus, Luther favored a more powerful role for rulers and a weaker church authority.

Many German princes who wanted freedom from the pope's authority favored Protestantism. Others remained Catholic because they depended on the support of the pope. Eventually, the differences between these German princes erupted in war. From 1546 to 1555, war raged between the Catholic and Protestant princes.

Finally, in 1555, a compromise, called the Peace of Augsburg, was reached. This compromise permitted each German prince to decide which religion would be allowed in his state. Most rulers of northern Germany chose Protestantism, and most in southern Germany remained Catholic. Many people had to move to states that allowed them to practice their own religion.

Lutheranism in Central Europe

Roman Catholic

Lutheran

By 1560, the Reformation was established in Germany and, as you can see on the map above, in much of the rest of Europe. Compare this map with that on page 531 of the Atlas showing the distribution of religions in the world today. What other countries can trace their religious roots to the ideas of the Reformation? ■

▲ *In what countries did Lutheranism become established by 1555?*

■ *Why did Protestantism spread throughout Germany between 1517 and 1560?*

Compare this map with that on page 531 of the Atlas

R E V I E W

1. **FOCUS** What was Luther's role in the Reformation?
2. **CONNECT** What similar task did John Wycliffe and Martin Luther undertake? What was the purpose of their work?
3. **HISTORY** How did Gutenberg's invention help spread Protestantism?
4. **POLITICAL SYSTEMS** How did Luther's reforms affect political events in Germany?
5. **CRITICAL THINKING** How do you think Martin Luther would have advised the European peasants to handle their problems with their landowners?
6. **ACTIVITY** Think of a topic you would like to debate. Then write out your position on the topic and post it on your class bulletin board. As in Martin Luther's time, invite other students to debate your viewpoint and exchange ideas.

Reformation and the Scientific Revolution

Identifying Patterns

Here's Why

Writers use different patterns to organize what they write. The chart on this page identifies four text patterns and gives clues for each. You will find examples of all four patterns in this chapter. Recognizing the patterns while reading helps improve your understanding.

Here's How

The section Challenges from Monarchs on page 339 is an example of a chronological or time-related pattern. This pattern describes events in the order in which they happened. Notice that several dates are used: "in 1305," "in 1376," and "in 1378." Dates and phrases that describe time periods, such as "for 70 years," are clues that the pattern is chronological. Words that describe time relationships—before, after, during—are clues too.

A cause-and-effect pattern shows what events made other events happen. Sometimes this pattern begins with the effect and then explains its causes. The section Corruption Within the Church on page 339 is an example of a cause-and-effect pattern. The first sentence alludes to the schism in the church. The rest of the paragraph describes actions taken by the bishops to restore the unity of the church.

Look for the cause-and-effect pattern in the paragraph that focuses on how corrupt practices severely weakened the church (page 340). The cause is the sale of indulgences to raise money. The effect is that some officials kept the money for themselves.

Spatial patterns describe people, places, things, and events. Such a pattern shows the relationship of the characteristics being described. The description of Luther and Tetzel on page 342 is an example of spatial organization.

Compare-and-contrast patterns show similarities and differences between two subjects. On pages 346–347 is a description of two groups' reactions to Luther's ideas. It contrasts the reactions of some social reformers with that of the German princes.

Writers use all of these patterns to organize their work. Often, especially in long passages, you will find a combination of several of these patterns.

Try It

Turn to A New Religion in Lesson 2. Tell what organizational pattern is used in this section. Explain how you identified the pattern.

Apply It

Find an article in a magazine or newspaper that uses one of the organizational patterns explained on this page. Name the pattern and explain how you identified it.

Pattern	Definition	Clue Words
Chronological	Tells the order in which events happened	as soon as, at last, first, second, third, next, then, before, after, finally, while, by 1565, until 7 P.M.
Spatial	Describes people, places, things, or events	above, across, beside, behind, below, beyond, east, farther, in front of, inside, lower, near, next to, north, outside, south, under, within, west; names of places
Cause-and-effect	Tells what events caused others	as a result, because, consequently, if, nevertheless, since, so, therefore, then
Compare-contrast	Compares or contrasts events, ideas, people, and so on	although, by contrast, by comparison, compared to, relatively, similarly, unlike

L E S S O N   3

Era of Reformation

H ere's an imaginary scene that might have occurred in 1560. A young Frenchman arrives in Geneva, Switzerland, and enters a Calvinist church—a plain wooden structure one story high. Inside, the people sing a hymn in French.

Looking around, the young man compares this church with the Catholic church he attended as a boy. Absent are brightly colored stained-glass windows, candles, ornate statues, paintings on the walls. The young man sees just one cross, a plain wooden one that hangs above the small altar table.

When the singing stops, the minister delivers a sermon on the importance of living a virtuous life.

The entire service is simple but serious, and the young man feels comfortable in this church.

THINKING
F O C U S

What effect did the Reformation have on religion in Europe?

Key Terms

- predestination
- Counter Reformation
- inquisition

◄ *Like Luther, Calvin was a persuasive writer and speaker who united many religious reformers.*

Calvin and the Reformation

In the early 1500s, reform spread throughout Europe. Three of Martin Luther's ideas became the center of debate. One idea was justification by faith. The second was the idea that the Bible was the only authority for Christians, rather than the laws of the Catholic church or papal bulls. The third was a belief in a priesthood of all Christians, denying the special powers that priests had in the Catholic church.

Around 1517, when Luther posted his *Ninety-Five Theses,* Ulrich Zwingli, a Swiss priest working in Zurich, brought the Reformation to that city. He urged Christians to study the Bible on their own and deepen their faith.

After Zwingli's death, John Calvin, a Frenchman educated in law, continued to teach the ideas of the Reformation. Forced to flee France in 1534, where the Catholic church had been harrassing

Protestants, Calvin moved to Switzerland. The city of Geneva soon became the center for a movement called Calvinism.

Calvinism differed from other movements of the Reformation in one important way. Calvin taught that God had already chosen, or predestined, a special group of believers for salvation. This theory is known as **predestination.** Luther also accepted predestination but thought that people could never know whom God had chosen.

Calvinism emphasized being devoted to God and leading a disciplined life. According to Calvinists, a person who could maintain such conduct was probably a member of God's chosen group.

Calvinist church services were plain. No images of saints hung on the walls; no organ accompanied the singing. Nothing appealing to the senses interfered with what the worshiper experienced as his or her spiritual link to God.

Calvinists also followed a strict code of moral behavior. Laughing

or making noise in church was prohibited. So were fortunetelling, gambling, and even dancing at social gatherings. Councils elected by church members enforced this code of behavior, as well as other laws of the Calvinist church. By the time Calvin died in 1564, Calvinism had taken root in Scotland, England, France, Italy, Bohemia, Poland, and the Dutch Netherlands. ■

➤ *For many believers, church reform involved trying to reach a new relationship with God. That struggle was sometimes agonizing, as seen here in Albrecht Dürer's* The Prodigal Son.

■ *What religious ideas and practices were important to Calvinists?*

Other Protestant Movements

▼ *Can you list some of the beliefs or practices central to each of the religions named here?*

One Protestant group, called the Anabaptists, lived by an even stricter moral code than that of the Calvinists. The Anabaptist movement began in Zurich around 1525 among a group of dissatisfied followers of Zwingli. They believed that the state was made up of sinners. Therefore, the Anabaptists believed, true Christians should withdraw from the state and form a separate community.

Both Catholics and Protestants openly opposed the Anabaptists. They resented the Anabaptists' claim that members of all other religious groups were sinners. Anabaptists were widely harassed, and many were executed. Those who survived fled to Poland and Holland.

Major Religions During the Reformation

Religion	Time Founded	Founder	Source of Authority
Roman Catholic	1st Century A.D.	Simon Peter	Pope, Cardinals, Bishops
Lutheran	1529	Martin Luther	Congregation
Church of England	1534	Henry VIII	King of England
Calvinist	1546	John Calvin	Presbytery (Council of Elders)

Not all religious reform movements had religious causes. In 1533, Henry VIII of England was excommunicated for divorcing his wife and marrying another woman. So, Henry set up a new church—the Church of England. In 1534, the English government recognized the monarch as the supreme head of the new church. Although independent of the pope, the English church remained basically very similar to the Catholic church in its principles and practices. Not until Henry's son, Edward VI, became king in 1547 did a Protestant religion gain a strong following in England.

Although these reform movements had different beliefs, they shared the same basic motivation: the desire to bring about changes in the church. And because those changes were not coming from within the church, the reformers created their own churches. ■

The Church's Response

During the 1400s, many priests recognized that reforms needed to be made. They realized that selling indulgences was corrupt, and they protested against such abuses.

Reforms came slowly. However, as more and more people left the Catholic church to join the Protestant movement, Catholic leaders urged Pope Paul III to assemble a general council to discuss church reform. The Council of Trent, held from 1545 to 1563, set two main goals: to rid the church of abuses and uphold traditional Catholic beliefs. This movement

UNDERSTANDING REFORM

The leaders of the Reformation first tried to change the Catholic church from within. Reform means to change an existing institution.

Participants in a revolution, on the other hand, seek to destroy or replace an existing institution. Therefore, the actions of the colonists in America against the English in 1776 were a revolution, not a reform movement.

Issues and Leaders

Reform movements start because people want to improve some aspect of society. In the mid-1800s, many people wanted to reform the United States voting system to allow women to vote. Leaders of this reform movement, such as Susan B. Anthony, campaigned for women's rights for more than 70 years. In 1920, the Nineteenth Amendment was added to the U.S. Constitution to guarantee women's right to vote.

The Results of Reform

Sometimes the changes brought about by reform movements go beyond what the reformers had in mind. For example, Luther's religious reformation helped to foster a climate of questioning that led to many social, political, and scientific changes during the following 300 years.

351

Christian Religions in Europe, 1600

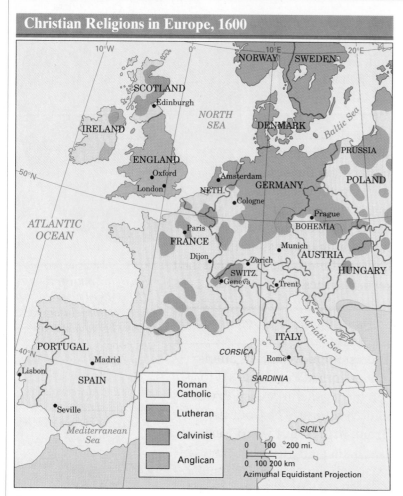

Roman Catholic
Lutheran
Calvinist
Anglican

0   100   200 mi.
0 100 200 km
Azimuthal Equidistant Projection

▲ *Most Anglicans lived in England in 1600. What is another name for this Protestant religion?*

■ *In what ways did the Catholic church try to reform from within?*

Jesuits *(JEHZ oo ihts)*, as the members of the order were called, took vows of poverty and obedience to the pope and fasted rigorously. The Jesuits were noted for their educational and missionary works. They worked tirelessly, spreading Catholicism in other sections of the world, to the peoples of the Americas, Africa, and Asia.

Reacting to Protestants

In addition to encouraging the spread of Catholicism, church officials tried to halt the spread of Protestantism. Their methods were often extremely harsh. For example, the officials in Rome revived the **Inquisition**—a church court to judge and convict heretics. However, this court often abused its power. Many Protestants who appeared before it were tortured. Others were sentenced to death when they refused to change their beliefs.

The church officials also established the *Index of Prohibited Books.* This list of banned books included books by Calvin and Luther.

The Counter Reformation helped to correct many church abuses. However, it could not stop the spread of Protestantism. Never again would a single religion dominate all of Europe. ■

within the church became known as the **Counter Reformation.**

Reaffirming the Faith

To rid the church of abuses, the church also encouraged the founding of new orders, or special religious groups. Many of these were modeled after the Society of Jesus, founded by a Spanish priest named Ignatius Loyola in 1540.

R E V I E W

1. **FOCUS** What effect did the Reformation have on religion in Europe?
2. **CONNECT** In what ways were the religious beliefs of Zwingli and Calvin similar to Martin Luther's beliefs?
3. **GEOGRAPHY** Suppose you were a follower of Martin Luther living in Spain in 1600. Use the map on this page to determine where you could go to live among people who shared your beliefs.

4. **CRITICAL THINKING** Why do you think the Anabaptists were persecuted by other Protestant groups?
5. **CRITICAL THINKING** In your opinion, was the Counter Reformation successful? Explain your answer.
6. **WRITING ACTIVITY** Imagine you are a 16th-century Calvinist. You have been charged with heresy and brought before the Inquisition in Rome. Write a one-minute speech to defend your beliefs.

LESSON 4

Scientific Revolution

Clearly, by 1543, Nicolaus Copernicus, the Polish physician and astronomer, did not have much longer to live. For years, Georg Joachim, his young assistant, had begged Copernicus to publish his revolutionary theories on planetary motion. Copernicus theorized that the sun, not the earth, was the center of the universe. Copernicus claimed he needed more time to provide mathematical and factual support for these theories. But, on his deathbed, he agreed to publish.

Copernicus died later that year. But on the day he died, Joachim brought him the first copy of his work, *On the Revolution of the Celestial Spheres.*

The publication of Copernicus's theory began a movement that would change people's view of the world. Theories that had been accepted for hundreds of years would be challenged by scientific experiment and observation.

THINKING FOCUS

What was the Scientific Revolution?

Key Terms

- Scientific Revolution
- scientific method
- hypothesis

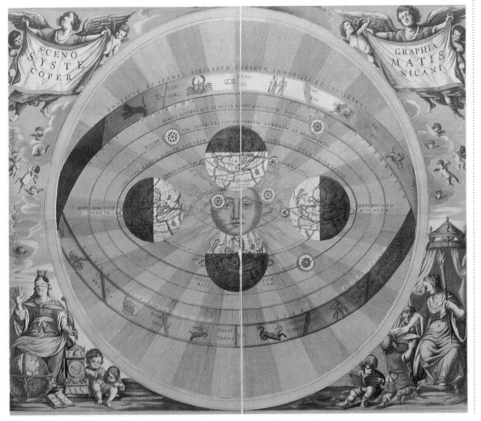

◀ *In Ptolemy's system, the earth is circled by water, air, fire, and seven planets—including the moon and sun. The plan shown here illustrates Copernicus's sun-centered theory.*

New Visions of the Natural World

Copernicus was one of the first European scientists to question theories about the universe that had been handed down from classical philosophers. For instance, educated Europeans had long accepted the theory of Egyptian astronomer Ptolemy *(TAHL uh mee),* which stated that the earth was at the center of a limited universe. Between the earth and the limits of the universe were the moon, the planets, and the sun.

The Universe

After years of observation and mathematical research, Copernicus concluded that the universe was sun-centered. Drawings demonstrating Copernicus's theory appear on the preceding page and on page 516 of the Minipedia. According to this theory, the planets, including earth, revolve around the sun in circular orbits. The German astronomer Johannes Kepler later proved that the planets' orbits were oval.

Protestant and Catholic leaders alike opposed Copernicus's theory. The Protestants claimed that the Bible said the earth stood still. The Catholics claimed that the earth and its human beings—not the sun—held the central place in the universe. In 1610, the Catholic church declared that all followers of Copernicus were heretics.

The Human Body

While Copernicus and Kepler explored the universe, Flemish physician Andreas Vesalius explored the human body. His observations challenged the works of Galen, a second-century physician whose theories based on the dissection of animals were widely accepted. Vesalius's thorough dissection of the human body enabled him to write a much more accurate description of human anatomy. Vesalius's book stimulated new research in the field of anatomy. Some results stemming from continued research are discussed in Making Decisions on pages 358 and 359.

Vesalius and Copernicus both dared to question and reevaluate accepted theories. Their emphasis on careful observation of the natural world marked a new era in scientific thinking, a period that became known as the **Scientific Revolution.** ■

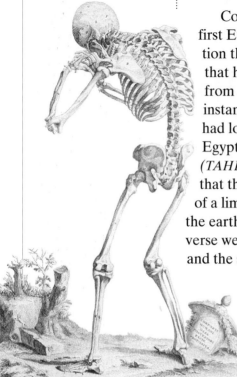

▲ *In order to carry out his experiments and make drawings such as this, Vesalius sometimes stole the bodies of people who had been hanged.*

■ *How did the scientific discoveries of Copernicus offer a new view on the world?*

Galileo and the Church

The Italian astronomer and physicist Galileo continued the work of Copernicus. He greatly admired the Polish astronomer's genius. Like Copernicus and Vesalius, Galileo recognized the importance of relying on observation rather than blindly trusting classical authorities.

Through observation and experimentation, Galileo tested the theory of falling bodies. This theory, which held that heavy objects fall faster than lighter objects, had been accepted since about 300 B.C. Galileo made his own observations by dropping objects of various weights and shapes from different heights. He then developed a mathematical formula showing that all bodies—no matter what their shape or weight—would fall at the same speed.

Galileo also applied his method of observation to astronomy. In 1609, he developed a telescope that was larger and more powerful than any made before. Galileo was the first person to observe sunspots, Jupiter's moons, and Saturn's rings. He also provided new information about the rough, crater-marked surface of our moon, which had previously been considered smooth.

Galileo's observations of one planet, Venus, provided strong support for Copernicus's theory. But when Galileo argued the point in his *Dialogue Concerning the Two Chief World Systems*, the Catholic church reacted. Because the idea of a sun-centered universe went against Catholic beliefs, the publication was placed on the *Index of Prohibited Books*. The inquisition in Rome condemned Galileo in 1616. Threatened with torture, Galileo, now an old man, denied his belief in Copernicus's ideas.

But his spirit was not broken. Upon leaving his trial, he is believed to have said of the earth, "but still it moves." Galileo spent the remaining eight years of his life under house arrest on his estate near Florence, where he continued his scientific activities.

The church's victory was short-lived. By the late 1630s, the theory of the sun-centered universe was well established, and the age of science was under way. ■

How Do We Know?

HISTORY *Church officials banned books whose ideas threatened the church's power and authority. By reading the books listed in the* Index of Prohibited Books, *modern scholars have determined which ideas the church considered to be most dangerous.*

■ *Why was the Catholic church threatened by Galileo's ideas?*

▼ *Using this compound microscope, Robert Hooke examined cork, snowflakes, and tiny organisms, such as the tick. His drawings were published in the book* Micrographia *in 1645.*

The Scientific Method

The Scientific Revolution was pioneered by Copernicus, Vesalius, and Galileo. Many other thinkers and writers also contributed to its success.

Francis Bacon

One such thinker was Francis Bacon, an English philosopher. In his book *Novum Organum*, published in 1620, Bacon stressed the importance of observation and experimentation leading to the statement of general principles about the natural world. This way of doing scientific research is now known as the **scientific method.**

A key part of this process, according to Bacon, was forming a hypothesis. A **hypothesis** is an assumption that can be tested by investigation. For example, Robert Hooke, an Englishman who developed the compound microscope in 1665, hypothesized that a microscope with two lenses could produce a clearer image of a magnified object.

This hypothesis was then tested by an experiment, and the results were recorded. Hooke experimented by adjusting and readjusting the placement of the lenses. Then he made accurate drawings based on his observation of the

▲ *Isaac Newton was praised by the English poet Alexander Pope in the following rhyme: "Nature, and nature's laws lay hid in night/ God said, 'Let Newton be!' and all was light."*

➤ *Newton's studies of how light passes through a prism helped explain how rainbows are formed.*

■ *What was revolutionary about the scientific method?*

magnified objects. Finally, the collected data were analyzed and a conclusion was drawn. Hooke's data indeed revealed that objects could be more closely observed using a microscope with two lenses.

Bacon's method helped others in the Scientific Revolution organize and formulate their research. The scientific method is still at the core of scientific research.

Isaac Newton

Sir Isaac Newton, English scientist, astronomer, and mathematician, also used the scientific method. Many scientists before Newton made observations and recorded data. However, Newton's biggest contribution was in providing an explanation for the universe that was very large in scope. His great ability lay in interpreting data and drawing accurate conclusions about the nature of the universe.

Born in 1642, the year Galileo died, Newton expanded and perfected many of Galileo's theories. Like Galileo, Newton was fascinated by falling objects. According to the story, while in the country one day, Newton saw an apple fall from a

tree branch. He hypothesized that there must be some force pulling the apple to the ground. He further hypothesized that the same force that pulls an object to earth keeps the moon and planets in orbit around the sun. After much observation and many experiments, Newton announced that a force called gravity holds the universe together. He described this theory and many others in the *Mathematical Principles of Natural Philosophy* published in 1687.

During the Reformation and the Scientific Revolution, people began to reexamine their spiritual and physical worlds. Freed from having to rely on accepted theories and beliefs, they sought new answers to old questions. This searching set the stage for further reformation in the 18th and 19th centuries. ■

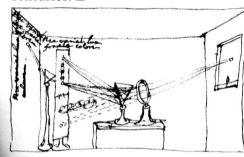

R E V I E W

1. **FOCUS** What was the Scientific Revolution?
2. **CONNECT** What did the new scientific thinkers and the leaders of the Reformation have in common?
3. **BELIEF SYSTEMS** Why was the publication of Vesalius's findings considered revolutionary?
4. **SCIENCE** How did Newton use the scientific method?
5. **CRITICAL THINKING** Which scientific achievements do you think were more important, those of Copernicus or those of Galileo? Explain.
6. **ACTIVITY** Use Bacon's scientific method to answer the following question: Which weighs more, a pound of apples or a pound of lettuce?

Making Hypotheses

Here's Why

You know that a hypothesis is an explanation, based on known facts, that can be tested as more facts become available. To develop a hypothesis, you gather all the information you can about a question or a problem. The hypothesis then becomes the basis of any further testing. You can test a scientific hypothesis through observation or experimentation, as discussed in Lesson 4.

Other subjects, such as history, also invite hypotheses. Some hypotheses about history can never be proved or disproved because of lack of evidence. However, you can continue to test a hypothesis when you find new information.

Suppose you want to explain why the church lost so much of the power it once had. You have read many facts about this in the chapter. You could use these facts to form a hypothesis.

Here's How

Look at the diagram below. It shows the steps involved in making a hypothesis.

The arrows indicate that each step leads to the next. To formulate a hypothesis of your own, follow these steps in order:

1. **Define the question.** You could ask, for example: What was the primary cause of the decline in church authority between 1300 and 1500?
2. **Gather evidence.** Read through the chapter and list events that caused the church's authority to decline. Your list may look something like this:
   - Secular rulers gained power.
   - The Great Schism caused confusion.
   - Corruption existed within the church.
   - Many groups were asking for reform in the church.
3. **Examine the clues.** Analyze the list. Can the clues be placed under a particular heading? How might the ideas be summarized?
4. **Make a hypothesis.** One example of a hypothesis that shows the primary cause of the decline in church authority between 1300 and 1500 is this: The church did not use its power wisely.
5. **Test the hypothesis.** You can test your hypothesis by reading more about the topic, either in your textbook or in outside sources.

Try It

Now form a hypothesis of your own that answers this question: Why did the Calvinists have such a strict code of behavior? Use what you have learned about the Calvinists in Lesson 3 to complete steps 2–4.

Apply It

Formulate a hypothesis which answers this question: Why do some seventh grade students. make excuses about late homework assignments? Use the five-step process to work out your hypothesis. Write down the facts you used to develop your hypothesis. When you learn new facts about the question, examine them and be prepared to alter your hypothesis to account for the new information.

Making a Hypothesis

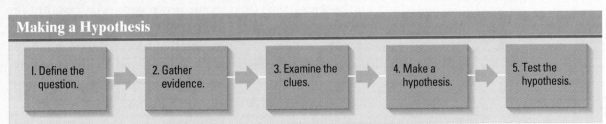

I. Define the question. → 2. Gather evidence. → 3. Examine the clues. → 4. Make a hypothesis. → 5. Test the hypothesis.

357

Scientific Discoveries

I n all corners of the world, I sought for the true and experienced arts of medicine. Not alone with doctors; but with barbers, surgeons, learned physicians, women, magicians, alchemists . . . , with the wise and the simple, I [gathered information] for a foundation of medicine which should be unspotted by fables or babble.

Paracelsus, a Swiss physician, 1493–1541

Background

In 1543, Flemish scientist Andreas Vesalius did a shocking thing. He published a book about human anatomy, showing detailed pictures of the bones, muscles, and organ systems. In doing so, he admitted that he had performed dissections. In those days, dissecting the human body was forbidden by the major religions—Judaism, Christianity, and Islam.

The Scientific Revolution, fueled by the courage of Galileo, Vesalius, and others, created an intellectual climate in which people began to question even the oldest and most accepted ideas. Doctors and scientists rejected what they could not prove to be true and formulated new theories based on their observations of the world.

For example, in 1796, English physician Edward Jenner made an observation about smallpox, a disease that terrorized Europe.

Milkmaids— young girls who milked cows—rarely contracted the disease. Jenner found that these girls had previously suffered from cowpox, a disease similar to smallpox, but much milder. Victims of both diseases developed infected sores on their skin.

Jenner did an experiment to find out if injecting a person with fluid from a cowpox sore prevented the person from contracting smallpox. A young boy volunteered to be the guinea pig. Several weeks after injecting the boy with fluid from a cowpox sore, Jenner injected the boy with material from smallpox sores. Jenner, the boy, and the boy's mother waited anxiously to see if the boy would come down with smallpox, but the boy remained healthy. By recognizing that cowpox and smallpox were related and conducting a daring experiment, Jenner had found a way to protect people from smallpox.

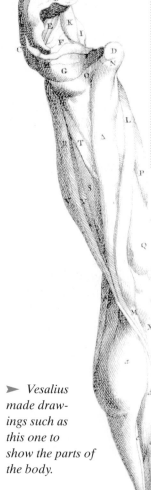

➤ *Vesalius made drawings such as this one to show the parts of the body.*

◄ *Magnetic resonance imaging produces pictures of the human body that enable doctors to pinpoint problems before surgery. Today, doctors are also able to use artificial hearts and cell-separation techniques to save lives.*

Knowledge and Responsibility

Jenner's discovery was not easy for people to accept at first. Even physicians found it unsettling to think of injecting people with material from infected sores. Was Jenner taking too many risks? Was he sure that injections could do no harm? Should people wait for more proof before submitting themselves to Jenner's procedure?

Decision Point

1. What were the risks and benefits of Jenner's treatment for smallpox? Do you think Jenner was right to test his procedure the way he did? Why?
2. If you had been alive in Jenner's day, would you have wanted to undergo Jenner's treatment? What would you want to ask him before you agreed to the procedure? List the questions you would ask before making this decision.
3. Suppose a researcher discovers a drug that helps cure heart disease. Its side effects are not yet fully known or understood. What information could help you decide whether this new drug should be given to patients? How could you find this information?

What should a doctor do with a new medicine that could save people's lives?

Withhold it for further tests	Make it available to a select group	Make it available to anyone
• Advantages • Disadvantages	• Advantages • Disadvantages	• Advantages • Disadvantages

Reformation and the Scientific Revolution

Chapter Review

Reviewing Key Terms

council (p. 340)
Counter Reformation (p. 352)
hypothesis (p. 355)
indulgence (p. 340)
inquisition (p. 352)
pamphlet (p. 345)
predestination (p. 350)
Protestant (p. 344)
Reformation (p. 344)
scientific method (p. 355)
Scientific Revolution (p. 354)

A. Write whether each of the following statements is true or false. Then rewrite the false statements to make them true.
1. Martin Luther was a leader in the Counter Reformation.
2. The Reformation was the Catholic movement to improve the Protestant church.
3. The scientific method involves a series of logical steps used in scientific research.
4. Councils of church leaders were created to meet and rule on matters of church law and faith and to restore unity and dignity to the Catholic church.
5. During the Scientific Revolution, accepted theories about the nature of the universe were challenged.

B. Write a sentence or two using the three terms in each group. The sentences should show how the terms are related.
1. indulgences, Protestant, predestination
2. Protestant, Reformation, inquisition
3. scientific method, hypothesis, Scientific Revolution

Exploring Concepts

A. In every age there are individuals who have a strong effect on historical events. Copy the chart below. Then fill in the boxes with the names of individuals who were important participants in this historical period. Add more boxes if necessary. Then choose two names from each category and summarize the contributions of each.

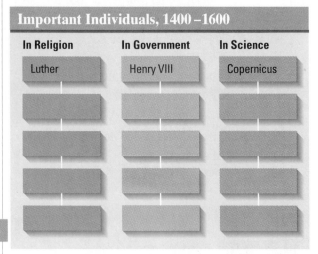

Important Individuals, 1400–1600

In Religion	In Government	In Science
Luther	Henry VIII	Copernicus

B. Support each statement with facts and details from the chapter.
1. The *Unam Sanctam* eventually led to a lessening of the authority of the Catholic church.
2. Many Catholics were confused by the French cardinals' election of Clement VII to the office of pope.
3. Some clergy engaged in corrupt practices, which further weakened the authority of the church.
4. October 31, 1517 was a day that began a new era in Christian religion.
5. The Council of Trent was an important part of the Catholic church's attempt to reform itself.
6. Scientists of the 1500s and 1600s and religious reformers questioned accepted theories and beliefs.
7. In addition to Martin Luther, there were other individuals and groups who broke away from the Catholic church.

Reviewing Skills

1. What organizational patterns are used in the text sections The Reformation Begins and Protestantism Spreads on pages 344 through 347? Explain how you know.
2. Copernicus believed that the sun was the center of the universe and the earth only one of the planets that revolved around the sun. However, he refused to publish the mathematical work and records of observation that supported his hypothesis until he knew that he was near death. Use the five-step process to formulate a hypothesis that explains why Copernicus did not publish his findings earlier. Read Lesson 4 to review the facts. Explain how your hypothesis accounts for all the facts you list.
3. Reread the quotation from Pope Boniface's *Unam Sanctam* on page 338. What was Pope Boniface's bias?
4. You are reading Protestant and Catholic primary sources on the Reformation. What factors can you think of that might affect factual reporting from both Protestant and Catholic sources?

Using Critical Thinking

1. The events of history are like a chain of causes and effects. What action of King Philip IV caused Pope Boniface VIII to issue the *Unam Sanctam?* What action did Philip take as a result of the pope's decree? What effect did Philip's action have on the Catholic church? If Philip IV hadn't responded to the *Unam Sanctam* as he did, what role might the church play in our lives and government today? Why?
2. "The pen is mightier than the sword" is an old saying. What does it mean? How would you apply the saying to the actions of Martin Luther?
3. Copernicus's theory on planetary motion was strongly opposed by certain leaders of his day. Suppose that a theory that is in direct opposition to a widely accepted scientific theory was proposed today. Do you think it would meet with the same kind of opposition? Why?
4. Modern Americans enjoy many important rights, including the freedom of religion and the freedom of speech. If the people you learned about in this chapter had these two rights, do you think the events in the chapter would have been any different? Explain what you mean.

Preparing for Citizenship

1. GROUP ACTIVITY Look at the map of world religions on page 529 of the Atlas. Choose one of the religions shown. Research its development and prepare a timeline showing dates of important events in its history. Display the timelines in the classroom. Also look for and display newspaper and magazine articles about that religion.
2. INTERVIEWING Interview a minister, a priest, a rabbi, or someone else in a religious role. Ask questions such as these: Why did you choose this profession? What type of schooling is required? What do you especially like about your work? What are some disadvantages? Present your information in brief talks called "Meet ____."
3. COLLABORATIVE LEARNING Meet with your class to plan a Living History in which important people introduced in this chapter discuss their contributions and achievements. Which people made the most important contributions? Use the chart you completed in Exploring Concepts as a guide. Select students for the following tasks: role-play the historical figures; write their scripts; make costumes and props; design and construct scenery; and make posters advertising the presentation. Then present the Living History.

Chapter 14
The Age of Exploration

Gold, silver, and silks glimmered in the North African sun. The fragrance of spices filled the air. The year was 1415. Portugal's Prince Henry, then a crusader, marveled at the riches in the city of Ceuta. These sights gave Henry a dream—to control the rich trade with Africa and Asia. The same dream sparked many adventurers of the 1400s and 1500s. Time after time, they risked voyages on uncharted waters to reach the valuable goods of Africa and Asia.

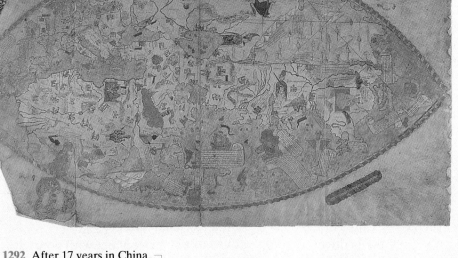

Throughout this period, explorers brave high waves, storms, rocky shallows, and their crews' fears that sea monsters lurk in the ocean.

1292 After 17 years in China, traveler Marco Polo returns to Venice and tells Europeans of China's wonders. A later geographer uses Polo's accounts to draw this map.

| 1250 | 1300 | 1350 | 1400 |

1250

c. 1400 Chinese trading ships sail to the Middle East and eastern Africa.

The Spice Trade

Europeans wanted more spice in their lives. Tired of bland food, nobles used spices to lend their dishes an exotic flavor. Spices were expensive because they were rare and passed through many hands on their way to market. The demand for tasty products pushed out the boundaries of the known world, as explorers rushed to find new routes to the spice lands.

Pepper plant, pepper berries, and dried peppercorns— native to India

One of the earliest known spices, pepper became popular because its fiery bite overpowered the taste of spoiled food.

Marco Polo in Pepperland shows the explorer helping to harvest the precious berries. Marco Polo tasted pepper for the first time in the East and brought some back to Europe in the 13th century. At one time in England, peppercorns were so valuable they were counted out one by one, and used as money.

Cinnamon—native to the island of Sri Lanka

Cloves —dried flowerbuds of a tree from Southeast Asia

Merchants, sailing ships like this one, traded Arabian frankincense for Indian pepper.

Peppercorns in meat

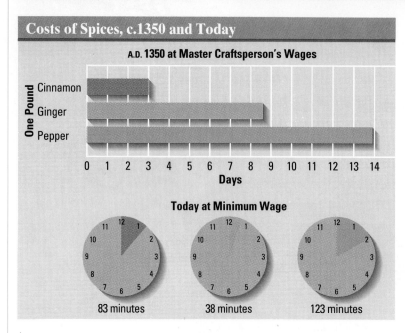

Costs of Spices, c.1350 and Today

A.D. 1350 at Master Craftsperson's Wages

One Pound
- Cinnamon
- Ginger
- Pepper

Days: 0 1 2 3 4 5 6 7 8 9 10 11 12 13 14

Today at Minimum Wage

83 minutes   38 minutes   123 minutes

This chart compares the amount of time it would have taken to earn enough money to buy these luxury items in 1350 with the amount of time it takes today. Which item remains the most expensive?

■ *How did Europeans obtain goods from the East?*

Along the way to ports such as Antioch and Alexandria the goods changed hands many times. Each trader covered only a portion of the route and then sold his cargo to the next trader.

Each Muslim, Arab, or Persian trader along the way raised the price of the items. Thus, by the time a piece of silk reached the Mediterranean, it might cost more than 100 times its original price.

In the bustling Mediterranean ports, cargoes from the East were loaded onto Italian merchant ships for the passage to Europe. Italian port cities such as Venice and Genoa played a key role in east-west trade.

Because their location was central to Mediterranean markets, the Italian city-states had long been home to the best seafarers, navigators, and shipbuilders in the West. Moreover, Italian merchants had long been involved in overseas trade with commercial centers in Muslim countries. As a result, Italian cities had flourished since the 1100s.

Venice was all-powerful in the eastern Mediterranean, while Genoa dominated western Mediterranean trade in the early 1300s. However, in the late 1300s, the two cities waged war to determine which of them would command trade on the Black Sea and the Aegean Sea. Despite some crushing defeats in battle, Venice maintained a **monopoly,** or complete control, over trade with the East. ■

Carrying Christianity Across the Sea

Europeans sought goods and profit, but they also wanted to spread Christianity among non-believers in other parts of the world. Some Christian explorers also hoped to find a mythical king named Prester John, who was rumored to rule a Christian kingdom in Africa. According to legend, Prester John had successfully defended his kingdom from Muslim attack. From the 1100s on,

the Portuguese spent great amounts of time, energy, and resources looking for this potential ally in the fight against the Muslims.

The Spanish and Portuguese had long been waging religious warfare against Islam. Since the early 700s, Muslims had invaded and occupied much of Spain and what would later become Portugal. Many battles were fought against the Muslims, but they were not finally driven out of southern Spain until 1492.

These religious wars influenced Spanish and Portuguese exploration. If people in newly discovered regions converted to Christianity, Spain and Portugal would have new allies in the fight against Islam. This was one reason missionaries usually accompanied the expeditions that explored or settled new regions.

Missionaries used education to convert the nonbelievers to Christianity. In the 1600s, Jesuit missionaries in China studied Chinese language and culture to better understand the people they wanted to convert. They also helped teach the Chinese and Europeans about each other's civilizations.

However, other missionaries were not so gentle. Some used torture to subdue nonbelievers in foreign lands. For instance, 16th-century missionaries in Central and South America forced native inhabitants to work on church-owned farms. This outraged many Christians. Bartolomé de Las Casas, a defender of the rights of the natives, wrote a book on acceptable methods of conversion. An excerpt from his work follows.

*H*earers, especially pagans, should understand that the preachers of the faith have no intention of acquiring power over them through their preaching. . . . [They] should understand that no desire for riches moves [preachers] to preach. . . . In speaking and conversing with their hearers, especially pagans, the preachers should show themselves so mild and humble, courteous and . . . goodwilled that the hearers eagerly wish to listen and hold their teaching in greater reverence.

Las Casas, *The "Only Method" of Converting the Indians*, 1530s

While missionaries on exploratory expeditions sought to make new converts, many of the explorers leading these expeditions were searching for new gold markets. If Spanish and Portuguese explorers could find new sources of gold, their governments might be able to break up the Venetian monopoly on trade. ∎

◄ *This 1422 painting is of a Jesuit missionary-astronomer who predicted an eclipse of the sun in China. The Chinese ruler ordered the missionary to teach his people Western science.*

∎ *What role did religion play during the new era of European exploration?*

Searching for New Markets

The Venetians delivered their cargoes of spices and other eastern goods by land or by sea to cities throughout Europe. In exchange for the eastern imports, Europeans exported wool, linen, timber, tin,

The Age of Exploration

copper, lead, and guns. Above all, some European countries needed gold to buy imported goods.

Portugal and Spain were active participants in east-west trade. However, the total cost of the goods Portugal imported was often higher than the total value of the goods it exported. Thus, the Portuguese government frequently owed a trade debt to other governments. Portugal had to pay these governments to maintain the **balance of trade,** or the difference between the total value of exports and the total value of imports. European trading countries demanded payment of debts in gold, which often took the form of **bullion.** Bullion was gold that had been melted and then molded into ingots, or bars, of specific weights.

As eastern imports increased, the Portuguese government needed more gold to pay for the goods. Portugal and Spain obtained most of their gold from North African traders at high prices. These traders had bought the gold from central and southern African gold producers and then carried it by caravan across the Sahara. Portugal wanted to bypass the North African traders and deal directly with the source, the gold producers. By trading directly, they could obtain gold more cheaply. So, in 1419, Portuguese explorers began sailing south along the west coast of Africa in search of gold markets.

Portugal needed gold, but it also needed good farmland and workers to cultivate the land. Nobles wanted to claim farmland in overseas regions to increase their wealth. And traders were eager to find new supplies of agricultural produce to sell in Portugal.

Eventually, some Portuguese began to hope for an even greater reward than gold and land: a sea route to the East. If they sailed directly to India and China, Portuguese traders could buy goods at their source and sell them in Europe at huge profits. Portugal could then break the Italian monopoly on east-west trade. Finding a sea route to the East and establishing a direct trading connection became the goal of many European explorers. ■

A Gold bullion is still used by countries today to pay debts and to settle accounts.

■ *Why did Portugal want to find new markets?*

R E V I E W

1. **FOCUS** Why did explorers in the 1400s risk their lives to explore unknown parts of the world?

2. **CONNECT** Travelers in the age of exploration began to view the world in new ways. How was their view of the world similar to that of thinkers during the Reformation and the Scientific Revolution?

3. **ECONOMICS** Why did the Portuguese want to find new sources of gold?

4. **BELIEF SYSTEMS** What did European Christians hope to achieve by exploring unknown lands?

5. **CRITICAL THINKING** Many non-Christians in different parts of the world rebelled against European attempts to convert them to Christianity. Why do you think they reacted this way?

6. **ACTIVITY** Hide a book or other object. Then draw a map that could be used to direct someone to the object's discovery. Be sure to indicate the proper positions and directions of things and places indicated on your map. Finally, see if a friend can use the map to find the object.

LESSON 2

Adventure and Profit

PRINCE HENRY OF PORTUGALL

CEUTA

Prince Henry of Portugal, or "Henry the Navigator" as he was known, was a leader in the early years of European exploration. In 1453, a historian described him as a curious and adventurous man.

The noble spirit of this Prince was ever urging him both to begin and to carry out very great deeds. . . . He had also a wish to know the land that lay beyond the isles of Canary and that Cape called Bojador [BAHJ uh dawr], for that up to his time, neither by writings, nor by the memory of man, was known with any certainty the nature of the land beyond that Cape. . . . It seemed to him that if he or some other lord did not endeavor to gain that knowledge, no mariners or merchants would ever dare to attempt it, for it is clear that none of them ever trouble themselves to sail to a place where there is not a sure and certain hope of profit.

Gomes Eannes de Azurara, from
Discovery and Conquest of Guinea, 1453

Prince Henry was determined to overcome the fear surrounding Cape Bojador. And the unknown beyond the Cape fascinated him.

THINKING FOCUS

How did Prince Henry's center for navigation help establish Portugal's trading empire in the 1500s?

Key Terms

- caravel
- capital
- colony

◄ *Prince Henry leads troops against the Muslim city of Ceuta in this painting from the 1400s. While in Ceuta, Henry became intrigued by descriptions of Africa's wealth.*

Prince Henry, Navigator

Henry could not guarantee that Portugal would profit from his exploration along the west coast of Africa. But he could vouch that gold and other luxury goods could be found in Africa. In 1415, he had been a crusader in the Muslim port city Ceuta *(SAY oo tah)* in North Africa. He had seen vast quantities of gold, silver, and grain, magnificent silks and tapestries, and fragrant spices. Camel caravans from sub-Saharan Africa brought these sumptuous goods to Ceuta.

371

Henry hoped to find the source of African gold by sailing south along the coast. He hoped to find new markets and new goods for Portugal as well. Perhaps he would even find the legendary Prester John or new believers for the Christian faith.

Henry was an unusual man—intensely religious and fascinated by the mystery beyond known boundaries. When he left Ceuta, he did not return to Lisbon and the luxurious life of a prince. Rather, Henry sailed to the small town of Sagres *(SAH greesh)*

on Cape St. Vincent, the southernmost point of Portugal. There, on the rocky, windswept peninsula, Henry established a center for navigation and exploration. He summoned shipbuilders, mapmakers, sea captains, and instrument makers from all over Europe to live and study in Sagres.

Henry also invited sailors, travelers, and scholars from Europe, Africa, and the Middle East to share their geographical knowledge. He financed expeditions to West Africa. Bit by bit, Henry's scholars added information to the maps developed at Sagres. ■

Preparations for Sailing

Explorers needed more than improved maps to find their way to unknown destinations in Africa and beyond. Out on the open sea, they had only the sun, moon, and stars to guide them. Ocean-going seafarers also had to deal with unpredictable winds and unseen

currents that could send them far off course. They didn't know what hardships lay ahead of them or how long it might take to get to their destination.

Prince Henry's experts improved and adapted for navigation such instruments as the compass

and then by the Guinea Current.

About halfway down the coast of Africa, however, da Gama would have encountered the Benguela Current. This current runs in the opposite direction of the route of da Gama's ships. What current affected the ships after they went around the tip of Africa?

For the final leg of the voyage, da Gama's ships crossed the northern Indian Ocean. The currents in this portion of the Indian Ocean change direction in response to strong seasonal winds called monsoons. From April to October, monsoons blow from the southwest, creating a current that flows in a clockwise direction. From November to March, monsoons create a current that runs in a counterclockwise direction. Since da Gama completed this last leg of the voyage in May, we can

assume that he was helped by both the wind and ocean currents in the northern Indian Ocean.

Try It

Look back at the map on page 378 that shows the routes taken by Christopher Columbus from Portugal to the Americas. Use that map with the one below to describe how wind and ocean currents affected one of the voyages.

Apply It

Suppose you wanted to sail from a port about halfway down the western coast of North America to the Philippines, and then back. Assume that you are making the voyage during the summer. What route would you take in order to use wind and ocean currents to speed your voyage? Suppose you wanted to sail from the tip of Florida to the coast of West Africa and back. What route would you take?

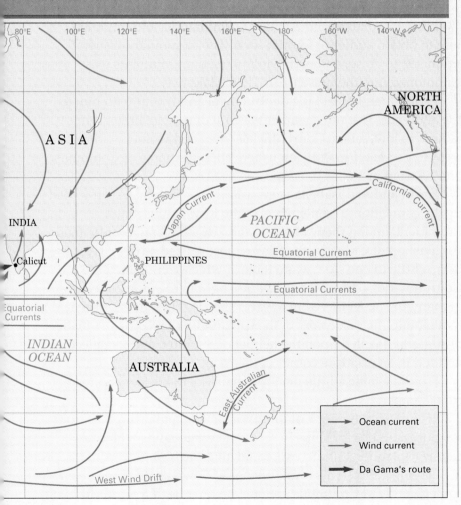

The Age of Exploration

The Audience

C. Walter Hodges

As you have learned in this chapter, the dream of wealth and the lure of riches drove Columbus and other explorers like him. They undertook journeys of unknown dangers and uncertain outcomes to pursue that dream. But they needed financial support. As you read this story, play the role of the audience— the King or Queen. Would you support Columbus? Why or why not?

In Lesson 3 you learned about Columbus's appeal to Ferdinand and Isabella. Here is an imaginative recreation of his second appearance before that King and Queen.

The town was taken, the Moors were driven out, the wars were at an end. Now, now at last there must be time to hear Columbus. Now at last the victorious Sovereigns would give him ships to sail in quest of his new horizon.

He went to his friend Alonzo de Quintanilla and implored him to obtain audience for him soon. The Accountant-General promised to do so, and on the following day Columbus was summoned into the presence of Their Majesties.

Father Juan Perez, Luiz de Santangel and I went with him to the audience. The antechamber was full of people, little groups talking in low voices, Court officials, men and women with petitions to present. Presently an usher called the name of Columbus, and he went in.

Ferdinand and Isabella were seated on a low dais, surrounded by the councillors and members of the Royal Household. Prominent among them was Fernando de Talavera, recently made Archbishop of Granada, the King's most trusted adviser. Near the dais, a little to one side, was a table at which were seated the Court notaries. There was a subdued light in the room, a feeling of many people gathered in a warm silence. Their dresses seemed to melt into the rich colors of the surrounding tapestries. A blade of sunlight dazzled upon the helmet of a soldier, and its reflection nodded in an opposite corner of the room.

From the table a little man rose halfway to his feet and read from a paper:

"Señor Christopher Columbus of Genoa, making application to Your Majesties for ships to seek out certain lands which he claims to stand yet undiscovered beyond the seas."

Having gabbled his formality he sat down again. The Queen smiled gently at Columbus and inclined her head towards him.

Then the King spoke:

"Señor Columbus is well known to us, I think; but if I remember rightly his proposals were examined by a Special Commission some years ago. Was it not so?"

"At Salamanca, sire."

"And the Commissioners rejected them," continued the King, "on the grounds that you could not bring forward sufficient evidence in support of your theory. Again, was it not so? And was not the Archbishop of Granada here in charge of that Commission?"

Columbus looked across at Talavera, and said nothing. The King continued:

"But since you bring your case again before us, señor, we must presume that you have fresh evidence in support of it. Or that you have fault to find with the method by which it was previously examined."

"Sire, it is not with the method but with the verdict that I have fault to find," said Columbus. "I believe that the members of the commission were all men of great renown for learning and scientific knowledge. But the greater their learning the greater was their error. They were wrong in their conclusions, and I dispute their verdict."

"And what says the Archbishop to that?" asked the King. Talavera shrugged.

"What can I say, sire, more than Señor Columbus has said? The men whom I assembled numbered among them some of our greatest scholars. Upon my word the hearing was fair and unprejudiced. Señor Columbus has his project much at heart, and it is natural that he should disagree with our findings upon it. Indeed I am sorry. But if he can bring forth further evidence . . ." He was silent. The King looked questioningly at Columbus. "Can you do that, señor?"

Columbus seemed for a second to be tongue-tied. Then he said, rather slowly:

"I can bring forward a few more traveler's tales, more strange reports; what else had I to do in all these years but to seek and collect them wherever they were to be found? I have no more real proofs than you have heard already. Nor will any man have, until he goes to find them where they exist beyond the horizons of the Ocean itself. Only give me my ships sire, and I will bring you proof enough."

There was whispering among the company, and someone laughed softly. But the King was obviously impatient. Drumming with his fingers on the arm of his chair, he said:

"We do not doubt your personal sincerity, señor. But you have heard the Archbishop. Without fresh evidence we cannot think it would be justifiable to re-open the inquiry."

Suddenly the Queen spoke.

"My Lord," she said, "perhaps Señor Columbus has not been quite fair to himself. He says he has no further proofs to bring. But since his proposals were first rejected by us he has faced much adversity without foregoing his convictions. Also he has made many friends who believe in him, men whose opinions should carry some weight. If constancy of itself is proof of nothing, at least it has the merit to be heard, even a second time."

The King looked at her and smiled slightly.

"I stand rebuked, madam," he said. "Certainly, if Señor Columbus wishes to speak, he shall be heard."

Again Columbus bowed; and he began to speak, at first slowly, then with increasing force.

"It is true what I have said. The evidence you have previously examined is still the only evidence I have to offer. But, sire, upon that very evidence I am willing to venture my life. I have shown you maps, drawn up not only by me, but by some of the greatest authorities ever known to have studied the mysteries of the Western Ocean; and I have offered to follow those maps till I have found a way for you across that ocean to the very shores of the Indies. I repeat, to do so is to venture my life; and not only my life, but the reputation I have spent so much of it to build. I can offer no other guarantee. But if Your Majesties will give me three ships, and accept the hazard, then it must be, if God so wills it, that according to all the known laws of science we shall find those shores that I have promised you, and Spain will become as wealthy as she is now victorious."

The King interrupted: "Spain is victorious, but she is also poor. The wars against the Infidel have drained the treasury dry. You say you demand three ships only. But what you really ask is for ships, men, provisions, cannon, ammunition, a thousand things, for a voyage lasting perhaps a year, perhaps even longer. It may be, as you yourself suggest, that I shall never see those ships again. Where is the money to come from?"

"From the Indies, sire!" cried Columbus, "where there is wealth enough in one province to beggar the combined treasuries of all Europe! This is testified by Marco Polo and Sir John Mandeville, and many other travellers from the East. They have seen kingdoms where swineherds fasten their rags with belts of gold and where the little street boys play in the mud with pearls. They have seen with their own eyes the princes of India riding in procession upon elephants whose thick hides are inset with jewels patterned like a carpet, whose tusks are carved to the fineness of lace, and whose ears are hung with bells of silver and gold which chime with every step in confused and wonderful harmonies! They say these beasts would seem like gods of splendor were it not for the splendor of the kings who ride them, under the tinkling and perfumed canopies that shade them from the sun. Is there another nation in Europe that would not gamble three ships for all that treasure? I tell you, for the people who first discover the Western way to the Indies, a thousand ships will not suffice to carry home the riches they will find, not even though their holds are crammed so full they spill upon the decks! All this I offer to Spain. But there is little time for Spain to choose. My plan is no secret. It is talked of everywhere, and is plainly written down for anyone to study. Am I the only man to consider the undertaking? Perhaps even now in Portugal, or France, or England, they are preparing ships for just such a voyage as mine. Perhaps in a few years the Atlantic will be an open road. Perhaps some other man, not I, will sail the ship that opens it. If this should happen it will be God's punishment for my pride, for I have lived all these years dreaming of the pride I should have when I, the first, shall strike the Spanish flag into the soil of the Indies.

"I have only one thing to add. Upon the floor here between us is a carpet. It is an Indian carpet such as has great value for us in Europe. The merchants who trade in such things grow richer every year. And from whom are they obtained? Not from the Indians. They are bought from the Muslims of Aleppo and

Alexandria, who alone control the channels of trade with the Far East. Thus, though you have driven the Infidel out of Spain, you must still buy in his bazaars and pay the price he asks. And as your ships return home from the Muslims of Aleppo they may be plundered and sunk by the Muslim pirates of Barbary, and their crews sold into slavery. Will you pay that price, and still not grant three ships for a venture such as mine?"

It was plain, long before he finished speaking, that Columbus held the imagination of the Court. Even those who could not believe him to be more than a half-crazy fanatic were moved by the forcefulness of his address. After his concluding words the assembly became aware of its own hesitancy, kept awkwardly silent and waited for the King to establish them again in their former opinions. But the King himself was hesitant. He cleared his throat and looked round at the Archbishop of Granada, and somehow it began to be clear, even from this, that Columbus had made his mark. In a moment the silence was relieved by the mutterings of conversation, and when at last the King spoke it was to make certain the good opinion in which the petitioner now found himself. The King inquired if Columbus had with him the papers and other material relating to the expedition, particularly of the estimated cost. Columbus produced two closely written scrolls, saying that the greater bulk of the material was at his lodging.

"Then señor," said the King, "if you will deliver it this evening to my secretary, I will see that the Council meets to discuss the matter within the next day or two, and I promise that it shall have every consideration."

More than this Columbus could not have desired. His joy was evident to everyone, and we, his friends, standing in the doorway of the room felt that at last his success was assured.

Our hopes were high. But in a few minutes they were to be brought down even lower than before! Where success had seemed certain, failure became inevitable out of the mouth, as it were, of Columbus himself. For, as we were about to leave the audience, the Archbishop spoke suddenly:

"Señor Columbus has stated his requirements for the expedition," he said, "but nothing for himself. Before the matter goes to Council we should know what reward he proposes to ask for his services. Supposing," he added, "that they are fruitful."

To this the King immediately assented, and the Court again waited for Columbus to speak. After a moment's hesitation he made the following demands:

"Firstly, my lords, I request that I receive a knighthood and the title of First Admiral. Secondly, if the expedition is successful, that I should be accorded the hereditary vice-regency of all the lands I may discover. And thirdly, that I receive a tenth part of all the revenues obtained from them."

The entire audience was aghast. No one had expected such extravagant demands. When he finished speaking Columbus found himself the center of a silence so deep that it seemed as though a blanket of deafness had enclosed the room. Not even the voice of anger could find itself. At last the King spoke, quietly, his words magnified by the hush.

"Can you not moderate those terms, señor?"

Columbus spread his hands. "They are reasonable, my lord," he said.

"Reasonable indeed!" a thick red-faced man spluttered out suddenly, unable to hold his wrath. "They are outrageous, monstrous, an insult! Has not this crazy adventurer the wits enough to know his place before the nobility of Spain? What is he but a weaver's son from the gutters of Genoa, and he demands to be made an Admiral and a knight! A peddler of inaccurate maps! He, an Admiral! And since when did tradesmen receive knighthoods? He should be whipped for his impertinence!"

"Sire," cried Columbus, addressing the King. "From whom should Spain most proudly accept her Empire: from the hands of a tradesman, or from her own Admiral, duly appointed by the State?"

The King shrugged his shoulders and said:

"Very well, señor. The Council shall consider the matter."

The audience was at an end. Columbus bowed and walked quickly from the room. We, his friends, went with him into the bright evening street through the crowd of idle soldiers at the gate. Here we parted company, no one saying a word.

Further Reading

Argosies of Empire. Ralph Bailey. Here are stories of sailors who explored the world's sea routes before Columbus.

Columbus Sails. C. Walter Hodges. The rest of Columbus's story by the writer of "The Audience." A sailor and a monk describe his story.

He Went with Vasco da Gama. Louise Andrews Kent. This is a story of how da Gama sailed around the Cape of Good Hope to reach the Indies. It also tells the story of Portuguese history.

I Challenge the Dark Sea. Olive W. Burt. Based on the life of Henry the Navigator, this story describes how Henry's support of science above superstition paved the way for many of the discoveries of his time.

Son of Columbus. Hans Baumann. Columbus's youngest son sails with his father and tells the story of his fourth and final voyage to the New World.

Chapter Review

Reviewing Key Terms

balance of trade (p. 370)
bullion (p. 370)
capital (p. 375)
caravel (p. 373)

circumnavigation (p. 380)
colony (p. 375)
monopoly (p. 368)

A. Each of the sentences below has words in italics that describe a key term. Read each sentence, and replace the words in italics with the correct key term from the list above.

1. Spain, Portugal, England, and France founded *settlements of their own citizens in foreign lands they explored.*
2. Portugal paid its foreign debts in *bars or blocks of gold.*
3. Spanish explorers in South America searched for gold so that Venice's *complete control of business activity* might be destroyed.
4. Ferdinand Magellan of Spain made the first *voyage around the earth.*
5. Prince Henry's ship designers created a *swift and easily maneuverable ship that could sail on the open sea.*
6. Portugal had to pay other countries to maintain the *difference between the total value of exports and the total value of imports.*
7. The rulers of Spain contributed the *money and material* to finance Columbus's voyage.

B. Write a sentence or two using each pair of words below. The sentences should show how the words are related.

1. bullion, monopoly
2. caravel, circumnavigation
3. capital, colony

Exploring Concepts

A. Copy the following chart on the age of exploration on your paper. List one or more reasons for each historical fact.

Historical Fact	Reason
1. Knowledge about the world grew (1200–1500).	Maps, travelers' tales
2. Portuguese exploration became easier.	
3. Spanish mistreated natives of Central and South America.	
4. Christianity spread.	
5. Portuguese sugar plantations were profitable.	

B. Tell why each statement below is false using facts and details from the chapter.

1. From 1200 to 1500, geographers had no idea of the size and shape of the world.
2. Vasco da Gama reached Mexico in May 1498.
3. Ptolemy's T-O maps were of little use to European mapmakers.
4. Few Europeans wanted to buy goods from the East during the 1200s and 1300s.
5. Venice and Genoa were isolated from profitable trade with the Middle East.
6. Jesuit missionaries in the 1600s were not interested in understanding the Chinese people whom they wanted to convert.
7. Prince Henry of Portugal had little interest in exploring other lands.
8. Spain had no colonies in the Americas.
9. Only Spain explored North and South America.

Reviewing Skills

1. Look at the wind and ocean current map on pages 382 and 383. In what direction do the prevailing winds blow in the Pacific Ocean off the eastern coast of South America? Would you expect this for wind currents in this area of the world? Why?

2. Look again at the map. Would it be difficult to sail from Australia to the southern tip of South America? Describe the winds and currents and their directions on such a voyage.

3. Suppose you are a partner in an English trading company in the early 1500s. Your company has just voted to finance an expedition to find the Northwest Passage. What are the advantages and disadvantages of such a decision? How did you vote?

4. If you wanted to find out how terrain helped people decide how to use land, what two types of maps would you compare?

Using Critical Thinking

1. As in Columbus's time, some people today argue that the exploration of the solar system and the universe is a waste of time and money. If you agree with these people, explain your reasons. If you do not agree, write down some arguments that could be used to convince them that they are mistaken about space exploration.

2. An old saying states that the people of one generation build on the accomplishments of the generations who lived before them. Explain how this saying was true of the European explorers between 1200 and 1500. Then discuss how the saying applies to the generations living today.

3. Prince Henry and Christopher Columbus both reached important goals in their lives. Examine and compare the lives of Prince Henry and Christopher Columbus. Think of what character trait or traits may have helped them succeed. Now think about goals you want to reach sometime in your future. How could you use one of the traits that helped them succeed to achieve your goal? Explain your answer.

4. Suppose you could travel back in time and live in Europe during the age of exploration described in this chapter. Would you like to live during that era? If so, what things would you like to do? If not, why not?

Preparing for Citizenship

1. ARTS ACTIVITY Choose an event from each lesson of this chapter that interests you. Draw or paint a picture to illustrate each event. You may want to select one of these: Vasco da Gama's voyage to India; Bartolomé de Las Casas defending the rights of native people to the King of Spain; Prince Henry's shipbuilders inspecting their first caravel; sailors on a ship in the "Green Sea of Darkness" near Cape Bojador; African slaves working on a sugar plantation on Madeira; Cabot, Verrazano, or Cartier searching for the Northwest Passage. See page 511 of the Minipedia for more ideas.

2. COLLABORATIVE ACTIVITY Meet with your class to plan a book of mini-biographies of people you learned about in this chapter. Have each biography explain how the person was involved with European exploration. First, decide on a title for the book. Then, choose groups to do the following jobs: research and write an introduction and the biographies; illustrate the biographies and design a cover; photocopy the biographies and bind them together in a book; distribute copies of the finished book to other classes in your school. Have all the groups work together to produce your book.

Unit 7
Civilizations of the Americas

Richly colored, this South American weaving is made of tropical bird feathers. What was it for? Archaeologists think it is an Inca cape of the A.D. 1400s, perhaps worn by priests. Such objects, left by small groups or great civilizations, tell of life in the Americas before 1500.

1800 B.C.

Detail of a feathered poncho with cotton base, Inca culture, north or central coast of South America, 15th century. The Textile Museum, Washington, D.C. 91.7

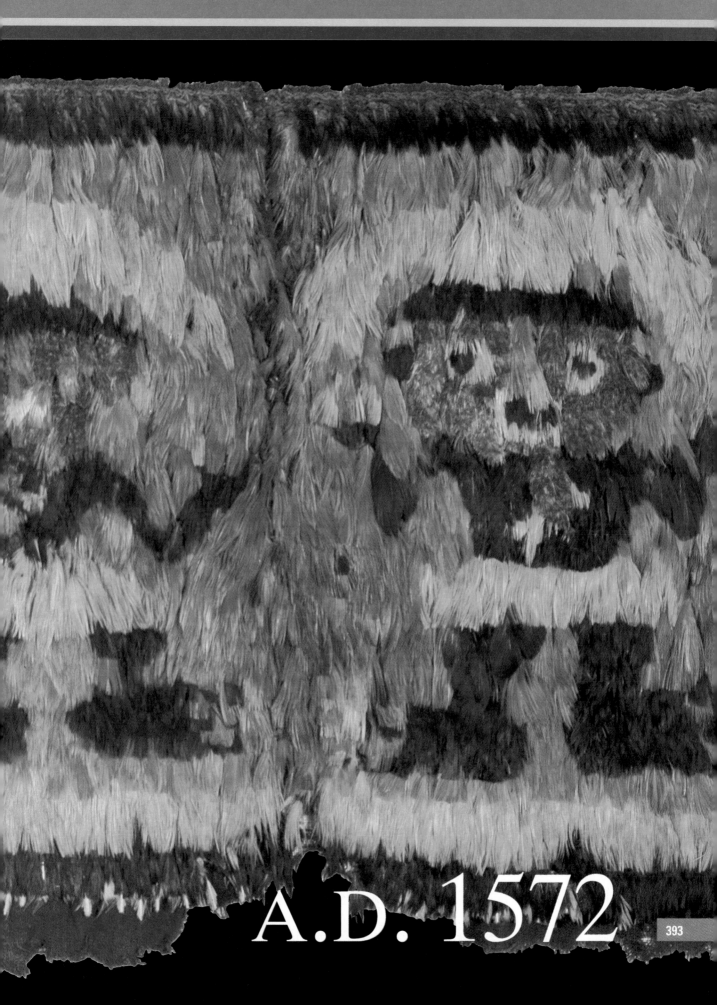

A.D. 1572

Chapter 15

Early American Civilizations

A prehistoric bone, a spear, a carved jade figure—all are clues in an age-old mystery: What were the earliest Americans like, those who settled North and South America between about 40,000 B.C. and A.D. 1300? Ancient tools and bones found by archaeologists help trace the paths of these first settlers. Carvings and sculptures, ornaments and massive temples show how later groups farmed, hunted, fought, and worshiped. All of these objects help unravel the mysteries of prehistoric America.

During this period, hunters migrated as far as southernmost South America. In Texas's Bonfire Cave archaeologists have found weapons and bones from about 13,000 to 10,000 B.C.

1200–400 B.C. The Olmec people build a great civilization in Mexico. Religion is important to the Olmec, who carve jade religious figures like the one shown here.

2000	1500	1000	500

563 B.C. Religious leader Siddhartha Gautama, later called the Buddha, is born in India.

1800 B.C.

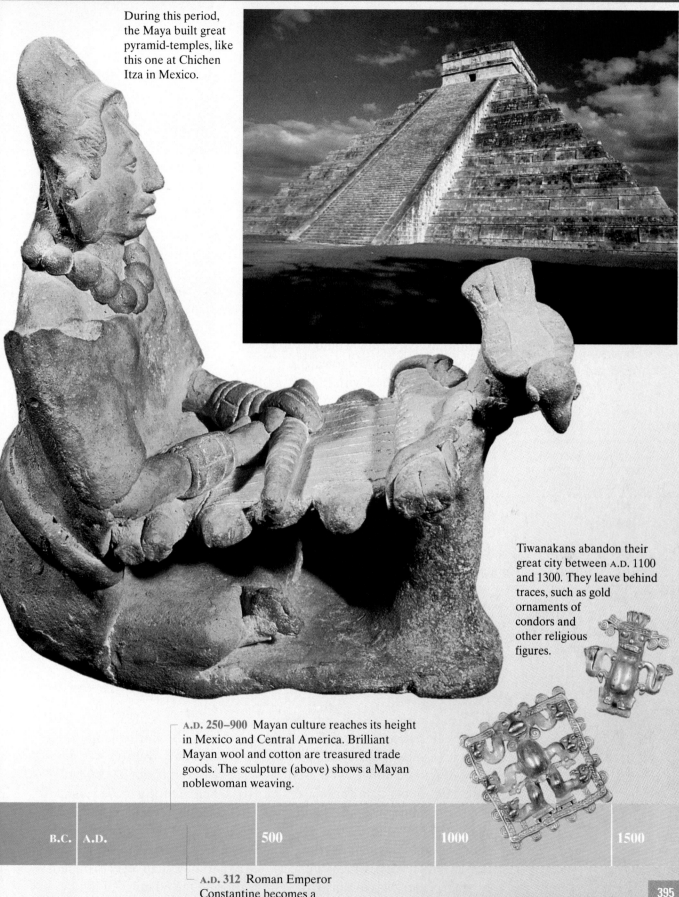

During this period, the Maya built great pyramid-temples, like this one at Chichen Itza in Mexico.

Tiwanakans abandon their great city between A.D. 1100 and 1300. They leave behind traces, such as gold ornaments of condors and other religious figures.

A.D. 250–900 Mayan culture reaches its height in Mexico and Central America. Brilliant Mayan wool and cotton are treasured trade goods. The sculpture (above) shows a Mayan noblewoman weaving.

B.C.	A.D.		500		1000		1500

A.D. 312 Roman Emperor Constantine becomes a Christian. Before the century ends, Christianity is the empire's official religion.

A.D. 1300

LESSON 1

Origins

Describe the development of early communities in the Americas.

Key Terms

- hunter-gatherer
- extinct
- sedentary

➤ *Many mammoths stood as tall as 14 feet at the shoulder. Their tusks grew to more than 13 feet in length.*

His heart was beating fast. Was it excitement or fear? Today, as a young man, he would finally join the hunt.

The men had sighted a herd of mammoths. Now they would try to drive the mammoths toward a steep ravine. Armed with flint-tipped wooden spears, they hoped to force some of the huge beasts off the cliff.

The boy gasped when he saw the mammoths. They were at least three times his height. Giant, curved tusks jutted from their jaws.

He tightened his grip on his spear. With a signal from his father, he rushed with the others toward the animals, startling them into a full run.

The mammoths pounded toward the cliff, but most of them veered to avoid the edge. One turned too late. When the hunters found their reward at the bottom of the cliff, the boy's eyes gleamed with pride. He had left the camp a boy; he would return a hunter.

Migrants from Asia

The first people to come to the Americas were hunters such as those described above, who used the bodies of big-game animals like the mammoth for food and clothing. They followed the animals back and forth across the Bering land bridge, which connected Siberia and Alaska during several Ice Ages.

Today, the Bering land bridge is under water. But this was not the case between about 33,000 and 10,000 B.C. During those years, glaciers one to two miles thick covered much of the northern hemisphere. So much water froze into ice that the ocean level dropped, exposing the 50 miles of land between Asia and North America.

396

Animals wandered across the land bridge to graze on the plants growing on each continent. From time to time, hunters from east Asia followed the animals across to North America. Over thousands of years, hunters and animals traveled south to the warmer forests and grasslands of North and Central America. Follow their migration routes on the map on page 398. By 9000 B.C., people were living at the southern tip of South America.

Archaeologists traced the path these early migrants took by studying ancient bones and artifacts, such as tools, pottery, and ornaments. They have discovered tools dating from 32,000 to 17,000 B.C. that are very similar to ancient stone tools found in Asia. From this evidence, archaeologists deduce that the people of South America migrated from Asia. ■

▲ *Islands between Siberia and Alaska are the parts of the Bering land bridge that are still above water.*

■ *Describe the migration of Asians to the Americas.*

Early Hunter-Gatherers

The hunters who migrated to North America made their own weapons and tools. They pounded pieces of stone into sharp points and attached them to long wooden spears or bones. As the hunters learned more about working with stone, they developed improved tools, like those shown below. Some of these tools have sharp edges, which means other stones were used as chisels to chip off one or both edges of the stone. Sharp points such as these were an improvement over the points used earlier in Asia. These improved points have been found at hunting sites, along with the bones of hundreds of animals apparently killed in one hunt.

These people moved from place to place following big-game animals. They hunted huge tusked mammoths like the one shown on page 396, mastodons, ground sloths as big as modern-day elephants, sabre-tooth cats, and bison. Usually they hunted these animals in groups of 20 to 50 people, since it took several spear points to kill a big-game animal.

The hunters also stalked smaller animals, such as bears, deer, foxes, and turkeys. And they gathered nuts, wild berries, and other foods from plants. Because these people obtained their food by hunting wild animals and gathering fruits of wild plants, scholars call them **hunter-gatherers.**

▼ *Early hunter-gatherers used points like these as tools and weapons. Each one could fit easily in your hand.*

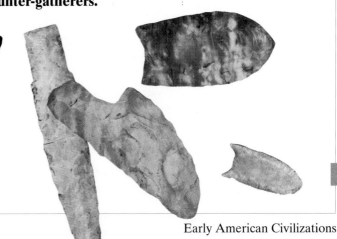

Early American Civilizations

By dating bones of big-game animals, archaeologists have established that the big game had died out by 8000 B.C. No one is certain why they disappeared, or became **extinct.** Some experts think that as the last Ice Age ended at about 8000 B.C., the climate grew warmer and drier. The grass fields where animals grazed turned brown and dried into dusty deserts. The lakes where hunter-gatherers fished, shrank or dried up. And as food and water supplies dwindled, so did the great herds. Others think the hunters killed off too many of the big animals when they developed better hunting methods. ■

■ *What did early hunter-gatherers eat, and how did they get their food?*

▼ *While the first Americans were migrating into South America, sheets of ice covered most of what is now Canada. How did this affect the migration routes of these people?*

Early Farmers

As the big game died out in the Americas, the hunter-gatherers adapted to their changing environment. They hunted smaller animals and gathered food within a smaller area than they had before. As they began to spend time in one place, they adopted a more **sedentary,** or settled, lifestyle.

To support this new lifestyle, the hunter-gatherers developed new tools. Those who lived near water wove nets and fashioned harpoons to catch fish. To store the food they gathered, they wove baskets from plant fibers. Using rocks, the hunter-gatherers crushed nuts and seeds into coarse meal to make flat cakes something like tortillas *(tawr TEE yuhs).*

As people searched for food closer to where they lived, they noticed that many of their food plants grew in the same places year after year. They probably saw plants sprout from discarded seeds. Eventually, they found they could grow their own plants using seeds from wild plants.

They probably also noticed that their plants grew best in open, sunny areas, so they began to create clearings with their stone axes. To plant their seeds, these first farmers used long, sturdy digging sticks. They harvested plants by hand. Gradually, as would happen all over the world, the hunter-gatherers became food producers. In the chart on page 399, you can see how their lives changed as

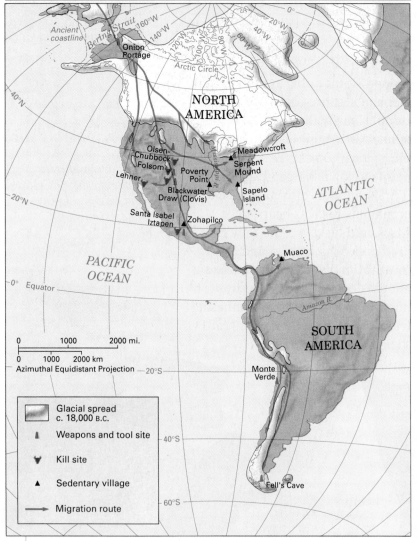

The Americans, 18,000–500 B.C.

Ancient coastline
Bering Strait
Onion Portage
Arctic Circle
NORTH AMERICA
Olsen-Chubbock
Folsom
Lehner
Poverty Point
Blackwater Draw (Clovis)
Meadowcroft
Serpent Mound
Sapelo Island
Santa Isabel Iztapen
Zohapilco
PACIFIC OCEAN
Equator
ATLANTIC OCEAN
Muaco
Amazon R.
SOUTH AMERICA
Monte Verde
Fell's Cave

0   1000   2000 mi.
0   1000   2000 km
Azimuthal Equidistant Projection

Glacial spread c. 18,000 B.C.
▲ Weapons and tool site
▼ Kill site
▲ Sedentary village
→ Migration route

Life in the Americas

	Hunter-Gatherers, c. 12,000–8500 B.C.	Sedentary Villagers, c. 8500–500 B.C.
Food	Some large game, but primarily smaller animals, such as moose and bear; fish; wild plants; and limited cultivated plants	Cultivated crops, including maize (corn), beans, squash, and chili peppers; domesticated animals, such as sheep, goats, and llamas; and some small wild game
Homes	Portable and easy to assemble (probably made of animal hides and wood)	Sturdy, built to endure over time (hardwood frames and foundations)
Tools	Projectile points, axes, scrapers (made of stone), wooden mortars, grinding stones, and small implements (made of shell and bone)	Cultivating tools, such as digging sticks and simple hoes; cooking pottery; weaving looms; and polished stone tools

◄ *What clues can you find on this chart to indicate that the people in the Americas lived a more settled life after about 8500 B.C.?*

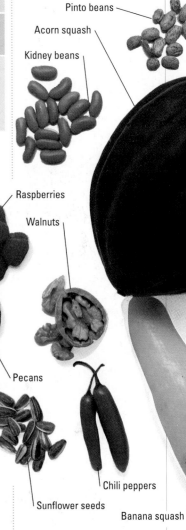

Pinto beans

Acorn squash

Kidney beans

Raspberries

Walnuts

Pecans

Chili peppers

Sunflower seeds

Banana squash

they began to rely more heavily on farming.

Farmers in regions now known as Mexico, Peru, and Bolivia began growing maize (corn), beans, and squash around 8500 B.C. These new foods were especially important because people could eat them fresh, or they could dry them and store them for later use.

People also domesticated wild animals that roamed near their settlements. In early Bolivia and Peru, for instance, people raised llamas and alpacas for food and wool. They also used such animals to transport heavy loads.

Freed from the demands of constant hunting, people had time for other activities. They used their free time to build durable dwellings and to perfect their crafts and toolmaking. They also built special structures for religious ceremonies. Religion became a community-wide activity, and religious events became social events as well.

As the settlers worked in their fields, good farmland became important, and people created permanent homes in fertile areas where they settled. Neighboring farmers began sharing duties and dividing up tasks. Some settlers developed specialties and traded tasks or goods with their neighbors. Thus, their simple settlements grew into established villages. As the villages prospered, their populations increased. These early communities became the basis for the first civilizations in the Americas. ■

■ *How did hunter-gatherers become food producers?*

R E V I E W

1. **FOCUS** Describe the development of early communities in the Americas.
2. **CONNECT** In what ways did the arrival of the early migrants in America differ from the arrival of the European explorers?
3. **GEOGRAPHY** What do you think caused big-game animals and hunters to migrate as far as South America?
4. **ECONOMICS** What did having a surplus of food enable the early hunter-gatherers to do?
5. **CRITICAL THINKING** How did the lifestyle of hunter-gatherers differ from that of early farmers?
6. **ACTIVITY** Look at the chart, Life in the Americas, on this page. On a separate sheet of paper, create a third column with a heading that describes your lifestyle, for example, Urban Dweller, and the year. Then list your food, home, and tools under this new heading.

399

Early American Civilizations

L E S S O N   2

The Olmec

THINKING FOCUS

What evidence suggests that the Olmec civilization was complex?

Key Terms

- elite
- hieroglyph

▼ *Huge stone heads such as this were first unearthed in 1862. They weigh 18 to 24 tons and stand 6 to 10 feet tall.*

A bout a league and a half's distance [four and a half miles] from a sugarcane hacienda (hah see EHN duh), on the western slopes of the Sierra de San Martin, a worker on this hacienda who was clearing jungle noticed on the surface of the ground what he took to be the bottom of a huge pot lying upside down. He told the owner of the hacienda of this discovery, and the latter ordered this object to be unearthed. . . . As a work of art, it is, without exaggeration, a magnificent sculpture. . . ."

This notice appeared in 1869 in a bulletin of the Mexican Geographical Society. The news it told introduced the modern world to a mysterious ancient world, one of the first American civilizations, the Olmec of Mexico.

The object was a colossal head, carved from stone. It was taller than a person and weighed several tons. Archaeologists wondered about the person with the helmet and stern face. Was he a king, a soldier, a priest, or some combination of the three? More mystifying, how had the Olmec obtained the massive stone that was used in the sculpture?

Archaeologists knew there were no large boulders in the area where the Olmec had settled. The closest stones were about 50 miles away in the Tuxtla (TOOST luh) Mountains. The Olmec must have brought the stones from the mountains. But how had they managed to move these huge stones?

After studying the geography of the area, archaeologists found an answer to their question. The Olmec probably rolled the huge slabs of rock on logs or dragged them 25 miles on wooden sleds down the mountainsides to a tributary of the Coatzacoalcos (koh aht suh koh AHL kuhs) River. Then they must have floated their cargo on rafts to the Gulf of Mexico and along the coast to the Tonala River. There they battled their way upriver 12 miles to their site at La Venta.

The lowlands were located in the central and northern part of the region. Some lowlands were covered with dense tropical forests with fertile soil. Others had only rough, dry grass or cactus and were not good for farming. But they were rich in the limestone the Maya needed for building and in the flint they used in stonework.

Archaeologists think the Maya may have begun farming the fertile areas of the lowlands as early as 1800 B.C. Between 1800 and 500 B.C., the Maya established small farming villages. They gathered food from the forests and also raised crops. Between 100 B.C. and A.D. 200, some of the villages grew into cities with impressive palaces and pyramids. Mayan artisans carved huge stone figures and pillars to adorn their cities.

During the height of Mayan civilization, between A.D. 250 and 900, about three million people lived in Mayan cities scattered throughout the empire. Look at the map at the above right to find the major cities.

Mayan cities were built around religious centers. At the heart of

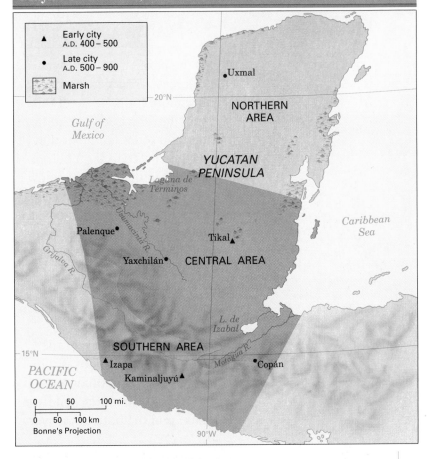

Mayan Civilization, A.D. 300–900

Early city
A.D. 400–500

Late city
A.D. 500–900

Marsh

Gulf of Mexico

20°N

NORTHERN AREA

YUCATAN PENINSULA

Laguna de Términos

Uxmal

Caribbean Sea

Palenque

Usumacinta R.

Grijalva R.

Tikal

Yaxchilán

CENTRAL AREA

L. de Izabal

15°N

SOUTHERN AREA

Izapa

Kaminaljuyú

Motagua R.

Copán

PACIFIC OCEAN

0   50   100 mi.

0   50   100 km

Bonne's Projection

90°W

the city, the Maya usually built tall limestone pyramids that were surrounded by large, open plazas. At the top of the pyramids they built temples. The Mayan priest-kings climbed the steps of the pyramids to perform religious ceremonies at these temples. ■

Find Copan on the map. Look at the Copan ball court below. Guess the size of the buildings by comparing them with the car in the background.

■ *What were Mayan cities like?*

An Economy Based on Agriculture

■ *What techniques enabled highland and lowland farmers to become more efficient?*

▼ *Mayan farmers built flat terraces on the slopes of the highlands to stop topsoil from being washed downhill. They built canals that descended the hills. The canals were an efficient way to provide water for irrigating the crops in the terraces.*

As the population of Mayan cities increased, farmers had to produce more food. To meet this demand, they devised ways to farm hillsides and other land that they had not been able to farm before. You can see in the diagram below that the Maya built flat terraces into the slopes of the highlands. In the wet lowlands, they built raised fields to improve drainage and, thus, water fields without flooding them. In densely forested areas, they burned off vegetation to clear land.

In the hot, dry region of the lowlands, where the soil was thin, the Maya used yet another technique. They scooped rich soil from the banks and the bottom of rivers and spread this over the rocky plains to create farmland. They also dug canals and moats to bring water to dry areas. Using these techniques, the Maya grew their crops of maize, beans, avocados, melons, and squash.

As the Maya became more efficient farmers, they developed a surplus of food. They traded their excess food and other products with other peoples living in Central America and Mexico. Mayan traders carried their goods on foot or in dugout canoes to places as far away as present-day Mexico City. In this way, they obtained things they could not produce themselves. For instance, they traded salt, honey, finely decorated cotton, and jaguar pelts with people in regions we know today as Guatemala and Honduras. In return, they received jade, brightly colored bird feathers, and cacao beans. From jade they carved jewelry and statues. They used the cacao beans to make chocolate and also as a form of money in trade. ■

High ground

Irrigation channel

Topsoil
Small, smooth gravel
Large, coarse gravel
Clay
Cobblestone base

Drainage channel

Field of level soil

Embankment

Limestone mountainside

Priests as Kings

The Maya worshiped many gods and believed their gods controlled the sun, rain, and other elements of nature. They sought to please the gods, hoping in return they would be blessed with good weather and bountiful harvests. They also worshiped their rulers, because they believed their rulers could influence the gods.

The Maya told about their rulers in hieroglyphs painted on tomb walls and carved into stone **steles,** or columns. One such ruler, named Pacal, began ruling the city-state Palenque at the age of six, with help from his mother. In A.D. 65, when he turned 12, he became king in his own right. During his 68-year reign, the city of Palenque flourished.

From pictures carved on the walls of Pacal's tomb, scholars have concluded that Pacal, like other Mayan rulers, was a priest as well as a warrior and ruler. As priests, Mayan kings sacrificed food, animals, and even human beings to please the gods. Sometimes the priest-kings pierced their own skin and shed their own sacred blood in the belief that this would keep their society healthy and productive. ◼

◄ *This Mayan death mask from about A.D. 700 was fashioned out of pieces of jade cemented together. The eyes are made of seashells. The Maya covered their king's face when he went to live with the gods.*

◼ *What do we know about Mayan rulers?*

Mayan Achievements

The Mayan civilization developed many cultural achievements, such as a number system and a writing system of hieroglyphs like those on the stele at the right. The priest-kings also created two calendars to record and plan their years. To learn more about the Mayan calendars, read A Closer Look on page 408.

The number system enabled the priest-kings

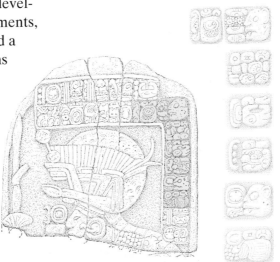

◄ *Mayan hieroglyphs are read from left to right, top to bottom. Scholars think this stele describes a person named Jaguar Claw, who is about to be sacrificed. The person shown here is probably the ruler of the Mayan city of Dos Pilas.*

The Mayan Calendar

Why do people have good days and bad days? Why do crops grow well one year and poorly the next? The Maya believed it was because different gods ruled each day. By consulting their two calendars and using the right mathematics, Mayan priests knew which gods ruled which days. Then the priests had to figure out what influence the gods would have.

On the 260-day religious calendar, each day was given a name and a number. The name *Imix* meant "water lily," and represented the ocean. *Ik* was named for the wind, and *Akbal* was named for the darkness of night.

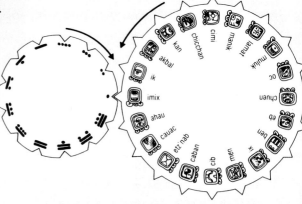

Historians use the diagram above to explain the 260-day religious calendar. Each name and each number was a divine being—two gods for every day. When you turn the wheels, you discover that the same name and the same number only fall together once every 260 days. Then the cycle starts all over again.

1 Imix—the New Year's day of the Mayan 260-day year

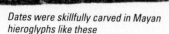

Dates were skillfully carved in Mayan hieroglyphs like these

Mayan priests interpreted the mood of the gods. If the gods on a particular day were grouchy—look out!

The other Mayan calendar was based on the earth's orbit around the sun and had 365 days like ours. Each of these days had a god, too. This calendar had 18 months of 20 days each, plus 5 extra days. It was considered bad luck to do anything on those 5 days, so people did very little. They didn't even eat!

Adapting to the Land

The Tiwanakans and Moche developed different ways to grow their crops that were well suited to their different environments. Look at the cross-sectional map below to get a sense of the terrain and elevation in the Tiwanakan and Moche regions.

Tiwanakan Adaptations

On the high plateau where the Tiwanakans lived, the nights are cold and the daylight sun is scorching. Water is scarce, except near the lakes. The Tiwanakans channeled water to their fields from nearby Lake Titicaca and from other lakes. They dug broad irrigation canals to enable water to flow around large raised beds of soil.

To make the soil beds, the Tiwanakans built a cobblestone base and covered it with a thick layer of clay. They poured on top of this three layers of gravel, each finer than the next. Finally, they covered the entire mound with a rich layer of soil. These raised beds provided a quality of both irrigation and drainage that today's technology cannot surpass.

The canals around the beds not only provided water for the plants but also protected them from the killing nightly frosts. Water and algae in the canals absorbed the sun's heat during the day and then radiated that warmth throughout the chilly nights.

The Tiwanakans could not grow maize, beans, squash, and other warm-climate crops. Instead, they grew hardy crops such as potatoes and grain suited to the cool climate.

Moche Adaptations

Because the land was too dry for farming, the Moche had to invent ways to get water to their crops. Using mud as their building material, the Moche constructed miles of aqueducts to carry river water to their fields. At least one of these channels was 70 miles long. Many are still in use today.

The Moche also found a way to grow crops on the steep slopes of the Andes foothills. They terraced the slopes into flat beds like steps of a giant staircase. In these fields the Moche grew corn, beans, peanuts, hot peppers, and squash. They also gathered shellfish from the sea and rivers and ate llama and guinea pig. ■

■ *Describe the methods the Tiwanakans and Moche used to bring water to their farmlands.*

▼ *Melting snow from the Andes forms a river that created the Moche Valley (previous page, left) leading into the Pacific coast. The Moche lived alongside the river. The environment below is called an "altiplano," or high plain. It is a windswept plain with a lake. Compare the elevation of the Moche and the Tiwanakans.*

Lake Titicaca

Tiwanaku (12,645 ft./ 7,857m)

ALTIPLANO

▲ *This four-cornered, brightly dyed Tiwanakan hat is made of llama wool. Hats like these were used by all for extra warmth at high elevations.*

► *Viracocha was the Tiwanakans' god of the sky and creation, and was often shown as the condor god with snake hair, as in this sandstone image.*

Living and Working

As the Tiwanakans improved their farming methods, their harvests grew in size. Their population also increased, and soon social classes began to form. Moche civilization also shows evidence of social classes.

Tiwanakan Lifestyle

Among the Tiwanakans, as in other early civilizations, the common people performed the hard labor. They also paid two types of taxes to support the government. They gave part of the food they harvested to the state and spent time each year working for the state. The women usually worked as weavers, and the men helped to build and maintain the raised fields and roads.

The Tiwanakan rulers ordered many miles of roads to be built to connect the villages and to make trading easier. To further promote trade, the government supplied llamas as pack animals in trade caravans and patrolled the roads to protect caravans from attack.

The llama caravans brought tropical fruits, wood, monkeys, and colorful bird feathers from the jungles of Bolivia. From Chile and Peru, they carried seafood, corn, hot peppers, copper, and gold dust. Outbound caravans hauled potatoes, grains, locally crafted textiles, pottery, and jewelry.

The holy city of Tiwanaku was the center of both trade and religion. Pilgrims came to worship at the Gateway of the Sun in this holy city. Archaeologists who have studied this carved gateway and other Tiwanakan carvings have deduced that the Tiwanakans honored the condor. This is not surprising, since great numbers of stately condors must have soared over Tiwanaku, seeming to watch over its land and subjects.

The condor is also associated with the ruling elite. Perhaps like the Maya, the Tiwanakans thought their rulers could influence the gods and, out of respect, treated them much like gods. Artisans crafted fine jewelry, crowns, pottery, and vivid textiles to honor them.What happened to these strong, creative people? How did their civilization come to an end?

Between 1100 and 1300, the city of Tiwanaku was abandoned.

Those who lived in and around Tiwanaku resettled in small groups on the mountainsides.

Archaeologists disagree about why people deserted the city. Some think a drought destroyed the city's fragile agricultural system. Others speculate that Lake Titicaca may have flooded and made the nearby fields unusable. Still others believe that outsiders invaded the city. Whatever the reason, by 1400, all that was left of Tiwanakan culture were ruins high in the Andes.

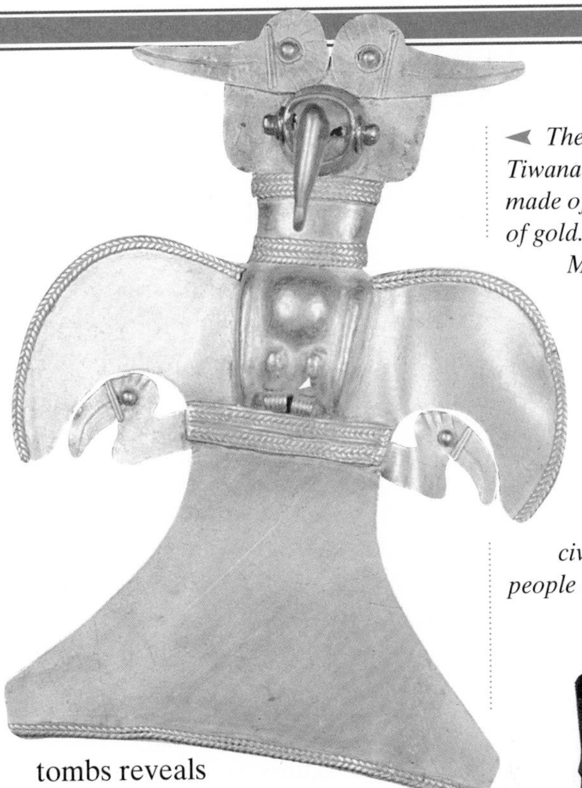

Moche Lifestyle

The ancient city of Moche was the civic and religious hub of the Moche civilization. It was located on Peru's Pacific coast in the midst of irrigated farmlands.

Much like the Tiwanakans, the Moche probably used great numbers of laborers from the lower class to do their work. These workers dug and maintained aqueducts and built great pyramids and temples. To build temples, the Moche mixed river mud and straw to form bricks called **adobe** (*uh DOH bee*).

Most commoners farmed or fished and hunted for food. Priests, artisans, warriors, and engineers were members of the elite.

We have no written record of Moche life, because the Moche did not have a system of writing. But Moche pottery recovered from tombs reveals much about their culture. Clay figures and painted pottery jars show people farming, cooking, weaving, and giving birth. These ceramics tell of war and sacrifice, of glorious rulers and many gods, but they do not tell us what caused the decline of Moche civilization.

Some experts think that the Moche culture was absorbed by other Andean cultures. Others believe the Moche were conquered by outsiders. But the truth remains unknown. In about 600, the Moche abandoned their city and moved to nearby areas. Six hundred years later, the Tiwanakans would do the same. ■

◄ The figure at left is a Tiwanakan condor god made of a beaten sheet of gold. The one-foot tall Moche pot below is decorated with the ruler's head at the top of the vessel. Examine each artifact carefully. What does each imply about that civilization, its people and their beliefs?

■ *Compare and contrast Tiwanakan and Moche lifestyles.*

R E V I E W

1. **FOCUS** In what ways did the Tiwanakans and the Moche adapt to the land?
2. **CONNECT** What did the Tiwanakan lifestyle have in common with other early civilizations in the Americas?
3. **CULTURE** What does Moche pottery tell us about Moche culture?
4. **CRITICAL THINKING** In what ways were the Moche and the Tiwanakans similar?
5. **ACTIVITY** The condor was an emblem of a Tiwanakan god. What symbols do we use in our society to represent important things? Make a list of modern symbols such as the American eagle and the American flag. Tell what each symbol represents.

Early American Civilizations

Recording Information

Here's Why

You may have made use of reference books, magazines, newspapers, or computer databases in the library in your school or community. To make the most effective use of such sources, you need to develop the skill of taking and organizing notes. Taking good notes will make the task of writing a report easier and will improve the quality of your reports.

Suppose you had to prepare a report about how the ancient Maya lived. Would you know how to take notes and organize them for your report?

Here's How

As you begin to gather information for your report, skim several general sources. This will give you an idea of some of the key topics and subtopics you might want to include in your report. You might begin by reading about the Maya on pages 404 through 409 of this book. Another general source would be an encyclopedia. From these general ideas, develop several questions you want your report to answer about the Maya. For example, you might decide to answer these questions: What did Mayan houses look like? What were they made of? How were they made? Revise and add to

these questions as you do further reading for your report.

Once you have several questions to answer, begin the note-taking process. Writing your notes on 4" x 6" cards will make it easy for you to keep track of your information and organize it for writing.

The text shown on the computer screen in the illustration is an example of a source you might use for notes. It tells about the homes of the Maya. This will be a subtopic in your report. Write the name of the subtopic on the first line, as shown on the

sample note card at the top of the next page.

On the note card under the subtopic name, list important details from the text. If you are listing many details about a subtopic, use a separate card for each category. Look again at the cards shown above. Notice that one card has information about how the Mayan huts were divided for use. What category of details does the other card contain?

As you make notes, be sure that you paraphrase what you have read. This means you must write the

Mayan huts were made from poles that were tied together with vines and plastered with mud. The roofs were made from palm leaves and the floor from packed earth.

5. **Mayan Huts**
   Single room
   Partition divides sleeping area from living area

5. **Mayan Huts**
   Walls of poles covered with mud
   Palm leaf roofs
   Packed earth floors

   The Mayans, p. 15

notes in your own words. Reread the information about Mayan huts shown on the computer screen below. Notice how this information has been condensed to three short phrases on the note card. The card simply notes the main ideas from the sentences.

Paraphrasing will help you to take notes more quickly and efficiently. It will also help to ensure that the report you turn in is your own work. You should copy directly from a source only if you want to use an exact quotation.

If you plan to include a quotation in your report, be sure you have copied the spelling, punctuation, and grammar from your source precisely. On your note card, be sure to put quotation marks at the beginning and the end of the quotation, so that you will be able to tell it from your paraphrased notes.

On each note card, include information about just one subtopic. If the source you are using includes information on more than one subtopic, put the information on separate cards. Keeping the information on different subtopics separate will make sorting your note cards much easier.

After you have written all of the details about one subtopic from a single source, write the source information on the card. Source information includes the source title and the page number on which you found the information. By recording this information, you make it easy to refer to the source again.

When you finish writing note cards, you might want to use a number-coding system to help organize your cards. Assign each subtopic a number, and write that number on any cards with notes about that subtopic. For example, the number 5 on the note cards above indicates that both cards contain information about the subtopic "Mayan huts."

You could also code your note cards with color. Use a magic marker of a different color to highlight each subtopic, or use note cards of different colors for each subtopic.

Try It

Turn to Lesson 3, page 404. Find the paragraph that begins with the sentence "As the Maya became more efficient farmers, they developed a surplus of food." Write a note card summarizing the information in the paragraph. Be sure to include a subtopic, notes that are paraphrased, and source information.

Apply It

Suppose you were writing a report about one of the groups you have read about in this chapter. Prepare five or six note cards on the material you find for your report. Remember to include the source of your information on each card. Organize your note cards using one of the methods mentioned in Try It.

417

Early American Civilizations

Chapter Review

Reviewing Key Terms

adobe (p. 415)   hieroglyph (p. 403)
altiplano (p. 412)   hunter-gatherer (p. 397)
codex (p. 409)   sedentary (p. 398)
elite (p. 401)   stele (p. 407)
extinct (p. 398)

A. Use a dictionary to find the origins of the following words. On your own paper, write one or two sentences explaining how each word got its meaning.

1. hieroglyph
2. altiplano
3. adobe
4. codex
5. stele
6. extinct

B. Each sentence below includes one or two key terms. Rewrite each sentence. Do not use any of the key terms in your new sentence.

1. Hunter-gatherers followed mammoths and other animals that have long been extinct.
2. The development of farming enabled people to adopt a sedentary way of life.
3. Fancy, complicated tombs found at Olmec burial sites probably belonged to members of the elite class.
4. The people who live on the altiplano today live a sedentary way of life, farming and keeping small herds.
5. Translating a Mayan codex requires tremendous dedication.

Exploring Concepts

A. The diagram below should show ways that each of the two groups, hunter-gatherers and sedentary villagers, adapt to their environment. Copy the diagram on your paper, and fill in four behaviors and characteristics of both hunter-gatherers and sedentary villagers. Use information from the chapter to complete the diagram.

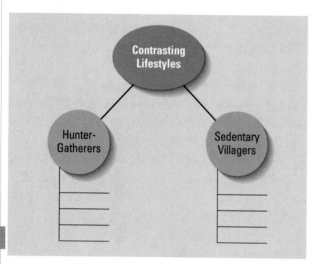

B. Write a sentence giving a piece of archaeological evidence that supports each statement below. The first one has been done for you.

1. People first came to the Americas from Asia. Answer: Tools found in South America are very similar to stone tools from the same time period found in Asia.
2. Olmec society was divided into classes.
3. In their rituals, Olmecs sacrificed people and animals.
4. Many ancient American cultures worshiped animals.
5. The Olmec traded with people as far away as 500 miles.
6. Mayan priest-kings developed two calendars, an understanding of astronomy, and a number system.
7. Food surpluses led to increasingly complex societies and cultures.
8. The Tiwanakans built raised beds of soil for farming that provided an exceptional quality of irrigation and drainage.

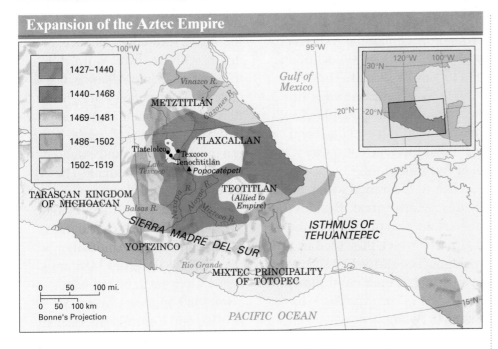

Adapting to the Land

The future looked grim for the Aztec. Because the land on their island was mostly swamp, they couldn't grow crops such as corn for food or cotton for clothing. Also, the timber and stone they needed to build huts was scarce on the small island.

The Aztec, however, learned to use what was around them to their advantage. They used reeds and mud from the swamp to make huts. They caught and ate birds and fish that lived on the island or in the water around it. From the tribes around them, the Aztec learned a method of farming that was especially suited to the swampy areas in which they lived.

This way of farming made use of **chinampas,** or "floating gardens." Chinampas are narrow strips of land about 300 feet long and 15 to 30 feet wide, almost completely surrounded by canals. The Aztec built these floating gardens around their central city. They used the rows of canals to tend the chinampas by boat. Look at the pictures of the floating gardens below. On these floating gardens, Aztec farmers were able to produce such vegetables as corn, squash, chili peppers, beans, and tomatoes.

▼ The Aztec were able to turn swampy ground into usable farmland with chinampas. Notice the types of soil that were piled in layers. Which layer do you think would have been most fertile? In the photograph at left, modern farmers are tending chinampas in south central Mexico.

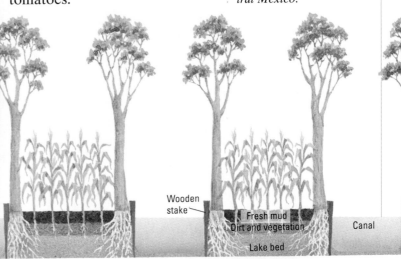

Wooden stake

Fresh mud
Dirt and vegetation

Canal

Lake bed

The Aztec used the canals around the chinampas to travel by canoe to the city of Tenochtitlan and to nearby islands. They also built three great causeways, or raised roads, to the mainland so they could also travel back and forth on foot. One causeway was over five miles long.

The Aztec traded with peoples in these nearby areas. Besides food items, they also obtained timber and stone, which they used in building. The Aztec had succeeded in adapting to their environment.

■ *How did the Aztec adapt to their swampy environment?*

Rising to Power

The Aztec not only adapted to the land, they also found ways to get along with their neighbors. According to Aztec legend, more powerful and more civilized tribes forced the Aztec to serve as soldiers in their armies. From these more powerful tribes, the Aztec learned to be skilled warriors.

As the number of Aztec warriors increased, so did the Aztec

reputation for military skill. In 1428, the Aztec formed an **alliance,** or union, with two other powerful tribes. This Triple Alliance increased Aztec military strength, and they began to build a huge empire that would one day cover the southern third of Mexico and extend into what is today Guatemala. The Aztec empire covered an area about 375 miles wide and 315 miles long.

One of the greatest rulers of the empire was Ahuitzotl *(ah WEE soh tl).* From 1486 until his death in 1502, he led Aztec armies in conquest throughout Mexico and Central America. He launched lightning-quick attacks that took his enemies by surprise. Ahuitzotl also oversaw the completion of the pyramid of the Great Temple, which he dedicated to the god Huitzilopochtli.

When Ahuitzotl died in 1502, his nephew, Montezuma, became the new ruler. Like Ahuitzotl, he led his warriors into battles of conquest. Under his rule, which lasted until 1520, the empire reached its greatest size, with a population of about 25 million people. ■

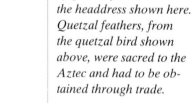

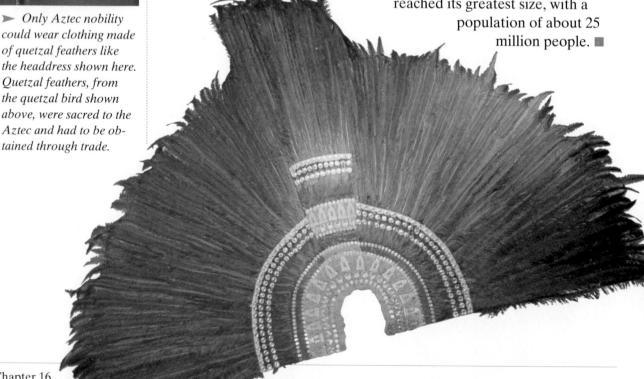

➤ *Only Aztec nobility could wear clothing made of quetzal feathers like the headdress shown here. Quetzal feathers, from the quetzal bird shown above, were sacred to the Aztec and had to be obtained through trade.*

Conquering and Controlling

Conquering a Region

How were the Inca able to conquer and control so many different peoples so far away from their capital? Superior organizational and administrative skills are a large part of the answer.

The Inca ruler first sent scouts to the region he wanted to take over. The scout judged the fertility of the region's land and the strength of its armies and defenses, and memorized its geography. Then the ruler and his military advisors devised a plan of attack based on the scout's report. Before attacking, though, the Inca ruler sent ambassadors to the enemy tribe to try to persuade them to join the empire peacefully. Usually, the tribes refused, and then the massive Inca armies attacked.

Once they conquered a region, the Inca made certain that it stayed under their control. They held both local religious idols and local princes hostage in Cuzco to discourage rebellion. The Inca also forced members of conquered tribes to join their army. The Inca offered rewards to new soldiers who proved successful in battle to ensure their loyalty. These rewards were taken from newly conquered areas.

The Inca stationed troops throughout their empire. If an uprising occurred far away from Cuzco, the Inca ruler could easily send a messenger to his army in that region to put it down. The rebellious people were then relocated closer to Cuzco or to another area where Inca rulers could keep a close eye on them. When tribes were peaceful, the Inca allowed the local rulers to stay in power. They also held feasts and festivals for loyal subject tribes.

The Inca also used other methods to maintain control of subject peoples. They made the Inca religion the official religion of the empire and they required all of their subjects to learn Quechua (KEHCH wuh), their native language. This helped promote unity in the empire.

Organizing the People

Inca rulers totally controlled the lives of their peoples. The Inca believed that their ruler was lord of all things—the land, the animals, the water, and the people. Everything belonged to him. A rigid social structure helped the emperor exercise this control.

The Inca had two classes—the nobility and the commoners. Most of the people in the empire were commoners. They lived in cramped adobe huts and worked the land from sunrise to sunset. This work was their tribute to the government. The nobles lived off the tribute but also served as governors of Inca subject tribes, political advisers, and public administrators. Government administrators organized huge public projects. Those commoners not needed for farming had to pay tribute by helping with these projects.

One such project was a highway system that spanned the

▲ *One of the first steps in organizing an area is to find out what exists there. The Inca used counting devices called quipus to keep track of everything from soldiers to food. The red strings were used to count warriors or record wars.*

▼ *Tribes conquered by the Inca generally had well-developed cultures of their own. This ceremonial cup was created by the Chimu people of northwest Peru.*

431

The Inca built many rope bridges that spanned steep-cliffed canyons and crossed over fast-flowing rivers. Today, many Inca descendants still rely on rope bridges. They often spin as much as 20,000 to 30,000 feet of rope from grass to build or repair their bridges.

■ *What methods did the Inca use to control their empire?*

▼ *The llama was very important to the Inca. Its wool, shown here, was spun into thread, which was used to make beautiful fabrics like the weaving below. These fabrics were used by all levels of society.*

length of the empire. Roads were built in the highlands and along the coast. When necessary, the roads included tunnels, causeways, and stone or even rope bridges. Built to quickly move the Inca army, the highways also helped transport crops and other goods throughout the empire. Scholars estimate that the Inca built nearly 10,000 miles of roads.

Under Inca rule, the commoners had few individual freedoms. They weren't allowed to travel without government approval. The government also decided when and whom they married. Marriage was encouraged, because only married couples were assigned plots of land

from which goods for tribute could be raised. ■

Working the Land

Though they enjoyed little freedom, Inca subjects rarely went hungry. The Inca's clever farming techniques allowed them to make full use of their varied lands. In addition, their strong organizational skills made them efficient producers and distributors of food.

Once the Inca conquered a region, they took total control of the land. They sent administrators, who were members of the nobility, to evaluate the geographic resources of the region. Then they divided the region's farmland into three parts. The commoners harvested one part of the farmland for government workers, one part to support Inca religious leaders, and one part for themselves.

The farmland varied greatly from region to region because the Inca Empire lay in and around the Andes. Some valleys lie as high as 8,000 feet above sea level. Others are only a few hundred feet above sea level.

Because soil, temperature, and other conditions change as altitude increases, only certain crops could be grown in

Inca terraces were such an effective farming technique that they are still used in modern-day Peru.

certain areas. In the low valleys, farmers grew maize (corn), beans, and squash. In the mountains, they raised llamas and alpacas for wool and meat. This growing of crops according to the height of the land is called a **vertical economy.**

The Inca were able to grow surplus amounts of food by using very productive farming techniques. One of these techniques was **terrace farming.** The soil on the mountain slopes in the highlands was thin and didn't receive enough rainfall. The Inca carried topsoil and gravel from the more fertile lowlands to the hillsides. There, they packed it into narrow farming terraces like the ones pictured above. To protect against drought, the Inca constructed elaborate canal systems for irrigation.

The government built huge warehouses to store surplus food in case of emergencies such as crop failure or war. The quipu camayocs recorded how much food was stored and where it was stored. Because the government distributed food and goods to the people, free trade and huge markets like those the Aztec enjoyed did not exist in the Inca Empire. ■

■ Why was Inca agriculture so productive?

Praying to the Ancestors

Not all of the commoners worked to produce food for the empire. Some commoners helped to build massive cities. To learn more about an Inca city, see A Closer Look on page 434.

Other commoners paid their tribute by making pieces of art and

Machu Picchu

Almost touching the clouds, the Inca city of Machu Picchu sits one and a half miles high on a mountain-top in Peru. Forgotten for hundreds of years, Machu Picchu was rediscovered in 1911 by explorer Hiram Bingham, who wrote: "It fairly took my breath away."

Clearing away the vines covering the city, Bingham searched for clues to its inhabitants. He made drawings of objects he found, like this knife with its little man pulling a fish on a rope.

Bingham thought that Machu Picchu must have been a special religious city because of the fine stonework. Archaeologists now think it may have been a kind of vacation resort for Inca nobles.

Climbing stairs was a way of life for the people who lived here. Over 3,000 steps connect the levels of the city and the farming terraces. Machu Picchu could only be reached by a log bridge on a sheer cliff. If enemies threatened, citizens could simply draw back the bridge.

Many mysteries about Machu Picchu remain. When, exactly, did people live here? Why were more women buried here than men? Historians still study Bingham's discoveries, like this jar which may have held a corn drink, to try to find answers.

434

jewelry from precious metals. Many of these precious works of art were placed in the palaces of dead rulers as well as the temples of the gods. In order to assure that their crops would grow, the Inca prayed to both gods and ancestors. They believed that there was life after death, and that dead rulers and nobility played a role in deciding the fate of the empire.

When an Inca ruler died, the Inca mummified, or preserved, his body. His relatives looked after his palace and estate. They believed the mummy's spirit would harm them if they didn't. The Inca believed mummies spoke to the living and to each other through priests. Mummies were brought out of their palaces for important ceremonies held during the harvest and planting seasons. A Spanish chronicler in the 1500s witnessed one of these ceremonies.

> They sat them [the royal mummies] all down in a row, in order of seniority, and the servants who looked after them ate and drank there. . . . In the fire they burned the food they had set before the mummies to eat; it was the same meal that [the family] themselves ate.

Inti, the god of the Sun, was the most important god of the Inca state. In all major cities of the empire, the Inca built temples for Inti, whom they portrayed as a golden disk with a human face. The Inca made animal or special food sacrifices to their gods. Only in times of crisis, such as flood or famine, did the Inca sacrifice humans.

Priests performed these sacrifices. In fact, priests played a large role in Inca everyday life. In Cuzco, the priests began each day with prayers, offerings to the gods, and predictions of the future. They predicted the future by "reading" the remains of animal sacrifices or flames in a fire. No matter how small the issue, Inca rulers often based their decisions on predictions of the priests.

The Inca were optimistic about the world and their place in it. They believed that, under the rule of their divine king, their empire would continue into eternity. The arrival of the Spanish, however, would prove them wrong. ■

▲ *Fine gold jewelry, like this necklace, was placed in the palaces of dead rulers. Inca children were often buried with dolls like the one below.*

■ *Why were mummies important to the Inca?*

R E V I E W

1. **FOCUS** In what ways were the Inca a technologically advanced civilization?
2. **CONNECT** How did the Inca method of conquering other tribes differ from the Aztec method?
3. **GEOGRAPHY** How did altitude and terrain affect Inca agriculture?
4. **SOCIAL SYSTEMS** What was everyday life like for the common people who lived in the Inca Empire?
5. **CRITICAL THINKING** Why do you think the Inca worshiped their ancestors?
6. **ACTIVITY** Choose a city that you feel best illustrates life in the United States. Make A Closer Look for the city you chose using photographs from magazines.

435

Two American Empires

Analyzing Elevation

Here's Why

You already know about topography, the natural surface features of the land. If you plan a bicycle route to avoid hills or to go around a lake, you are considering topography.

Studying topography doesn't only provide information about possible routes. Topography can also help you explore cultures and history. For example, you can learn about the Inca culture by analyzing the elevation of the Inca Road.

Here's How

Suppose you want to go from Lima to Jauja on the Inca Road. The map below uses color to show different ranges in elevation, or height above sea level.

Elevation is part of the topography of a region. The key beside the map shows the elevations represented by each color.

From Lima, you travel south for about 35 miles. The elevation during this portion of your trip is low and unchanging.

Now you turn to the east, toward Huarochiri. In the 45 miles to Huarochiri, you climb first to an elevation of over 5,000 feet and then to over 10,000 feet. This is higher than Mount St. Helens in Washington.

In Huarochiri, you continue east and soon reach an elevation of over 15,000 feet. This is higher than Mount Whitney in California.

As you leave Huarochiri, the elevation drops to the 10,000-foot range. In the 50 miles between Huarochiri and Jauja, you are never below 10,000 feet and are often as high as 15,000 feet.

Try It

Suppose you wanted to travel from Nazca to Cuzco, going through Andahuaylas, on the Inca Road. Use the map to trace your route. Use the vertical profile to describe the topography that you would encounter.

Apply It

Locate a topographic map of your state in an atlas. Use the map to describe a bicycle or hiking route between two areas that show either a very great or very small change in elevation over 50 miles.

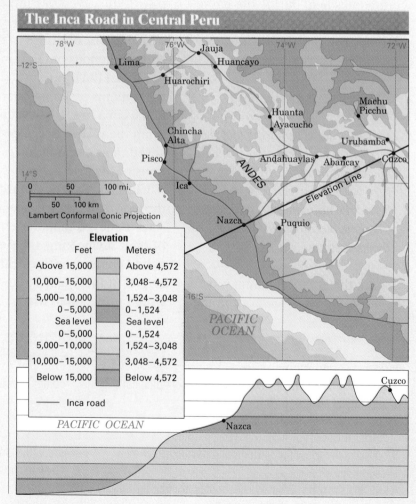

The Inca Road in Central Peru

Elevation

Feet		Meters
Above 15,000		Above 4,572
10,000–15,000		3,048–4,572
5,000–10,000		1,524–3,048
0–5,000		0–1,524
Sea level 0–5,000		Sea level 0–1,524
5,000–10,000		1,524–3,048
10,000–15,000		3,048–4,572
Below 15,000		Below 4,572

—— Inca road

Lambert Conformal Conic Projection

Chapter 16

empires. Not only did disease drastically reduce their armies, it killed off many leaders, leaving the Aztec and Inca even more vulnerable.

The Spanish conquest all but destroyed the Aztec and Inca populations. Spanish nobles took over the land and forced the Aztec and Inca into slavery. As slaves, they labored on farms and in silver mines. In some areas more than 90 percent of the population died as the result of the Spanish takeover. The chart on this page shows the population decline among the Aztec and the Inca after the arrival of the Spanish.

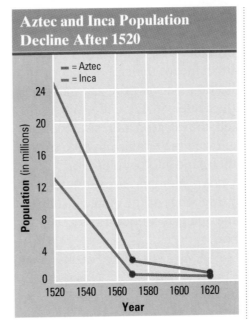

◄ *Note the dramatic drop in both the Aztec and Inca populations after the Spanish arrived.*

UNDERSTANDING EPIDEMICS

*I*t attacked people, beat them down all over the city and killed enormous numbers. Those afflicted lay about helpless, like corpses on their beds. . . . If they tried to move they cried out in pain." A Spanish chronicler describes the effects of a smallpox epidemic that killed millions of Aztec and Inca in the 1500s. An epidemic is a highly contagious disease that infects many people at the same time. Because of the numbers they affect, epidemics disrupt societies and help shape the development of history.

The Spanish had built up immunity, or resistance, to diseases like the measles and smallpox. Native Americans had no immunity to the Spanish diseases, which devastated their peoples.

Epidemics in History

Major epidemics have had significant impact on other civilizations. An outbreak of the bubonic plague, or Black Death, swept through Europe in the 1300s. Nearly half the population of Europe died. Due to the plague, life in both cities and the countryside was hard hit. Trade and production slowed, and governments found it difficult to raise money.

Epidemics Now

Epidemics still occur today. In the late 1980s,

Acquired Immune Deficiency Syndrome, or AIDS, infected approximately 1,000,000 people in the United States. Researchers are looking for a cure, but experts predict that by 2010, 1.6 million people will have died from AIDS. No one knows what the full impact of the epidemic will be in this country, but in some parts of Africa, entire villages have been wiped out.

In general, epidemics are much rarer today. Medicines now exist that prevent the diseases that devastated the Aztec and the Inca. But the discovery of such drugs came too late to prevent epidemics from playing a role in the conquest of the New World.

The Aztec and Inca, however, responded differently to the invaders. The capture of Tenochtitlan meant the end of Aztec civilization, because the city had been the center of Aztec life. When it fell, they ceased all resistance and allowed the Spanish to take over their land and people.

An anonymous poet described the feelings of the Aztec just after the Spanish conquest in 1521:

There is nothing but grief and suffering
in Mexico and Tlatelolco,
where once we saw beauty and valour.
Have you grown weary of your servants?
Are you angry with your servants, O Giver of Life?

The Inca, on the other hand, did not give up after their capital city was conquered. Resistance to Spanish rule continued for 40 years. Some scholars believe this is because the Inca rulers took much better care of their subject tribes. They provided their subjects with both food and land. By spreading their culture, religion, and language throughout their empire, the Inca bonded their subjects together.

The Spanish destroyed temples, artwork, and anything else that represented Inca culture. But Inca traditions survived. Today, some 20 million Inca descendants still speak Quechua, celebrate ancient religious ceremonies, and farm in small villages. The Inca people below live much as their ancestors did. ■

■ *Which of the following contributed most significantly to the defeat of the Aztec and Inca empires: disease, civil war, cultural differences, or Spanish military strength? Defend your answer.*

➤ *Both the Aztec and the Inca continued to exist after the Spanish conquest. The people in the near photo are descendants of the Aztec. Those to the far right are descendents of the Inca.*

R E V I E W

1. **FOCUS** Why were the Spanish able to take over the Aztec and Inca empires so quickly?
2. **CONNECT** Why did civil wars occur in the Aztec and Inca empires?
3. **HISTORY** Spaniards wrote most accounts of the conquest. Why do you think it would be hard for historians to reconstruct the truth about what happened?
4. **CRITICAL THINKING** Do you think the defeat of the Aztec and Inca by the Spanish could have been prevented? Explain.
5. **WRITING ACTIVITY** Write a news broadcast describing either the arrival of Cortés in the Aztec Empire or the arrival of Pizarro in the Inca Empire.

Identifying Values

Here's Why

Do you sometimes wonder why people act as they do? If you can identify the values that underlie their actions, you may better understand those actions.

When the Aztec and the Spanish conquistadors first faced each other in 1519, they knew nothing about each other's values. As the painting below shows, the Aztec welcomed Cortez with gifts, as they would a returning hero or a god. Compare the weapons carried by the Aztec and by the Spanish soldiers. What does this suggest to you?

The reasons why the Spanish were able to conquer the Aztec within two years are complex: technical advantages of cannons and muskets over stone knives, political instability of the Aztec Empire, and a disastrous outbreak of smallpox among the Aztec.

If the Aztec and the Spaniards had known more about each other's values, that might not have been enough to change the outcome of the battles. However, from your viewpoint, looking back into the past, you can see how their values influenced their actions.

Here's How

Turn to page 440 and read the section Two Empires Destroyed. Identify statements that refer to values of the Spanish and the Aztec. Explain the differences in values and how these might have affected their actions. For example, look now at the statement, "The two groups even fought by different rules." The Aztec valued the taking of captives in battle; the Spanish did not. Therefore, the Spaniards who were captured frequently escaped and could fight again. Because of the differences in values, the Aztec were more likely to die on the battlefield.

Try It

Use the text on pages 431, 432, and 442 to identify values of the Inca. List those you think affected the Inca's responses to the Spaniards.

Apply It

Write down the values you and your classmates hold in common on these topics: air pollution, environmental waste, diet, clothes, exercise. Compare your list with others'.

The Legend of the Lake

Retold by Douglas Gifford

Lake Titicaca, the largest freshwater lake in South America, lies nearly 4,000 meters up on the Altiplano. There it straddles the border between Bolivia and Peru. To the Inca, the lake was a holy place. According to legend, it was there that the children of the Sun first descended to earth. This story, set in a region where earthquakes are still a common occurrence, tells how the lake first came into being.

Long ago in the high plains lay a vast, rich city built by a proud and arrogant people. They were so pleased with their city and so satisfied with their progress that they would never admit that any improvement was possible. "We are the lords of all creation," they said loftily, "and all people must obey us. There is no city like ours in all the world."

One day a group of ragged Indians arrived in the city. Although they looked poor, they soon began to attract attention to themselves by prophesying that the city would be destroyed. "Prepare," they told the people, "for ruin will come by earthquake and flood and fire. The smell of death is on this city!"

"What nonsense," scoffed the city people. "Why don't you go away? We are the greatest of all people. Look at our buildings. There are none like them in the world. Look at our water system and irrigation. Where will you find any to equal them? We are a modern, progressive race: we know how to deal with floods and earthquakes. Go away with your old wives' tales."

The ragged band of Indians persisted in their warnings and eventually, tired of their nagging, depressing voices, the city people had them flogged and thrown out of the city. Only the priests were anxious.

"These were holy men," they said, "and who knows, they may be right. Perhaps they can see further than we can."

Some of the priests took the Indians' words so seriously that they, too, left the city and retired to their temple on the hill. There they lived as hermits, cutting themselves off from the city people completely.

"Look at them," mocked the city people. "What good do they think they are doing up there? All they can do is preach; they've never done an honest day's work in their lives. If anyone is doomed it is they. That hill is the very place for lightning to strike. How we'll laugh when that happens."

Then, one peaceful afternoon, one of the city people saw a small red cloud on the horizon. At first he could not tell whether it was a real cloud or just a puff of smoke from a burning house but it grew larger and larger. Soon it was obvious that it was a real cloud and that there were others massing together with it, red clouds and dark clouds the color of lead. When night came there was no darkness, for the sky and the earth below were lit up by a glaring red light from the clouds. An eerie silence hung over the whole land.

Suddenly, there was a flash and a rumble, then an ear-splitting crash as the earth jolted violently. Many of the buildings stood firm, for they had been well constructed of stone but almost immediately a red rain started to pour from the clouds and the earth shook again, more violently even than before. Building after building crashed to the ground and the red rain grew to a continual cloudburst. The carefully constructed water and irrigation systems were completely destroyed; mountain rivers were jolted from their courses and a great flood rose over the buildings of the city.

Today the great Lake of Titicaca covers the proud city. Not one of its mocking inhabitants survived and it is said that some died with their unbelieving smiles still on their faces. Only the priests in their humble straw huts were saved. Their temple on the hill stood firm against the earthquake and the hill itself rose above the flood waters. Today it is the Island of the Sun.

The ragged prophets, too, survived for they watched sadly from a high place as the waters rose and the city was destroyed. Some of their descendants became the Callawayas, the wise men of the valleys by the Altiplano, travelling doctors and healers famous for their skills.

Further Reading

The Captive. Scott O'Dell. A young seminary student joins a Spanish expedition to the New World. He joins the Maya and assumes the identity of a Mayan god.

The Feathered Serpent. Scott O'Dell. This book continues the chronicle begun in *The Captive*.

Temple of the Sun. Evelyn Lampman. This is a story of how the Aztec Indians tried to resist being conquered by Cortés.

Warriors, Gods and Spirits from Central and South American Mythology. Retold by Douglas Gifford. A collection of stories about Central and South American peoples.

Chapter Review

Reviewing Key Terms

alliance (p. 424) conquistador (p. 437)
calpulli (p. 425) terrace farming (p. 433)
chinampa (p. 423) tribute (p. 425)
civil war (p. 438) vertical economy (p. 433)

The following sentences contain clues to the key terms. On your own paper, write the key term each sentence suggests. Then use the key term in a different sentence.

1. Fighting between different parts of the empire was a problem for both the Aztec and the Inca empires.
2. Inca living at different altitudes grew products and raised livestock suited to different altitudes and conditions.
3. In the Aztec Empire, nobles lived off a kind of tax that could be paid to them in goods and services.
4. The Aztec converted swampy land to floating gardens.
5. Aztec families of different social ranks lived in each settlement.
6. Cortés and Pizarro were Spanish conquerors who conquered the Aztec and Inca.
7. To enlarge their empire, the Aztec formed a union with other tribes.
8. In order to grow crops at high altitudes, the Inca carried rich topsoil from low areas and packed it into flat-topped mounds of earth in the higher areas.

Exploring Concepts

A. Copy and complete the following outline using information from the chapter.

I. The Aztec
   A. Building an empire
   B. _____
   C. Fighting for the gods
II. The Inca
   A. Rising to power
      1. _____
      2. _____
   B. _____
   C. Working the land
   D. _____
III. The arrival of the Spanish
   A. _____
   B. Old and new worlds clash
   C. Two empires destroyed
      1. _____
      2. _____
      3. _____

B. Support each of the following statements with facts and details from the chapter.

1. Both the Aztec and the Inca used imaginative farming methods to grow crops.
2. Historians have a different way of learning about early Aztec history than they do about early Inca history.
3. The Inca Empire was larger than the Aztec Empire.
4. The Inca and Aztec behaved differently when they conquered other tribes.
5. The Inca used various methods for maintaining control over conquered tribes.
6. Lives differed for Inca nobility and commoners.
7. The Aztec and the Inca had different motivations for human sacrifice.
8. More social classes existed in the Aztec Empire than in the Inca Empire.
9. The Inca engaged in ancestor worship.
10. Conquistadors conquered the Aztec and the Inca for many of the same reasons.

Reviewing Skills

1. Refer to the map of the Inca Road on page 436. Use this map to trace a route from Chincha Alta to Andahuaylas. Then describe what this route is like as if you were telling a group of travelers what they can expect.

2. Study the overall network of roads shown on the map of Inca Road. In general, do you think it is easier to travel east-west or north-south on the Inca Road? Explain your answer.

3. Find the head Rising to Power on page 424. Reread this part of the chapter and explain what values the Aztec seem to have learned from neighboring tribes.

4. Tell how each of these sections of Lesson 1 helps to identify the moral values of the Aztec people:
   Social Classes—pages 425 and 426
   Human Sacrifices—page 427 and 428
   War and Religion—page 428

5. How might differences in the way conquered peoples were treated in the Aztec and Inca empires be explained by differences in the political values and objectives of the two empires?

6. Before the arrival of the Spanish conquistadors in the Inca Empire in 1532, the Inca were confident that their empire would continue on into eternity. Form a hypothesis to explain this belief. Be sure to give evidence from the chapter to support your hypothesis.

7. If you were planning a trip from one side of the Andes Mountains to the other and wanted to see where mountain peaks and valleys were located, what kind of map would you use?

Using Critical Thinking

1. Both the Aztec and Inca solved the major problem of feeding their people in spite of poor farming conditions. Modern farmers have also had to solve problems to grow crops. For example, the dry climate in the American Southwest presented problems, so farmers developed ways to irrigate crops. How does this solution compare to that of the Aztec and Inca?

2. The Aztec government allowed only certain goods to be sold in each market. There might have been one market for feathers and jewels and another market for slaves. Evaluate how this system might affect store owners and shoppers today in your community if all the shoe stores were in one area, sporting goods stores in another area, bookstores in still another, and so on.

Preparing for Citizenship

1. **WRITING ACTIVITY** Write a report in which you compare the way the Inca emperors ruled with the way our leaders govern today. For example, how would each type of leader accomplish large building projects such as the construction of roads, sewage treatment plants, or large public monuments?

2. **COLLABORATIVE LEARNING** The Aztec created beautiful hieroglyphic books called codices that told about various aspects of Aztec life. Create a codex to tell about life in your school. As a class, decide which aspects to include, such as school sports, the art department, the choir or chorus, the band or orchestra, the school newspaper, and various clubs such as language clubs. Then break into small groups to cover each aspect. Each group should decide what each member will contribute. One might research the various school departments for ideas about what to draw; another might draw the hieroglyphs; another might write translations of the hieroglyphs. All the codices can then be bound into a book for the whole class to use.

Unit 8

Europe: 1600-1789

The 1600s and 1700s were the Age of Monarchs, when powerful kings ruled Europe. Witness the splendor of Louis XIV's magnificent palace at Versailles, France, shown on these pages. But power and splendor would bring their own destruction. How long would subjects pay the high taxes needed to support a lavish royal court? New ideas began to spread. A government that does not serve its people must be overthrown, one writer insisted. In the late 1700s, such ideas began coming to life.

1600

Versailles, by Pierre Patel, 1668.

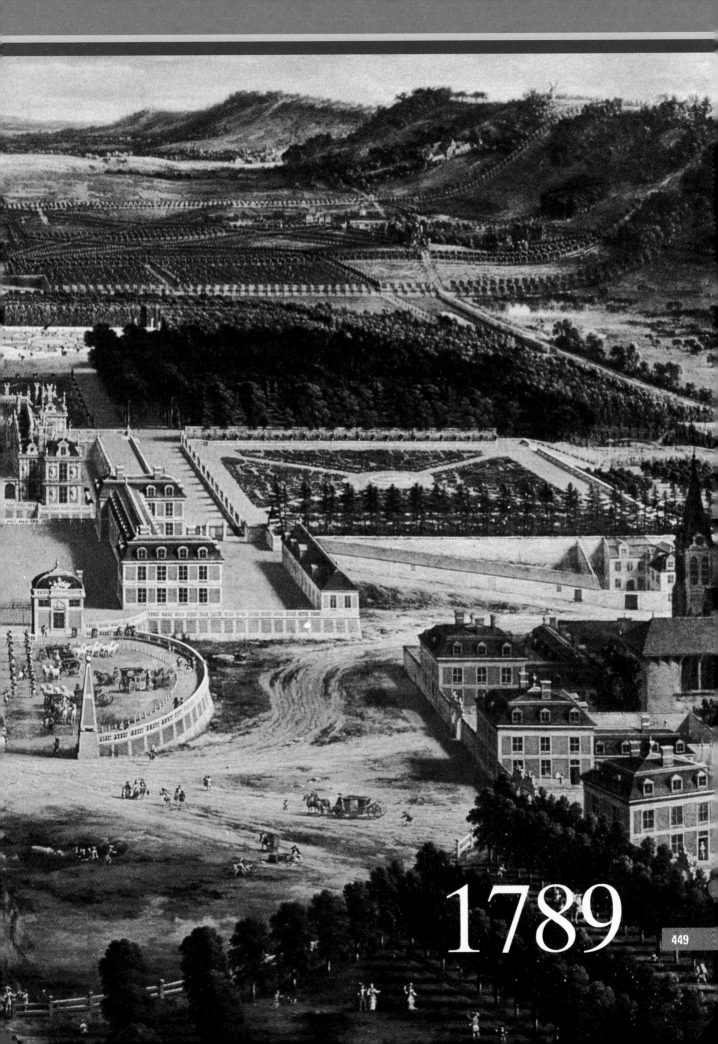

1789

Chapter 17

European Rule and Expansion

"I have loved war too much," confessed King Louis XIV of France. The period after the Reformation was a stormy time in Europe. Catholics and Protestants fought for their beliefs. Kings plotted against their enemies. Nations battled for land. Meanwhile, European explorers tested uncharted waters and claimed new lands. In time, the Europeans carried their disputes across the ocean to the New World.

During the 1500s, Spanish officials in the Americas put Indians to work on farms and in mines. This emerald-studded cross was made of gold mined in the Americas.

1498 Portuguese explorers make Goa, a port in India, a center for trade and Catholic missionaries. This painting shows St. Francis Xavier sailing into Goa in 1542.

1400	1475	1550

1505 Portuguese ships attack key African ports and try to control East African trade.

King Charles I of England, shown with Queen Henrietta, lost a power struggle with Parliament. He was beheaded for treason in 1649.

In the 1700s, the kings of France held grand parties at the palace in Versailles. Women dressed in the latest fashions, such as this silk and lace gown from about 1770.

1661–1715 King Louis XIV outlaws the Protestant faith and wages war against England and Spain. This portrait of the king was painted on the lid of a snuffbox.

1625

1700

1775

1635 The Japanese shogunate bans European trade.

1763

L E S S O N   1

The French Monarchy

THINKING FOCUS

What part did religion play in French history?

Key Terms

- prime minister
- absolute monarch
- divine right

➤ *All three of Catherine's sons became kings of France. Catherine was the mother and unofficial adviser of Francis II, Charles IX, and Henry III.*

W ithin weeks after the wedding, it became known as the "scarlet nuptials," because of the amount of blood that had been spilled. But at first it had seemed like a chance to unite French Catholics and Protestants.

In 1572, Henry, King of Navarre, arrived in Paris to marry Marguerite, the sister of the Catholic king of France, Charles IX. Henry was a leader of the French Huguenots *(HYOO guh nahts),* or French Protestants, a small but fast-growing group that some Catholics feared would eventually control the government.

One person who had much to lose if the Huguenots gained power in France was Catherine de Medici, the mother of the bride. But Catherine was also the niece of the Pope, the widow of the French king, Henry II, and the mother and adviser of King Charles IX. She pressured her son to have one of the Huguenot leaders killed so that the others would flee Paris.

King Charles submitted to the pressure and ordered a few of his nobles to commit murder. When the plot failed, Charles's nobles spread rumors that Huguenots were seeking revenge against all Catholics.

The following morning, St. Bartholomew's Day, Catholics who

were convinced the Huguenots were about to kill them murdered hundreds of Huguenots in their beds. The Huguenots fought back, but in one month's time 20,000 Huguenots died. Henry, the new husband of the king's sister, was spared on the condition that he renounce his Protestant faith and become a Catholic.

Religious Wars Divide France

Since the Reformation began in 1517, Christians had a choice of being Protestant or Catholic. Making the choice often involved serious consequences, even death.

After convincing his French in-laws that his conversion to Catholicism was sincere, Henry returned to Navarre in 1576. There he resumed his leadership of the Huguenots and his membership in the Protestant church.

In 1589, Charles IX's brother, King Henry III of France, was dying without a direct descendant. The dying king named his sister's husband as his successor. Henry of Navarre became King Henry IV of France.

Henry's Second Conversion

But Catholics refused to allow a Protestant to rule France. So Henry took religious instruction, converted to Catholicism, and was crowned at Chartres Cathedral.

Both Catholics and Huguenots claimed Henry had given up his faith for political gain. But Henry replied, "I wish to give peace to my subjects, and rest to my soul."

The Edict of Nantes

In 1598, Henry met with Protestant leaders in Nantes (nants), France. Together they created a

document known as an edict, or order, that gave Protestants the same civil rights as Catholics:

> And we permit those of the so-called Reformed religion to live and dwell in all the towns and districts of this our kingdom and the countries under our rule, without being annoyed, disturbed, molested.
>
> Edict of Nantes, 1598

In 1610, a religious fanatic who did not agree with the edict assassinated Henry IV. ■

The Edict of Nantes allowed Protestants such as the Huguenots of Lyon to build a church and worship openly.

■ *Why did Henry IV issue the Edict of Nantes?*

Cardinal Richelieu Builds the Monarchy

At the time of Henry IV's death, his son, Louis XIII, was only nine years old. Louis XIII depended upon a council of advisers. By 1624, the king's chief adviser, or **prime minister,** was a cardinal named Richelieu *(RISH uh loo).*

From 1624 to 1642 he ruled France for Louis XIII.

Gaining Power for the King

Richelieu was both a cardinal of the Catholic church and a brilliant politician. His goals were to

These three views of Richelieu were painted as a study in preparation for a sculpture of him.

■ *Why did Richelieu want to limit the nobles' power?*

make the king the undisputed ruler of France and to increase the power of France in Europe.

Richelieu did not want the nobility to share the king's power. In 1626, he ordered the army to destroy the nobles' castles, except those border and coastal castles needed for defense against invasion. He felt that their castles gave the nobility too strong a power base.

Richelieu thought that the Huguenots also threatened the king's power. He personally led the French troops in taking the Huguenots' weapons. But he allowed the Huguenots to keep their freedom of worship.

Waging War on Spain

In the 1630s, Richelieu turned his attention to the Thirty Years War, involving France in this conflict. This war had started in 1618 as a religious dispute between the Catholic and Protestant nations of Europe. By the 1630s, it had become a political battle to obtain land.

Richelieu commanded the French Catholic forces to fight the Spanish Catholic forces. Since Spain and its territories in the Netherlands nearly surrounded France, Richelieu was worried about the possibility of Spain invading France. He was also anxious to increase French landholdings. Although France acquired more land through these battles, Richelieu had to triple taxes between 1635 and 1638 to finance the war. ■

Louis XIV Reigns Supreme

When Louis XIII died at age 42 in 1643, his son, Louis XIV, was only 4 years old. For 18 years, he was advised by Cardinal Mazarin, who had succeeded Richelieu as prime minister. When Cardinal Mazarin died in 1661, Louis—then 22 years old—announced that he would rule without a prime minister, although he would have advisers.

Louis was an **absolute monarch,** an all-powerful king. For the next 54 years, he devoted himself to his task eight hours a day (and often longer), controlling everything from court etiquette to troop movements. He described the position of monarch in a letter to his son:

A Huguenot cartoon shows King Louis XIV, the "Sun King," as the "Sun Avenger" out to bring death to all Protestants.

I *n a well-run state, all eyes are fixed upon the monarch alone. . . . Nothing is undertaken, nothing is expected, nothing is done except through him alone.*

Louis XIV stated the theory that he ruled by **divine right,** that his power came from God and he was responsible only to God. Louis XIV's great power earned him the title "the Sun King."

Nobles and Huguenots

The nobility of France could have challenged Louis's power. But in 1661, Louis began to build a new palace near Paris. Find out about Louis's life at Versailles (*vuhr SY*) by studying A Closer Look on the next page.

Morning at Versailles

All France revolved around the palace at Versailles, and life at Versailles revolved around King Louis XIV. Every morning a crowd of nobles gathered anxiously outside the king's bedroom. Inside, the ceremonial "Rising of the King" was beginning.

If the king woke up in a bad mood, the news spread throughout the palace in minutes.

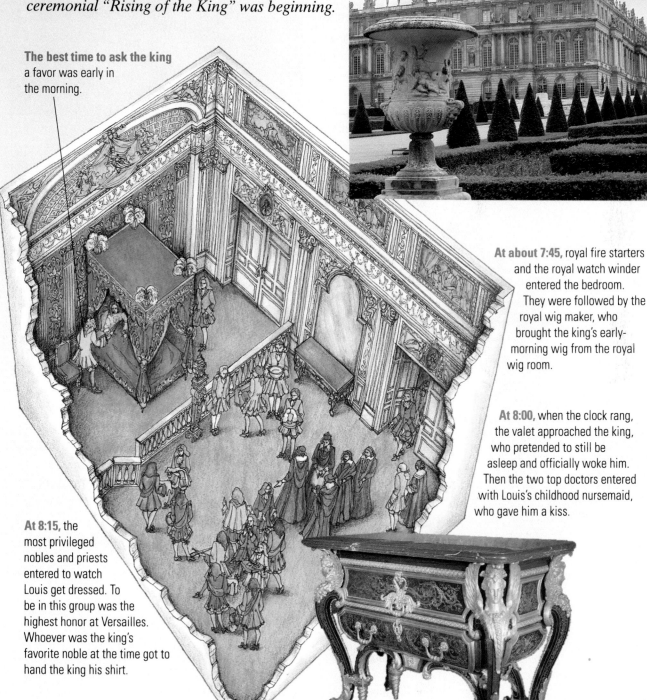

The best time to ask the king a favor was early in the morning.

At about 7:45, royal fire starters and the royal watch winder entered the bedroom. They were followed by the royal wig maker, who brought the king's early-morning wig from the royal wig room.

At 8:00, when the clock rang, the valet approached the king, who pretended to still be asleep and officially woke him. Then the two top doctors entered with Louis's childhood nursemaid, who gave him a kiss.

At 8:15, the most privileged nobles and priests entered to watch Louis get dressed. To be in this group was the highest honor at Versailles. Whoever was the king's favorite noble at the time got to hand the king his shirt.

This chest held the king's clothes for the day

455

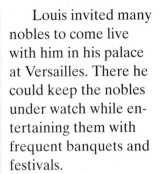

➤ *This portrait shows Louis XIV wearing his fleur-de-lis robe. According to legend, the fleur-de-lis represents a lily that an angel gave to Clovis, the first Germanic king to accept Christianity.*

▼ *A wig such as this was worn by Louis XIV in his later years. The fashion of the day was for younger men to wear dark wigs and for men over forty to wear white wigs.*

■ *In what ways did Louis XIV govern as an absolute monarch?*

Louis invited many nobles to come live with him in his palace at Versailles. There he could keep the nobles under watch while entertaining them with frequent banquets and festivals.

The other challenge to Louis's power might have come from the Huguenots. For in 1685, he abolished the Edict of Nantes. Since Louis was convinced he ruled by God's authority, he believed that his first duty as ruler was to uphold the Catholic faith. Therefore, he made it illegal to be Protestant in France. Nearly 200,000 Huguenots moved to other countries.

Peasants

Louis wanted to make France the greatest military power in Europe. Thus, he increased taxes to finance wars against England and Spain.

Peasant farmers had the most difficulty paying taxes, since they also paid rents to their landlords for use of the land they farmed.

The peasants lived in fear of bad harvests that would limit their produce and leave little money for taxes. Many of the peasants' noble landlords lived at Versailles with the king and were out of touch with the peasants.

By 1715, at the end of Louis XIV's 72-year reign, wars had killed many Frenchmen and the government was bankrupt. On his deathbed, Louis XIV confessed, "I have loved war too much." ■

R E V I E W

1. **FOCUS** What part did religion play in French history?
2. **CONNECT** In what ways were Louis XIV's idea of divine right and the beliefs of the Incas about their ruler alike?
3. **POLITICAL SYSTEMS** How did Cardinal Richelieu increase the power of the monarch?
4. **HISTORY** Compare the ways in which Louis XIII and Louis XIV ruled France.
5. **CRITICAL THINKING** Was building the palace at Versailles an appropriate use for the tax money that Louis XIV collected from the people? Why?
6. **WRITING ACTIVITY** Look at the picture of Louis XIV on this page. Write a paragraph describing your impressions of the personality of this absolute monarch.

money, Charles agreed to the Petition of Right. But the following year, he dismissed Parliament again when it refused to approve more war funds. For the next 11 years, Charles ruled alone and did not call Parliament.

In 1640, Charles needed money to fight the Scots, who were invading England. He was forced to accept Parliament's demands to get the money. By now, Puritan candidates had gained power in Parliament. They introduced laws to make the king call Parliament into session every three years.

In 1642, Charles made a final effort to assert his power. He ordered the arrest of five powerful members of the House of Commons. To defend itself, Parliament took control of the army. Charles fled north with his own army, and Parliament took over the central government. The clergy and most of the nobles, who benefited from Charles's religious policies and taxes, supported the king. Puritans and many merchants supported Parliament. Thus began the English Civil War.

Cromwell Leads Parliament

The war lasted seven years until Oliver Cromwell, a devout Puritan and a brilliant military leader, led Parliament's forces to victory. At the end of the war in 1649, Parliament put Charles on trial. They accused him of treason, charging "that by a tyrannical power he had endeavoured to overthrow the rights and liberties of this people." Charles claimed that, because he was king, no court had authority over him. Nevertheless, Parliament found him guilty and ordered him beheaded.

For the next four years, Cromwell and a Parliament dominated by Puritans ran the government. The leaders called the nation a **commonwealth,** because the government was a group working for the common good of all people.

However, in 1653, Cromwell was angered by the failure of Parliament to adopt proposed reforms. He responded by dismissing Parliament and abolishing the commonwealth. He then formed a new government, called the Protectorate, gave himself the title Lord Protector, and continued to rule England.

Cromwell ruled much like a military dictator. He imposed his Puritan values on England, limiting freedom of the press and enforcing strict moral standards. He

▲ *A memorial locket picturing Charles I contains a piece of linen stained with his blood.*

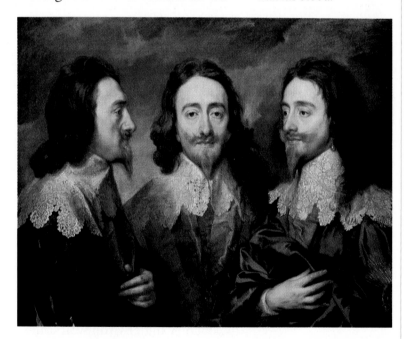

prohibited gambling, horse racing, dancing on the village greens, fancy dress, and going to the theater. Because of such harsh policies, the public hated him as much as they ever hated Charles. However, Cromwell still controlled the military.

▲ *This is a portrait of Charles I in three poses. Studies of this type were usually done in preparation for a sculpture of the model.*

1624–1649 Charles I

1625

1649–1658 Oliver Cromwell

1650

1658–1660
Richard Cromwell

1660–1685 Charles II

■ *Why did Charles I and Parliament quarrel?*

When Cromwell died in 1658, his son, Richard, attempted to run the country. But Richard did not have the leadership ability to manage the new government, and in 1659, Parliament took sole control of the government. By that time, the English were weary of political and religious conflict but were still in need of a leader. So in 1660, Parliament invited Charles, the son of the executed king, to return from exile in France to become King Charles II. ■

The Glorious Revolution

Historians call this return to monarchy the Restoration. It was not an absolute monarchy, however. When Charles II became king, the authority to govern was divided more equally between the monarch and Parliament.

A Period of Uncertainty

After what happened to his father, Charles II knew better than to try to force Parliament to do as he willed. He ruled England peaceably for 25 years. During his reign, many people rejected the Puritan ways that had dominated the country under Cromwell's rule. Parliament restored the Church of England as the state church and passed laws restricting the religious practices of Puritans, preventing them from assembling in groups of five or more persons.

After Charles II died in 1685, he was succeeded by his brother, King James II. However, at the age of 25, James had converted to Catholicism. Many in England feared that he would try to make England Catholic again. He did appoint Catholics to public office, against Parliament's wishes. He also stationed soldiers near London to scare Parliament.

To many, it looked as if James was preparing to rule as an absolute monarch. However, the people were willing to put up with James, because they expected that eventually he would be succeeded by his Protestant daughter, Mary. Mary had been raised a Protestant by James's first wife. Then, in June 1688, James's second wife, a Catholic, had a son. Because males succeeded to the throne before females, the new heir to the throne would be Catholic.

Parliament was unwilling to govern in partnership with another

1702–1714 Anne

1700

1689–1702 William; 1689–1694 Mary

1685–1688
James II

1714–1727 George I

1725

Catholic king. A group of lords invited Mary, daughter of James II, whom they had originally hoped would become their monarch, to become the new queen. They also asked Mary's husband, William of Orange, to be their king. William was the Protestant son of a prince of the Netherlands.

William arrived on English shores with an army of 14,000 soldiers and was welcomed by the English people. King James II, powerless, fled to France without putting up a fight. This became known as the Glorious Revolution because power changed hands without blood being shed.

A Constitutional Monarchy

Although William and Mary became joint rulers of England in 1689, they did so only after agreeing to accept Parliament's Bill of Rights. This document limited the power of the English monarch in a number of ways.

First, the monarch could appoint to public office only persons who were acceptable to a majority of Parliament. Second, the monarch could not keep an army in peacetime, nor could he suspend any laws without the consent of Parliament. Third, Parliament was required to hold regular meetings so that the king could never govern without Parliament. Finally, a Catholic could no longer become king of England.

With the passage of this Bill of Rights, Parliament finally had direct political power over the government of England, making England a **constitutional monarchy.** A constitutional monarchy is one in which the monarch's power is limited by law. ■

King Louis XIV ruled France for 72 years. During that time England had nine leaders.

■ *What was the Glorious Revolution, and why was it so named?*

R E V I E W

1. **FOCUS** What events led to Parliament's becoming a major power in English government?
2. **CONNECT** How did the power of the English monarchs in the 1600s and early 1700s compare with the power of the French monarchs during the same period?
3. **HISTORY** Why did Parliament want William of Or-

ange, rather than James II, to be king?

4. **CRITICAL THINKING** In what ways is a constitutional monarchy different from an absolute monarchy?
5. **WRITING ACTIVITY** Study the portrait of the young Queen Elizabeth I on page 459. Imagine you have just written a book of poems dedicated to the queen. Write a flattering description of the queen that could

463

European Rule and Expansion

LESSON 3

European Expansion

THINKING FOCUS

Why did European nations establish colonies throughout the world?

Key Terms

- encomienda system
- mercantilism
- charter

► *This illustration shows how slave revolts were handled on board ship and suggests the extreme violence associated with slave trade.*

Shielding their eyes from the blazing African sun, the men from the Portuguese ship approached the chief of the tribe. After an exchange of greetings and some gifts, the ship's captain got down to business: Did the chief have any slaves to sell? Yes, there were slaves.

With a signal from the chief, guards brought the slaves forward, chained to each other at the wrists. The captain inspected them carefully to find the healthy ones, for only healthy ones would survive the trip back to Lisbon. Then he pointed to the ones he wanted, and the barter began. When the dealing was finished, weapons and trinkets were exchanged for human beings, and families were separated forever.

On board ship, the slaves had to lie on planks that were stacked between the decks. Each was in a space only two feet by five feet. They were allowed to walk around the deck once each day for exercise. They ate twice a day if there was enough food. Those who rebelled on the way were killed by being tossed overboard. One out of six died anyway from disease, spoiled food, or starvation.

Slave trade was only one part of a trading empire that linked the small country of Portugal to colonies in Africa, South America, India, and China. In the 1400s, Portugal's Prince Henry, known as the Navigator because of his interest in sea exploration, led all other European monarchs in setting up an overseas empire.

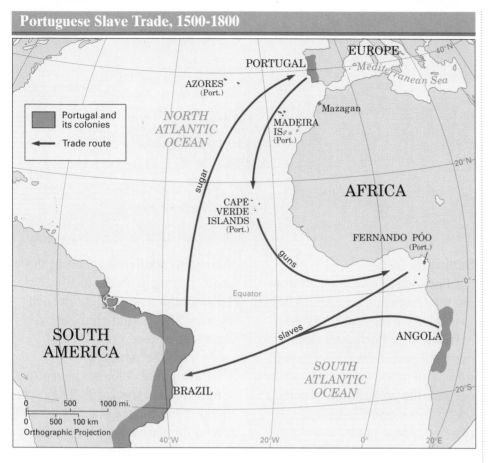

Portuguese Slave Trade, 1500-1800

Legend:
- Portugal and its colonies
- → Trade route

The exchange of goods and slaves among Africa, South America, and Europe formed a triangle of trade.

The Portuguese brought back cinnamon, peppercorn, and cloves from the Indies.

Growth of the Portuguese Empire

The Portuguese wanted to establish a sea route to the Indies. Most Europeans at that time used the term *East Indies* to refer to India and the islands southeast of it. The Portuguese were tired of relying on Italian merchants who, since the Crusades, had dominated trade in spices and other products from the East Indies.

The Portuguese also wanted to spread Christianity. By the mid-1200s, Muslims had been expelled from Portugal. The Christian government was eager to spread the Catholic faith to new lands.

Exploring the Seas

On their early voyages in the mid-1400s, Portuguese explorers cautiously hugged the west coast of Africa as a way of directing their course. By 1488, explorers had rounded the southern cape, or tip, of Africa and headed up the east coast. The Portuguese exploration voyages reached India in 1498.

In 1500, a Portuguese ship captain supposedly drifted off course and landed on the east coast of South America in an area known today as Brazil. However, he may have been secretly exploring lands south of where the Spanish had been. The Portuguese laid claim to a large area of South America for their king. On the map above, estimate how close Africa and South America are to each other.

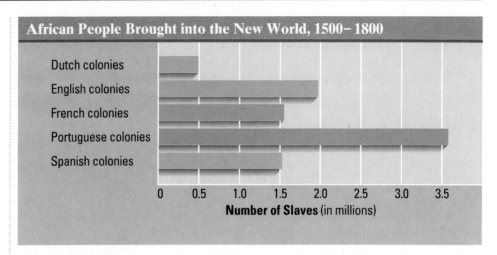

African People Brought into the New World, 1500–1800

Dutch colonies
English colonies
French colonies
Portuguese colonies
Spanish colonies

0   0.5   1.0   1.5   2.0   2.5   3.0   3.5
Number of Slaves (in millions)

➤ *All countries having colonies in the New World imported slaves to the Americas. The largest percentage of the slaves were brought to Brazil by the Portuguese. Which country was second in bringing slaves to the New World?*

How Do We Know?

HISTORY *We know about the Portuguese involvement in the spice trade through* The Book of Duarte Barbosa, *written by a government official in India between 1501 and 1517. He noted where each spice grew and the price it sold for in different markets.*

■ *Why did the Portuguese seek new trade routes to the Indies?*

Setting Up Trade

Portuguese merchants following the newly mapped routes began to establish a far-reaching trade network. The Portuguese government supported merchant expeditions with money, ships, and sailors, because the government wanted to set up a monopoly over trade. If the Portuguese held a monopoly, the government could make more money. The government got a share of the profits made by merchants, so when merchants made more money, the government also made more money.

The Portuguese set up their first trading posts along the west coast of Africa. Portuguese merchants stationed agents at the posts to trade with the local people. The merchants traded items such as guns, knives, and cloth. In exchange they received gold and ivory from the Africans.

Portuguese colonists began to settle Brazil in the 1530s. They set up large sugar cane plantations and forced the native people to work on them. Many native people died from diseases brought by the Europeans, such as smallpox and measles. As the native population dwindled, Portuguese traders brought slaves from Africa to Brazil. These slaves were then forced to work on the plantations in place of the natives. ■

Expansion of the Spanish Empire

In 1492, the Spanish government funded its first explorer on an expedition—an Italian, Christopher Columbus. By going west around the globe, Columbus hoped to avoid the Portuguese and gain access to the spice trade in the Indies. Columbus had no idea that a continent existed between Europe and the East Indies.

In a journal entry, Columbus described the lush lands he had just discovered:

I t seems to me that there could never be under the sun [lands] superior in fertility, in mildness of cold and heat, in abundance of good and pure water; and the rivers are not like those of Guinea, which are all pestilential.

Christopher Columbus, December 5, 1492

From 1492 to 1504, Columbus made four voyages to and from the

Americas. During each voyage, he explored and claimed islands, including those now known as the Bahamas, Cuba, and Haiti. He called these islands the West Indies and the inhabitants Indians.

The Encomienda System

News of Columbus's discoveries attracted many Spanish explorers to these new lands. By 1550, Spain controlled Mexico, Central America, part of South America, most islands in the Caribbean, and part of what is now the southwestern United States.

The Spanish government gave away land under an arrangement known as the **encomienda** *(ehn koh mee EHN dah)* **system,** named after a Spanish word meaning "to entrust." Under this system, a Spanish official received from his government a grant of land and all the Indians who lived on it. In exchange, the official was entrusted to house and feed the Indians and instruct them in the Catholic faith. For their part, the Indians were expected to mine the land and do enough farming to feed the people.

However, many Indians died from the hard labor the Spaniards forced them to perform, as well as from the diseases carried by the Spaniards. In fact, so many Indians died that the Spaniards, like the Portuguese, eventually imported black slaves from Africa to replace Indian laborers.

Mercantilism

The Spanish and Portuguese governments both followed an economic policy called **mercantilism** *(MUR kuhn tee lihz uhm)*. According to this policy, a country set up

colonies for the purpose of obtaining raw materials and developing new markets that would trade only with the ruling country. The colonies provided the ruling country with the raw materials they produced. Likewise, the colonies bought manufactured goods from the country that ruled them.

By 1600, vast amounts of silver had been shipped back to Spain. When the supply of precious metals declined, the Spaniards concentrated on agriculture as a source of income.

Spanish slave traders bought sugar, tobacco, and cotton and shipped them to Spain. There they traded these agricultural products for manufactured goods, such as cloth and guns. Then the traders took these goods to Africa and exchanged them for slaves to bring to the Americas. From 1520 to 1800, European traders shipped as many as 12 million slaves from Africa to the mines and plantations of the New World. ■

The Spanish used slaves to mine gold during the 1500s in South America. Slave laborers on plantations produced cash crops such as sugar, tobacco, and cotton (below).

■ *How were the native people of Mexico treated by the Spanish under the encomienda system?*

European Rule and Expansion

➤ *A painted cotton wall hanging from India, done in the 1600s, shows the Portuguese in India. The Portuguese can be identified by their European dress.*

⚜ *This coat of arms of the East India Company includes the Latin motto "God shows the way."*

Dutch, English, and French Competition

Because they were busy with civil and national wars, the Dutch, English, and French lagged behind Portugal and Spain in developing overseas trade and establishing colonies. However, beginning in about 1600, the Dutch began taking control of Portuguese colonies along the African coast, in the East Indies, and in China. They also began setting up new colonies in North America.

Trade in the East

Not only did the Dutch take over many of Portugal's colonies, they also took over Portugal's trade routes. The Dutch, English, and French founded large trading companies. Private investors joined together to finance these companies, such as the East India Company. They could invest more

money than the government or an individual alone could afford.

Furthermore, the government granted **charters,** official documents that gave companies the right to do things that normally only a government would do. They could maintain an army and navy, declare war, and govern new territories. The Portuguese, more limited in power, were no match for these well-equipped rivals.

In 1662, the English won trading rights to Bombay, an important colony on the west coast of India. In 1690, they founded another major colony, Calcutta, on the east coast of India. Meanwhile, in 1674, the French set up a post near Madras on the Indian south coast. England and France then battled each other throughout the next century for control of trade in

India. In 1763, English troops decisively defeated the French forces.

Colonies in the West

Spain's hold over its colonies in the Americas proved strong. Therefore, the other European powers began to establish colonies away from the Spanish on the Atlantic coast of North America.

England was the first to establish a North American colony. In 1607, the English made a permanent settlement at Jamestown. The London Company, granted a charter by King James I, provided the money for the ship and crew. Some people came to seek wealth, while others, such as the Puritans, came to escape religious persecution. By 1763, the English colonies had nearly three million inhabitants. Under mercantilism, people in the colonies exchanged raw materials, such as tobacco and furs, for manufactured goods from England, such as cooking utensils, tools, and cloth. Colonists were not allowed to manufacture any product that England could sell to them.

The Dutch also settled in North America. In 1624, they founded New Netherland, which covered parts of today's states of New York, New Jersey, Connecticut, and Delaware.

Many colonists in New Netherland made a living by trapping animals and selling the pelts to merchants. The furs were shipped to the Netherlands to be made into hats and coats for the Dutch. However, the Netherlands and England competed for the fur trade. In 1664, the Dutch lost New Netherland to England,

The English boasted the sun never set on their Union Jack flag. A jack is a small flag flown at the front of a ship on a jack, or a staff.

UNDERSTANDING COLONIALISM

Colonialism did not begin with the Portuguese in Africa in the 1400s. The Greeks established colonies along the coast of Italy in 750 B.C.

Why Colonies Existed

Colonialism is a policy in which one country forcibly takes control of the people and land of another country, known as its colony. The ruling country often uses the colony as a source of wealth.

A colony is a separate country; however, a colony is not a separate nation, because it does not govern itself.

During the 1800s, Europeans began to explore and claim land in Africa's interior. Africa was ruled by Italy, Belgium, France, England, Germany, Spain, and Portugal. By 1914, there were only two independent countries left in Africa—Liberia and Ethiopia.

Colonialism Runs Its Course

In the early 1900s, many African colonies began to demand self-government. In 1975, Portugal, the last European country with holdings in Africa, gave up its colonies. The last British colony, Hong Kong, will return to Chinese control in 1997.

In the Western Hemisphere, most colonies won their independence in the 1700s and early 1800s. In many cases the struggle for independent status involved a colony in a war with the ruling country. Freeing its colony meant a loss of economic benefits to the ruling country.

469

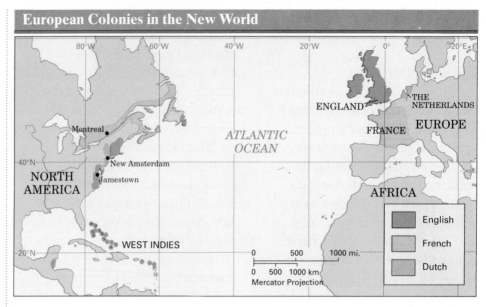

European Colonies in the New World

ENGLAND
THE NETHERLANDS
FRANCE
EUROPE
ATLANTIC OCEAN
Montreal
New Amsterdam
NORTH AMERICA
Jamestown
AFRICA
WEST INDIES

English
French
Dutch

0   500   1000 mi.
0   500 1000 km
Mercator Projection

➤ *The colonies increased the territory of the monarchs and produced new resources for Europe.*

when English warships entered the harbor of New Amsterdam and demanded the city's surrender.

In 1608, England's other rival, France, founded its first North American settlement of Quebec in present-day Canada. Later, Louis XIV did not allow Huguenots to settle there, because he wanted colonists to be loyal to the king and to the Catholic faith. Although sparsely populated, French territory included all the land along the Mississippi River Valley down to the Gulf of Mexico.

Conflict in the West

The English wanted this French territory as well as control of the prosperous fur trade in the

north. So, beginning in 1689, the English fought the French in a series of wars of expansion known in America as the French and Indian Wars. These wars were fought in both the British colonies and the French territories. They also happened at the same time that the French and English were fighting each other in Europe.

The English finally defeated the French in 1763. As a result, the American colonies felt less dependent militarily on the English, who had been protecting them from the French and the Indians. Now, the American colonists began to question the rules of mercantilism which limited their rights to trade and manufacture. ■

■ *Why did the Dutch, English, and French settle in North America?*

REVIEW

1. **FOCUS** Why did European nations establish colonies throughout the world?
2. **CONNECT** Compare the way the French and English monarchs felt about religious minorities in their colonies.
3. **GEOGRAPHY** What valuable resources did the Spanish export from South, Central, and North America?
4. **ECONOMICS** Why did the Dutch, English, and French set up trading companies?

5. **CRITICAL THINKING** Was the encomienda system a good way to manage Spain's colonies in the New World? Why?
6. **WRITING ACTIVITY** Suppose that you have been asked to establish a colony for your country. What type of site would you choose? How would you manage the colony? What would you do if natives already lived on the site? Write a proposal discussing these three issues.

Identifying Stereotypes

Here's Why

A stereotype is an oversimplified idea about a group of people. For example, "Scandinavians are blond" is a stereotype. It is oversimplified. Not all Scandinavians are blond.

Because they are often based on partial truths, stereotypes can be hard to recognize. You may have some oversimplified and only partly true ideas about people from a certain country or of a certain race, religion, age, or sex. Some stereotypes, such as that of blond Scandinavians, may be harmless; others are not. During the 1500s, Europeans made slaves of the peoples of Africa and the Americas. Because these Europeans accepted the stereotype of Africans and Indians as less than human, they did not treat them as fellow humans.

Relating to people as individuals rather than as members of groups will help you to overcome stereotypes. Many of the events described in this chapter would not have been possible if people of the 1500s and 1600s had been able to recognize and overcome the stereotypes they held about people of certain religions or people of certain races.

Here's How

The picture below shows an American family from the 1950s packing their car for a vacation. Look carefully at the picture to see what it tells you about the stereotypes people had about boys and girls at this time. Notice that the girl holds a doll; the boy, a baseball bat. Like her mother, the girl wears a skirt and dressy shoes. The boy wears clothing more suitable for play. Some stereotypes about sex roles that this picture suggests are that boys play active games and girls wear pretty dresses and play quietly with dolls.

Try It

What stereotypes about sex roles did people have during other periods in history?

Look through this textbook for pictures of men or women. Think about what the men and the women are doing in the pictures. Notice that many pictures include no women at all.

What stereotypes about sex roles do the pictures represent? Write a paragraph about one or two of the most interesting examples. Compare your observations with those of your classmates.

Apply It

Much of the humor in television situation comedies is based on stereotypes. Make a list of stereotypes that you see in a show you watch. Discuss your list with others in your class.

Chapter Review

Reviewing Key Terms

absolute monarch (p. 454)
charter (p. 468)
commonwealth (p. 461)
constitutional monarchy (p. 463)
divine right (p. 454)

encomienda system (p. 467)
mercantilism (p. 467)
Parliament (p. 458)
prime minister (p. 453)

A. Rewrite the sentences below using key terms in place of the underlined words.
1. A <u>ruler who believes in doing whatever he or she wants</u> has complete freedom of rule and answers to no one.
2. Louis XIV ruled by believing in <u>God-granted power</u>.
3. The <u>members of an elected group of representatives</u> made the laws in England.
4. England was called a <u>government where people governed for their common good</u>.

5. A <u>system that allows those of the faraway country to supervise natives</u> might not be popular with the natives.
6. Under a <u>government where a king or queen rules a country</u>, power is restricted by a constitution and laws.

B. The statements below are false. Rewrite them to make them true.
1. A ruler owes allegiance first to the prime minister who appoints him or her.
2. Colonies receive more benefits than the ruling country under mercantilism.
3. The only reason that governments granted charters to private investors was out of a desire to help businesses grow.

Exploring Concepts

A. Copy and complete the following chart on your own paper.

People	Main Religions	Countries Fought	Lands Colonized
French	Catholic Protestant (Huguenot)	England Spain	N. America India Africa
English			
Spanish			
Portuguese			
Dutch			

B. Answer each question with information from the chapter.
1. Henry IV of France took an important step for religious freedom. What was it?
2. Richelieu wanted to increase the king's power. How did he do this?
3. Louis XIV ruled by divine right, with no prime minister. What was the form of government?
4. Was Elizabeth considered a successful Queen of England? Explain.
5. What did Charles I do when Parliament would not approve his requests for money?
6. What was it called when William arrived to take over England and James II fled? Why?
7. Why did Portugal encourage exploration?
8. Were the Spaniards in the Americas fair or unfair rulers? Explain.
9. Why did the English, French, and Dutch establish colonies away from Spain's in North America?

Reviewing Skills

1. Read the first paragraph in the text section on page 458 of Lesson 2 that begins with The Reign of Elizabeth I. Predict what actions Elizabeth will take to solve the religious problems in England. Explain the stated facts and other knowledge that you used to make your prediction.
2. Under the encomienda system, the Spanish government gave Spanish officials grants of land with power over all the Indians who lived on it. What might you predict could happen when a person has this much power over other people?
3. How did the Spanish government view Indians? How might that have made it easier for the Spanish to adopt a policy of giving away Indians with land grants?
4. When there is a struggle for power in a war or over succession to a throne, people often view those on the other side in a stereotyped way. How might this make it easier for one side to fight the other?
5. Read pages 452 and 453. How did the religious values of the leaders of France affect the citizens of France? How did these values make it hard for the people to understand each other?
6. When reading about the actions of a character in a story, what skill would you use to guess what will happen?

Using Critical Thinking

1. When kings were absolute monarchs they caused much bloodshed and turmoil. Do you think it is possible for an absolute monarch to be a wise, fair, honest king or queen? Would an absolute monarchy work in today's world? Explain your opinion.
2. When a Spanish official received land and the Indians living on that land, he was expected to provide something in return: to care for them and teach them Catholicism. Evaluate the strengths and weaknesses of this system. Do you think people would want to live under this system today?
3. Choosing a religion in the 16th century was a dangerous business. If your choice was not the accepted religion, you might face death. Think about why some people chose to practice unpopular religions they knew might endanger their lives. Were they stereotyped because of their religious choices? Are all people the same who practice a certain religion?

Preparing for Citizenship

1. **WRITING ACTIVITY** Imagine you live in England during the Glorious Revolution. Today you witnessed the arrival of William of Orange accompanied by 14,000 soldiers. A group of lords invited him to rule peacefully with his wife, Mary, the Protestant daughter of James II. Describe the scene and express your thoughts about this revolution.
2. **COLLABORATIVE LEARNING** Your class will stage two debates set in England in 1642. Both debates will present the Puritans and merchants who support Parliament against the nobles and clergy who support King Charles. But the two debates will have different outcomes: the first debate will stage the actual outcome—the English Civil War; and the second debate will stage an imaginary outcome—peace. Divide the class into four sections. The first two sections' debate will lead to the actual outcome. The other two sections will "rewrite" history and show a peaceful outcome. In each section, have some students research the information (or create new ideas for the peaceful outcome), some moderate the debate, and some do the actual debating. You might create simple costumes and a painted mural background for your debates.

473

Chapter 18
The Enlightenment

To enlighten *means "to shine a light on." During the 18th century, the time known as the Enlightenment, great thinkers did just that. They shed new light on old ideas by using their powers of reasoning and helped bring about great change. Scientists made great discoveries. Inventors created marvelous new machines. Revolutionaries even overthrew kings and built new governments with the inspiration of Enlightenment ideas.*

Jean Jacques Rousseau (right) comes to Paris and meets Enlightenment thinkers in the 1740s. Rousseau's ideas help spark the French Revolution.

1717 At the age of 23, the writer Voltaire is jailed for making fun of the French government. Voltaire goes on to become a great Enlightenment thinker.

1700

1720

1740

1733 Georgia becomes Britain's 13th colony along North America's Atlantic coast.

1700

New Ideas about Government

Among the thinkers whose ideas were included in the volumes of *Encyclopédie* were three philosophes—John Locke of England, Baron de Montesquieu of France, and Jean-Jacques Rousseau of Switzerland. These three men concerned themselves with the question of what the best form of government was.

In *Two Treatises of Government* (1690), Locke wrote that government was a **contract,** or agreement, between the people and their ruler. The people allowed the ruler power as long as he or she governed fairly. Locke believed that if a ruler did not honor this contract, then the people had a right to overthrow the ruler.

Locke was willing to accept a monarch as ruler as long as he or she protected the rights of the people. Locke considered these **natural rights**—the rights every person was entitled to by nature—to be life, liberty, and the protection of property.

Baron de Montesquieu thought that government worked best when the power of the monarch was limited. Montesquieu argued that good government was best divided into three equal branches—legislative, executive, and judicial. If government were not divided, he feared:

> There would be an end of everything, were the same man or the same body . . . to exercise those three powers, that of enacting laws, that of executing the public resolutions, and of trying the causes of individuals.
>
> Montesquieu,
> *The Spirit of the Laws*, 1748

Rousseau criticized the idea of an absolute monarch even more strongly than Montesquieu. Rousseau believed that the people should participate directly in the government they elected:

> The deputies of the people . . . are not and cannot be its representatives. . . . Every law the people have not ratified [approved] in person is null and void—is, in fact, not a law.
>
> *The Social Contract*, 1762

Like Locke, Rousseau believed that government was a contract between the rulers and the people. He argued that the people could cancel the contract if they believed the government was not serving their needs. However, they could not sever the contract for trivial reasons. ■

▼ *Rousseau was an important philosophe during the Enlightenment. This playing card from the 1700s shows Rousseau dressed as a champion of democracy.*

■ *How were Locke, Montesquieu, and Rousseau alike and different in their philosophies of government?*

R E V I E W

1. **FOCUS** How did the Age of Enlightenment reflect a spirit of optimism?
2. **CONNECT** Why do you think the philosophes were critical of Louis XIV's absolute monarchy?
3. **HISTORY** What role did the *Encyclopédie* play in spreading the views of the philosophes?
4. **CRITICAL THINKING** How was the focus of the Enlightenment different from the focus of Renaissance humanism?
5. **WRITING ACTIVITY** Imagine that you have just been at one of the famous salons in Paris in the 1700s. Write a brief description of what you heard.

L E S S O N   2

Ideas in Action

THINKING
F O C U S

How did the ideas of the Enlightenment affect governments in Europe and America?

Key Term

• enlightened despot

➤ *Voltaire, the figure on the left in the engraving, often provided advice to Frederick the Great, shown at right.*

H e [the king] should often remind himself that he is a man just as the least of his subjects." With these words, Frederick II of Prussia, shown here with Voltaire, defined the new type of leader envisioned by the philosophes. An avid reader of the philosophes, Frederick especially admired Voltaire. Frederick even invited Voltaire to come live at his court. Voltaire must have thought highly of Frederick as well, for he called him the "Philosopher King." Eventually they quarreled, but not before Frederick had adopted many of the ideas of the philosophes. In an essay, he wrote:

I f [a king] is the first judge, the first general, the first financier, the first minister of the nation . . . it is in order to fulfill the duties which these titles impose upon him. He is only the first servant of the state, obliged to act with fairness, wisdom, and unselfishness, as if at every instant he would have to render an account of his administration to his citizens.

Essay on the Forms of Government, 1788

Attempts at Reform

Frederick wanted to use his power and wisdom to improve the lives of his people. Because Frederick supported the ideals of the Enlightenment while remaining an all-powerful ruler, or despot, he is called an **enlightened despot.** But

Frederick was not the only European monarch to adopt Enlightenment ideals. Catherine the Great of Russia and Joseph II of Austria were also enlightened despots of the late 1700s. Locate the areas they ruled on the map on page 481.

Reform in Europe

Frederick made important changes in Prussia during his rule from 1740 to 1786. His interest in recent scientific advancements resulted in the use of new crops, such as potatoes and clover in Prussia. He also encouraged the use of new planting methods and new equipment, such as crop rotation and iron plows.

As an enlightened ruler, Frederick also worked to increase religious tolerance. He welcomed Catholics into Lutheran Prussia and gave them nearly full equality. He even built a large Catholic church in Berlin and once said that he would erect a mosque if Muslims came to Prussia.

Under Frederick's rule, Prussia's legal system was vastly improved. The laws were simplified, and Frederick worked to ensure just sentences by trying to end the bribing of judges.

Elsewhere in Europe other enlightened despots supported reforms. In Russia, Catherine the Great ruled from 1762 to 1796. She tried to modernize Russia by importing architects, musicians, and intellectuals from western Europe. When the French government banned Diderot's *Encyclopédie*, Catherine offered to publish it. Catherine also restricted cruel punishment of serfs and allowed some religious tolerance.

Most progressive of all the enlightened despots was Joseph II of Austria, who ruled from 1780 to 1790. Determined to improve life for his subjects, he abolished serfdom and allowed peasants to own land. He taxed all classes equally and offered complete religious freedom to all faiths.

The Failure of Reform

Although these monarchs tried up to a point to help their people, most of the gains they made were small or short-lived. In Prussia, Frederick was intolerant of Jews. He made Jews pay special taxes, and tried to keep them from holding government offices. In Russia,

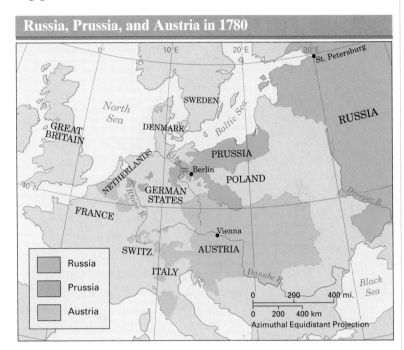

Russia, Prussia, and Austria in 1780

a peasant revolt caused Catherine to strengthen oppression of the serfs. And in Austria, nearly all of Joseph's reforms were reversed after his death at the age of 49. Nobles regained their privileges, and peasants lost their rights.

It was clear that the European nobility, who held the power and the money, were not going to give up their favored position easily. Since a monarch's power depended on the nobility's support, enlightened despots found it difficult to fulfill Enlightenment ideals. Montesquieu described this interdependence between the monarch and the nobles in a brief phrase: "No monarchy, no nobility; no nobility, no monarchy." ■

The rulers of Russia, Prussia, and Austria all tried to use the ideas of the philosophes when governing their countries. Where were these countries in relation to France?

■ *Why were the reforms of enlightened despots largely unsuccessful?*

481

Influences in America

Leaders of the British colonies in North America adopted Enlightenment ideas with more success. Two leaders, Thomas Jefferson and Benjamin Franklin, had studied European ideas and traveled in Europe. The philosophes' ideas impressed them.

Like the philosophes, Jefferson and Franklin had a wide range of intellectual, political, and scientific interests. Jefferson was a writer and a student of the classical languages, literature, and architecture. Franklin—a talented printer, writer, scientist, politician, and inventor—corresponded with many of the philosophes.

Since the mid-1760s, Jefferson, Franklin, and other British colonists in North America had been enraged by attempts to raise taxes. Parliament wanted the colonists to pay a share of the expense from fighting the Seven Years' War with France. The colonists disagreed. Since they were British citizens, they reasoned, they should not be taxed unless they were represented in Parliament.

Convinced that their rights were being violated, the colonists made a bold decision. In 1776, they decided to reject British rule. Then Thomas Jefferson headed a committee to draft a Declaration of Independence. On July 4, 1776, the Declaration was formally adopted.

In this document the colonists declared that "governments are instituted among men" to secure "certain inalienable rights, that among these are life, liberty, and the pursuit of happiness." These guaranteed rights follow directly from Locke's belief in natural rights.

The Declaration also stated that "governments [derive] their just powers from the consent of the governed." Therefore, when a government fails to respect the people's rights, "it is the right of the people to alter or to abolish it and to institute new government." This again echoes Locke's belief that the people have a right to overthrow a king who violates the contract between subjects and ruler. The American Revolution would be fought to defend these declarations of Enlightenment thought. ■

▲ *Some Americans, such as Franklin, were influenced by Enlightenment thought. Here Franklin, at right, is shown on a snuff box with Rousseau and Voltaire to illustrate that all three shared many of the same ideals.*

■ *How does the Declaration of Independence reflect the influence of Enlightenment thinkers?*

The French Revolution

In 1787, France's government was deeply in debt from supporting the colonists during the Revolutionary War. Poor harvests in 1788 led to food shortages, rising food prices, unemployment, and starvation. But still the government continued to collect taxes from the poor, while French nobles paid almost no taxes. The anger of the French people grew.

In 1789, King Louis XVI, needing money to pay off his debts, decided to raise taxes. He called a meeting of the Estates General. The Estates General was made up of representatives from three groups of people, or estates. The First Estate was the clergy, the Second Estate was the noblility, and the Third Estate included everyone else. Members of the Third Estate had virtually no power in the government but paid almost all the taxes.

A Struggle for Power

On June 17, 1789, the representatives of the Third Estate broke away from the Estates General and formed a new group called the National Assembly. They swore to meet separately until France became a constitutional monarchy. Some members of the First and Second Estates joined them. In need of a unified group to have new taxes passed, Louis gave in to the Assembly's demands. He then urged the rest of the nobles and clergy to join the Assembly.

In July 1789, Louis gathered troops near Paris. The people of Paris feared that he was going to seize power from the Assembly and go back to his old methods of absolute rule. In retaliation, on July 14, a crowd stormed the Bastille, a fortress-prison that held arms and a few prisoners. They tore down the prison, took the weapons, and liberated its prisoners. This event marked the beginning of the French Revolution. The French woman in A Moment in Time on page 484 is part of a group that is presenting the demands of the people to King Louis XVI.

Waging a Revolution

In August 1789, the Assembly began drafting a new constitution. They adopted the Declaration of the Rights of Man and of the

▲ *The poor in France paid almost all the taxes. This French cartoon from the 1700s shows a poor person carrying a noble and a churchman.*

▼ *Governor De Launay (center) is arrested by the angry crowd during the storming of the Bastille.*

Parisian Market Woman

*7:19 P.M., October 5, 1789
In the royal clock room of the
palace at Versailles*

Eyes
She's amazed by the bright, white room decorated with real gold. Never in her life did she dream that she would be demanding the king's help.

Apron
She had no time to change before she joined the huge march to see the king. She sells the fish her husband catches, and a fishy smell clings to her clothes.

Stomach
She's hungry, very hungry. It's not just because she hasn't eaten since early morning today. It's been weeks since she's been able to put bread on her family's table.

Hand
Trembling with excitement and fear, she is holding her skirt to bow to her king. She wishes her hands weren't so chapped from her hard daily work.

Pamphlet
Tucked under her apron, a crudely printed page demands, "We want bread!" In the market people say that the king's army is not letting wheat wagons into Paris.

Skirt
Her hem got caked with mud on the rainy 12-mile march from Paris to Versailles. The angry marchers waited for hours at the gates of the palace before a small group of women was allowed inside.

Citizen. At the top of their list of natural rights, they placed "liberty, property, security, and resistance to oppression." They wrote that "the source of all sovereignty [power] resides essentially in the nation" rather than the king. France, home of the philosophes, was beginning to put their ideas to use.

In the next few years, the Assembly began numerous reforms in France. For instance, the nobility and clergy now had to pay taxes. In 1791, the Assembly established a constitutional monarchy and extended religious tolerance to Jews and Protestants.

In 1792, Louis plotted with the rulers of Austria and Prussia to overthrow the new government. The plot was discovered, and Louis and his family were imprisoned in August. A crowd of Parisians heard that the armies of Prussia and Austria were advancing into France and went wild. Afraid of a foreign invasion and suffering from yet another food shortage, the crowd massacred over half the prisoners they had previously taken.

In September, the people ended the monarchy, and France became a republic. Louis was guillotined for treason in January 1793. After the death of Louis, a period of disorder and violence swept through France. This Reign of Terror, which lasted almost a year, was spurred on by fears that the European monarchies were attempting to defeat the French revolutionaries. Anyone suspected of treason or hostility to the revolution was imprisoned and, in many cases, was executed. More than 18,000 men, women, and children received the death sentence, including the former French queen, Marie Antoinette.

The revolutionary period ended when General Napoleon Bonaparte seized control of the government in 1799. He defeated the Austrians and convinced the other European powers to make peace with France. Although the revolution had been bloody and terrifying, it marked a turning point in French history. ■

◄ *The artist Jacques Louis David drew this pencil sketch of Marie Antoinette on the way to the guillotine during the Reign of Terror.*

Across Time & Space

The storming of the Bastille is celebrated in France on Bastille Day. Observed on July 14, it is France's most important national holiday. This day of remembering freedom and independence, much like the Fourth of July in the United States, is traditionally celebrated with parades, music, and dancing.

■ *How are the reforms that took place during the French Revolution representative of Enlightenment ideals?*

R E V I E W

1. **FOCUS** How did the ideas of the Enlightenment affect governments in Europe and America?
2. **CONNECT** How did the enlightened despots in Europe differ from the constitutional monarchs in Britain?
3. **ECONOMICS** What were some of the economic and agricultural crises that helped to bring about the French Revolution?
4. **CRITICAL THINKING** Montesquieu wrote: "No monarchy, no nobility; no nobility, no monarchy." What do you think he meant by this statement?
5. **WRITING ACTIVITY** Imagine you have participated in the events in France of July 14, 1789. Write a letter in which you describe your day to a friend.

To the Assembly for Protection

Elizabeth Powers

Fifteen-year-old Marie Therese Charlotte began writing the story of her life in a journal when she and her family were imprisoned in revolutionary France. The daughter of Louis XVI and Marie Antoinette, Madame Royale, as Marie Therese was known, gives us an eyewitness account of the French Revolution. This story is from The Journal of Madame Royale, *a book based on the real journal kept by Marie Therese. What are Madame Royale's feelings about the French Revolution?*

Roederer (reh DRAIR)
Tuileries
(TWEE luh reez)

Mme　Madame

M.　Monsieur

At midnight on the ninth of August, Attorney General Roederer and others came to my father and warned him that there would be another march on the Tuileries. He urged my father to take his family to the National Assembly hall that adjoined the Tuileries and had been, in fact, the indoor riding school of the palace. There we would be under the protection of the deputies. My father left the room without answering.

My mother sent a message for Mme de Tourzel to awaken my brother and me and bring us to her. We came, along with kind Mme de Lamballe who had been safely out of the country but who had returned from England to be with my mother in her bad moments.

It was so hot that the leaves had fallen off the trees, and my mother had not been able to sleep.

Now she said, "This is a conflict of forces. We have come to the point where we must know which is going to prevail—the King and the Constitution, or the rebels."

At this point there was shouting and booing in the garden and drummers were beating the call to arms. M. Roederer put his head out of the window. He said, "My God, it is the King they are booing! What the devil is he doing down there? Come quickly, let us go to him!" He and his men ran down the stairs.

My father was brought back, out of breath and red in the face. It seems he had gone down to rally his guards, but when he got there he did not know what to say, so he only made matters worse. Some artillery men had even dared to turn their cannon against their King!

My poor father. I remembered then what I had heard my mother say once to Mme Campan, her first lady of the bedchamber: "The King is not a coward; he possesses an abundance of passive courage, but he is overwhelmed by an awkward shyness, a mistrust of himself, which proceeds from his education as much as from his disposition. He is afraid to command, and above all things, dreads speaking to assembled members. He lived like a child, and was always ill at ease under the eyes of Louis XV until the age of twenty. This constraint confirmed his timidity."

After M. Roederer returned with my father he pleaded, "Sire, your Majesty has not five minutes to lose."

My mother said that we had a strong force in the palace but he answered, "Madame, all Paris is on the march." Then he turned to my father, who was sitting staring at the floor, and asked permission to escort us to the Assembly.

My father raised his head and looked at M. Roederer. Then he turned to my mother and said, "Let us be going." As he rose to his feet, my aunt came from behind his chair and said, "M. Roederer, will you answer for the life of the King?"

He said yes, that he would walk in front, but that there should be no one from the Court, and there should be no other escort than the members of the department who would surround the Royal Family, and the men of the National Guard who would march in line on both flanks as far as the National Assembly.

"Very well," my father said. "Will you give the orders?"

My mother said, "What about Mme de Tourzel, my son's governess? And Madame de Lamballe?"

Yes, he said. They could come, too.

When we reached the bottom of the great staircase my father stopped and said, "What is going to happen to all the people remaining up there?" No one answered.

Mme Campan had remained in my mother's apartments. We learned later that some men with drawn sabres rushed up the stairs, seized her and thrust her to their feet. But some of the Queen's other waiting women threw themselves at the ruffians' feet and held their blades away from her. Just then someone called from the bottom of the staircase, "What are you doing up there? We don't kill women." Her assailant quitted his hold on her and said, "Get up; the nation pardons you."

When we were under the trees we sank up to our knees in the piled up leaves. "What a lot of leaves," my father remarked, "they have begun to fall very early this year."

My brother, holding my mother's hand, was amusing himself by kicking the leaves against the legs of the persons walking in front of him. My aunt was holding tight to my hand and Mme de

Lamballe (lah BAHL)

Tourzel and her daughter were supporting Mme de Lamballe who was trembling so she could hardly walk.

When we reached the hall, my father made an address. He said: "I have come here to prevent a great crime from being committed, and I am convinced that I could not be in a safer place than in your midst, gentlemen."

The president of the Assembly replied that the King could depend on the firmness of the National Assembly, but that they were sworn to defend with their lives the rights of the people and the constitutional authorities. They also said that it was against the rules for them to proceed with their debates with us there.

They then took us to the minute-writer's office. This room was so low the grown-up people could not even stand up straight. It had two or three stools and a bench, and an iron grating separated it from the hall. Not a breath of air could enter, and we were compelled to spend eighteen hours in this steaming cubbyhole.

All at once the boom of the gunnery was heard and men were saying it was coming from the Tuileries. Then someone shouted, "Here come the Swiss Guards!" Soon we heard the rattle of gunfire. There were shouts and cries coming from outside and inside now, saying that the King's Swiss Guards had fired on the people—had lured the citizens and then shot them down. There were curses and shouts demanding the death of the King.

My father sent an order for the Swiss Guards to cease firing, but before morning more than a thousand lives had been lost.

All at once, to our horror, we saw some of the faithful guards and nobles being chased into the Assembly hall by rogues who struck them down without mercy. They brought in my father's own servants who, with the utmost impudence, gave false testimony against him, while others boasted of vile things they had done. These were followed by looters who triumphantly strewed silverware, cashboxes, letters, even our toys, and anything else they could pick up over the desk of the president of the Assembly.

We listened as men mounted the tribune to lie about and denounce my mother and father. They cried, "Death to the Austrian woman!" "Death to the King!" and "Death to the Aristocrats!" We heard my father, the King, deposed and his veto abolished.

At last some one brought us food and water. My mother took a glass of water; my father ate; my brother and I fell asleep. My mother did not break her fast until we were taken to the Convent of the Feuillants, which had been confiscated and where bedrooms were made up for us. Next day we were taken back and heard the King and Queen branded as oppressors of the people. We heard them discuss what should be done with the King and where he should be kept.

Feuillants
(fuh YAHNTS)

For three long days we listened until it was declared that the King was suspended from his functions and a new municipal government, the Commune, was formed.

It was decreed that the Temple was the only place to ensure our safety. We were to be conducted there "with all the respect due to misfortune." The attorney for the new Commune, M. Manuel, was to accompany us. The Temple—so-called because in olden days it had been the fortress of the Knights Templar—was as sinister-looking as the Bastille. It consisted of a small castle with a round tower at each corner, narrow windows, and an inner court which, we would find, the sun hardly ever reached. We were to live in this fortress.

Towards three in the afternoon, Manuel, accompanied by Petion, came to take the Royal Family away. They made us all get in a carriage with eight seats. Then they crowded in with their hats on their heads, shouting "Long Live the Nation!" They had the driver go slowly, as throngs pressed themselves against the carriage, shrieking, spitting, and hurling insults. They had the cruelty, too, to point out to my parents things that would distress them—for instance, the statues of the kings of France thrown down from their pedestals, even that of Henri IV, before which they stopped and compelled us to look.

We learnt that the guillotine, the official instrument to cut off people's heads, had been set up in the Place du Carrousel.

Further Reading

Fear No More. Hester Chapman. This story is about the mysterious life and death of Louis Charles, the son of Louis XVI.

Jacobin's Daughter. Joanne S. Williamson. This story about the French Revolution focuses on its leaders and the conflicts among the political factions of the time.

Marie Antoinette, Daughter of an Empress. This biography focuses on the life of the woman who was queen of France in the 18th century. It also tell the story of her mother, the dominating Maria Theresa, Empress of Austria.

Victory at Valmy. Geoffrey Trease. This is an adventure story that takes place in the early days of the French Revolution.

LESSON 3

Economic Changes

**THINKING
FOCUS**

*How did the agricultural
and industrial revolutions
change life in Britain during the 1700s?*

Key Terms

- agricultural revolution
- crop rotation
- enclosure
- industrial revolution
- capitalist

➤ *Gleaners are seen
hard at work in this painting by Jean François Mil-
let. Gleaning was
backbreaking labor. But
some families could not
grow enough on their
small plots for their own
needs. So they gleaned to
survive.*

The British farm women bent over to gather the gleanings, or the grain remaining on the ground after harvest. These women and their families before them had gathered gleanings from these fields, which were owned by an aristocratic family, for hundreds of years. The women's families farmed small plots of land. But they depended on gleanings because their own lands were simply too small to provide their families with enough food.

But these were perhaps the last gleanings that the women would ever collect. Parliament had decreed that large landowners could fence in and redistribute the

land. The women and those like them had staged demonstrations, complained, argued and pleaded, but with no result.

Where would they go in the spring? Perhaps their families would go to the city to look for work. Perhaps they could be hired hands for a wealthy neighbor. Neither future appealed to them. They wanted things to stay the same.

The Agricultural Revolution

The French Revolution was not the only revolution that occurred during the 1700s. In Britain two different revolutions would change life in Europe forever.

The first major change took place on farms. By the end of the

1700s, British farmers had learned how to increase the amount of food they could grow by using a number of new methods. These new methods were so significant that together they are called the **agricultural revolution.**

Improved farm tools like horse-drawn seed drills were eventually replaced by gasoline-powered machines.

The agricultural revolution began in Britain in the 1500s. It started slowly and gathered momentum in the 1600s. By 1750, when the population of Britain began to grow rapidly, the changes were well under way. Experimentation resulted in more food to feed a hungry population.

Crop Rotation

In medieval Britain, farmers had used a three-field system when planting their crops. Each year, they would plant one field with wheat or rye and another with barley or oats. They would not plant any crop on the third field, allowing the soil to rest. The next year they would switch which crops were grown in which field. Under this system, called **crop rotation,** the soil in a field rested every third year.

Beginning in the 1500s, British farmers introduced changes in crop rotation. In the 1600s, they began to grow new crops, such as turnips or clover, on the field that had previously been left unplanted. Such crops actually nourished the soil, making it more fertile. Now fields were productive every year instead of lying unused every third year.

Turnips and clover also increased the amount of fodder, or food for animals, that was grown. The new crop rotation allowed farmers to raise more cows, sheep, and horses than before, making meat more plentiful. More animals also meant more manure, an important soil fertilizer. The more fertile soil produced more food.

Farm Tools

Another change in farming during the 1700s was the use of more efficient farming tools. One such tool was the horse-drawn seed drill pictured above. Developed by Jethro Tull in the 1730s, the drill planted evenly spaced seeds at a consistent depth and immediately covered them with soil. Space was left between rows so that the ground could be broken by a horse-drawn hoe. In this way the soil absorbed more air and water, helping plants grow better.

Enclosure

Perhaps the most significant change accompanying the agricultural revolution was **enclosure** of land—breaking up large unfenced common fields into smaller, fenced-in plots. Traditionally, peasants held their land scattered equally in the three fields in their village. Once the grain in one field was harvested, poor farmers could collect gleanings from the lands. Once the gleaning was finished, villagers could pasture their animals on the stubble. They also had

Across Time & Space

Historians are not sure why the population of Britain increased during the 1700s. One reason for the increase was that fewer people were catching the plague and dying.

491

The Enlightenment

common rights to village pastureland and meadowland. Without these sources of food, farmers had trouble providing for their families.

But during the 1600s and 1700s, large landowners began buying up the holdings of small landowners and then fencing in, or enclosing, the land. Once the land was enclosed, the owner could farm it any way he liked. Landowners introduced new agricultural techniques, which boosted the amount of food produced on the same amount of land. But many peasants were left without land of their own. They bitterly resented enclosure but could not stop it. Deprived of land, many headed to cities to find work. ■

■ *What developments changed agriculture in Britain?*

The Industrial Revolution

As the population of Britain grew, the demand for goods, such as clothing, also increased. British manufacturers could not meet this demand using only the traditional method of making cloth by hand. In response, inventors began producing machines that could manufacture goods faster and more cheaply. Some were operated by people who had been driven off the land by the agricultural revolution. These improvements brought about an **industrial revolution,** a change in the way goods were produced and the way people lived.

New Technology

Like other Enlightenment figures, British inventors hoped to apply scientific principles to the problem of producing more goods. Many inventions in the 1700s affected the textile industry. Prior to the 1700s, spinning and weaving had been done with spinning wheels and hand looms. In 1733, John Kay invented a flying shuttle, a mechanical loom that allowed one person to do the work of two.

With the flying shuttle, workers used up thread so quickly that a better machine was needed for spinning. In 1764, James Hargreaves invented the jenny, a device that spun eight spools of thread at once. Between 1750 and 1800, England went from importing 3 million to 50 million pounds of raw cotton per year to make cloth.

▼ Adam Smith's idea of specialization of labor can be applied to making shoes. By specializing in a particular step, each worker becomes faster at it. Also, dividing the process into simple steps opens the door to mechanization. The cotton gin (right), invented by Eli Whitney in 1793, separated cotton fiber from seed 50 times faster than workers could do it by hand.

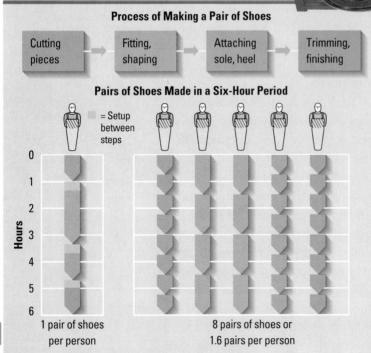

Specialization of Labor

Process of Making a Pair of Shoes

Cutting pieces → Fitting, shaping → Attaching sole, heel → Trimming, finishing

Pairs of Shoes Made in a Six-Hour Period

■ = Setup between steps

Hours: 0, 1, 2, 3, 4, 5, 6

1 pair of shoes per person

8 pairs of shoes or 1.6 pairs per person

Capital and Labor

Capital and labor, or money and workers, were two of the important elements in the industrial revolution. The British government encouraged individuals called **capitalists** to invest their money in new industries. Competition among individual producers led them to produce the best product at the cheapest price. It was important for producers to do this, so that they would have the most customers and make the greatest profit.

A British economist named Adam Smith wrote about some of the changes in the economy. Smith showed how having workers specialize in a task could increase the number of goods they could produce. The chart on page 492 illustrates Smith's argument.

Conditions of Life

Although the new industries provided jobs, they damaged the living and working conditions of many laborers. Workers—even children under 10 years of age—spent 12 or 14 hours, six days a week, performing monotonous tasks. Some children were crippled by unsafe machines.

The increase in the number of people in British cities caused new problems. So many people burned coal for heat that the skies turned black with smoke. Charles Dickens described the intense overcrowding and dirtiness of these cities:

> *I*t was a town of machinery and tall chimneys, out of which interminable [never ending] serpents of smoke trailed themselves for ever and ever. . . . It had a black canal in it, and a river that ran purple with ill-smelling dye, and vast piles of buildings.
>
> Charles Dickens, *Hard Times*

For better or worse, the industrial revolution made Britain the workshop of the world. ■

The first steam-powered loom was invented by Edmund Cartwright in 1786. Early power looms were most effective for weaving tough cotton fibers.

What conditions contributed to the growth of industry in the late 1700s?

REVIEW

1. **FOCUS** How did the agricultural and industrial revolutions change life in Britain during the 1700s?
2. **CONNECT** How did crop rotation in Britain during the 1700s differ from that used during the Middle Ages?
3. **ECONOMICS** How did an increase in the population during the 1700s help bring about changes in agriculture and industry?
4. **CRITICAL THINKING** If you had been a British peasant in the late 1700s, would you have preferred to remain a farmer or work in a textile factory? Explain.
5. **WRITING ACTIVITY** Referring to the text and a dictionary, write a definition of *capitalist* in your own words, and give an example from the present or the past.

493

Industrial Growth

> The city's destiny and expanse finally bred a sense of captivity. . . . Its ugliness finally obscured its grandeur; the wretchedness of most of its inhabitants mocked the luxury of the few. In the workers' quarters it was a sink of vice and disease. . . . It was crowded with rootless, anonymous strangers.
>
> Richard D. Altick, 20th-century historian

▼ *The textile factory below was one of the first examples of industrial growth in England. Notice the huge machines in this cloth factory. Modern industrial growth often results in other community projects, such as schools, museums, and shopping centers like the one at the right.*

Background

The English agricultural and industrial revolutions led to higher living standards and new expectations and desires. Thousands of people moved from rural areas to cities in search of work and a brighter future. The cities, however, were not ready to accommodate them. London, Birmingham, and other English cities were filled with people desperate for work. As described in the quote at the top of this page, poverty and overcrowding made these industrial cities places that bred despair.

On the other hand, industrialization affected the people in some very positive ways. Because of improvements in agricultural technology, food production increased. The increase in the number of new industries gave people a wider choice of how to make a living.

In cities, people were exposed to music, art, and other forms of culture that were less available in the countryside. Nevertheless, debates raged over whether the advantages of industrialization actually outweighed the disadvantages.

Concerns About Growth

The same debate rages today. When a major industry considers opening a plant or large office in a small or medium-sized community, some people in the community are for such growth; others are against it.

Those who welcome the new facility promote it with a number of arguments. For one thing, new industry creates new jobs. Its owners and the people who move to the town to work at the new facility will pay taxes to the town. These taxes can be used to build new schools, repair streets, and improve city services. The larger population will attract other new businesses: restaurants, hotels, clothing stores, groceries.

Those who do not want the new industry in their community have other arguments. A larger population will require more city services, such as more teachers, wider streets, more sewers, and larger police and fire departments. To get enough money to pay for all this will involve increasing taxes, at least at first. Opponents also argue that heavier traffic may lead to congestion, confusion, and frustration. Life may become more hectic and less enjoyable for the people in the town.

HELP WANTED

▲ *Greater job opportunities result from industrial growth.*

Decision Point

1. What goals and values would cause residents to support the bringing of a new industrial facility to their community? What goals and values would cause these residents to oppose the idea?

2. Suppose a manufacturing company plans to build a new factory in your town or city. What do you think you would want to know about this new facility? Where could you find the information you want?

3. Imagine that a new industry is going to be based in your community. What one problem could this help to solve? (Consider unemployment, young people leaving the community, inadequate support for local businesses.)

4. What is one problem that a new industry in your area might create? Can you think of a way to prevent this problem from arising and still allow the industry to develop in your area?

Presenting Primary Sources

Here's Why

You will probably speak to groups several times while you are in school. If you know how to prepare an interesting oral report, your presentations will be less stressful and more well received.

One way to make oral reports more accurate and interesting is to use primary sources. As you know, primary sources are documents that are produced at the time of the event, like newspaper articles. Many people you have read about in this chapter left written accounts of events that occurred during their lifetimes. Benjamin Franklin, for example, is well known for his fascinating autobiography. John Locke, Jean Jacques Rousseau, Adam Smith, and Voltaire also wrote extensively about events and ideas of their time. Suppose you wanted to make an oral report about one of these people. How would you use primary sources to make your report interesting?

Here's How

You can use primary sources in any of several different ways. You would not use all of these methods in one report, but using any one of them will certainly improve your report.

1. Use a primary source to limit your topic. For example, a specific journal entry could become the basis for an oral report about Benjamin Franklin.
2. Use quotations from a primary source to help bring your report alive. For example, you could frame your report with quotations at the beginning and the end. Or you could use quotations throughout the report to support specific points.
3. Broaden the perspective of your report by using several primary sources. For example, if you were preparing a report about the Constitutional Convention, you might choose quotations from the writings of Thomas Jefferson, Benjamin Franklin, and John Adams.

Review the steps below for preparing and presenting an oral report. Think about how you might use primary sources as you work your way through the steps.

Try It

Use the steps listed below to prepare an oral report about one of the people mentioned in Here's Why. Be sure to use primary source materials that will spark your listeners' interest.

Apply It

Find examples of primary sources used in oral reports on radio or television. Explain how the reports used those primary sources.

1. Pick a topic
2. Narrow your topic
3. Find information
4. Read, take notes
5. Make an outline
6. Prepare note cards
7. Practice your report
8. Face your audience and speak clearly.

LESSON 4

After the American Revolution

fter the North American colonists overthrew Britain's authority, government in the new nation was founded on the Articles of Confederation. Adopted in 1777, the Articles only loosely united the 13 states. Each state was like a separate country, with its own government, army, trade, and currency.

Many leaders, including George Washington, felt that the nation needed a more powerful central government than it had. They hoped that such a government would unite the states. The leaders also believed that the natural rights of the people had to be outlined to protect the freedoms that had so recently been won. In 1787, the leaders of the nation met to provide the nation with a new and responsive government.

THINKING FOCUS

What Enlightenment ideals did the founders of the government of the United States share with the philosophes?

Key Terms

- checks and balances
- immigrant

◄ *George Washington was unanimously approved as president of the Constitutional Convention held at Philadelphia in 1787.*

A New Constitution

e the people of the United States, in order to form a more perfect union, establish justice, insure domestic tranquility, provide for the common defense, promote the general welfare, and secure the blessings of liberty to ourselves and our posterity, do ordain and establish this Constitution for the United States of America.

497

▲ *The three branches of the U.S. Government are also separated physically in Washington D.C.—the executive White House (top right), the judicial Supreme Court (top left), and the legislative Capitol (bottom).*

How Do We Know?

HISTORY *In 1792, British author Mary Wollstonecraft extended the theory of natural rights to include women. In her book* A Vindication of the Rights of Women, *she stresses the importance of education in bringing about equality between men and women.*

■ *What ideas in the Constitution are similar to the ideals of the philosophes?*

The quote you just read begins the Constitution. It expresses the purpose of the document. The influence of the Enlightenment can be clearly seen in the first three words, "We the people." Americans had come to believe in Locke and Rousseau's theory that government is basically a "social contract" between the people and their ruler.

The Constitution goes on to identify the branches of government and to define these branches' roles. The three branches were the legislative, executive, and judicial. The framers of the Constitution wanted to keep any one of the branches of

government from becoming too powerful. As the French philosophe Montesquieu had written, "It is necessary from the very nature of things that power should be a check to power."

Those writing the Constitution developed a system of **checks and balances** between government power centers. For example, the president can veto, or refuse to pass, bills passed by the Congress. But if Congress passes the bill again by a two-thirds vote, it becomes law.

Similarly, the president can nominate judges to the Supreme Court, but the Senate can refuse to approve the persons chosen by the president. The Supreme Court can also cancel laws that have been passed by Congress if they are judged to be in conflict with the Constitution. ■

We the People

◄ *Ideas flowed from Europe to the United States. So did symbols of those ideas. The Statue of Liberty was built in France and was given to the United States. The workers in the photo were working near the left arm of the statue.*

UNDERSTANDING PROGRESS

When Alexander Hamilton, one of the delegates at the Constitutional Convention, tried to convince Americans to ratify the Constitution, he used a typical philosophe argument. The government of the United States would be better than past governments, he argued, because "the science of politics . . . like most other sciences, has received great improvement." Much like other thinkers of the Age of Enlightenment, Hamilton believed in progress. What is progress? And how do we measure progress?

What Is Progress?

Progress implies improvement, or forward movement toward a desirable goal. Although progress involves change, not all change involves progress. When the Roman Empire broke up, most of western Europe became isolated from the learning and culture of the larger world community. The Middle Ages were certainly a time of change but, in many ways, not a time of progress.

How Is Progress Measured?

Progress is not always easy to measure, because in some societies it occurs for some people but not for others. Ancient Greece is often considered a model of political, economic, and social progress. But this progress applied only to free white men, not to women or slaves. The opening up of the American West brought progress to pioneers but certainly not to American Indians.

Is Progress Always Good?

The philosophes of the 18th century looked forward to a perfect world. They did not realize that progress often has a cost. For instance, although the Industrial Revolution provided many people with jobs and goods, it also brought pollution, oppressive working conditions, and overcrowding to the cities. It is important to evaluate progress in terms of its benefits as well as its costs.

The Enlightenment

Hope for the Future

The framers of the Constitution shared many of the goals of the Enlightenment: individual freedom, religious tolerance, protection from tyrants, and direct participation of the people in their government. Europeans watched the young country carefully, eager to see how successful a government founded on such principles would be. It soon became clear that the new nation was not only surviving but thriving. Many Europeans moved from their homelands to the Americas during the 1800s.

These **immigrants**—people who leave one country to settle in another—permanently resettled in America for many different reasons. Many of them came to escape poverty, unemployment, and crowded living conditions in cities. Others came to escape religious or political persecution.

The United States has been called a nation of immigrants. This is because so many immigrants have settled in this country. The Statue of Liberty, which stands on Liberty Island in New York Harbor, was built to honor the religious and political freedom offered in the United States. Given to the United States by France, *Liberty Enlightening the World* stands as an example of the powerful impact of Enlightenment ideas on the world. ■

➤ *The Statue of Liberty has been a symbol of liberty, freedom, and democracy for over a hundred years.*

■ *What attracted immigrants to the United States?*

R E V I E W

1. **FOCUS** What Enlightenment ideals did the founders of the government of the United States share with the philosophes?

2. **CONNECT** What were the similarities between the Constitution and the Declaration of the Rights of Man and of the Citizen?

3. **HISTORY** How did the United States Constitution reflect a belief in progress?

4. **CRITICAL THINKING** How does the separation of powers into three branches of government, and checks and balances among those branches, help to guarantee freedom?

5. **WRITING ACTIVITY** Imagine that you are an immigrant arriving in the United States in the 1800s. Write a description of why you left your home and what you hope to find when you arrive in the United States.

Chapter Review

Reviewing Key Terms

Age of Enlightenment (p. 477)
agricultural revolution (p. 490)
capitalist (p. 493)
checks and balances (p. 498)
contract (p. 479)
crop rotation (p. 491)
enclosure (p. 491)

enlightened despot (p. 480)
immigrant (p. 500)
industrial revolution
(p. 492)
natural right (p. 479)
philosophe (p. 477)
reason (p. 476)

A. Rewrite each sentence. Use a key term in place of the phrase in italics.
1. Sir Isaac Newton used *logical thought* to discover the laws of motion.
2. Joseph II was an *absolute ruler who supported the ideals of the Enlightenment.*
3. Many *people from foreign lands* came to the United States seeking jobs and land.
4. The framers of the Constitution developed a system of *maintaining a balance of power between the three branches of government.*
5. *Breaking up large open, common fields into smaller, fenced-in plots* was an important part of the agricultural revolution.
6. *People willing to invest their money in new industries* were essential to the industrial revolution.

B. Write a sentence or two for each pair of words showing how the words are related.
1. Age of Enlightenment, philosophe
2. contract, natural right
3. agricultural revolution, crop rotation
4. industrial revolution, capitalist

Exploring Concepts

A. Copy the diagram and fill in the names of the people or documents.

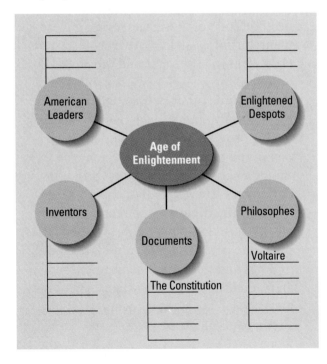

B. Support each statement with facts and details from the chapter.
1. Many of the philosophes hoped to discover a better way to govern.
2. Both Martin Luther and Thomas Jefferson challenged authority in order to make positive changes in their world.
3. Frederick II admired Voltaire and adopted many of his ideas.
4. During the reign of Joseph II, many Austrians were freer than ever before.
5. The Declaration of the Rights of Man and the Citizen included ideas from the writings of John Locke and Jean-Jacques Rousseau.
6. One of the effects of the agricultural revolution was an increased supply of workers for the Industrial Revolution.
7. Ideas expressed by the philosophes can be found in American government.
8. Many immigrants came to the United States seeking religious and political freedom.

Reviewing Skills

1. Reread the section in Lesson 3 entitled The Industrial Revolution. Choose one invention that would make a good oral report. What would you want to cover in your report? Make an outline. What primary sources might you use? Indicate in your outline where you would use information from primary sources.

2. Turn to Lesson 3, page 490. Find the section of the lesson with the heading The Agricultural Revolution. Use note cards to take notes summarizing the information found in this section. Remember to include subtopics, the source of information, and your page references.

3. You have to give an oral report on a recent event that occurred in your city, state, or country. What might you use as a source of information for your oral report?

Using Critical Thinking

1. In 1764, Voltaire wrote: "In general, the art of government consists in taking as much money as possible from one class of citizens to give to another." He was referring to the way that the king of France taxed the Third Estate. Does this statement describe government in the United States today? Why?

2. People living during the Age of Enlightenment believed that poverty, intolerance, and injustice could be ended. But we still have those problems today. What can citizens of this century do to help end them?

3. Inventions such as the flying shuttle greatly changed the British textile industry. Goods were produced more cheaply and quickly, but under terrible working conditions. Think of other inventions that have had a profound effect on other industries. Name some positive effects of those inventions. Name some negative effects.

Preparing for Citizenship

1. GROUP ACTIVITY Stage a panel discussion between philosophes and enlightened despots. You may portray Locke, Voltaire, Catherine the Great, or other figures from the chapter. Your purpose should be to include the points that the two groups agreed on, but also show how they differed. You may want to consult other resources such as biographies or the encyclopedia for additional ideas.

2. WRITING ACTIVITY Analyze a part of the Declaration of Independence to find ideas from the philosophes. On the left half of a large poster, write passages from the Declaration. On the right half, write the name of the philosophe on whose ideas the passage is based.

3. COLLABORATIVE LEARNING As a class, choose a recent period from history and put together a three-volume encyclopedia of the thinking from that period similar to Diderot's *Encyclopédie.* Each volume will be about one of these categories: government, business, or science. Decide as a class what the page size and the cover design of the encyclopedie will be. Team up with three other people. Divide the team into two pairs. Each pair is responsible for providing an illustrated article in one of the three categories. Each pair should choose a topic and research it in periodicals, encyclopedias, and other resources. The topic may be related to people, ideas, events, inventions or discoveries. Then one person should summarize the findings and the other illustrate the summary. Get together with other teams who have chosen the same category, bind all the pages into one volume and cover them.

Time/Space Databank

Architecture

Architectural terms

Ambulatory is a continuous aisle in a circular building. In a church, the ambulatory serves as a semicircular aisle that encloses the apse.

Apse is a semicircular area. In most churches, the apse is at one end of the building and contains the main altar.

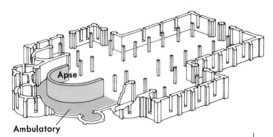

Arcade refers to a series of arches supported by columns or piers. A passageway formed by the arches is also called an arcade.

Arch is a curved structure used to support the weight of the material above it. A stone at the top of an arch, called the *keystone,* holds the other parts in place.

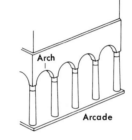

Architrave makes up the lowest part of an entablature. It rests on the capital of a column. For a drawing of an architrave, see Entablature on the opposite page.

Buttress is a support built against an outside wall of a building. A *flying buttress* is an arched support that extends from a column or pier to the wall.

Buttress   Flying Buttress

Cantilever is a horizontal projection, such as a balcony or a beam, which is supported only at one end.

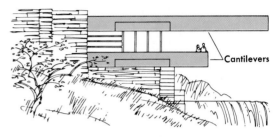

Cantilevers

Capital, in an order, forms the upper part of a column. It separates the shaft from the entablature.

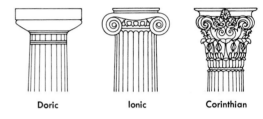

Doric   Ionic   Corinthian

Colonnade means a row of columns, each set an equal distance apart.

Column is a vertical support. In an order, it consists of a shaft and a capital and often rests on a base.

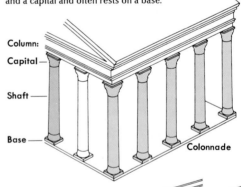

Column:
Capital
Shaft
Base
Colonnade

Composite order is a Roman order. It resembles the Corinthian order but has a capital that combines the Corinthian acanthus leaf decoration with volutes from the Ionic order.

Corinthian order became the last of the three Greek orders. It resembles the Ionic order but has an elaborate capital that is decorated with carvings of leaves of the acanthus plant.

Composite Order   Corinthian Order

Cornice forms the upper part of an entablature and extends beyond the frieze.

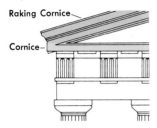

Raking Cornice

Cornice

Doric order was the first and simplest of the three Greek orders. The Doric is the only order that normally has no base.

Doric Order

Entablature refers to the upper horizontal part of an order between a capital and the roof. It consists of three major parts—the architrave, frieze, and cornice.

Entablature:

Cornice

Frieze

Architrave

Facade is the front of a building. Most facades contain an entrance.

Frieze forms the middle part of an entablature and is often decorated with a horizontal band of relief sculpture.

Ionic order was the second of the three Greek orders. It has a capital decorated with carved spiral scrolls called *volutes.*

Module is a measurement, such as the diameter of a column, which architects use to establish the proportions of an entire structure.

Ionic Order

Nave is the chief area within a church. It extends from the main entrance to the transept.

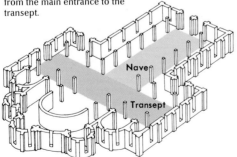

Nave

Transept

Order, in classical architecture, consisted of a column and an entablature. Orders served as the basic elements of Greek and Roman architecture and influenced many later styles.

Pediment is a triangular segment between the horizontal entablature and the sloping roof at the front of a classical-style building.

Pediment

Pendentive is a curved support shaped like an inverted triangle. Pendentives hold up a dome.

Dome

Pendentive

Pier refers to a large pillar used to support a roof.

Post and lintel is a method of construction in which vertical beams (posts) support a horizontal beam (lintel).

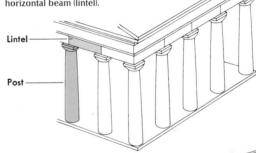

Lintel

Post

Shaft is the main part of a column below the capital. Many shafts have shallow vertical grooves called *fluting.*

Transept forms the arms in a T- or cross-shaped church.

Tuscan order, a Roman order, resembles the Doric order, but the shaft has no fluting.

Vault is an arched brick or stone ceiling or roof. A *barrel vault,* the simplest form of vault, is a single continuous arch. A *groined vault* is formed by joining two barrel vaults at right angles. A *ribbed vault* has diagonal arches that project from the surface.

Tuscan Order

WORLD BOOK illustrations by Robert Keys

Barrel Vault

Groined Vault

Ribbed Vault

City

Comparing the sizes of cities

A city determines its population by counting the people who live within its political boundaries. But cities of the world define their city limits differently, making population comparisons difficult. United States cities fix their limits so that they do not overlap or include other cities and towns. Some foreign cities include other urban and rural areas.

Countries also determine metropolitan areas in various ways. In the United States, metropolitan area boundaries follow county lines. Each metropolitan area includes a county with a large city and perhaps nearby counties. But in most countries, a metropolitan area does not have definite political boundaries.

In these countries, metropolitan areas include the major city and urban and rural areas that are socially or economically identified with the city.

Mexico City has the largest population of any city in the world. Mexico City also has the largest metropolitan area population in the world.

Some governments do not report separate city and metropolitan area populations in their censuses and population estimates. In such cases, the same city proper figure appears in both the cities and the metropolitan areas tables, *below*, to show the existence of a metropolitan area.

50 largest cities in the world

1. Mexico City 10,061,000	27. Ho Chi Minh City 3,419,978
2. Seoul 9,645,932	28. Wuhan 3,340,000
3. Tokyo 8,353,674	29. Calcutta 3,305,006
4. Moscow 8,275,000	30. Madras 3,276,622
5. Bombay 8,227,332	31. Guangzhou 3,220,000
6. New York City 7,071,639	32. Madrid 3,123,713
7. São Paulo 7,033,529	33. Berlin (East and West) .. 3,062,979
8. Shanghai 6,880,000	34. Chicago 3,005,072
9. London 6,767,500	35. Yokohama 2,992,644
10. Jakarta 6,503,449	36. Sydney 2,989,070
11. Cairo 6,052,836	37. Baghdad 2,969,000
12. Beijing 5,760,000	38. Los Angeles .. 2,968,579
13. Teheran 5,734,199	39. Lahore 2,952,689
14. Hong Kong 5,705,000	40. Alexandria 2,917,327
15. Istanbul 5,475,982	41. Buenos Aires 2,908,001
16. Tianjin 5,300,000	42. Rome 2,830,569
17. Karachi 5,208,170	43. Chongqing 2,730,000
18. Bangkok 5,153,902	44. Melbourne 2,645,484
19. Rio de Janeiro 5,093,232	45. Pyongyang 2,639,448
20. Delhi 4,884,234	46. Osaka 2,636,260
21. Leningrad 4,295,000	47. Harbin 2,590,000
22. Santiago 4,225,299	48. Hanoi 2,570,905
23. Lima 4,164,597	49. Chengdu 2,540,000
24. Shenyang 4,130,000	50. Bangalore 2,476,355
25. Bogotá 3,982,941	
26. Pusan 3,516,807	

50 largest metropolitan areas in the world

1. Mexico City ... 15,505,000	26. Bangkok 5,153,902
2. São Paulo 12,588,439	27. Leningrad 4,827,000
3. Shanghai 12,050,000	28. Philadelphia .. 4,716,818
4. Tokyo 11,618,281	29. Lima 4,608,010
5. Cairo 10,000,000	30. Detroit 4,488,072
6. Buenos Aires 9,927,404	31. Madras 4,289,347
7. Seoul 9,645,932	32. Santiago 4,225,299
8. Beijing 9,470,000	33. Shenyang 4,130,000
9. Calcutta 9,194,018	34. Bogotá 3,982,941
10. Rio de Janeiro 9,018,637	35. Pusan 3,516,807
11. Paris 8,706,963	36. Toronto 3,427,168
12. Moscow 8,537,000	37. Ho Chi Minh City 3,419,978
13. New York City 8,274,961	38. Wuhan 3,340,000
14. Bombay 8,227,332	39. Caracas 3,310,236
15. Tianjin 7,990,000	40. Washington, D.C. 3,250,822
16. Los Angeles- Long Beach . 7,447,503	41. Guangzhou ... 3,220,000
17. London 6,767,500	42. Madrid 3,123,713
18. Jakarta 6,503,449	43. Berlin (East and West) .. 3,062,979
19. Chicago 6,060,387	44. Athens 3,027,331
20. Manila 5,926,000	45. Yokohama 2,992,644
21. Teheran 5,734,199	46. Sydney 2,989,070
22. Delhi 5,729,283	47. Baghdad 2,969,000
23. Hong Kong 5,705,000	48. Lahore 2,952,689
24. Istanbul 5,475,982	49. Bangalore 2,921,751
25. Karachi 5,208,170	50. Montreal 2,921,357

50 largest cities in the United States

1. New York City ... 7,071,639	26. St. Louis 452,801
2. Chicago 3,005,072	27. Kansas City, Mo. 448,033
3. Los Angeles 2,968,579	28. El Paso 425,259
4. Philadelphia 1,688,210	29. Atlanta 425,022
5. Houston 1,595,138	30. Pittsburgh 423,959
6. Detroit 1,203,399	31. Oklahoma City .. 403,484
7. Dallas 904,078	32. Cincinnati 385,457
8. San Diego 875,538	33. Fort Worth 385,164
9. Phoenix 789,704	34. Minneapolis 370,951
10. Baltimore 786,741	35. Portland, Ore. ... 366,383
11. San Antonio 786,023	36. Honolulu 365,048
12. Indianapolis 700,807	37. Long Beach 361,355
13. San Francisco .. 678,974	38. Tulsa 360,919
14. Memphis 646,174	39. Buffalo 357,870
15. Washington, D.C. 638,432	40. Toledo 354,635
16. Milwaukee 636,297	41. Miami 346,865
17. San Jose 629,531	42. Austin 345,890
18. Cleveland 573,822	43. Oakland 339,337
19. Columbus, O. ... 565,032	44. Albuquerque ... 332,239
20. Boston 562,994	45. Tucson 330,537
21. New Orleans ... 557,927	46. Newark 329,248
22. Jacksonville, Fla. 540,920	47. Omaha 327,558
23. Seattle 493,846	48. Charlotte 314,447
24. Denver 492,365	49. Louisville 298,694
25. Nashville 455,651	50. Birmingham ... 284,413

50 largest cities and towns in Canada

1. Montreal 1,015,420	28. Markham 114,597
2. Calgary 636,104	29. Halifax 113,577
3. Toronto 612,289	30. Thunder Bay ... 112,272
4. Winnipeg 594,551	31. Richmond 108,492
5. Edmonton 573,982	32. St. John's 96,216
6. North York 556,297	33. Nepean 95,490
7. Scarborough ... 484,676	34. Montréal-Nord .. 90,303
8. Vancouver 431,147	35. Glouster 89,810
9. Mississauga ... 374,005	36. Sudbury 88,717
10. Hamilton 306,728	37. Saanich 82,940
11. Etobicoke 302,973	38. Gatineau 81,244
12. Ottawa 300,763	39. Sault Ste. Marie 80,905
13. Laval 284,164	40. Cambridge 79,920
14. London 269,140	41. Delta 79,610
15. Windsor 193,111	42. Guelph 78,235
16. Brampton 188,498	43. Saint John 76,381
17. Surrey 181,447	44. Brantford 76,146
18. Saskatoon 177,641	45. St.-Léonard 75,947
19. Regina 175,062	46. La Salle 75,621
20. Quebec 164,580	47. Sherbrooke 74,438
21. Kitchener 150,604	48. Niagara Falls 72,107
22. Burnaby 145,161	49. Ste.-Foy 69,615
23. York 135,401	50. Coquitlam 69,291
24. Longueuil 125,441	
25. Oshawa 123,651	
26. St. Catherines .. 123,455	
27. Burlington 116,675	

506

Sources: 1980 census for the United States cities; 1986 census for Canadian cities; 1976-1990 censuses and estimates for other cities.

Highlights in the history of communication

Prehistoric people used paintings and drawings to tell stories.

The Semites developed the first real alphabet.

| About 20,000 B.C. | About 3500 B.C. | About 1500-1000 B.C. | 59 B.C. |

The Sumerians developed the first known system of writing.

The Romans began a handwritten newssheet that was a forerunner of today's newspapers.

WORLD BOOK illustration by Richard Hook

Deutsches Museum, Munich, West Germany

Deutsches Museum, Munich, West Germany

Smoke signals were one of the earliest forms of long-distance communication. Such signals could send only limited information—a warning, for example.

Cuneiform writing consists of wedge-shaped characters stamped on clay. The clay cylinder above was inscribed during the 500's B.C. in Babylon.

Wax tablets were once a common writing surface. The early Greeks wrote on such tablets with a pointed tool called a *stylus* and laced the tablets together.

T'sai Lun, a Chinese government official, invented paper.

The German metalsmith Johannes Gutenberg reinvented movable type.

Printed newssheets called *corantos* appeared.

| About A.D. 105 | About 1045 | Mid-1400's | Mid-1500's | 1600's |

Pi Sheng, a Chinese printer, invented movable type.

The English made the first pencils of *graphite,* the substance used today.

Detail of an Italian manuscript (about 1331) by Giovanni de' Nuxiglia; Biblio-thèque Nationale, Paris (SCALA/EPA)

Bettmann Archive

During the Middle Ages, artists copied books by hand, letter by letter. They covered their work with gold, silver, and colored decorations called *illumination.*

Printing from movable type was invented in Asia during the 1000's and in Europe during the 1400's. A shop of the 1600's is shown above. At the left, typesetters assemble type to form pages. In the background, an assistant inks a page. At the right, a printer turns a huge screw on the printing press to push paper against the type.

Communication

The French engineer Claude Chappe developed a visual telegraph.

Joseph Nicéphore Niépce, a French physicist, made the first permanent photograph.

○ Late 1700's   ○ 1811   ○ 1826   ○ 1830's

Friedrich Koenig, a German printer, invented a steam-powered printing press.

The French painter Louis J. M. Daguerre developed an improved photograph.

American Antiquarian Society, Worcester, Mass.

Postal service was established in many nations during the 1700's. This postrider carried mail between Boston and other cities in the American Colonies.

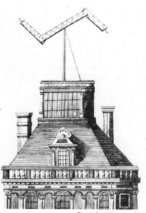

Deutsches Museum, Munich, West Germany

The Chappe telegraph consisted of a series of towers. An operator in each tower moved a crossbar and two large, jointed arms to send coded messages.

Detail of *Intérieur d'un Cabinet de Curiosités*; Société Française de Photographie, Paris

A daguerreotype was an early type of photograph printed on a metal plate. Louis J. M. Daguerre took this picture of a collection of rare objects in 1837.

Thomas A. Edison developed the first practical phonograph.

Ottmar Mergenthaler, a German-born mechanic, patented the Linotype machine.

○ 1877   ○ 1880's   ○ 1884   ○ 1895

The German physicist Heinrich Hertz discovered electromagnetic waves.

The Italian inventor Guglielmo Marconi developed the *wireless telegraph* (radio).

Bettmann Archive

Thomas A. Edison's phonograph recorded sound on a cylinder covered with foil. This picture shows the inventor with an early version of his phonograph.

Historical Pictures Service

Linotype machines used a keyboard to set type mechanically. Their introduction sped the production of newspapers and other publications.

The Marconi Company

Guglielmo Marconi combined the ideas of several scientists to send signals through the air. His invention, the *wireless telegraph,* led to present-day radio.

Communication

The American painter Samuel F. B. Morse patented his electric telegraph.

The first successful transatlantic telegraph cable linked Europe and North America.

Alexander Graham Bell patented a type of telephone.

| 1840 | 1864 | 1866 | 1868 | 1876 |

The British physicist James Clerk Maxwell reported his theory of electromagnetism, which led to radio.

Three American inventors patented the first practical typewriter.

Bettmann Archive

Bettmann Archive

Bettmann Archive

Samuel F. B. Morse developed one of the first successful electric telegraphs. He also developed Morse code, a system of sending messages by dots and dashes.

An early typewriter was patented in the 1860's by three American inventors—Carlos Glidden, Christopher Latham Sholes, and Samuel W. Soulé.

Alexander Graham Bell designed one of the first successful telephones and demonstrated it at the 1876 Centennial Exposition in Philadelphia.

Reginald A. Fessenden, a Canadian-born physicist, transmitted voice by radio.

Vladimir K. Zworykin, a Russian-born physicist, demonstrated the first all-electronic TV system.

| 1906 | 1907 | 1929 | 1936 |

The American inventor Lee De Forest patented the *triode,* an improved vacuum tube.

The British Broadcasting Corporation made the world's first TV broadcasts.

Bettmann Archive

Bettmann Archive

British Broadcasting Corporation

A motion picture camera of about 1915 was used to film silent movies. Several inventors developed movie cameras in the late 1800's and early 1900's.

Radio became a major source of family entertainment during the 1920's. This photograph shows a singer making a broadcast during the early days of radio.

One of the first TV broadcasts was a demonstration of self-defense techniques. It appeared in 1936 on the British Broadcasting Corporation (BBC).

Communication

Bell Telephone Laboratories developed the transistor.	Television networks began to record programs on videotape.	Xerox Corporation perfected *xerography,* a copying process.

1947 — **Mid-1950's** — **1960**

Dennis Gabor, a British engineer, invented *holography* (3-D photography).

Echo 1 became the first satellite to receive radio signals from a ground station and reflect them back to earth.

Ampex Corporation

American Telephone & Telegraph Co.

WORLD BOOK photo

Tape recorders that recorded sounds on magnetic tape were developed in the 1930's. This 1948 recorder was the first one manufactured in the United States.

Telstar I, a communications satellite launched in 1962, relayed telephone calls, TV shows, and other communications between the United States and Europe.

Computers revolutionized communication in the 1960's and 1970's. A computer terminal at an airport, *above,* relays information about flights and reservations.

Corning Glass Works produced the first optical fiber suitable for long-range communication.	The first mailgram was transmitted by satellite.	

1970 — **1970's** — **1974** — **Early 1980's**

Several manufacturers developed cassette videotape recorders.

Several companies began marketing cellular mobile telephones.

WORLD BOOK photo

WORLD BOOK photo

© Paul Robert Perry

Fiber-optic communication uses a laser to send signals through glass strands called *optical fibers,* shown above.

A home computer, *above,* helps a girl practice arithmetic problems. Small computers that perform a variety of jobs gained popularity in the late 1970's.

A cellular mobile telephone enables a motorist to make and receive calls. These devices, introduced in the 1980's, greatly improved mobile phone communication.

Famous ancient and medieval explorers

Explorer	Nationality	Main achievements	Date
* Alexander the Great	Macedonian	Reached Afghanistan, western India.	c.331 B.C.-326 B.C.
* Eric the Red	Norwegian	Sailed to Greenland from Iceland.	c.982
* Ericson, Leif	Norwegian	Probably the first European to reach mainland North America.	c.1000
* Ibn Batuta	Arabian	Traveled through the Middle East and India; visited China and the East Indies.	1325-1354
Odoric of Pordenone	Italian	Traveled in Turkey, Iran, across central Asia, and in the Indian and South Pacific oceans.	c.1314-c.1330
* Polo, Marco	Italian	Visited Sri Lanka, China, India, Iran, and Sumatra.	1271-1295
* Pytheas	Greek	Sailed from the Mediterranean Sea to the North Atlantic Ocean.	c.300 B.C.
Rubruck, William of	Flemish	Traveled through central Asia to Mongolia.	1253-1255
Zhang Qian	Chinese	Traveled from China to central Asia.	128-126 B.C.

*Has a separate biography in WORLD BOOK.

Explorers of the great age of European discovery

Explorer	Nationality	Main achievements	Date
* Balboa, Vasco Núñez de	Spanish	Led expedition across Isthmus of Panama; sighted Pacific Ocean.	1513
* Cabeza de Vaca, Álvar Núñez	Spanish	Explored Gulf Plains from Texas to Mexico.	1528-1536
* Cabot, John	Italian	Sailed across the North Atlantic to what is now Canada.	1497-1498
* Cabot, Sebastian	Italian	Explored South American coast to the Río de la Plata.	1526-1530
* Cabral, Pedro Álvares	Portuguese	Reached Brazilian coast; sailed around Africa to India.	1500-1501
* Cartier, Jacques	French	Sailed up the St. Lawrence River.	1535
* Columbus, Christopher	Italian	Made four voyages to the West Indies and Caribbean lands.	1492-1504
* Coronado, Francisco de	Spanish	Explored the American Southwest.	1540-1542
* Cortés, Hernando	Spanish	Conquered Mexico.	1519-1521
* Da Gama, Vasco	Portuguese	First European to reach India by sea.	1498
* De Soto, Hernando	Spanish	Explored American Southeast; reached Mississippi River.	1539-1542
* Dias, Bartolomeu	Portuguese	First European to round the Cape of Good Hope.	1487-1488
* Drake, Sir Francis	English	First English explorer to sail around the world.	1577-1580
* Frobisher, Sir Martin	English	Searched North American coast for a Northwest Passage.	1576-1578
* Magellan, Ferdinand	Portuguese	Commanded first globe-circling voyage, completed in 1522 after his death.	1519-1521
* Oñate, Juan de	Spanish	Explored American Southwest.	1598-1605
* Orellana, Francisco de	Spanish	Explored Amazon River.	1541
* Pizarro, Francisco	Spanish	Conquered Peru; founded Lima.	1531-1535
* Ponce de León, Juan	Spanish	Explored Florida.	1513
* Verrazano, Giovanni da	Italian	Searched for a Northwest Passage.	1524
* Vespucci, Amerigo	Italian	Sailed to the West Indies and South America.	1499-1504

*Has a separate biography in WORLD BOOK.

Famous explorers of Africa

Explorer	Nationality	Main achievements	Date
Bruce, James	Scottish	Rediscovered source of the Blue Nile.	1770
* Burton, Sir Richard	English	Explored Arabia and East Africa; reached Lake Tanganyika.	1853-1858
Caillié, René	French	Explored western Africa; crossed the Sahara.	1826-1828
Clapperton, Hugh	Scottish	Explored northern Nigeria and Lake Chad region.	1822-1827
* Emin Pasha	German	Explored east-central Africa.	1878-1892
Laing, Alexander Gordon	Scottish	Explored Niger River Basin; reached Timbuktu.	1822; 1826
* Livingstone, David	Scottish	Traced upper course of the Zambezi River; reached Victoria Falls and Lake Ngami.	1849-1873
* Park, Mungo	Scottish	Explored course of the Niger River.	1795-1797; 1805-1806
Speke, John Hanning	English	Reached Lake Tanganyika and Lake Victoria.	1858
* Stanley, Sir Henry	Welsh	Explored the Congo River.	1874-1889

*Has a separate article in WORLD BOOK.

Explorers of Australia and the Pacific Ocean

Explorer	Nationality	Main achievements	Date
Bougainville, Louis Antoine de	French	Led first French expedition around the world.	1766-1769
Burke, Robert O'Hara	Irish	One of the first explorers to cross Australia from south to north, with William John Wills.	1860-1861
* Cook, James	English	Explored South Pacific.	1768-1779
* Dampier, William	English	Explored coasts of Australia, New Guinea, and New Britain.	1691-1701
Eyre, Edward John	English	Explored southern coast of Australia.	1840-1841
Jansz, Willem	Dutch	First known European to sight and land in Australia.	1606
Stuart, John McDouall	Scottish	Made six trips into the interior of Australia.	1858-1862
Sturt, Charles	English	Explored southeastern Australia; reached Darling River.	1829-1830
* Tasman, Abel Janszoon	Dutch	Sailed to Tasmania and New Zealand.	1642
Warburton, Peter Egerton	English	Crossed Australia from Alice Springs to Roebourne.	1873
Wills, William John	English	One of the first explorers to cross Australia from south to north, with Robert O'Hara Burke.	1860-1861

*Has a separate article in WORLD BOOK.

Extracted from the Exploration article in *World Book*. Copyright © 1990 by World Book, Inc.

Heraldry

Symbols of heraldry

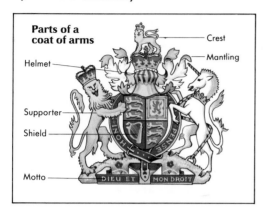

Parts of a coat of arms

- Crest
- Mantling
- Helmet
- Supporter
- Shield
- Motto

DIEU ET MON DROIT

The displaying of arms

Coats of arms were first displayed on the shields of knights. Later, arms appeared on flags, clothes, and other possessions.

WORLD BOOK illustrations by Oxford Illustrators Limited

Symbols used on a coat of arms

Coats of arms were developed during the 1100's as a way to help a knight's followers recognize him on the battlefield. The colors, designs, lines, and *cadency* (status) symbols shown below became standard and were used in different combinations according to specific rules.

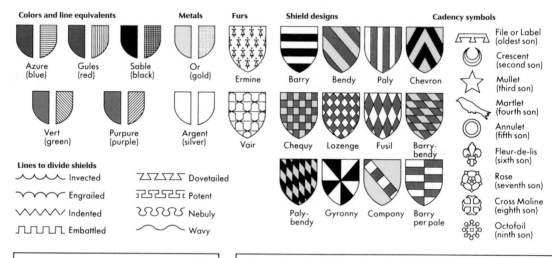

Colors and line equivalents

- Azure (blue)
- Gules (red)
- Sable (black)
- Vert (green)
- Purpure (purple)

Metals

- Or (gold)
- Argent (silver)

Furs

- Ermine
- Vair

Shield designs

- Barry
- Bendy
- Paly
- Chevron
- Chequy
- Lozenge
- Fusil
- Barry-bendy
- Paly-bendy
- Gyronny
- Compony
- Barry per pale

Cadency symbols

- File or Label (oldest son)
- Crescent (second son)
- Mullet (third son)
- Martlet (fourth son)
- Annulet (fifth son)
- Fleur-de-lis (sixth son)
- Rose (seventh son)
- Cross Moline (eighth son)
- Octofoil (ninth son)

Lines to divide shields

- Invected
- Engrailed
- Indented
- Embattled
- Dovetailed
- Potent
- Nebuly
- Wavy

Kinds of charges

A charge is a symbol of an object or figure that appears on a shield. Animals are among the most popular charges.

- Swords
- Ship
- Tower
- Unicorn
- Lion
- Dragon
- Arms
- Wolf's head
- Tortoise

Patterns of family relationships

Two or more arms were sometimes combined on one shield in order to show family relationships. The earliest methods of *marshalling,* as this procedure is called, are shown below. The arms of two families are placed side by side or one within the other.

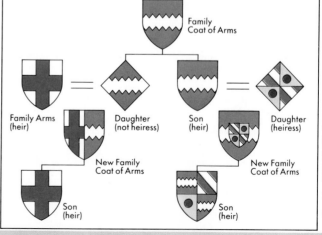

- Family Coat of Arms
- Family Arms (heir)
- Daughter (not heiress)
- Son (heir)
- Daughter (heiress)
- New Family Coat of Arms
- New Family Coat of Arms
- Son (heir)
- Son (heir)

Independent countries of the world*

Name	Area In sq. mi.	Area In km²	Rank in area	Population†	Rank in population	Capital
Afghanistan	251,773	652,090	38	15,885,000	50	Kabul
Albania	11,100	28,748	122	3,248,000	107	Tiranë
Algeria	919,595	2,381,741	10	25,174,000	33	Algiers
Andorra	180	465	156	49,000	163	Andorra
Angola	481,354	1,246,700	21	10,000,000	65	Luanda
Antigua and Barbuda	171	442	158	86,000	160	St. John's
Argentina	1,073,400	2,780,092	8	32,361,000	29	Buenos Aires
Australia	2,966,150	7,682,300	6	16,365,000	49	Canberra
Austria	32,377	83,855	105	7,493,000	78	Vienna
Bahamas	5,385	13,878	135	251,000	148	Nassau
Bahrain	265	688	153	516,000	137	Manama
Bangladesh	55,598	143,998	87	116,000,000	8	Dhaka
Barbados	166	430	159	260,000	147	Bridgetown
Belgium	11,783	30,519	120	9,895,000	67	Brussels
Belize	8,867	22,965	129	182,000	151	Belmopan
Benin	43,484	112,622	93	4,737,000	95	Porto-Novo
Bhutan	17,950	46,500	114	1,513,000	124	Thimphu
Bolivia	424,165	1,098,581	26	7,311,000	80	La Paz; Sucre
Botswana	224,607	581,730	42	1,283,000	126	Gaborone
Brazil	3,286,488	8,511,965	5	150,557,000	6	Brasília
Brunei	2,226	5,765	142	277,000	146	Bandar Seri Begawan
Bulgaria	42,823	110,912	96	8,985,000	71	Sofia
Burkina Faso	105,869	274,200	66	8,996,000	70	Ouagadougou
Burma	261,218	676,552	37	41,279,000	24	Rangoon
Burundi	10,747	27,834	124	5,450,000	91	Bujumbura
Cameroon	183,569	475,442	47	11,236,000	60	Yaoundé
Canada	3,849,674	9,970,610	2	26,279,000	31	Ottawa
Cape Verde	1,557	4,033	144	378,000	140	Praia
Central African Republic	240,535	622,984	40	2,911,000	112	Bangui
Chad	495,755	1,284,000	19	5,674,000	89	N'Djamena
Chile	292,258	756,945	35	13,185,000	55	Santiago
China	3,696,032	9,572,678	3	1,100,258,000	1	Beijing
Colombia	440,831	1,141,748	25	31,863,000	30	Bogotá
Comoros	863	2,235	147	518,000	136	Moroni
Congo	132,047	342,000	56	2,183,000	119	Brazzaville
Costa Rica	19,730	51,100	112	3,017,000	110	San José
Cuba	42,804	110,861	97	10,279,000	63	Havana
Cyprus	3,572	9,251	141	701,000	135	Nicosia
Czechoslovakia	49,373	127,876	90	15,659,000	51	Prague
Denmark	16,632	43,077	115	5,119,000	93	Copenhagen
Djibouti	8,958	23,200	128	337,000	144	Djibouti
Dominica	290	751	150	98,000	158	Roseau
Dominican Republic	18,816	48,734	113	7,172,000	82	Santo Domingo
Ecuador	109,484	283,561	65	10,782,000	61	Quito
Egypt	386,662	1,001,449	28	53,522,000	21	Cairo
El Salvador	8,124	21,041	130	5,655,000	90	San Salvador
Equatorial Guinea	10,831	28,051	123	411,000	138	Malabo
Ethiopia	471,778	1,221,900	23	48,630,000	22	Addis Ababa
Fiji	7,056	18,274	132	772,000	133	Suva
Finland	130,559	338,145	57	4,981,000	94	Helsinki
France	210,026	543,965	44	56,236,000	19	Paris
Gabon	103,347	267,667	68	1,172,000	128	Libreville
Gambia	4,361	11,295	138	820,000	132	Banjul
Germany, East	41,828	108,333	99	16,645,000	48	East Berlin
Germany, West	96,005	248,651	70	60,471,000	14	Bonn
Ghana	92,100	238,537	73	15,020,000	53	Accra
Great Britain	94,248	244,100	72	57,293,000	16	London
Greece	50,962	131,990	88	10,053,000	64	Athens
Grenada	133	344	161	96,000	159	St. George's
Guatemala	42,042	108,889	98	9,117,000	69	Guatemala City
Guinea	94,926	245,857	71	6,871,000	86	Conakry
Guinea-Bissau	13,948	36,125	118	985,000	130	Bissau
Guyana	83,000	214,969	77	868,000	131	Georgetown
Haiti	10,714	27,750	125	5,777,000	88	Port-au-Prince
Honduras	43,277	112,088	94	5,144,000	92	Tegucigalpa
Hungary	35,920	93,032	102	10,545,000	62	Budapest
Iceland	39,800	103,000	100	250,000	149	Reykjavík
India	1,269,219	3,287,263	7	853,532,000	2	New Delhi
Indonesia	741,101	1,919,443	14	180,594,000	5	Jakarta
Iran	636,300	1,648,000	16	56,800,000	17	Teheran
Iraq	169,235	438,317	51	18,048,000	44	Baghdad
Ireland	27,136	70,283	109	3,637,000	103	Dublin
Israel	8,019	20,770	131	4,585,000	96	Jerusalem
Italy	116,320	301,268	63	57,380,000	15	Rome
Ivory Coast	124,504	322,463	61	12,053,000	58	Abidjan
Jamaica	4,244	10,991	139	2,520,000	115	Kingston
Japan	145,870	377,801	55	123,749,000	7	Tokyo
Jordan	35,475	91,880	103	3,065,000	109	Amman
Kampuchea	69,898	181,035	82	6,993,000	85	Phnom Penh
Kenya	224,081	580,367	43	25,081,000	35	Nairobi
Kiribati	277	717	152	69,000	162	Tarawa
Korea, North	46,540	120,538	91	22,965,000	39	Pyongyang
Korea, South	38,625	99,106	101	43,650,000	23	Seoul
Kuwait	6,880	17,818	133	2,096,000	120	Kuwait
Laos	91,430	236,800	75	4,070,000	101	Vientiane
Lebanon	4,015	10,400	140	2,947,000	111	Beirut
Lesotho	11,720	30,355	121	1,757,000	122	Maseru
Liberia	43,000	111,370	95	2,552,000	114	Monrovia
Libya	679,362	1,759,540	15	4,356,000	97	Tripoli
Liechtenstein	62	160	165	28,000	166	Vaduz
Luxembourg	998	2,586	146	367,000	142	Luxembourg
Madagascar	226,658	587,041	41	11,969,000	59	Antananarivo
Malawi	45,747	118,484	92	8,198,000	75	Lilongwe
Malaysia	127,317	329,749	59	17,344,000	46	Kuala Lumpur
Maldives	115	298	163	215,000	150	Male

See footnotes at end of table.

World

Independent countries of the world* (concluded)

Name	Area In sq. mi.	Area In km²	Rank in area	Population†	Rank in population	Capital
Mali	478,841	1,240,192	22	8,278,000	74	Bamako
Malta	122	316	162	350,000	143	Valletta
Mauritania	397,956	1,030,700	27	2,021,000	121	Nouakchott
Mauritius	788	2,040	148	1,105,000	129	Port Louis
Mexico	756,067	1,958,201	13	88,560,000	11	Mexico City
Monaco	0.73	1.9	169	29,000	165	Monaco
Mongolia	604,250	1,565,000	17	2,185,000	118	Ulan Bator
Morocco	177,117	458,730	49	25,169,000	34	Rabat
Mozambique	308,642	799,380	32	15,627,000	52	Maputo
Nauru	8	21	168	9,000	168	—
Nepal	56,827	147,181	86	19,157,000	43	Kathmandu
Netherlands	14,405	37,310	117	14,765,000	54	Amsterdam
New Zealand	103,883	269,057	67	3,402,000	106	Wellington
Nicaragua	50,200	130,000	89	3,606,000	104	Managua
Niger	489,200	1,267,000	20	7,905,000	84	Niamey
Nigeria	356,669	923,768	30	112,765,000	10	Lagos
Norway	149,405	386,958	54	4,213,000	99	Oslo
Oman	82,030	212,457	78	1,469,000	125	Muscat
Pakistan	307,374	796,095	33	113,163,000	9	Islamabad
Panama	30,193	78,200	107	2,421,000	117	Panama City
Papua New Guinea	178,704	462,840	48	3,824,000	102	Port Moresby
Paraguay	157,048	406,752	52	4,278,000	98	Ascunción
Peru	496,225	1,285,216	18	22,330,000	40	Lima
Philippines	116,000	300,000	64	62,446,000	13	Manila
Poland	120,728	312,683	62	38,441,000	26	Warsaw
Portugal	34,340	88,941	104	9,903,000	66	Lisbon
Qatar	4,416	11,437	137	369,000	141	Doha
Romania	91,700	237,500	74	23,279,000	38	Bucharest
Rwanda	10,169	26,338	127	7,222,000	81	Kigali
St. Christopher and Nevis	101	261	164	48,000	164	Basseterre
St. Lucia	238	616	155	143,000	154	Castries
St. Vincent and the Grenadines	150	388	160	117,000	156	Kingstown
San Marino	24	61	166	23,000	167	San Marino
São Tomé and Príncipe	372	964	149	123,000	155	São Tomé
Saudi Arabia	830,000	2,149,690	12	12,939,000	56	Riyadh
Senegal	75,750	196,192	79	7,360,000	79	Dakar
Seychelles	175	453	157	71,000	161	Victoria
Sierra Leone	27,699	71,740	108	4,146,000	100	Freetown
Singapore	239	618	154	2,704,000	113	Singapore
Solomon Islands	10,639	27,556	126	329,000	145	Honiara
Somalia	246,201	637,657	39	7,106,000	83	Mogadishu
South Africa	471,445	1,221,037	24	36,696,000	27	Cape Town; Pretoria; Bloemfontein
Spain	194,897	504,750	46	39,623,000	25	Madrid
Sri Lanka	25,333	65,610	110	16,779,000	47	Colombo
Sudan	967,500	2,505,813	9	23,797,000	37	Khartoum
Suriname	63,037	163,265	85	408,000	139	Paramaribo
Swaziland	6,704	17,364	134	779,000	134	Mbabane
Sweden	170,250	440,945	50	8,346,000	73	Stockholm
Switzerland	15,943	41,293	116	6,509,000	87	Bern
Syria	71,498	185,180	81	12,471,000	57	Damascus
Taiwan	13,900	36,000	119	20,454,000	41	Taipei
Tanzania	364,900	945,087	29	25,955,000	32	Dar es Salaam
Thailand	198,115	513,115	45	55,760,000	20	Bangkok
Togo	21,925	56,785	111	3,451,000	105	Lomé
Tonga	289	748	151	101,000	157	Nukualofa
Trinidad and Tobago	1,980	5,128	143	1,283,000	127	Port-of-Spain
Tunisia	63,170	163,610	84	8,095,000	76	Tunis
Turkey	300,948	779,452	34	56,549,000	18	Ankara
Tuvalu	10	26	167	8,000	169	Funafuti
Uganda	91,074	235,880	76	17,593,000	45	Kampala
Union of Soviet Socialist Republics	8,649,500	22,402,000	1	288,239,000	3	Moscow
United Arab Emirates	32,278	83,600	106	1,731,000	123	Abu Dhabi
United States	3,618,770	9,372,571	4	250,372,000	4	Washington, D.C.
Uruguay	68,500	177,414	83	3,130,000	108	Montevideo
Vanuatu	4,706	12,189	136	164,000	153	Port-Vila
Vatican City	0.17	0.44	170	1,000	170	—
Venezuela	352,145	912,050	31	19,744,000	42	Caracas
Vietnam	127,242	329,556	60	67,084,000	12	Hanoi
Western Samoa	1,093	2,831	145	170,000	152	Apia
Yemen (Aden)	128,587	333,038	58	2,486,000	116	Aden
Yemen (Sana)	75,300	195,000	80	7,993,000	77	Sana
Yugoslavia	98,766	255,804	69	23,853,000	36	Belgrade
Zaire	905,365	2,344,885	11	35,330,000	28	Kinshasa
Zambia	290,586	752,614	36	8,459,000	72	Lusaka
Zimbabwe	150,804	390,580	53	9,700,000	68	Harare

*Each country listed has a separate article in *World Book.*
†Populations are 1990 estimates based on the latest figures from official government and United Nations sources.

Major developments from A.D. 500 to about 1500

WORLD BOOK illustrations by Tak Murakami

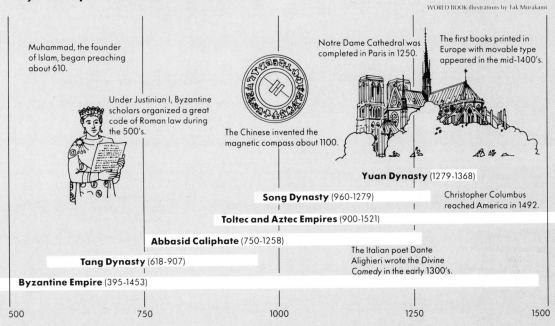

Muhammad, the founder of Islam, began preaching about 610.

Under Justinian I, Byzantine scholars organized a great code of Roman law during the 500's.

The Chinese invented the magnetic compass about 1100.

Notre Dame Cathedral was completed in Paris in 1250.

The first books printed in Europe with movable type appeared in the mid-1400's.

Yuan Dynasty (1279-1368)

Song Dynasty (960-1279)

Christopher Columbus reached America in 1492.

Toltec and Aztec Empires (900-1521)

Abbasid Caliphate (750-1258)

The Italian poet Dante Alighieri wrote the *Divine Comedy* in the early 1300's.

Tang Dynasty (618-907)

Byzantine Empire (395-1453)

500   750   1000   1250   1500

Between 500 and 1500, new civilizations appeared in Africa and the Americas. In the Middle East, the Muslim Arabs rose to power and conquered a huge empire by the mid-700's. In the 1200's, Mongol warriors swept through Asia, creating one of the largest empires in history.

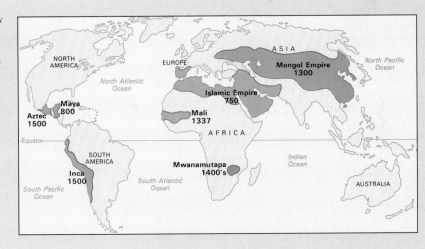

WORLD BOOK map

Important dates

527-565 The Byzantine Empire reached its greatest extent under Emperor Justinian I.

622 Muhammad, founder of Islam, fled from Mecca to Medina. His flight, called the Hegira, marks the beginning of the Islamic calendar.

700's-mid-1000's The Ghana Empire, the first great black empire in western Africa, flourished as a trading state.

732 Charles Martel and the Franks defeated invading Muslims in fighting in west-central France. The victory prevented the Muslims from overrunning Europe.

750 The Abbasids became the caliphs of the Islamic world.

800 Pope Leo III crowned Charlemagne, ruler of the Franks, emperor of the Romans.

c. 988 Vladimir I converted the Russians to Christianity.

1054 Rivalries between the church in Rome and the church in Constantinople resulted in their separation as the Roman Catholic Church and Eastern Orthodox Churches, respectively.

1192 Yoritomo became the first shogun to rule Japan.

1215 English barons forced King John to grant a charter of liberties called Magna Carta.

1279 The Mongols gained control of all China.

1300's The Renaissance began in Italy.

1368 The Ming dynasty began its nearly 300-year rule of China.

1453 The Ottoman Turks captured Constantinople (Istanbul) and overthrew the Byzantine Empire.

World, History of the

Major developments from A.D. 1500 to about 1900

WORLD BOOK illustrations by Tak Murakami

Nicolaus Copernicus proposed in 1543 that the sun is the center of the universe.

Michelangelo completed painting the ceiling of the Sistine Chapel in the Vatican in 1512.

William Shakespeare wrote many of the world's greatest dramas between 1590 and 1616.

Charles Darwin published his theory of evolution in 1859 in *The Origin of Species.*

European Colonial Expansion in Africa and Asia (1870-1914)

Latin-American Wars of Independence (1791-1824)

French Revolution (1789-1799)

Revolutionary War in America (1775-1783)

Industrial Revolution (1700-mid-1800's)

Manchu Rule of China (1644-1912)

Ludwig van Beethoven composed many of his greatest symphonies between 1800 and 1815.

Tokugawa Shogunate in Japan (1603-1867)

Mogul Empire (1526-1707)

Alexander Graham Bell invented the telephone in 1876.

Voyages of Discovery (1400's-1500's)

Ottoman Empire (1326-1922)

Renaissance (1300-1600)

1500   1600   1700   1800   1900

European colonial empires had spread over much of the world by the late 1800's. The largest empires of the period belonged to Great Britain, France, and Germany.

- Belgium
- France
- Germany
- Great Britain
- Italy
- Netherlands
- Portugal
- Spain

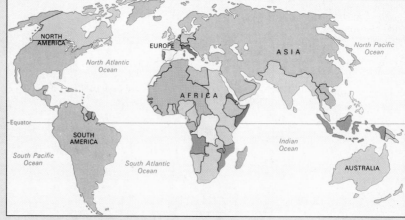

WORLD BOOK map

Important dates

1500's The Reformation led to the birth of Protestantism.

1519-1521 Ferdinand Magellan commanded the first globe-circling voyage, completed in 1522 after his death.

1521 The Spanish conquistador Hernando Cortés defeated the Aztec Indians of Mexico.

1526 Babar, a Muslim prince, invaded India and founded the Mogul Empire.

1588 The Royal Navy of England defeated the Spanish Armada, establishing England as a great naval power.

1644-1912 The Manchus ruled China as the Qing dynasty.

1776 The 13 American Colonies adopted the Declaration of Independence, establishing the United States of America.

1789 The French Revolution began.

1815 Napoleon Bonaparte was defeated in the Battle of Waterloo, ending his attempt to rule Europe.

1853-1854 Commodore Matthew Perry visited Japan and opened two ports to U.S. trade, ending Japan's isolation.

1858 Great Britain took over the rule of India from the East India Company after the Sepoy Rebellion.

1865 Union forces defeated the Confederates in the American Civil War after four years of fighting.

1869 The Suez Canal opened.

1871 Germany became united under the Prussian king, who ruled the new empire as Kaiser Wilhelm I.

1898 The United States took control of Guam, Puerto Rico, and the Philippines following the Spanish-American War.

Major developments from 1900 to 1990

WORLD BOOK illustrations by Tak Murakami

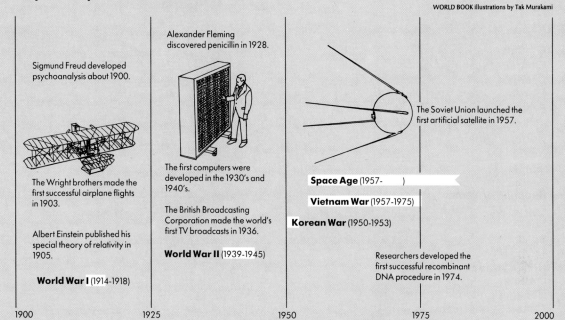

Sigmund Freud developed psychoanalysis about 1900.

The Wright brothers made the first successful airplane flights in 1903.

Albert Einstein published his special theory of relativity in 1905.

World War I (1914-1918)

Alexander Fleming discovered penicillin in 1928.

The first computers were developed in the 1930's and 1940's.

The British Broadcasting Corporation made the world's first TV broadcasts in 1936.

World War II (1939-1945)

The Soviet Union launched the first artificial satellite in 1957.

Space Age (1957-   )

Vietnam War (1957-1975)

Korean War (1950-1953)

Researchers developed the first successful recombinant DNA procedure in 1974.

1900   1925   1950   1975   2000

The wealth of nations can be compared on the basis of each country's *gross national product* (GNP). The GNP is the value of all goods and services produced by a country in a year. The developing countries of Africa and Asia have the lowest GNP per person.

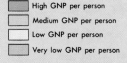

High GNP per person
Medium GNP per person
Low GNP per person
Very low GNP per person

WORLD BOOK map
Map is based on U.S. government
GNP estimates for 1982.

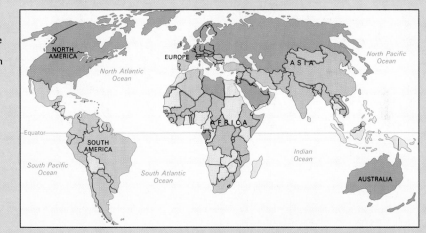

Important dates

1914 The assassination of Archduke Francis Ferdinand of Austria-Hungary started World War I.

1917 The Bolsheviks (Communists) seized power in Russia.

1933 Adolf Hitler became dictator of Germany.

1939 Germany invaded Poland, starting World War II.

1941 The Japanese attacked Pearl Harbor, and the United States entered World War II.

1945 The United Nations was established.

1945 The first atomic bombs used in warfare were dropped by U.S. planes on Hiroshima and Nagasaki.

1945 World War II ended in Europe on May 7 and in the Pacific on September 2.

1949 The Chinese Communists conquered China.

1950 North Korean Communist troops invaded South Korea, starting the Korean War.

1957 The Vietnam War started when South Vietnamese rebels known as the Viet Cong attacked the U.S.-backed South Vietnamese government.

1962 The Soviet Union agreed to U.S. demands that its missiles be removed from Cuba, ending a serious Cold War crisis.

1969 U.S. astronauts made the first manned moon landing.

1975 The Vietnam War ended when South Vietnam surrendered to the Viet Cong and North Vietnam.

1979 Soviet troops invaded Afghanistan to support the leftist Afghan government against rebel tribes.

1989 The Soviet Union completed withdrawal of its troops from Afghanistan.

WORLD: *Political*

ABBREVIATIONS

CEN. AFR. REP.
  Central African Republic
DEN. Denmark
FR. France
GR. Greece
IT. Italy
N. North, Northern
NETH. Netherlands
P.D.R. YEMEN
  People's Democratic
  Republic of Yemen
PORT. Portugal
S. South
SP. Spain
TERR. Territory
U.A.E. United Arab
  Emirates
U.K. United Kingdom
U.S. United States
W. Western

— National boundary

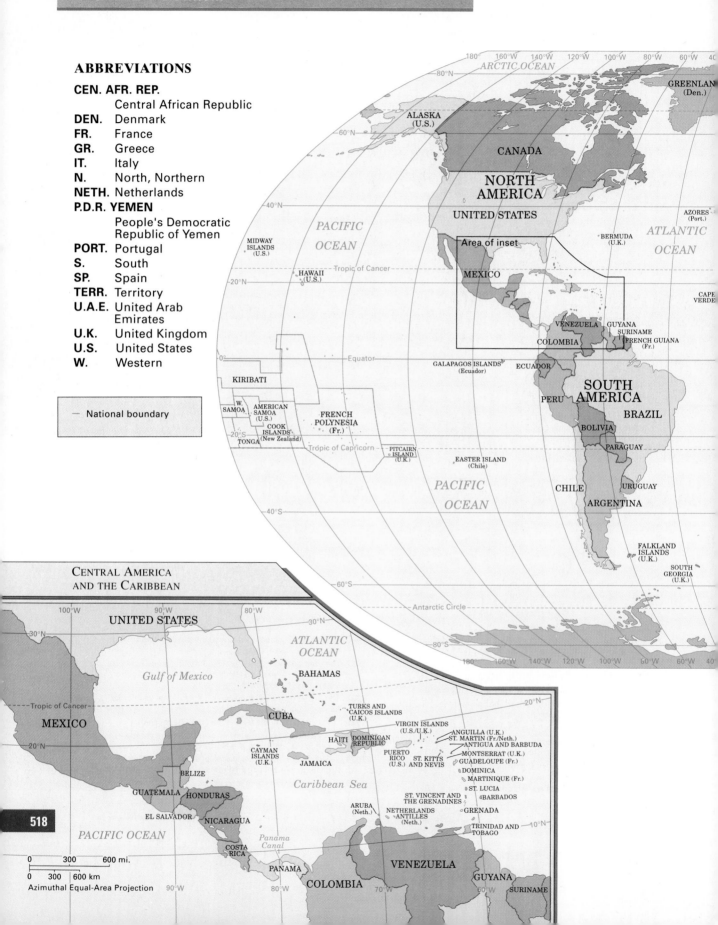

CENTRAL AMERICA AND THE CARIBBEAN

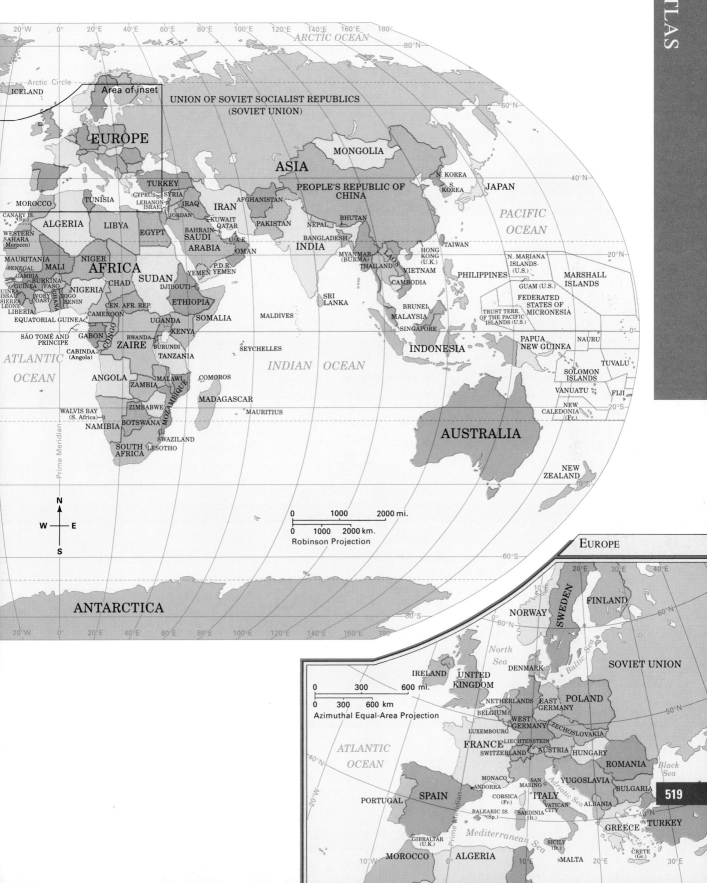

20°W 0° 20°E 40°E 60°E 80°E 100°E 120°E 140°E 160°E 180°

ARCTIC OCEAN

80°N

Arctic Circle

ICELAND

Area of inset

UNION OF SOVIET SOCIALIST REPUBLICS
(SOVIET UNION)

60°N

EUROPE

MONGOLIA

ASIA

PEOPLE'S REPUBLIC OF
CHINA

N. KOREA
S. KOREA

JAPAN

40°N

MOROCCO

TUNISIA

TURKEY

CYPRUS SYRIA
LEBANON
ISRAEL

IRAQ

IRAN

AFGHANISTAN

PACIFIC
OCEAN

CANARY IS.
(Sp.)

ALGERIA

LIBYA

JORDAN

KUWAIT
QATAR

PAKISTAN

NEPAL

BHUTAN

WESTERN
SAHARA
(Morocco)

EGYPT

SAUDI
ARABIA

BAHRAIN
U.A.E.
OMAN

INDIA

BANGLADESH

TAIWAN

20°N

MAURITANIA

NIGER

P.D.R.

MYANMAR
(BURMA)

HONG
KONG
(U.K.)

SENEGAL
GAMBIA

MALI

AFRICA

CHAD

SUDAN

YEMEN YEMEN

THAILAND

LAOS

N. MARIANA
ISLANDS
(U.S.)

GUINEA
BISSAU

BURKINA
FASO

DJIBOUTI

VIETNAM

GUINEA
SIERRA
LEONE

NIGERIA

CAMBODIA

GUAM (U.S.)

PHILIPPINES

MARSHALL
ISLANDS

IVORY
COAST

TOGO
BENIN

CEN. AFR. REP.

ETHIOPIA

SRI
LANKA

LIBERIA

EQUATORIAL GUINEA

CAMEROON

UGANDA

SOMALIA

MALDIVES

BRUNEI

FEDERATED
STATES OF
MICRONESIA

TRUST TERR.
OF THE PACIFIC
ISLANDS (U.S.)

0°

SÃO TOMÉ AND
PRINCIPE

GABON

KENYA

MALAYSIA

CONGO

ZAIRE

RWANDA
BURUNDI

SINGAPORE

CABINDA
(Angola)

TANZANIA

SEYCHELLES

INDONESIA

PAPUA
NEW GUINEA

NAURU

ATLANTIC

INDIAN OCEAN

OCEAN

ANGOLA

MALAWI

COMOROS

TUVALU

ZAMBIA

SOLOMON
ISLANDS

WALVIS BAY
(S. Africa)

ZIMBABWE

MADAGASCAR

MOZAMBIQUE

MAURITIUS

VANUATU

FIJI

NEW
CALEDONIA
(Fr.)

20°S

NAMIBIA

BOTSWANA

SWAZILAND

SOUTH
AFRICA

LESOTHO

AUSTRALIA

NEW
ZEALAND

40°S

N
W E
S

0 1000 2000 mi.

0 1000 2000 km.

Robinson Projection

60°S

ANTARCTICA

80°S

20°W 0° 20°E 40°E 60°E 80°E 100°E 120°E 140°E 160°E 180°

EUROPE

20°E 30°E 40°E

10°E

SWEDEN

FINLAND

NORWAY

0°
60°N

60°N

North
Sea

DENMARK

Baltic Sea

SOVIET UNION

IRELAND

UNITED
KINGDOM

0 300 600 mi.

NETHERLANDS

EAST
GERMANY

POLAND

0 300 600 km

BELGIUM

50°N

Azimuthal Equal-Area Projection

LUXEMBOURG

WEST
GERMANY

CZECHOSLOVAKIA

FRANCE

LIECHTENSTEIN

AUSTRIA

HUNGARY

SWITZERLAND

ATLANTIC

ROMANIA

OCEAN

40°N

MONACO

SAN
MARINO

YUGOSLAVIA

Black
Sea

ANDORRA

Adriatic Sea

PORTUGAL

SPAIN

CORSICA
(Fr.)

ITALY

BULGARIA

ALBANIA

VATICAN
CITY

BALEARIC IS.
(Sp.)

SARDINIA
(It.)

GREECE

TURKEY

GIBRALTAR
(U.K.)

SICILY
(It.)

CRETE
(Gr.)

MOROCCO

ALGERIA

Mediterranean Sea

MALTA

10°W 0° 10°E 20°E 30°E

519

ARCTIC OCEAN
Beaufort Sea
GREENLAN
Baffin
Bay
Mt. McKinley
Bering
Sea
Gulf of
Alaska
ROCKY MOUNTAINS
NORTH
AMERICA
Hudson
Bay
ALEUTIAN
ISLANDS
NEWFOUNDLAND
PACIFIC
OCEAN
GREAT PLAINS
APPALACHIAN MTS.
AZORES
Mt. Whitney
ATLANTIC
OCEAN
BERMUDA
Gulf of
Mexico
Tropic of Cancer
HAWAIIAN
ISLANDS
BAHAMAS
YUCATAN CUBA
PEN.
HISPANIOLA
CAPE VERD
ISLAND:
Caribbean Sea
WEST
INDIES
CENTRAL
AMERICA
Equator
GALAPAGOS
ISLANDS
GUIANA
HIGHLANDS
AMAZON
BASIN
POLYNESIA
ANDES
SOUTH
AMERICA
BRAZILIAN
HIGHLANDS
ATACAMA
DESERT
Tropic of Capricorn
PACIFIC
OCEAN
Mt. Aconcagua
PAMPAS
PATAGONIA
FALKLAND
ISLANDS
Cape Horn
Antarctic Circle

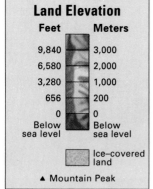

Land Elevation

Feet		Meters
9,840		3,000
6,580		2,000
3,280		1,000
656		200
0		0
Below sea level		Below sea level

Ice–covered land

▲ Mountain Peak

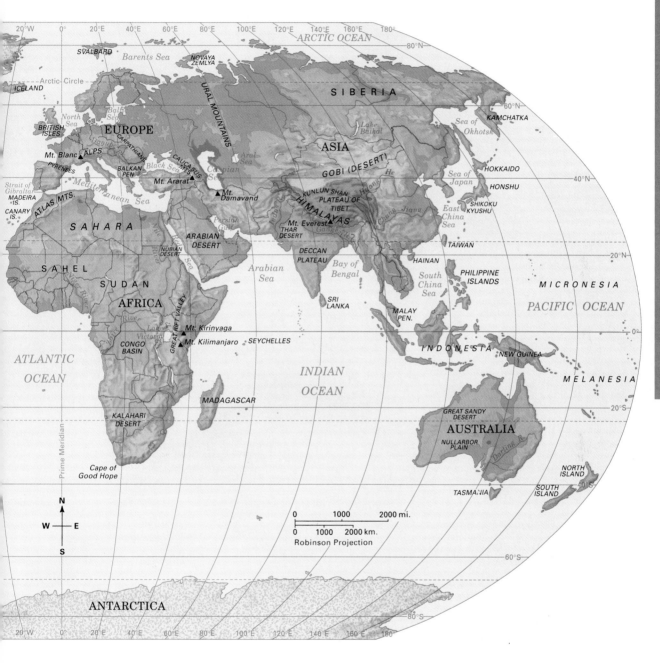

20°W 0° 20°E 40°E 60°E 80°E 100°E 120°E 140°E 160°E 180°

ARCTIC OCEAN

80°N

SVALBARD *Barents Sea* NOVAYA ZEMLYA

ICELAND — Arctic Circle —

SIBERIA

60°N

KAMCHATKA

BRITISH ISLES *North Sea* Baltic Sea URAL MOUNTAINS

EUROPE CARPATHIANS Lake Baikal *Sea of Okhotsk*

ASIA

HOKKAIDO

Mt. Blanc ALPS CAUCASUS MTS. *Aral Sea* GOBI (DESERT) He *Sea of Japan*

PYRENEES BALKAN PEN. *Black Sea* Caspian Sea HONSHU

40°N

Strait of Gibraltar *Mediterranean Sea* Mt. Ararat KUNLUN SHAN Huang *East China Sea* SHIKOKU KYUSHU

MADEIRA IS. ATLAS MTS. Mt. Damavand PLATEAU OF TIBET Chang Jiang

CANARY IS.

SAHARA ARABIAN DESERT HIMALAYAS Mt. Everest TAIWAN

Persian Gulf THAR DESERT Ganges R. 20°N

NUBIAN DESERT DECCAN PLATEAU HAINAN

SAHEL *Arabian Sea* *Bay of Bengal* *South China Sea* PHILIPPINE ISLANDS MICRONESIA

SUDAN PACIFIC OCEAN

AFRICA SRI LANKA MALAY PEN.

Nile River Mt. Kirinyaga 0°

ATLANTIC OCEAN GREAT RIFT VALLEY Mt. Kilimanjaro SEYCHELLES INDONESIA NEW GUINEA

CONGO BASIN Lake Victoria MELANESIA

INDIAN OCEAN

MADAGASCAR 20°S

KALAHARI DESERT GREAT SANDY DESERT

Prime Meridian

AUSTRALIA

Cape of Good Hope NULLARBOR PLAIN Darling R. NORTH ISLAND

N 0 1000 2000 mi. SOUTH ISLAND

W—E 0 1000 2000 km. TASMANIA 40°S

S Robinson Projection

60°S

ANTARCTICA

80°S

20°W 0° 20°E 40°E 60°E 80°E 100°E 120°E 140°E 160°E 180°

NORTH
AMERICA

90°W   75°W   60°W   45°W   30°W   15°W   0°   15°E   30°E   45°E   60°E   75°E

SVALBARD
(Norway)

FRANZ JOSEPH LAND

75°N

*Barents
Sea*

NOVAYA ZEMLYA

Arctic Circle

Norwegian Sea

Murmansk

Reykjavik   ICELAND

*White
Sea*

Trondheim
NORWAY

Helsinki

FINLAND

Leningrad

60°N

UNION OF SOVIE

Oslo

Stockholm

*Volga
River*

Novosibirsk

*ATLANTIC
OCEAN*

North Sea

Copenhagen
DENMARK

Moscow

URAL MOUNTAINS

*Ob
River*

Edinburgh

Gdansk

Minsk

Kuybyshev

*Irtysh
River*

Dublin
IRELAND

UNITED
KINGDOM

Amsterdam
The
Hague   NETH.

Berlin

Warsaw

Kiev

Kharkov

KIRGHIZ STEPPE

*Lake
Balkhash*

London

BELG.

E.
GER.

POLAND

Don River

Volgograd

Brussels

Bonn
LUX.

W. GER.
Prague
CZECH.

Vienna

Budapest

*Aral
Sea*

Tashkent

Paris

LIECH.

Bern
SWITZ.

ALPS   AUST.

HUNG.

ROMANIA

Dniester R.

45°N

Sea of
Biscay

FRANCE

Venice

Belgrade

Bucharest

Black Sea

CAUCASUS MTS.

Caspian Sea

PAMIRS

MONACO
ANDORRA
CORSICA
(Fr.)

SAN
MARINO

APENNINES

YUGOSLAVIA

BULGARIA
Sofia

Tbilisi

ARMENIA

KUNL

Barcelona

PYRENEES

Tirane

Sea of Azov

AZERBAIJAN

HINDU KUSH

Islamabad

PORTUGAL
Lisbon

Madrid

Rome
ITALY
ALB.

Istanbul

Ankara

ASIA
MINOR

TURKEY

KURDISTAN

ELBURZ
MTS.
Teheran

Kabul
AFGHANISTAN

HIMALAY

SPAIN

SARDINIA
(Italy)

*Tyrrhenian
Sea*

GREECE
Athens

ZAGROS

PLATEAU
OF
IRAN

*Ionian
Sea*

BALEARIC
ISLANDS
(Sp.)

SICILY
(Italy)

*Aegean
Sea*

Nicosia
CYPRUS

SYRIA

Baghdad

IRAN

New
Dehli

Katman

MALTA

MOUNTAINS

PAKISTAN

NEP

30°N

Mediterranean Sea

Beirut
LEBANON
Damascus

IRAQ

Ganges

Jerusalem

Amman
JORDAN

THAR
DESERT

INDIA

ISRAEL

NEUTRAL ZONE

Kuwait

Karachi

Persian Gulf

KUWAIT

BAHRAIN

QATAR

Abu Dhabi

Tropic of Cancer

*Red
Sea*

Riyadh

SAUDI ARABIA

U.A.E.

Muscat

DECCAN
PLATEAU

Bombay

WESTERN GHATS

EASTERN GHATS

OMAN

Madra

RUB AL KHALI
(DESERT)

*Arabian
Sea*

15°N

Sana
YEMEN

PEOPLE'S
DEMOCRATIC
REPUBLIC
OF YEMEN

LACCADIVE
ISLANDS
(India)

SRI
LANKA

AFRICA

Aden

SOCOTRA
(P.D.R. Yemen)

Gulf of Aden

Colombo

Male

MALDIVES

0°   Equator

INDIAN   OCEAN

Prime Meridian

* National capital

• Major city

— National boundary

N

W   E

S

0   400   800 mi.

0   400   800 km.

Robinson Projection

15°S

0°   15°E   30°E   45°E   60°E   75°E

ARCTIC OCEAN

75°N

NORTH
AMERICA

S I B E R I A

60°N

SOCIALIST REPUBLICS

Yenisei

River

Lena River

STANOVOI RANGE

Amur River

Bering Sea

Sea of
Okhotsk

SAKHALIN
(U.S.S.R.)

Lake
Baikal

● Irkutsk

KURIL ISLANDS

ALTAI MTS.

DA HINGGAN LING

● Ulan Bator

MONGOLIA

Harbin ●

45°N

180°

GOBI (DESERT)

● Vladivostok

● Sapporo

SHAN

Huang He

● Beijing

N. KOREA
● Pyongyang

Sea of
Japan

JAPAN

PLATEAU
OF
TIBET

● Seoul
S. KOREA

● Tokyo

PEOPLE'S REPUBLIC
OF CHINA

Jiang

Chang

Yellow
Sea

● Osaka

Brahmaputra R.

● Shanghai

● Thimbu
BHUTAN

East
China
Sea

30°N

BANGLADESH
● Dacca

Irrawaddy R.

Xi Jiang

● Taipei
TAIWAN

PACIFIC

● Calcutta

MYANMAR
(BURMA)

LAOS

● Guangzhou

MACAO
(Port.)

● Hanoi
Gulf
of
Tonkin

HONG
KONG
(U.K.)

OCEAN

Bay of
Bengal

● Vientiane

HAINAN

Mekong R.

● Rangoon
THAILAND

● Da Nang

Philippine

Sea

15°N

● Bangkok

VIETNAM

● Manila

PHILIPPINES

ANDAMAN
ISLANDS
(India)

CAMBODIA

Phnom ●
Penh

● Ho Chi Minh City
(Saigon)

NICOBAR
ISLANDS
(India)

South China
Sea

Bandar Seri
Begawan

MALAYSIA

BRUNEI ●

● Kuala Lumpur

MALAYSIA

SUMATRA

Singapore
● SINGAPORE

BORNEO

0°

CELEBES

INDONESIA

Java Sea

NEW GUINEA

● Jakarta

JAVA

Arafura Sea

15°S

Timor
Sea

523

AUSTRALIA

90°E 105°E 120°E 135°E 150°E 165°E

90°E 105°E 120°E 135°E 150°E 165°E 180° 165°W 150°W 135°W 120°W

MIDDLE EAST: *Political/Physical*

EUROPE

ASIA

AFRICA

Black Sea

Istanbul
Bosporus
Sea of Marmara
Dardanelles

PONTIC MOUNTAINS

Ankara

TURKEY

Izmir

Aegean Sea

Tuz Lake

TAURUS MTS.

Nicosia
CYPRUS

ARMENIA

Murat River
Lake Van

KURDISTAN

Aleppo

SYRIA

Caspian Sea

Lake Urmia

ELBURZ MTS.
Teheran

DASHT-E-KAVIR
(DESERT)

PLATEAU OF IRAN

Mediterranean Sea

LEBANON
Beirut
Damascus
Jordan River
SYRIAN DESERT

Tigris River
Euphrates River

Baghdad

ZAGROS MOUNTAINS

IRAN

DASHT-E-LUT
(DESERT)

ISRAEL
Tel Aviv
Jerusalem
Port Said
Gaza
Alexandria

WEST BANK
Amman
Dead Sea
NEGEV DESERT
JORDAN

IRAQ

AN NAFUD
(DESERT)

QATTARA DEPRESSION
Cairo

Suez Canal

SINAI PEN.

Gulf of Suez

EGYPT

SAHARA

LIBYAN DESERT

ARABIAN DESERT

Nile River

Gulf of Aqaba

Tropic of Capricorn

Lake Nasser

Red Sea

Medina

Jidda
Mecca

KUWAIT
Kuwait

NEUTRAL ZONE

Persian Gulf

Manama
BAHRAIN

Riyadh

SAUDI ARABIA

Doha
QATAR

Strait of Hormuz

Abu Dhabi

UNITED ARAB EMIRATES

Gulf of Oman

Muscat

OMAN

RUB AL KHALI
(DESERT)

HADRAMAUT

PEOPLE'S DEMOCRATIC REPUBLIC OF YEMEN

Arabian Sea

Sana

YEMEN

Aden

SOCOTRA
(P.D.R. Yemen)

Bab el Mandeb

Gulf of Aden

N
W E
S

⊛ National capital

• Major city

— National boundary

0   200   400 mi.

0   200   400 km
Lambert Conformal Conic Projection

INDIAN OCEAN

AFRICA: *Political/Physical*

EUROPE

ASIA

Mediterranean Sea

Strait of Gibraltar

Suez Canal

Tunis
Algiers
TUNISIA
Tripoli

MADEIRA ISLANDS (Port.)
Casablanca
Rabat
Marrakech
ATLAS
MOUNTAINS
MOROCCO

CANARY ISLANDS (Sp.)

WESTERN SAHARA (Morocco)

ALGERIA
LIBYA

Alexandria
QATTARA DEPRESSION
Cairo

EGYPT

S A H A R A

AHAGGAR MOUNTAINS

Nile River

Red Sea

Tropic of Cancer

MAURITANIA
Nouakchott

MALI

TIBESTI MOUNTAINS

NUBIAN DESERT

Cape Verde

Timbuktu

NIGER

SAHEL

CHAD

NILE BASIN

Khartoum

Bab el Mandeb

ERITREA

Gulf of Aden

Dakar
SENEGAL
Banjul
GAMBIA
Bissau
GUINEA-BISSAU
Bamako
BURKINA FASO
Niamey
Ouagadougou
BENIN
GUINEA
Conakry
TOGO
Freetown
SIERRA LEONE
IVORY COAST
GHANA
Monrovia
LIBERIA
Abidjan
Accra
Lomé
Porto Novo
Lagos

NIGERIA

Kano
N'Djamena

S U D A N

SUDAN

DJIBOUTI
Djibouti

AMHARA

Addis Ababa

PLATEAU

ETHIOPIA

SOMALIA

L. Volta

Gulf of Guinea
Malabo
EQUATORIAL GUINEA
Yaounde

CAMEROON
Bangui

CENTRAL AFRICAN REPUBLIC

Zaire River
Lake Albert

UGANDA
Kampala

KENYA
Nairobi

Mogadishu

SÃO TOMÉ AND PRINCIPE
São Tomé

ANNOBÓN (Equatorial Guinea)

Libreville
GABON

CONGO

CONGO BASIN

Kigali
RWANDA
Bujumbura
BURUNDI

Lake Victoria

SERENGETI PLAIN

GREAT RIFT VALLEY

INDIAN OCEAN

Victoria
SEYCHELLES

Equator

ATLANTIC OCEAN

Kasai R.

Brazzaville
Kinshasa

CABINDA (Angola)

ZAIRE

MITUMBA MTS.

L. Tanganyika

TANZANIA

ZANZIBAR
Dar es Salaam

ASCENSION (U.K.)

Luanda

Cuanza R.

KATANGA PLATEAU

Lubumbashi

Moroni
COMOROS

ST. HELENA (U.K.)

N
W E
S

ANGOLA

ZAMBIA

MALAWI
Lilongwe

Lake Malawi

MAYOTTE (Fr.)

Lusaka

Zambezi

Harare

L. Kariba

Victoria Falls

MOZAMBIQUE

Mozambique Channel

MADAGASCAR

Antananarivo

Port Louis
MAURITIUS
RÉUNION (Fr.)

NAMIB DESERT

NAMIBIA

OKAVANGO BASIN

ZIMBABWE

Windhoek

BOTSWANA

WALVIS BAY (S. Africa)

KALAHARI DESERT

Gaborone

Limpopo River

Pretoria
Maputo
Mbabane
SWAZILAND

Tropic of Capricorn

Johannesburg

Orange River

Vaal R.

LESOTHO
Maseru

Durban

DRAKENSBERG MTS.

SOUTH AFRICA

GREAT KAROO

Cape Town
Cape of Good Hope
Cape Agulhas

Legend

⊛ National capital
• Major city
— National boundary

0   400   800 mi.
0   400   800 km

Azimuthal Equal-Area Projection

30°W 20°W 10°W 0° 10°E 20°E 30°E 40°E 50°E 60°E

50°N 40°N 30°N 20°N 10°N 0° 10°S 20°S 30°S 40°S

NORTH AMERICA: *Political/Physical*

EUROPE

ASIA

ARCTIC OCEAN

Bering Strait

Bering Sea

BROOKS RANGE

Yukon River

QUEEN ELIZABETH ISLANDS

ELLESMERE ISLAND

GREENLAND (Denmark)

Beaufort Sea

BANKS ISLAND

VICTORIA ISLAND

Baffin Bay

ALASKA RANGE · Fairbanks

BAFFIN ISLAND

ALEXANDER ARCHIPELAGO

·Anchorage

Gulf of Alaska

KODIAK ISLAND

Great Bear Lake

Mackenzie River

Labrador Sea

QUEEN CHARLOTTE ISLANDS

COAST MOUNTAINS

Great Slave Lake

LAURENTIAN SHIELD

UNGAVA PENINSULA

Hudson Bay

LABRADOR

VANCOUVER ISLAND

ROCKY

·Edmonton   CANADA

NEWFOUNDLAND

Vancouver
Puget Sound
Seattle

·Calgary

Lake Winnipeg

PRINCE EDWARD ISLAND

CAPE BRETON ISLAND

Portland

Columbia River

·Winnipeg

Quebec

St. Lawrence River

·Montreal
Ottawa ✹

Bay of Fundy

M O U N T A I N S

Snake River

Missouri River

BLACK HILLS

Minneapolis·

Lake Superior

Lake Huron

Toronto·

L. Ontario

Boston
Cape Cod

San Francisco·

SIERRA NEVADA

Great Salt Lake

Salt Lake City

Milwaukee·

Lake Michigan

·Detroit

New York

ATLANTIC OCEAN

COAST   RANGES

Omaha·

Chicago·

Cleveland·

Lake Erie

·Philadelphia

·Denver

Indianapolis·

APPALACHIAN MTS.

·Baltimore
✹Washington

Kansas City·

St.
Louis·

Ohio River
·Louisville

Colorado River

UNITED STATES

Los Angeles·

MOJAVE DESERT

·Wichita

Nashville· ·Charlotte

Cape Hatteras

·BERMUDA (U.K.)

San Diego·

GRAND CANYON

·Phoenix

Red   River

Fort Worth·

Atlanta·

Birmingham·

PACIFIC OCEAN

Ciudad Juárez·
Chihuahua·

Rio Grande

·San Antonio

Austin·

·Houston

Jacksonville·

New Orleans·

Cape Canaveral

Tropic of Cancer

BAJA CALIFORNIA

·Monterrey

SIERRA MADRE ORIENTAL

Gulf of Mexico

·Miami

✹Nassau
·BAHAMAS

Gulf of California

SIERRA MADRE OCCIDENTAL

MEXICO

PLATEAU OF MEXICO

Cabo San Lucas

Guadalajara·

Havana✹

CUBA

San Juan

VIRGIN ISLANDS (U.S., U.K.)

ANGUILLA (U.K.)

ANTIGUA AND BARBUDA

Mexico City✹
Puebla·

·Veracruz

YUCATÁN PENINSULA

Santiago de Cuba·

CAYMAN ISLANDS (U.K.)

Port-au-Prince✹
HAITI

DOMINICAN REPUBLIC

PUERTO RICO (U.S.)

ST. KITTS-NEVIS

GUADELOUPE (Fr.)

MARTINIQUE (Fr.)

Acapulco·

ISTHMUS OF TEHUANTEPEC

✹Belmopan
BELIZE

JAMAICA

Kingston✹

Santo Domingo

DOMINICA Roseau✹

Castries✹ ST. LUCIA

Bridgetown

Caribbean Sea

ST. VINCENT AND THE GRENADINES

BARBADOS

GUATEMALA

HONDURAS

NETHERLANDS ANTILLES (Neth.)

St. George's✹
GRENADA

Port of Spain✹
TRINIDAD AND TOBAGO

Guatemala City✹
San Salvador✹
EL SALVADOR

✹Tegucigalpa
NICARAGUA

ARUBA (Neth.)

MOSQUITO COAST

N

Managua✹

Lago de Nicaragua

W   E

San José✹
COSTA RICA

ISTHMUS OF PANAMA

Panama City✹

S

PANAMA

SOUTH AMERICA

| ✹ National capital |
| • Major city |
| — National boundary |

0   400   800 mi.

0   400   800 km

Azimuthal Equal-Area Projection

Equator

SOUTH AMERICA: *Political/Physical*

CENTRAL
AMERICA

Caribbean Sea

*ATLANTIC
OCEAN*

Barranquilla
Cartagena
•Maracaibo   Caracas⊛

LLANOS
VENEZUELA

Orinoco River

Georgetown•
GUYANA Paramaribo•
SURINAME Cayenne•
FRENCH
GUIANA
(Fr.)

Medellín•
⊛Bogotá

COLOMBIA

Angel Falls

GUIANA HIGHLANDS

MALPELO.
(Colombia)

OCCIDENTAL MTS.

Rio   Negro

AMAZON

•Belém

⊛Quito
Guayaquil•ECUADOR
*Gulf of
Guayaquil*

Iquitos•

BASIN

Manaus•

Amazon   River

Fortaleza•

GALAPAGOS
ISLANDS
(Ecuador)

Equator

Solimões   River

Madeira River

Tapajós River

Xingu River

Trujillo•

PERU

BRAZIL

Recife•

São Francisco River

Lima⊛

Cuzco•

A N D E S

Lake Titicaca

La Paz⊛

PLATEAU OF
MATO GROSSO

BRAZILIAN

Arequipa•

BOLIVIA

⊛Sucre

⊛Brasília

HIGHLANDS

Salvador•

PACIFIC

OCEAN

ALTIPLANO

Paraguay River

Belo Horizonte•

Antofagasta•

ATACAMA DESERT

GRAN CHACO

PARAGUAY

Paraná River

São Paulo•   Rio de Janeiro•
Santos•

Tropic of Capricorn

SAN FELIX
ISLAND
(Chile)   SAN AMBROSIO
ISLAND
(Chile)

Asunción⊛

Salado River

Paraná River

Pôrto Alegre•

Córdoba•

JUAN FERNANDEZ
ISLANDS
(Chile)

CHILE

Rosario•

URUGUAY

Valparaíso•
Santiago⊛

Buenos Aires• ⊛Montevideo

Rio de la Plata

*ATLANTIC

OCEAN*

Concepción•

ARGENTINA

PAMPAS

Valdivia•

Colorado R.

Bahía Blanca•

Gulf of San Matias

N
W ⊕ E
S

PATAGONIA

Comodoro Rivadavia•
Gulf of San Jorge

⊛ National capital

• Major city

— National boundary

0   400   800 mi.
0   400   800 km
Azimuthal Equal-Area Projection

*Strait of
Magellan*
FALKLAND
ISLANDS
(U.K.)
TIERRA
DEL FUEGO

527

SOUTH GEORGIA
(U.K.)

Cape Horn

Drake Passage

PACIFIC RIM: *Political/Physical*

ARCTIC OCEAN

Arctic Circle

ALASKA
(U.S.)
• Anchorage

UNION OF SOVIET
SOCIALIST REPUBLICS

60°N

Bering Sea

CANADA

KAMCHATKA

ASIA

SAKHALIN

Vancouver NORTH
• Seattle AMERICA

MONGOLIA

Vladivostok

KURIL IS.
(U.S.S.R.)

PACIFIC
OCEAN

60°

NORTH
Beijing KOREA
✹ ✹Pyongyang
✹Seoul
SOUTH
KOREA

PEOPLE'S
REPUBLIC
OF CHINA

San
Francisco

UNITED
STATES

Washington
✹

Ottawa
✹

JAPAN
✹Tokyo

• Los Angeles

30°N

Shanghai

East
China
Sea RYUKYU
IS.

MIDWAY ISLANDS
(U.S.)

Tropic of Cancer

BAHAMAS

MEXICO

Hanoi

✹Taipei

VOLCANO IS.
(Japan)

WAKE ISLAND
(U.S.)

Honolulu

Mexico City

CUBA

HONG
KONG
(U.K.)

TAIWAN

Philippine
Sea

NORTHERN
MARIANA
ISLANDS
(U.S.)

HAWAII
(U.S.)

GUATEMALA
EL SALVADOR

BELIZE
HONDURAS
NICARAGUA

LAOS
VIETNAM
THAILAND
CAMBODIA

Manila
PHILIPPINES

MARSHALL
ISLANDS

International Date Line

COSTA RICA
PANAMA

Bogotá
✹

South
China Sea

MICRONESIA

GUAM (U.S.)

✹Kolonia

Majuro
✹

Kuala
Lumpur BRUNEI
✹MALAYSIA

TRUST TERR.
OF THE PACIFIC
ISLANDS (U.S.)

FEDERATED STATES
OF MICRONESIA

Tarawa
✹

Equator

COLOMBIA
Quito✹
GALAPAGOS IS.
(Ecuador)

ECUADOR
Guayaqu

SINGAPORE

Yaren
✹
NAURU

INDONESIA

NEW
GUINEA

PAPUA
NEW GUINEA

SOLOMON
ISLANDS

TUVALU

KIRIBATI

POLYNESIA

PERU

Lima
✹

Jakarta

Arafura
Sea

Funafuti
✹

WESTERN
SAMOA

AMERICAN
SAMOA
(U.S.)

FRENCH
POLYNESIA
(Fr.)

SOUTH
AMERICA

INDIAN
OCEAN

Timor
Sea
Gulf of
Carpentaria

✹Port
Moresby

Great
Barrier
Reef

✹Honiara

VANUATU

WALLIS AND
FUTUNA IS. (Fr.)

COOK
ISLANDS
(N.Z.)

TONGA

GREAT
SANDY
DESERT

Coral Sea

✹Port
Vila

✹Suva
FIJI

✹Nuku'alofa

Tropic of Capricorn

EASTER I.
(Chile)

PITCAIRN I.
(U.K.)

CHILE

MACDONNELL
RANGE

NEW CALEDONIA
(Fr.)

AUSTRALIA

Great
Australian
Bight

NORFOLK I.
(Aust.)

KERMADEC
ISLANDS
(N.Z.)

PACIFIC

Valparaíso✹
Santiago✹

30°S

• Sydney
✹Canberra

Auckland

OCEAN

TASMANIA

NEW
ZEALAND

✹Wellington

Tasman
Sea

CHATHAM IS.
(N.Z.)

0   1000   2000 mi.

0 1000 2000 km
Miller Cylindrical Projection

60°S

Antarctic Circle

⊛ National capital

• Major city

— National boundary

ANTARCTICA

528

120°E   150°E   180°   150°W   120°W   90°W

WORLD: *Religions*

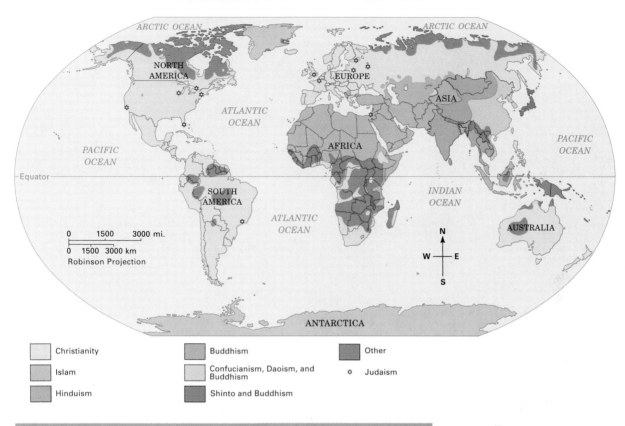

Christianity	Buddhism	Other
Islam	Confucianism, Daoism, and Buddhism	✿ Judaism
Hinduism	Shinto and Buddhism	

WORLD: *Languages*

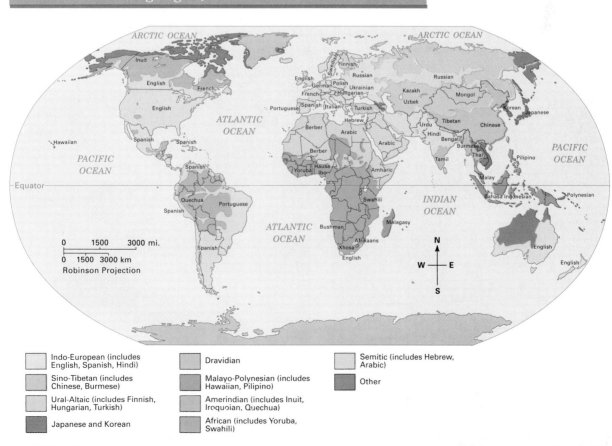

Indo-European (includes English, Spanish, Hindi)	Dravidian	Semitic (includes Hebrew, Arabic)
Sino-Tibetan (includes Chinese, Burmese)	Malayo-Polynesian (includes Hawaiian, Pilipino)	Other
Ural-Altaic (includes Finnish, Hungarian, Turkish)	Amerindian (includes Inuit, Iroquoian, Quechua)	
Japanese and Korean	African (includes Yoruba, Swahili)	

WORLD: *Vegetation*

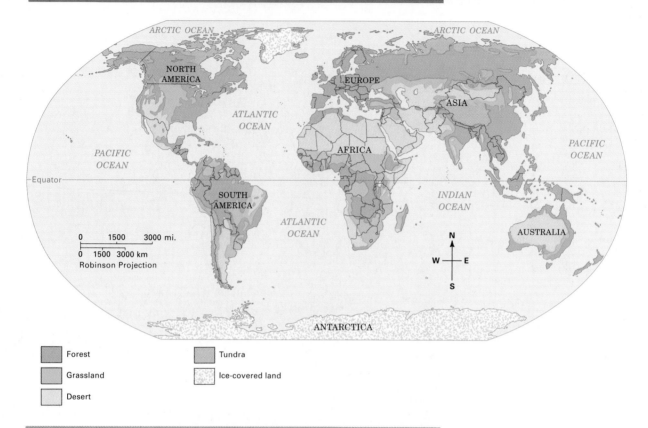

ARCTIC OCEAN

NORTH AMERICA

ATLANTIC OCEAN

PACIFIC OCEAN

Equator

SOUTH AMERICA

ATLANTIC OCEAN

ARCTIC OCEAN

EUROPE

ASIA

AFRICA

PACIFIC OCEAN

INDIAN OCEAN

AUSTRALIA

ANTARCTICA

0   1500   3000 mi.
0 1500 3000 km
Robinson Projection

N
W — E
S

- Forest
- Grassland
- Desert
- Tundra
- Ice-covered land

WORLD: *Climate*

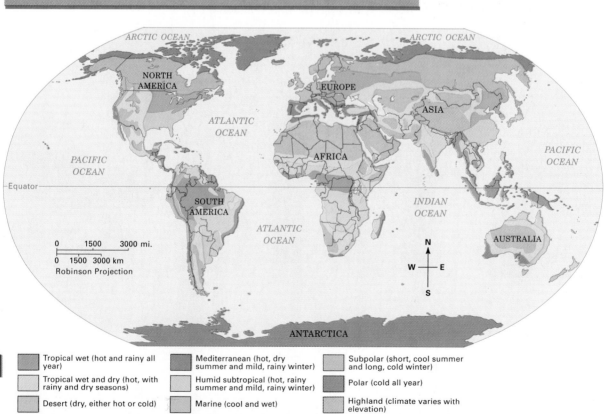

ARCTIC OCEAN

NORTH AMERICA

ATLANTIC OCEAN

PACIFIC OCEAN

Equator

SOUTH AMERICA

ATLANTIC OCEAN

ARCTIC OCEAN

EUROPE

ASIA

AFRICA

PACIFIC OCEAN

INDIAN OCEAN

AUSTRALIA

ANTARCTICA

0   1500   3000 mi.
0 1500 3000 km
Robinson Projection

N
W — E
S

- Tropical wet (hot and rainy all year)
- Tropical wet and dry (hot, with rainy and dry seasons)
- Desert (dry, either hot or cold)
- Semiarid (short rainy season)
- Mediterranean (hot, dry summer and mild, rainy winter)
- Humid subtropical (hot, rainy summer and mild, rainy winter)
- Marine (cool and wet)
- Continental (hot summer, cold winter)
- Subpolar (short, cool summer and long, cold winter)
- Polar (cold all year)
- Highland (climate varies with elevation)

WORLD: *Population*

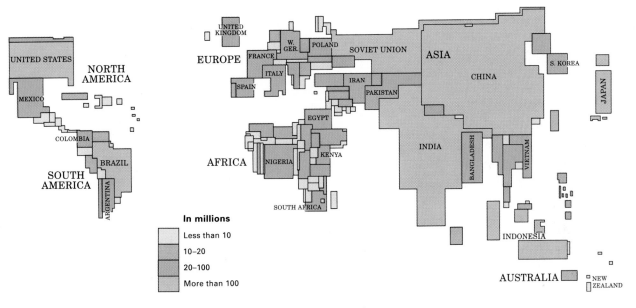

In millions

Less than 10
10–20
20–100
More than 100

Each country's size in the cartogram represents the size of its population compared with those of other countries in the world. Based on information in the *1985 Demographic Yearbook* (1987).

WORLD: *Land Use and Resources*

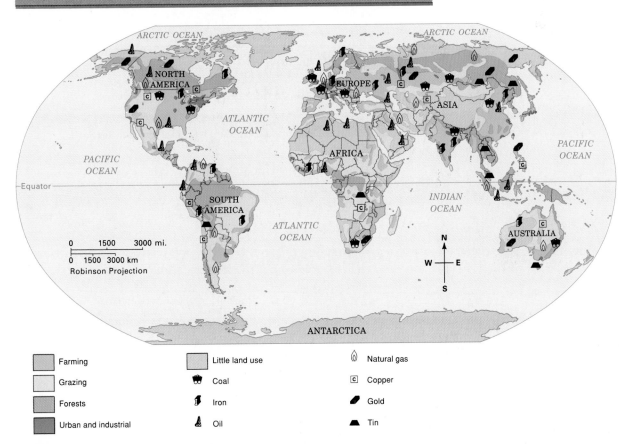

Farming

Grazing

Forests

Urban and industrial

Little land use

Coal

Iron

Oil

Natural gas

Copper

Gold

Tin

THE WORLD: A.D. 750

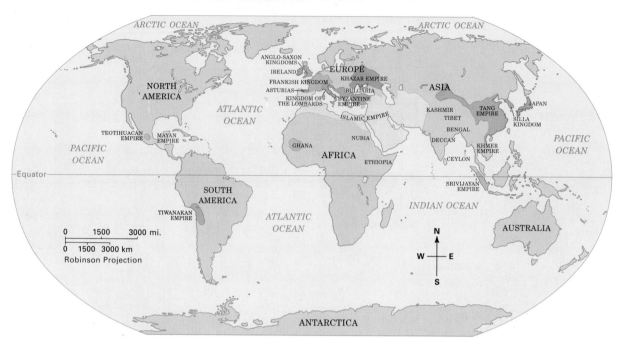

ARCTIC OCEAN   ARCTIC OCEAN

NORTH AMERICA

ANGLO-SAXON KINGDOMS

IRELAND

EUROPE

FRANKISH KINGDOM

ASTURIAS

KHAZAR EMPIRE

BULGARIA

KINGDOM OF THE LOMBARDS

BYZANTINE EMPIRE

ASIA

ISLAMIC EMPIRE

KASHMIR

TIBET

TANG EMPIRE

JAPAN

ATLANTIC OCEAN

NUBIA

BENGAL

DECCAN

SILLA KINGDOM

TEOTIHUACAN EMPIRE

MAYAN EMPIRE

PACIFIC OCEAN

GHANA

AFRICA

ETHIOPIA

KHMER EMPIRE

CEYLON

PACIFIC OCEAN

Equator

SOUTH AMERICA

TIWANAKAN EMPIRE

ATLANTIC OCEAN

SRIVIJAYAN EMPIRE

INDIAN OCEAN

AUSTRALIA

0   1500   3000 mi.

0   1500   3000 km

Robinson Projection

N   W — E   S

ANTARCTICA

World Civilizations: A.D. 500–1700

The map above shows the world at A.D. 750. The timeline indicates major civilizations during, before, and after this time period.

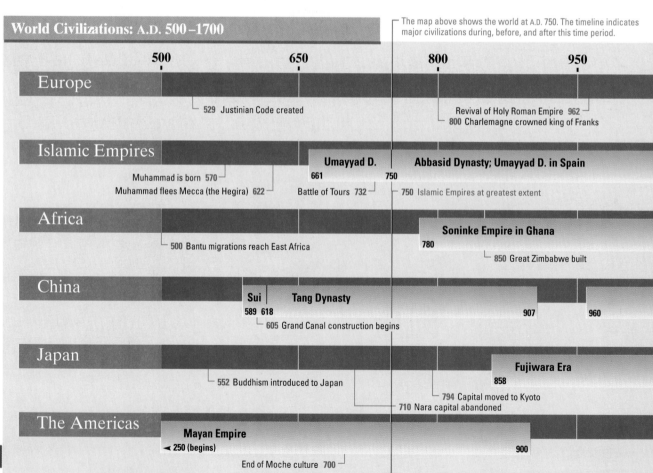

	500	650	800	950

Europe
- 529 Justinian Code created
- Revival of Holy Roman Empire 962
- 800 Charlemagne crowned king of Franks

Islamic Empires
- Umayyad D. 661
- 750
- Abbasid Dynasty; Umayyad D. in Spain
- Muhammad is born 570
- Muhammad flees Mecca (the Hegira) 622
- Battle of Tours 732
- 750 Islamic Empires at greatest extent

Africa
- 500 Bantu migrations reach East Africa
- Soninke Empire in Ghana 780
- 850 Great Zimbabwe built

China
- Sui 589 618 Tang Dynasty
- 605 Grand Canal construction begins
- 907
- 960

Japan
- 552 Buddhism introduced to Japan
- Fujiwara Era 858
- 794 Capital moved to Kyoto
- 710 Nara capital abandoned

The Americas
- Mayan Empire ◄ 250 (begins)
- End of Moche culture 700
- 900

THE WORLD: *A.D. 1492*

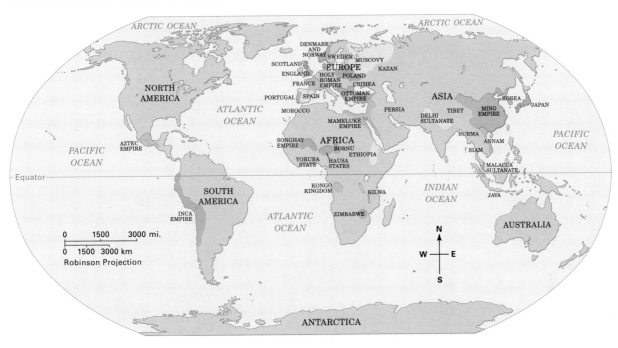

ARCTIC OCEAN

ARCTIC OCEAN

DENMARK
AND
NORWAY
SWEDEN
MUSCOVY
SCOTLAND
EUROPE
KAZAN
ENGLAND
HOLY
POLAND
FRANCE
ROMAN
EMPIRE
CRIMEA
PORTUGAL
SPAIN
OTTOMAN
EMPIRE
ASIA
KOREA
JAPAN

NORTH
AMERICA
ATLANTIC
OCEAN
MOROCCO
PERSIA
TIBET
MING
EMPIRE
DELHI
SULTANATE
MAMELUKE
EMPIRE
BURMA
ANNAM

PACIFIC
OCEAN
AZTEC
EMPIRE
SONGHAY
EMPIRE
AFRICA
BORNU
SIAM
MALACCA
SULTANATE
PACIFIC
OCEAN
YORUBA
STATE
HAUSA
STATES
ETHIOPIA

Equator

SOUTH
AMERICA
KONGO
KINGDOM
KILWA
INDIAN
OCEAN
JAVA

ATLANTIC
OCEAN
ZIMBABWE
AUSTRALIA
INCA
EMPIRE

0   1500   3000 mi.
0   1500 3000 km
Robinson Projection

N
W — E
S

ANTARCTICA

The map above shows the world at A.D. 1492. The timeline indicates major civilizations during, before, and after this time period.

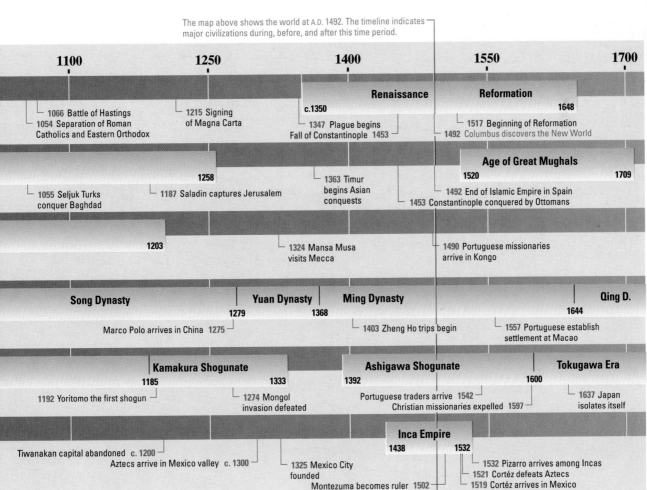

1100	1250	1400	1550	1700

Renaissance   **Reformation**
c.1350   1648

1066 Battle of Hastings
1054 Separation of Roman
Catholics and Eastern Orthodox
1215 Signing
of Magna Carta
1347 Plague begins
Fall of Constantinople 1453
1517 Beginning of Reformation
1492 Columbus discovers the New World

Age of Great Mughals
1520   1709

1055 Seljuk Turks
conquer Baghdad
1187 Saladin captures Jerusalem
1258
1363 Timur
begins Asian
conquests
1492 End of Islamic Empire in Spain
1453 Constantinople conquered by Ottomans

1203
1324 Mansa Musa
visits Mecca
1490 Portuguese missionaries
arrive in Kongo

Song Dynasty   **Yuan Dynasty** **Ming Dynasty**   **Qing D.**
1279   1368   1644

Marco Polo arrives in China 1275
1403 Zheng Ho trips begin
1557 Portuguese establish
settlement at Macao

Kamakura Shogunate   **Ashigawa Shogunate**   **Tokugawa Era**
1185   1333   1392   1600

1192 Yoritomo the first shogun
1274 Mongol
invasion defeated
Portuguese traders arrive 1542
Christian missionaries expelled 1597
1637 Japan
isolates itself

Inca Empire
1438   1532

Tiwanakan capital abandoned c. 1200
Aztecs arrive in Mexico valley c. 1300
1325 Mexico City
founded
Montezuma becomes ruler 1502
1532 Pizarro arrives among Incas
1521 Cortéz defeats Aztecs
1519 Cortéz arrives in Mexico

GLOSSARY OF GEOGRAPHIC TERMS

cape
a narrow, curved area of land extending into an ocean or lake

(river) mouth
the place where a river flows into a lake or ocean

sea level
the level of the surface of the ocean

volcano
an opening in the earth, usually raised, through which lava and gasses from the earth's interior escape

harbor
a sheltered area of water, a safe docking place for ships

flood plain
flat land near the edges of rivers formed by mud and silt deposited by floods

strait
a narrow strip of water connecting two large bodies of water

bay
part of an ocean or lake extending into the land

island
a body of land surrounded by water

delta
a triangular area formed by deposits at the mouth of a river

oasis
a spot of fertile land in a desert, fed by water from wells or underground springs

desert
a dry area where few plants grow

tributary
a stream or river that flows into a larger river

savanna
a region containing scattered trees and vegetation

sahel
in Africa, a strip of dry grassland between a desert and a savanna

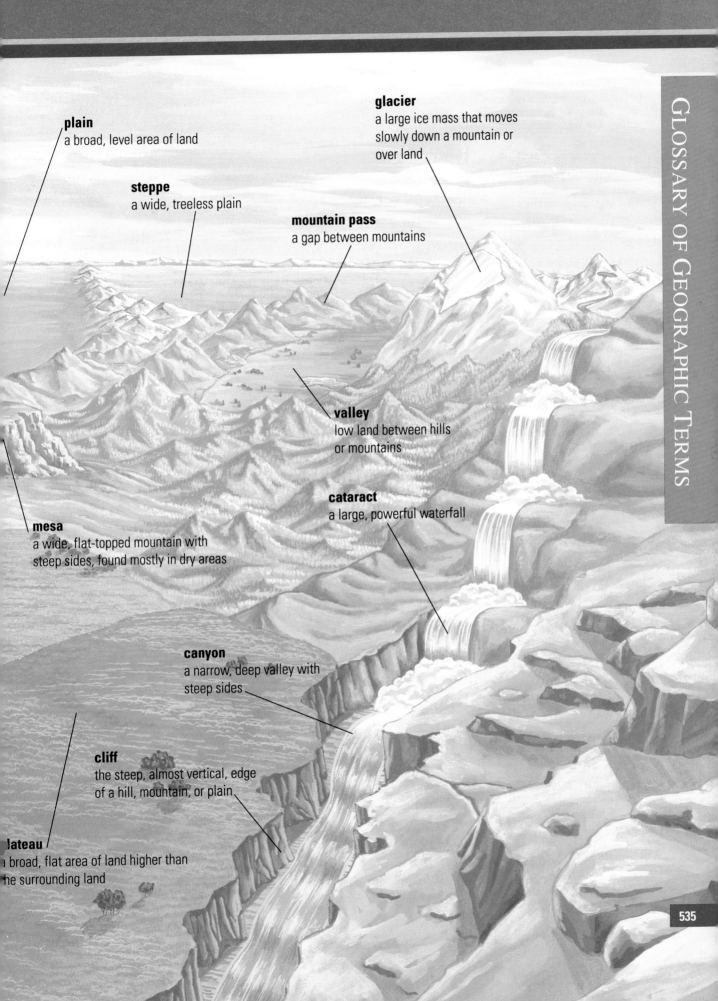

plain
a broad, level area of land

glacier
a large ice mass that moves slowly down a mountain or over land

steppe
a wide, treeless plain

mountain pass
a gap between mountains

valley
low land between hills or mountains

cataract
a large, powerful waterfall

mesa
a wide, flat-topped mountain with steep sides, found mostly in dry areas

canyon
a narrow, deep valley with steep sides

cliff
the steep, almost vertical, edge of a hill, mountain, or plain

plateau
a broad, flat area of land higher than the surrounding land

This Gazetteer will help you locate many of the places discussed in this book. Latitude and longitude given for large areas of land and water refers to the centermost point of the area; latitude and longitude of rivers refers to the river mouth. The page number tells you where to find each place on a map.

PLACE	LAT.	LONG.	PAGE
A			
Aachen (Charlemagne's capital; W. Germany)	51°N	6°E	260
Aegean Sea (part of Mediterranean)	16°N	65°E	290
Agra (early capital of Mughal Empire; India)	27°N	78°E	179
Alps (mountain range in S. and central Europe)	46°N	9°E	296
Antioch (ancient Syrian capital; Turkey)	36°N	36°E	10
Arguin (island discovered by Portuguese off W. Africa)	21°N	17°W	374
Augsburg (city connected with Reformation; Germany)	48°N	11°E	347
Avignon (papal city in France)	44°N	5°E	311
B			
Baghdad (capital of Abbasid caliphate; Iraq)	33°N	44°E	87
Bering Strait (waterway that separates Asia and N. America)	65°N	170°W	398
Berlin (capital of Brandenburg; Germany)	53°N	13°E	481
Black Sea (opens onto Aegean Sea through Bosporus)	43°N	32°E	36
Bojador, Cape (W. Africa; W. Sahara)	26°N	15°W	374
Bombay (city in W. India where English first traded)	19°N	73°E	468
Bosporus (waterway connecting Black Sea and Sea of Marmara; Turkey)	41°N	29°E	296
Bruges (important trading city in Flanders; Belgium)	51°N	3°E	330
Bursa (early capital of Ottoman Empire; Turkey)	40°N	29°E	171
C			
Cairo (capital of Fatamid caliphate; Egypt)	30°N	31°E	171
Calcutta (English colony in India)	23°N	88°E	468
Calicut (city da Gama visited first in India)	11°N	76°E	374
Caribbean Sea (W. Indies, Central and S. America)	15°N	76°W	378
Caucasus Mts. (mountain range; USSR)	43°N	45°E	36
Ceuta (Spanish port important in the gold trade; Morocco)	36°N	5°W	97

PLACE	LAT.	LONG.	PAGE
Chang Jiang (Yangtze R.; major river of China)	36°N	115°E	193
Changan (Xi'an; capital of China under Han and Tang dynasties)	34°N	109°E	193
Clermont (city where crusades originated; France)	46°N	3°E	296
Congo Basin (central Africa)	6°N	20°E	525
Constantinople (Istanbul; capital of Byzantine and Ottoman empires; Turkey)	41°N	29°E	67
Cordoba (capital of Umayyad caliphate; Spain)	38°N	5°W	97
Cuzco (capital of Inca Empire; Peru)	14°S	72°W	430
D			
Damascus (capital of Umayyad caliphate; Syria)	34°N	36°E	81
Dardanelles (waterway connecting Sea of Marmara and the Aegean Sea; Turkey)	40°N	26E	290
Delhi (capital of Mughal Empire; India)	29°N	77°E	179
E			
Edessa (Urfa; city held by crusaders; Turkey)	37°N	39°E	296
Edo (Tokyo; center of Tokugawa shogunate; Japan)	36°N	140°E	230
F			
Fernando Póo (island off W. Africa)	4°N	9°W	465
Flanders (region noted for woolen trade; France, Belgium)	51 N	3°E	330
Florence (cultural center of Renaissance Italy)	44°N	11°E	317
Fustat (Cairo; capital of Fatamid caliphate; Egypt)	30°N	31°E	80
G			
Gao (capital of Songhai Empire; Mali)	16°N	74°W	121
Geneva (center of Calvinism; Switzerland)	46°N	6°E	352
Genoa (port on Mediterranean; Italy)	44°N	9°E	290

PLACE	LAT.	LONG.	PAGE
Ghent (cloth weaving city in Flanders; Belgium)	51°N	4°E	**330**
Goa (Portuguese colony in India)	16°N	74°E	**142**
Good Hope, Cape of (S. Africa)	34°S	18°E	**374**
Granada (capital of Islamic kingdom; Spain)	37°N	4°W	**97**
Great Rift Valley (stretches from Jordan to S.E. Africa)	0°N	36°E	**525**
Great Zimbabwe (capital of ancient Zimbabwe; Africa)	20°S	31°E	**146**
Guinea, Gulf of (part of Atlantic; W. Africa)	2°N	1°E	**109**

H

PLACE	LAT.	LONG.	PAGE
Hangzhou (capital of China during late Song dynasty)	30°N	120°E	**167**
Hattin (battle where crusaders were defeated; Israel)	33°N	36°E	**299**
Heian (early name for Kyoto; Japan)	35°N	136°E	**230**
Himalayas (mountain range in Asia)	30°N	85°E	**179**
Hindu Kush (mountain range in Afghanistan)	36°N	72°E	**522**
Horn, Cape (tip of S. America)	56°S	67°W	**527**
Huang He (Yellow R.; N. central China)	34°N	117°E	**193**

I

PLACE	LAT.	LONG.	PAGE
Izapa (ruins of early Mayan city; Mexico)	15°N	92°W	**405**

J

PLACE	LAT.	LONG.	PAGE
Jamestown (English settlement in Virginia)	37°N	77°W	**470**
Jenne-jeno (Djénné; trading city in W. Africa; Mali)	14°N	5°W	**109**
Jerusalem (holy city of Jews, Christians, and Muslims; Israel)	32°N	35°E	**299**

K

PLACE	LAT.	LONG.	PAGE
Kaifeng (capital of China under Song dynasty)	35°N	114°E	**204**
Karakhota (caravan city; N. China)	42°N	101°E	**366**
Karakorum (ruined capital of Genghis Khan's empire; Mongolia)	47°N	103°E	**167**

PLACE	LAT.	LONG.	PAGE
Khanbalik (Beijing: Kublai Khan's capital; China)	40°N	116°E	**167**
Kilwa (port in E. Africa)	9°S	39°E	**142**
Koumbi (capital of ancient kingdom of Ghana)	15°N	8°W	**121**
Kyoto (Heian; city that was early home of Japan's emperors)	35°N	136°E	**230**

L

PLACE	LAT.	LONG.	PAGE
La Rochelle (port and Huguenot center; W. France)	46°N	1°W	**330**
Lisbon (capital of Portugal)	39°N	9°W	**374**
Luoyang (capital of China under Tang and Song dynasties)	35°N	113°E	**204**

M

PLACE	LAT.	LONG.	PAGE
Machu Picchu (ruined Inca citadel; Peru)	13°S	73°W	**430**
Madras (city in S. India; fought over by British and French)	13°N	80°E	**468**
Malacca (trading city; Malaysia)	2°N	102°E	**142**
Malindi (ancient E. African port; Kenya)	3°S	40°E	**142**
Marmara, Sea of (separates Europe and Asia; Turkey)	41°N	28°E	**290**
Mazagan (Al-Jadida: port founded by Portugal; Morocco)	33°N	9°W	**465**
M'Banza (capital of Kongo Kingdom; central Africa)	5°S	15°E	**150**
Mecca (holiest city of Islam; Saudi Arabia)	21°N	40°E	**67**
Medina (holy city of Islam; Saudi Arabia)	24°N	40°E	**67**
Milan (city-state in N. Italy)	45°N	9°E	**317**
Moche (site of ancient civilization; N. Peru)	8°S	79°W	**412**
Mombasa (E. African port)	4°S	40°E	**142**
Montreal (French settlement; Canada)	46°N	74°W	**470**
Mpinda (port on Zaire R.; Angola)	6°S	12°E	**150**

N

PLACE	LAT.	LONG.	PAGE
Nanjing (southern capital of Ming emperors; China)	32°N	119°E	**193**
New Amsterdam (Dutch settlement; New York)	41°N	74°W	**470**

This dictionary lists many of the important people introduced in this book. The page number refers to the main discussion of that person in the book. For more complete references see the Index.

Pronunciation Key

This chart presents the system of phonetic respellings used to indicate pronunciation in the Biographical Dictionary and in the chapters of this book.

Spellings	Symbol	Spellings	Symbol	Spellings	Symbol
pat	a	kick, cat, pique	k	thin, this	th
pay	ay	lid, needle	l	cut	uh
care	air	mum	m	urge, term, firm, word, heard	ur
father	ah	no, sudden	n		
bib	b	thing	ng	valve	v
church	ch	pot, horrid	ah	with	w
deed, milled	d	toe	oh	yes	y
pet	eh	caught, paw, for	aw	zebra, xylem	z
bee	ee	noise	oy	vision, pleasure, garage	zh
life, phase, rough	f	took	u		
gag	g	boot	oo	about, item, edible, gallop, circus	uh
hat	h	out	ow		
which	hw	pop	p	butter	ur
pit	ih	roar	r		
pie, by	eye, y	sauce	s	Capital letters indicate stressed syllables.	
pier	ihr	ship, dish	sh		
judge	j	tight, stopped	t		

A

Abd al Malik *(ahb dul mah LIHK)* c. 646–705, Umayyad caliph of Baghdad, 685–705 (p. 83).

Abd al Rahman I *(ahb al ra MAHN)* 731–788, escaped Abbasid massacre of 750 in Baghdad, Umayyad emir in Cordoba, 756–788 (p. 95).

Abd al Rahman III 891–961, Umayyad caliph of Cordoba, 929–961 (p. 96).

Abu Bakr 573–634, first caliph of Islam after death of Muhammad, 632–634 (p. 65).

Affonso I ?–c. 1550, ruler of the Kongo Kingdom in Africa (p. 152).

Ahuitzotl *(ah WEE soh tl)* ?–1502, Aztec ruler, 1486–1502 (p. 424).

Akbar, Akbar the Great 1542–1605, emperor of Mughal Empire, 1556–1605, (p. 181).

Alcuin 735–804, English scholar (p. 259).

Alfonso VI, Alfonso the Valiant ?–1109, king of Castile in Spain, 1072–1109 (p. 100).

Ali c. 600–661, fourth caliph of Islam, 656–661 (p. 66).

Anna Comnena c. 1083–1148, Byzantine author (p. 19).

Atahualpa *(ah tah WAHL pah)* c. 1500–1533, last ruler of the Inca Empire in Peru, killed by Pizarro's troops (p. 438).

Augustus 63 B.C.–A.D. 14, first Roman emperor, 29 B.C.–A.D. 14 (p. 26).

Aurangzeb *(AWR ung zehb)* 1618–1707, emperor of Mughal Empire, 1658–1707 (p. 185).

B

Babur 1483–1530, founder of Mughal dynasty of India, emperor, 1526–1530 (p. 180).

Bacon, Francis 1561–1626, English philosopher (p. 355).

Balboa, Vasco de 1475–1519, Spanish explorer of Isthmus of Panama and Pacific Ocean (p. 380).

Bayezid II 1447–1513, son of Mehmed II, Ottoman sultan, 1481–1512 (p. 175).

Boniface VIII c. 1235–1303, pope, 1294–1303, had power struggle with Philip IV of France (p. 338).

Brueghel, Pieter, the Elder *(BROO guhl)* c. 1530–1569, Flemish artist (p. 329).

Brunelleschi, Filippo *(broo nuh LEHS kee)* 1377–1446, Italian Renaissance architect (p. 322).

C

Cabot, John 1450–1498, Italian navigator and explorer of North America for English (p. 380).

Calvin, John 1509–1564, French theologian and reformer (p. 349).

Cão, Diego c. 1400s, Portuguese navigator and explorer of Congo River (p. 149).

Cartier, Jacques 1491–1557, French explorer (p. 381).

Catherine II, Catherine the Great 1729–1796, Russian empress, 1762–1796 (p. 480).

Charlemagne, Charles the Great 742–814, king of the Franks, 768–814, and emperor of the West, 800–814 (p. 258).

Ibn Sina, Avicenna *(av ih SEHN uh)* 980–1037, Abbasid doctor (p. 90).

Ignatius Loyola 1491–1556, Spanish priest, founder of Jesuits (p. 352).

Isabella I, Isabella the Catholic 1451–1504, queen of Aragon and unified Spain, 1479–1504 (p. 378).

J

Jahangir *(juh hahn GEER)*, Conqueror of the World 1569–1627, Mughal emperor, 1605–1627 (p. 182).

James I 1566–1625, king of England, 1603–1625, began colonization of America (p. 460).

James II 1633–1701, king of England, 1685–1688, deposed in Glorious Revolution (p. 462).

Jefferson, Thomas 1743–1826, third president of the United States, 1801–1809 (p. 482).

Joan of Arc 1412–1431, French farm girl who led French against English in 1429 (p. 312).

John 1167–1216, king of England, forced by barons to set his seal to the Magna Carta (p. 270).

John II, John the Perfect 1455–1495, king of Portugal, 1481–1495, supported exploration (p. 149).

Joseph II 1741–1790, German king, 1764–1790 (p. 480).

Julius Caesar 100 B.C.–44 B.C., Roman general and dictator, 49 B.C.–44 B.C. (p. 26).

Justinian I 483–565, Byzantine emperor, 527–565 (p. 291).

K

Kay, John 1742–1826, English inventor of the flying shuttle, 1733 (p. 492).

Kepler, Johannes 1571–1630, German astronomer (p. 354).

Khwarizmi, al *(al KWAH rihz mee)* c. 780–850, Arab mathematician lived in Baghdad (p. 90).

Kublai Kahn 1216–1294, Mongol leader, 1260–1294 (p. 167).

L

Laozi 606 B.C.–530 B.C., Chinese philosopher and founder of Taoism (p. 197).

Las Casas, Bartolomé de 1474–1566, Spanish Dominican missionary and historian (p. 369).

Leo III c. 680–741, Byzantine emperor, 717–741 (p. 293).

Leo III c. 750–816, pope, 795–816, crowned Charlemagne emperor of Holy Roman Empire (p. 258).

Leo IX 1002–1054, pope, 1049–1054, excommunicated patriarch of Constantinople (p. 293).

Leo X 1475–1521, pope, 1513–1521, pope during start of Protestant Reformation (p. 344).

Leonardo da Vinci *(VEEN chih)* 1452–1519, Italian artist and scientific thinker (p. 319).

Li Yuan 565–635, founder and first emperor of Tang Dynasty of China, 618–626 (p. 203).

Locke, John 1632–1704, English philosopher (p. 479).

Louis VI, Louis the Fat 1081–1137, king of France, 1108–1137, friend of Abbot Suger (p. 284).

Louis VII, Louis the Young c. 1120–1180, king of France, 1137–1180, joined crusade (p. 299).

Louis XIII 1601–1643, French king, 1610–1643, assisted by Cardinal Richelieu (p. 53).

Louis XIV 1638–1715, king of France, 1643–1715, absolute monarch; built Versailles (p. 454).

Louis XVI 1754–1793, French king, 1774–1792, executed during French Revolution (p. 82).

Luther, Martin 1483–1546, German religious reformer (p. 341).

M

Magellan, Ferdinand c. 1480–1521, Portuguese navigator of the world (p. 380).

Mahmud of Ghazna c. 971–1030, Turkish sultan, 997–1030 (p. 178).

Mansa Musa ?–1332, ruler of Mali, 1307–1332 (p. 119).

Mansur, Abu Jafur al c. 712–775, Abbasid caliph of Baghdad, 754–775 (p. 86).

Mary I 1516–1558, English queen, 1553–58, daughter of Henry VIII's first wife (p. 459).

Mary II 1662–1694, English queen, 1689–1694, became queen during Glorious Revolution (p. 462).

Mehmed II, Mehmed the Conqueror 1432–1481, Ottoman sultan, 1451–1481 (p. 172).

Michelangelo Buonarroti *(BWAN nahr raw tih)* 1475–1564, Italian artist (p. 322).

Montesquieu, Charles *(MAHN teh skyoo)* 1689–1755, French lawyer and political philosopher (p. 479).

Montezuma c. 1480–1520, Aztec emperor (p. 437).

More, Thomas 1478–1535, English statesman and author (p. 332).

Muawiya *(mu AH wih ya)* ?–680, Umayyad caliph, 661–680 (p. 67).

Muhammad 570–632, founder of Islam, prophet of Allah (p. 58).

Mwene Mutapa c. 1400s, king of Monomutapa in Africa (p. 148).

N

Newton, Isaac 1642–1727, English scientist, astronomer, and mathematician (p. 356).

O

Oda Nobunaga 1534–1582, general who unifed Japan (p. 238).

541

Odoacer c. 434–493, barbarian ruler of Italy, 476–493 (p. 256).

Ogadei *(ahg ah DY)* 1185–1241, Mongol leader, 1229–1241 (p. 166).

Osman I 1259–1326, founder of Ottoman Empire (p. 171).

P

Paul III 1468–1549, pope, 1534–1549, (p. 351).

Pepin, Pepin the Short c. 714–768, king of the Franks, 751–768 (p. 258).

Peter ?–c. 64, first bishop of Rome (p. 290).

Philip II 1165–1223, king of France, 1180–1223, went on Third Crusade (p. 300).

Philip IV, Philip the Fair 1268–1314, king of France, 1285–1314; moved papacy to Avignon (p. 338).

Pizarro, Francisco c. 1476–1541, Spanish conquerer of Peru (p. 438).

Polo, Marco c. 1254–c. 1324, Italian traveler to China (p. 365).

Ptolemy *(TAHL uh mee)* 90–168, Roman geographer (p. 365).

R

Rabelais, François *(rah BLEH)* c. 1490–1553, French writer and physician (p. 331).

Richard I, Richard Lion Heart 1157–1199, English king, 1189–1199, went on Third Crusade (p. 300).

Richelieu, Armand *(RISH uh loo)* 1585–1642, cardinal and chief minister of Louis XIII (p. 453).

Romulus Augustulus 461–?, last Roman emperor of the West, 475–476 (p. 256).

Rousseau, Jean-Jacques *(roo SOH)* 1712–1778, French philosopher (p. 479).

S

Saladin c. 1137–1193, Muslim warrior and Egyptian sultan (p. 299).

Selim I 1467–1520, son of Bayezid II, dethroned father, Ottoman sultan 1512–1520 (p. 175).

Shah Jahan *(SHAH ju HAHN)* 1592–1666, emperor of Mughal Empire, 1628–1658 (p. 183).

Shakespeare, William 1564–1616, English poet, actor, and playwright (p. 458).

Shotoku, Taishi 573–621, Japanese Soga prince and regent, 593–621 (p. 226).

Sinan c. 1489–1587, Suleiman's architect, designed over 300 buildings including the Taj Mahal (p. 176).

Stephens, John 1805–1852, American traveler and author (p. 404).

Suger *(SOO zhair)* 1081–1151, French abbot of Abbey of St. Denis, 1122–1151 (p. 283).

Suleiman *(SOO lay mahn)*, Suleiman the Magnificent 1494–1566, sultan, 1520–1566 (p. 175).

T

Taizu *(ty TSOO)* 1328–1398, founder and emperor of Ming Dynasty of China, 1368–1398 (p. 211).

Timur the Lame, Tamerlane c. 1336–1405, Mongol conqueror, founder of Timurid Dynasty (p. 168).

Theodosius I, Theodosius the Great c. 346–395, Roman general and emperor, 379–395 (p. 31).

Tokugawa Ieyasu 1543–1616, Japanese shogun, 1603–1605, established shogunate (p. 238).

U

Umar c. 581–644, second caliph of Islam, 634–644 (p. 66).

Urban II c. 1042–1099, pope, 1088–1099, called for the First Crusade (p. 294).

Urban VI c. 1318–1389, pope, 1378–1389, first pope during Great Schism with France (p. 339).

Uthman ?–656, third caliph of Islam, 644–656 (p. 66).

V

Van Eyck, Jan *(van ik)* c. 1390–1441, Flemish painter (p. 332).

Verrazano, Giovanni da c. 1485–c. 1528, Italian navigator of North America for French (p. 381).

Voltaire *(vohl TAIR)*, Francois Marie Arouet *(a REH)* 1694–1778, French writer (p. 477).

W

William I, William the Conqueror 1027–1087, king of England, 1066–1087, first Norman king (p. 261).

William III, William of Orange 1650–1702, king of England, 1689–1702 (p. 463).

Wycliffe, John c. 1320–1384, English scholar (p. 340).

X

Xian Di *(shehn tee)* ?–220, last Han emperor of China, 189–220 (p. 192).

Xuanzang c. 600–664, Chinese traveler (p. 130).

Y

Yang Jian, Emperor Wen 541–604, founder of Sui dynasty, emperor, 581–604 (p. 195).

Yoritomo 1147–1199, Japanese shogun, 1192–1199 (p. 232).

Z

Zacharias ?–752, pope, 741–752 (p. 258).

Zheng Ho c. 1371–c. 1433, Chinese admiral and diplomat (p. 213).

Zwingli, Ulrich 1484–1531, Swiss priest (p. 349).

Pronunciation Key

This chart presents the pronunciation key used in this Glossary. For a key to the phonetic respellings used to indicate pronunciation in the text of the chapters, see page 539.

Spellings	Symbol	Spellings	Symbol	Spellings	Symbol
pat	ă	kick, cat, pique	k	thin	th
pay	ā	lid, needle	l	this	*th*
care	âr	mum	m	cut	ŭ
father	ä	no, sudden	n	urge, term, firm, word, heard	ûr
bib	b	thing	ng		
church	ch	pot, horrid	ŏ	valve	v
deed, milled	d	toe	ō	with	w
pet	ě	caught, paw, for	ô	yes	y
bee	ē	noise	oi	zebra, xylem	z
life, phase, rough	f	took	o͝o	vision, pleasure, garage	zh
gag	g	boot	o͞o		
hat	h	out	ou	about, item, edible, gallop, circus	ə
which	hw	pop	p		
pit	ĭ	roar	r	butter	ər
pie, by	ī	sauce	s		
pier	îr	ship, dish	sh	Primary stress ´	
judge	j	tight, stopped	t	Secondary stress ´	

A

absolute monarch (ăb´sə-lŏot´mŏn´ ərk´) a ruler who has no restrictions of any kind on his or her power (p. 454).

adobe (ə-dō´ bē) bricks formed of mud mixed with straw (p. 415).

Age of Enlightenment (āj ŭv ěn-līt´n-mənt) a movement in Europe during the 1700s that critically analyzed ideas and institutions, using human reason (p. 477).

age set (āj sĕt) a social unit in which all the members of the group are the same age, particularly the Kikuyu people of Africa (p. 139).

agricultural revolution (ăg-rĭ-kŭl´chər-əl rěv´ə-lōō´ shən) a series of agricultural developments in Europe during the 1700s that improved both farming methods and the yield of the land (p. 490).

alliance (ə-lī´əns) a pact or union between states in a common cause (p. 424).

altiplano (äl´tĭ-plä´nō) the land on a high, flat plateau in South America (p. 412).

ancestor worship (ăn´sĕs´tər wûr´shĭp) honor and reverence paid to one's deceased relatives, based on the belief that their spirits live on and can influence the gods in one's favor (p. 126).

archaeology (är´kē-ŏl´ə-jē) the recovery and study of physical remains from past human life and culture (p. 17).

aristocrat (ə-rĭs´tə-krăt´) a member of a privileged class having inherited wealth and high social position (p. 204).

B

balance of trade (băl´əns ŭv trād) the difference in value between the total imports and total exports of a nation (p. 370).

barbarian (bär-bâr´ē-ən) in the ancient Roman Empire, people living along the empire's borders; a person considered by another group to have a primitive culture (p. 29).

bazaar (bə-zär´) an open-air market with shops and goods for sale (p. 56).

Buddhism (bōō´dĭz´əm) a religion based on the teachings of Gautama Buddha; Buddhism stresses that suffering is a basic part of life and that life is a cycle of death and rebirth (p. 194).

bullion (bŏŏl´yən) gold or silver in the form of bars or ingots of a specific weight (p. 370).

bureaucracy (byŏō-rŏk´rə-sē) a type of organization structured like a pyramid, with one person at the top and many at the bottom; workers at each level supervise those below them (p. 82).

bushido (bōōsh´ĭ-dō´) a Japanese code of ethics involving courage, loyalty, and commitment to military life; "the way of the warrior" (p. 273).

C

caliph (kā´lĭf) the civil and religious ruler of a Muslim state (p. 66).

calligraphy (kə-lĭg´rə-fē) the art of fine handwriting, such as that practiced in Islamic art and writing (p. 88).

calpulli (kăl-pōō′lē) an Aztec settlement in which families of different social classes lived and shared the land (p. 425).

capital (kăp′ĭ-tl) wealth in the form of money or property used for the production of more wealth (p. 375).

capitalist (kăp′ĭ-tl-ĭst) an investor of money, or capital, in business (p. 493).

caravan (kăr′ə-văn′) a single file of pack animals journeying together to transport goods (p. 11).

caravel (kăr′ə-vĕl′) a swift, maneuverable sailing ship used for exploration by the Spanish and the Portuguese in the 1500s and 1600s (p. 373).

charter (chär′tər) a document issued by a monarch or other authority, creating a public or private corporation with special rights (p. 468).

checks and balances (chĕks ənd băl′əns-əz) the system of maintaining a balance of power between various branches of a government (p. 498).

chinampa (chĭ-năm′pə) narrow strips of land about 300 feet long and 30 feet wide built in swampy land and used for farming in Central America, particularly by the Aztec (p. 423).

chivalry (shĭv′əl-rē) qualities such as honor, courtesy, loyalty, and fair treatment of the weak, idealized by knights in the Middle Ages (p. 273).

circumnavigation (sûr′kəm-năv′ĭ-gā′shən) the act of sailing around the world (p. 380).

city-state (sĭtē-stāt′) an independent state made up of a city and the territory that surrounds it (p. 143).

civil war (sĭv′əl wôr) a war between factions or regions within a country (p. 438).

clan (klăn) a group of families who claim descent from a common ancestor (p. 163).

classic (klăs′ĭk) a work of art or literature from ancient Greece or Rome; something considered to be of the highest rank or excellence (p. 291).

clergy (klûr′jē) the group of people who have been ordained for religious service (p. 283).

codex (kō′dĕks′) a manuscript volume; record books kept by early Central American peoples such as the Maya and Aztec (p. 409).

colony (kŏl′ə-nē) a settlement in a distant land whose citizens keep close ties to their parent country (p. 375).

commerce (kŏm′ərs) trade, or the buying and selling of goods, on a large scale (p. 45).

commonwealth (kŏm′ən-wĕlth′) a nation governed by the people (p. 461).

Confucianism (kən-fyōō′shən-ĭz′əm) a set of beliefs, based on the teachings of Confucius, that focused on proper conduct, respect for elders, scholarship, and government service (p. 194).

conquistador (kŏn-kwĭs′tə-dôr′) the Spanish term for conqueror used in reference to Spaniards who came to the New World in the 1500s in search of wealth (p. 437).

constitutional monarchy (kŏn′stĭ-tōō′shə-nəl mŏn′ər-kē) a monarchy in which the powers of the ruler are restricted to those granted under the constitution and laws of the nation (p. 463).

contract (kŏn′trăkt′) an agreement between two or more parties, particularly one that is written and enforceable by law (p. 479).

council (koun′səl) an assembly called to help pick the next Muslim caliph (p. 67); a series of meetings of Roman Catholic Church leaders in the 1400s dealing with issues of church law and faith (p. 340).

Counter Reformation (koun′tər ref′ər-mā′shən) the reform movement within the Roman Catholic Church whose goals were to abolish abuses and reaffirm traditional beliefs (p. 352).

courtier (kôr′tē-ər) a person who takes part in the highly refined social life of a court (p. 228).

crop rotation (krŏp rō-tā′shən) the planting of crops such as turnips, wheat, and clover in alternate years to keep soil fertile (p. 491).

crusade (krōō-sād′) any of the military expeditions undertaken by European Christians from c. 1100 to c. 1400 to regain the Holy Land from the Muslims (p. 296).

currency (kûr′ən-sē) any form of money being used as a medium of exchange (p. 150, 206).

D

daimyo (dīm′yō′) the lord of a large agricultural estate in feudal Japan who supported the shogun (p. 232).

Daoism (dou′ĭz′əm) a belief system based on the teachings of Laozi; Daoists emphasize living in harmony with nature and being content with one's life (p. 197).

delta (dĕl′tə) a triangle-shaped landform of mud and silt deposited at a river's mouth (p. 110).

despot (dĕs′pət) a ruler who holds absolute power and uses it abusively (p. 212).

dissent (dĭ-sĕnt′) to disagree, especially with the accepted doctrine of an established religion (p. 82).

divan (dĭ-văn′) a governing council in a Muslim country, especially the Ottoman Imperial Council (p. 173).

divine right (dĭ-vīn′ rīt) the right of a monarch to rule, based on the belief that this right comes directly from God and that the monarch is responsible only to God (p. 454).

diviner (dĭ-vīn′ər) a person who is believed to communicate with the spirit world and to help other people interact with their gods (p. 126).

dowry (dou′rē) money, land, servants, or any other valuable property given by a bride's family to her husband at marriage (p. 328).

dynasty (dī′nə-stē) a succession of rulers from the same family or line (p. 32)

E

electronic communication (ĭ-lĕk-trŏn´ĭk kə-myōō´ nĭ-kā´shən) communication devices, such as the telephone, television, and computer that have reduced the time necessary for transmitting information (p. 7).

elite (ĭ-lēt´) a small, privileged group at the top of a society (p. 401).

emir (ĭ-mîr´) a prince, chieftain, or governor, especially in the Middle East (p. 82).

empire (ĕm´pīr´) a political unit often made up of a number of territories, states, or nations, ruled by a single supreme authority (p. 78).

enclosure (ĕn-klō´zhər) the fencing in of common land to form larger estates in England during the 1700s (p. 491).

encomienda system (ĕn-kō´mē-ĕn´də sĭs təm) a system in which a parcel of New World land and its inhabitants was granted to Spanish colonists, who were responsible for supervising the land and instructing the inhabitants in the teachings of Roman Catholicism (p. 467).

enlightened despot (ĕn-līt´nd dĕs´pət) a European ruler in the 1700s with absolute power who tried to support Enlightenment ideals such as tolerance and freedom (p. 480).

excommunication (ĕks´kə-myōō´nĭ-kā´shən) the act that deprives someone of membership in the church (p. 285).

extinct (ĭk-stĭngkt´) no longer existing or living (p. 398).

F

faction (făk´shən) a group of persons forming a minority in disagreement with the larger group (p. 91).

feudalism (fyōōd´l-ĭz´əm) a European political and economic system in which large landholders or lords gave protection to people in return for their service to the landholder (p. 261).

fief (fēf) a large feudal estate, particularly in medieval Europe (p. 261).

G

ghazi (gä´zē) a Muslim warrior who has fought against nonbelievers to expand the frontiers of Islam (p. 171).

grand vizier (grănd vĭ-zîr´) the senior adviser or prime minister who advises the sultan on state matters (p. 172).

griot (grē´ō) a West African storyteller (p. 118).

guild (gĭld) an association of tradespeople made up of merchants, craftspeople, or artisans, particularly in the Middle Ages (p. 269).

H

haiku (hī´kōō) an unrhymed Japanese poem consisting of three lines with five, seven, and five syllables, respectively (p. 241).

heretic (hĕr´ĭ-tĭk) a person who has controversial opinions, especially one who publicly disagrees with the accepted beliefs of the Roman Catholic Church (p. 313).

hierarchy (hī´ə-rär´kē) a group of people organized or classified by rank and authority (p. 261).

hieroglyph (hī´ər-ə-glĭf´) a system of writing that uses picture symbols for concepts, objects, or words (p. 403).

history (hĭs´tə-rē) a record of past human events; the study of the past, including explanations of the events (p. 17).

homage (hŏm´ĭj) an expression of public honor or respect; in feudalism, the ceremonial recognition of allegiance to a lord shown by a vassal (p. 263).

humanism (hyōō´mə-nĭz´əm) a doctrine or attitude that is concerned primarily with human beings and their values, capacities, and achievements (p. 319).

hunter-gatherer (hŭn´tər-găth´ər-ər) early people who obtained their food by hunting wild animals and gathering wild plants, roots, nuts, and berries (p. 397).

hypothesis (hī-pŏth´ĭ-sĭs) an assumption that accounts for a set of facts and that can be tested by investigation (p. 355).

I

icon (ī´kŏn´) a picture or representation of a sacred Christian person, itself regarded as sacred (p. 292).

idol (īd´l) an image used as an object of worship (p. 55).

immigrant (ĭm´ĭ-grənt) a person who leaves one country to settle permanently in another country (p. 500).

individualism (ĭn´də-vĭj´ōō-ə-lĭz´əm) personal independence; the idea that every person should be free to develop and pursue his or her own goals (p. 315).

indulgence (ĭn-dŭl´jəns) certificates, issued by the pope, which were said to reduce or cancel punishment for a person's sins (p. 340).

industrial revolution (ĭn-dŭs´trē-əl rĕv´ə-lōō´shən) major improvements in industry, especially those in Europe during the 18th century (p. 492).

infidel (ĭn´fĭ-dəl) one who is an unbeliever in respect to some religion, especially Islam or Christianity (p. 296).

Inquisition (ĭn´kwĭ-zĭsh´ən) a Roman Catholic Church court revived during the Counter Reformation for the purpose of trying and convicting heretics (p. 352).

Islam (ĭs-läm´) a religion based on the teachings of the prophet Muhammad that believes in one god, Allah; the laws of Islam are found in the Koran and the Sunna (p. 60).

isolation (ī´sə-lā´shən) the condition of being separated from a group (p. 223).

J

janissary (jăn´ĭ-sĕr´ē) a soldier of Christian birth in the elite Ottoman infantry called the janissaries (p. 173).

K

khan (kän) a Mongol ruler (p. 165).

kinship (kĭn´shĭp´) the relationship among family members (p. 127).

knight (nīt) an armed, mounted soldier of the feudal period who gives military service to a lord (p. 261).

Koran (kə-răn´) the sacred book of Islam that is believed to contain the revelations made to Muhammad by Allah (p. 58).

L

lateen sail (lə-tēn´ sāl) a triangular sail (p. 12).

legacy (lĕg´ə-sē) something handed down from an ancestor; something from the past (p. 98).

literacy (lĭt´ər-ə-sē) the ability to read and write (p. 291).

M

magnetic compass (măg-nĕt´ĭk kŭm´pəs) a device used to determine geographical direction, using a magnetic needle that is free to pivot until aligned with the magnetic field of the earth (p. 12).

malaria (mə-lâr´ē-ə) a tropical disease carried by the anopheles mosquito and characterized by chills, fever, and sweating (p. 148).

mandate (măn´dāt´) a command or instruction from an authority; an order to govern (p. 204).

manor (măn´ər) the castle and estate of a feudal lord (p. 266).

matrilineal (măt´rə-lĭn´ē-əl) relating to the system of tracing descent through the females of a family (p. 117).

mercantilism (mûr´kən-tē-lĭz´əm) a European economic system based on establishing colonies as a source of raw materials and as the market for goods from the ruling country (p. 467).

mercenary (mûr´sə-nĕr´ē) a professional soldier who is hired by a foreign country (p. 318).

meritocracy (mĕr´ĭ-tŏk´rə-sē) a system in which people are chosen for jobs and promoted on the basis of their performance (p. 204).

migrate (mī´grāt´) to move from one area or country to another and settle there (p. 137).

millet (mĭl´ā) a partially self-governing group of non-Muslims in the Ottoman Empire; the most common millets were Armenian, Greek Orthodox, and Jewish (p. 174).

missionary (mĭsh´ə-nĕr´ē) a person sent to a foreign country to do religious or charitable work (p. 152).

monarchy (mŏn´ər-kē) a strong central government ruled by a king or a queen (p. 312).

monastery (mŏn´ə-stĕr´ē) a place in which a community of religious people, particularly monks, lives (p. 257).

money economy (mŭn´ē ĭ-kŏn´ə mē) an economy in which cash is the most common item exchanged for goods (p. 206.)

monopoly (mə-nŏp´ə -lē) the total control by one group of the means of producing a service (p. 368).

monotheism (mŏn´ə-thē-ĭz´əm) the belief that there is only one God (p. 59).

monsoon (mŏn-soon´) a wind system that switches direction seasonally and brings dry and wet seasons, especially the Asiatic monsoon that brings wet and dry seasons to India and southern Asia (p. 141).

mosaic (mō-zā´ĭk) a picture or design made from small colored pieces of glass or quartz embedded in plaster (p. 43).

mosque (mŏsk) a Muslim house of worship (p. 60).

Muslim (mŭz´ləm) a believer in Islam (p. 60).

N

natural right (năch´ər-əl rīt) one of the rights believed by many to be guaranteed to all people by nature, including life, liberty, and the right to own property (p. 479).

nomad (nō´măd´) a member of a group that has no fixed home and moves from place to place in search of food, water, and grazing land for their herds (p. 53).

O

oasis (ō-ā´sĭs) a small area in the desert watered by springs and wells (p. 53).

oath of fealty (ōth ŭv fē´əl-tē) a feudal oath of loyalty sworn to a lord in exchange for an award of land (p. 261).

oral tradition (ôr´əl trə-dĭsh´ən) the legends, myths, and beliefs that a culture passes from generation to generation by word of mouth (p. 148).

P

pamphlet (păm´flĭt) an unbound published work such as an essay, usually on a current topic (p. 345).

parliament (pär´lə-mənt) a national representative body having the highest law-making powers within the state, particularly in England (p. 458).

patriarch (pā´trē-ärk´) the male leader of a family or tribe (p. 292).

patrician (pə-trĭsh´ən) a member of the highest class of society in Italian city-states during the Renaissance; an aristocrat (p. 327).

patrilineal (păt´rə-lĭn´ē-əl) relating to the system of tracing descent through the males of a family (p. 117).

patron (pā´trən) a person who financially supports scholars or artists (p. 327).

philosophe (fē´lə-zôf´) any of the leading philosophical, political, and social writers of the French Enlightenment of the 1700s from either the aristocracy or the middle class (p. 477).

pilgrimage (pĭl´grə-mĭj) a journey to a sacred place or shrine (p. 57).

plague (plāg) a highly infectious, usually fatal, epidemic disease (p. 310).

plantation (plăn-tā´shən) a large farm where crops are grown (p. 152).

plateau (plă-tō´) a raised and relatively flat area of land (p. 146).

predestination (prē-dĕs´tə-nā´shən) the belief that God has determined all things in advance, including the salvation of souls (p. 350).

prehistory (prē-hĭs´tə-rē) history that took place before the development of writing (p. 17).

primary source (prī´mĕr´ē sôrs) a source for historical study that was written by someone who participated in or observed the event being recorded (p. 17).

prime minister (prīm mĭn´ĭ-stər) the chief government official appointed by a ruler (p. 453).

Protestant (prŏt´ĭ-stənt) a reformer who protested against the abuses of the Catholic church in the 1500s; a member of a church descended from those that seceded from the Roman Catholic Church during the 1500s (p. 344).

province (prŏv´ĭns) in the ancient Roman empire, any of the lands outside Italy conquered and ruled by the Romans (p. 27).

R

realism (rē´ə-lĭz´əm) an artistic style dating from the Renaissance that attempts to visually represent people and objects as they exist naturally (p. 322).

reason (rē´zən) the capacity for logical thought (p. 476).

Reformation (rĕf´ər-mā´shən) the reform movement of the 1500s that resulted in the separation of the Protestant churches from the Roman Catholic Church (p. 344).

regent (rē´jənt) a person who rules for a monarch during periods of illness or absence, or during the monarch's extreme youth (p. 228).

Renaissance (rĕn´ĭ-säns´) the revival of attention to classical Greek and Roman art, literature, and learning that originated in Italy in the 14th century and later spread through Europe. (p. 317).

republic (rĭ-pŭb´lĭk) a political order whose head of state is not a monarch and in which supreme power lies in a body of elected citizens (p. 317).

S

Sahel (sə-hāl´) a strip of dry grasslands on the southern border of the Sahara; also known as "the shore of the desert" (p. 109).

salary (săl´ə-rē) a fixed payment for services paid on a regular basis (p. 181).

salvation (săl-vā´shən) the deliverance of the soul from the penalties of sin (p. 285).

samurai (săm´ə-rī´) the feudal military aristocracy of Japan, from the term meaning "those who serve" (p. 232).

satellite (săt´l-īt´) a relatively small object orbiting a planet or moon; a manufactured object orbiting the earth, often used to transmit information (p. 7).

savanna (sə-văn´ə) a region of grasslands containing scattered trees and vegetation (p. 109).

schism (sĭz´əm) a separation or division into factions, especially a formal separation within a Christian church (p. 293).

scientific method (sī´ən-tĭf´ĭk mĕth´əd) a series of logical steps formulated by Francis Bacon and used in scientific research that stressed observation and experimentation (p. 355).

Scientific Revolution (sī´ən-tĭf´ĭk rĕv´ə-lōō´shən) the era of scientific thought in Europe during which careful observation of the natural world was made, and accepted beliefs were questioned (p. 354).

secondary source (sĕk´ən-dĕr´ē sôrs) a source for historical study that was written after the event it describes, usually with the aid of a primary source (p. 17).

sect (sĕkt) a subdivision of a religious group (p. 234).

secular (sĕk´yə-lər) worldly, rather than religious, in nature (p. 332).

sedentary (sĕd´n-tĕr´ē) characterized by remaining in one place and not migrating (p. 398).

serf (sûrf) a peasant; a member of the lowest feudal class, bound to the land and owned by a lord (p. 266).

Shiite (shē´īt´) a member of the branch of Islam that supports the descendants of Muhammad as his rightful successors (p. 67).

Shinto (shĭn´tō) a Japanese religion whose followers believe that all things in the natural world are filled with divine spirits (p. 225).

shogun (shō´gən) a line of military leaders who ruled Japan under the nominal leadership of the emperor until 1868 (p. 232).

stele (stē´lē) an upright stone column with inscribed hieroglyphs used as a monument, particularly by early peoples of Central America (p. 407).

steppe (stĕp) a vast semiarid grass-covered plain, usually lightly wooded, as found in southeastern Europe and Siberia (p. 162).

sternpost rudder (stûrn´pōst´ rŭd´ər) a paddlelike device under a ship and connected to a handle on deck, for steering sailing ships (p. 12).

stirrup (stûr´əp) a loop or ring hung from either side of a horse's saddle to support the rider's foot in riding and mounting (p. 11).

succession (sək-sĕsh´ən) the sequence in which one person after another succeeds to a title, throne, or estate (p. 238).

sultan (sŭl´tən) the ruler of a Muslim country, especially the former Ottoman Empire (p. 172).

Sunna (soon´ə) traditional Islamic law observed by orthodox Muslims and based on the teaching of Muhammad (p. 61).

Sunni (soon´ē) the branch of Islam that follows orthodox tradition and accepts the validity of the caliphs elected as successors to Muhammad (p. 68).

T

terrace farming (tĕr´ĭs fär´mĭng) the building of raised banks of earth on steep land for farming (p. 433).

tithe (tīth) a tenth of one's income contributed voluntarily to a church (p. 285).

tribe (trīb) any system of social organization made up of villages, bands, or other groups with a common ancestry, language, culture, and name (p. 55).

tribute (trĭb´yoot) a kind of tax paid in goods or services to the ruling government (p. 425).

U

university (yoo´nə-vûr´sĭ-tē) an institution of higher learning with teaching and research facilities as well as graduate and professional schools (p. 287).

V

vassal (văs´əl) a person who receives land and protection from a feudal lord in return for loyalty to that lord (p. 261).

vertical economy (vûr´tĭ-kəl ĭ-kŏn´ə-mē) the growing of crops according to the altitude of the land, particularly in South America (p. 433).

Acknowledgments *(continued from page 559)*

401 © Mike Mazzaschi, Stock Boston. **402** © Lee Boltin. **403** © Justin Kerr (l,r). **404** Laurie Platt Winfrey Inc. (t); F. Catherwood (b). **405** © Andrew Holbrooke. **406** © Antoinette Jongen (t); © G. Gallant, TIB (r). **407** © Lee Boltin. **408** British Museum, Michael Holford (l); © Lee Boltin (r). **410** © Justin Kerr. **411** © Joseph Devenney, TIB (t); RJB (b). **412** David L. Brill, © National Geographic Society. **413** SuperStock. **414** © Lee Boltin (t); © Julian Brown, International Film Foundation (b). **415** Museum of the American Indian, Heye Foundation (t); © Nick Saunders (c). **416** RJB (c,b). **417** RJB. **420** Michael Holford, Private Collection (l); British Museum (r). **421** Werner Forman Archive (tl); © George Holton, Photo Researchers, Inc. (tr); LPW (b). **422** LPW **423** © Justin Kerr. **424** © George D. Dodge, Dale R. Thompson, Bruce Coleman, Inc. (c); © Lee Boltin (b). **425** The National Palace, Mexico City (t); © LPW (b). **426** Garfield Park Conservatory, Chicago, RJB (l); RJB (tl,tr,cl,c,b). **427** LPW (t); National Museum of Copenhagen, NB (b). **428** LPW (l,r). **429** RHPL. **431** American Museum of Natural History (t); British Museum, Michael Holford (b). **432** © Hans W. Silvester, Photo Researchers, Inc.(t); RJB (c,bl); American Museum of Natural History (br). **433** Comstock, Inc. (l); RHPL (r). **434** © Francisco Hidalgo, TIB (l); NB (trcr,br). **435** Museo de America, Madrid (t); © Delacorte Gallery, New York, Lee Boltin (b). **437** Biblioteca Nacional, Madrid. **438** Museo de America, Madrid. **439** Biblioteca Nacional, Madrid, NB (t); LPW (b). **440** © Loren McIntyre, Woodfin Camp & Associates (l); Gilcrease Institute, NB (r); AR (b). **442** © Merrell Wood, TIB (l); © Susan Malis, Gartman Agency (r). **443** Biblioteca Nacional, Madrid. **448–49** The Granger Collection; **450** Museu Nacional de Arte Antiga, Lisbon, Michael Holford (l); Bermuda News Service (r). **451** Galleria Palatina, Florence, AR (t); Private Collection, NB (b); The Metropolitan Museum of Art (r). **452** Victoria & Albert Museum, Bridgeman Art Library. **453** Bibliotheque Publique et Universitaire, Geneva. **454** National Gallery, London, AR (t); The Mansell Collection (b). **455** Comstock, Inc. (t); AR (b). **456** RJB (l); Photo Service de Documentation, RHPL (r). **458** British Library. **459** Private Collection, NB (t); Her Majesty's Stationery Office, England (b). **460** National Maritime Museum, Greenwich, England (t); Victoria & Albert Museum (b). **461** National Museum of Scotland (t); The Royal Collection (b). **462** AR (l); Private Collection (lc); The Granger Collection (rc); The National Portrait Gallery, London (r). **463** The National Portrait Gallery, London (l,rc,r); The New-York Historical Society (lc). **464** New York Public Library, Rare Book Division. **465** RJB. **467** The Folger Shakespeare Library (t); RJB (b). **468** British Museum, Bridgeman Art Library, AR (l); The Brooklyn Museum (r). **469** RJB. **471** © Willinger, FPG International. **474** © Robert Descharnes, Les Delices, Geneva (l); Musee Carnavalet, Paris (r). **475** © H. Andrew Johnson, Thomas Jefferson Memorial Foundation, Inc. (l); SCALA, AR (r). **476** British Museum, Bridgeman Art Library, AR. **477** Trinity College, Cambridge, England (t); The Granger Collection (b). **478** Giraudon, AR (t); The Cleveland Museum of Art (b). **479** Bettmann Archive. **480** Biblioteca Nacional, Madrid. **482** The Metropolitan Museum of Art, Gift of William H. Huntington, 1883. **483** Musee Carnavalet, Paris, Giraudon, AR (t,b). **485** Louvre, NB. **490** AR. **491** The Newberry Library, Chicago. **492** Smithsonian Institution. **493** LPW (l); RJB (r). **494** The Newberry Library, Chicago (t); © Eddie Hironaka, TIB (b). **495** © Stephen Wilkes, TIB. **496** RJB. **497** © Photri. **498** © Don Carl Steffan, Photo Researchers, Inc. (tl); © Bill Ross, Westlight (tr); © Craig Aurness, Westlight (c); The National Archives (b). **499** New York Public Library, NB. **500** © Pete Turner, TIB.

Picture Research Assistance by Carousel Research, Inc., Meyers Photo-Art, and Jim Lillie.

Italic numbers refer to pages on which illustrations appear.

Text *(continued from page iv)*

ii Excerpt from December 30, 1941, speech by Winston Churchill to the Canadian Senate and the House of Commons. Reprinted by permission of Curtis Brown Ltd. on behalf of the estate of Sir Winston Churchill. **10** From *Parthian Stations by Isidore of Charax*, translated by Wilfred H. Schoff, Philadelphia: Commercial Museum, 1914. **13** From *Journals of Hsuan-Tsang*, in *Chinese Accounts of India* by Samuel Beal, Calcutta, India: S. Gupta, 1958. **13** From *Travels of Ibn Batuta in Bengal, China, and the Indian Archipelago*, in *Cathay and the Way Thither*, by Sir Henry Yule, London: University Press, 1916. **19, 297** From *Memoirs* by Anna Comnena, in *The Crusades*, edited by Régine Pernoud, New York: G.P. Putnam's Sons, 1962. **19** From letter by Saladin, in *The Muslim Discovery of Europe* by Bernard Lewis, New York: W.W. Norton & Co., 1982. **26** From letter by Cyprian, Bishop of Carthage, in *Barbarian Europe* by Gerald Simons, New York: Time-Life Books, 1968. **35** From epic poem by Kalidasa, in *Hinduism* by Louis Renou, editor, New York: G. Braziller, 1962. **38** Excerpts from "The King's Adviser" in *Kalilah and Dimnah* ed. by Hassan Techranchian. Copyright © 1985 by Crown Publishers, Inc. **74** Excerpt from "The Voyage of Sinbad the Sailor" © Oxford University Press 1982. Reprinted from *One Thousand and One Arabian Nights* by Geraldine McCaughrean (1982) by permission of Oxford University Press. **84** From *A Source Book in Geography*, by George Kish editor, Cambridge, Massachusetts: Harvard University Press, 1978. **89** "You Departed From My Sight" from *Lyrics from Arabia* edited and translated by Ghazi A. Algosaibi. Copyright © 1983 by Ghazi A. Algosaibi. Published by Three Continents Press. Reprinted by permission of Three Continents Press. **90** From "Text 3: The Autobiography" by Avicenna, in *Avicenna and the Aristotelian Tradition*, Leiden, The Netherlands: E.J. Brill, 1988. **115** From *Book of the Roads and Kingdoms*, in *The Story of Africa* by Basil Davidson, London: Mitchell Beazley, 1984. **118** From a tale recorded by D.T. Niane of Mali, in *History of African Civilization* by E. Jefferson Murphy, New York, Thomas Y. Crowell Co., 1972. **125** From *Things Fall Apart* by Chinua Achebe, New York: Ballantine Books, 1959. **128** "The Cow-Tail Switch" from *The Cow-Tail Switch and Other West African Stories* by Harold Courlander and George Herzog, copyright 1947, 1974 by Harold Courlander. **141** "The Periplus of the Erythraean Sea" from *The East African Coast* by G.S.P. Freeman-Grenville. (Oxford University Press, 1962) Reprinted by permission of the author. **144** From a chronicler's observation of the destruction of Mombasa, in *The Story of Africa* by Basil Davidson, London: Mitchell Beazley, 1984. **144** "He Who Wants to String Pearls" from *Four Centuries of Swahili Verse* edited by Jan Knappert. Copyright © 1979 by Jan Knappert. Reprinted by permission of Heinemann Educational Books Ltd. **145** From "The Early Days of Mashonaland and a Visit to the Zimbabwe Ruins" by J.W. Posselt, in *Nada*, 1924. **148** From annals by Joãs de Barros, in *Introduction to African Civilizations* by John G. Jackson, New York: University Books, 1970. **153** From letter by Affonso of Congo to King John of Portugal, in *The African Past* by Basil Davidson, Boston: Little, Brown and Co., 1964. **154** From letter by Affonso of Congo to King John of Portugal, in *The Kingdom of Kongo* by Anne Hilton, Oxford: Clarendon Press, 1985. **162** From a history by Ibn al-Athir, in *A Literary History of Persia, Vol. 2* by Edward G. Browne, Cambridge University Press, 1902. **166** Quote by Genghis Khan, from *East Asia, Tradition and Transformation* by K. Fairbank, E.O. Reischauer, and A.M. Craig, Boston: Houghton Mifflin, 1973. **170** From *Histoire des Mongols* by Rashid ad-Din, in *The Empire of the Steppes* by Rene Grousset, translated by Naomi Walford, New Brunswick, New Jersey: Rutgers University Press, 1970. **172** From Mehmed quotation regarding legalization of fratricide (1460), in *A History of the World* by Stanley Chodorow, New York: Harcourt Brace Jovanovich, 1986. **175** From historical annals (1453) by Kritovoulos, in *The Global Experience*, edited by Philip F. Riley, Englewood Cliffs, New Jersey: Prentice-Hall, 1987. **176** From 1538 inscription, in *The World* by Geoffrey Parker, New York: Harper and Row. **176** "Elegy for Suleiman" by Baki from *Istanbul and the Civilization of the Ottoman Empire* by Bernard Lewis. Copyright © 1963 by the University of Oklahoma Press. Reprinted by permission of the University of Oklahoma Press. **178** From Chronicler of Mahmud, in *A Concise History of India* by Francis Watson, New York: Charles Scribner's Sons, 1975. **178** From *The Book of Kings* by Firdawsi, in *A History of the World* by Stanley Chodorow, New York: Harcourt Brace Jovanovich, 1986. **195** "On Compulsive Urges" and "Twin Verses" from *The Dammapada* translated by Eknath Easwaran. Copyright © 1986 by the Blue Mountain Center of Meditation. Reprinted by permission of Nilgiri Press, Petaluma, CA. **198** From *The Great Wall of China* by Robert Silverberg, Philadelphia: Chilton Books, 1965. **200** Poems by Yang Wan-Li, translated by Jonathan Chaves from *Heaven My Blanket, Earth My Pillow*. Copyright © 1976 by John Weatherhill. Used by permission of Charles Tuttle, Tokyo. **202** "Quiet Night Thoughts" from *China's Imperial Past* by Charles O. Hucker. Copyright © 1975 by the Board of Trustees of the Leland Stanford Junior University. Reprinted with the permission of the publishers, Stanford University Press. **203** From *Introduction to Painting* by Wang Wei, in *Sources of Chinese Tradition* by Wm. Theodore de Bary, New York: Columbia University Press, 1960. **206** From *Continuation of the Comprehensive Mirror for Aiding Government*, in *The Pattern of the Chinese Past* by Mark Elvin, London: Eyre Methuen, 1973. **208** From a Chinese sailor's report (1119), in *The History of Invention* by Trevor I. Williams, New York: Facts on File, 1987. **208** From *The Pattern of the Chinese Past* by Mark Elvin, London: Eyre Methuen, 1973. **208** From the *Tearful Records of the Battle of Qizhou* (1221), in *The History of Invention* by Trevor I. Williams, New York: Facts on File, 1987. **209** "Kubilai Khan" from *The Travels of Marco Polo*, translated by Ronald Latham. Copyright © 1958 by Ronald Latham. Reprinted by permission of Penguin Books Ltd. **226** "Here I Lie on Straw" from *Anthology of Japanese Literature*, edited by Donald Keene. Copyright © 1955 by Grove Press. Reprinted by permission of Grove Weidenfeld. **228** "This Perfectly Still" from *Anthology of Japanese Literature*, edited by Donald Keene. Copyright © 1955 by Grove Press. Reprinted by permission of Grove Weidenfeld. **227, 229** From *The Diary of Murasaki Shikibu*, in *Anthology of Japanese Literature*, edited by Donald Keene, New York: Grove Press, 1955. **231, 232** From *The Tale of the Heike*, translated by Helen Craig McCullough, Stanford, California: Stanford University Press, 1988. **237** Oda Nobunaga quotation from *Hoan Nobunaga-ki*, in *Sources of Japanese Tradition* by Ryusaku Tsunoda, New York: Columbia University Press, 1958. **241** "Old Pond" from *Introduction to Haiku* by Harold G. Henderson. Copyright © 1958 by Harold G. Henderson. Reprinted by permission of Doubleday, a division of Bantam, Doubleday, Dell Publishing Group, Inc. **250** Excerpt from "The Story of Roland" in *Charlemagne and His Knights* told by Katharine Pyle. (J.P. Lippincott) Copyright, 1932 by Harper & Row, Publishers, Inc. Reprinted by permission of Harper & Row, Publishers, Inc. **287** "The Canticle of Brother Sun" from *Saint Francis of Assisi* by Lawrence Cunningham. Copyright © 1981 by Lawrence Cunningham. Reprinted by permission of Scala Books/Philip Wilson Ltd. **303** From *Christian Society and the Crusades, 1198–1229*, edited by Edward Peters, Philadelphia: Univ. of Pennsylvania Press, 1971. **311** Quotation from Sienese chronicler Agnolo di Tura Del Grasso, in *The Oxford Illustrated History of Medieval Europe*, edited by George Holmes, New York: Oxford University Press, 1988. **313** From *The Trial of Jeanne d'Arc*, translated by W.P. Barrett, London: George Routledge, 1931. **338** From *Unam Sanctam* (1302), in *The Western Tradition* by Eugen Weber, Lexington, Massachusetts: D.C. Heath & Co., 1972. **341** "The Book of Margery Kempe" in *The Medieval Mystics of England* by Eric Colledge. Copyright © 1961 by Charles Scribner's Sons. Reprinted with permission of Charles Scribner's Sons, an imprint of Macmillan Publishing Company. **345** From *Milestones of History* by Neville Williams, New York: Newsweek Books, 1974. **369** From *Bartolomé de Las Casas*, translated and edited by George Sanderlin, New York: Knopf, 1971. **379** From *The Log of Christopher Columbus*, translated by Robert H. Fuson, Camden, Maine: International Marine Publishing Co., 1987. **384** "The Audience" by C. Walter Hodges, reprinted by permission of Coward-McCann, Inc., from *Columbus Sails* by Walter Hodges, copyright 1939 by Coward-McCann, Inc., copyright renewed © by C. Walter Hodges. **400** From a bulletin of the Mexican Geographical and Statistical Society (1869), in *The Olmecs* by Jacques Soustelle, translated by Helen R. Lane, New York: Doubleday, 1984. **422** From *The Ancient American Civilizations* by Friedrich Katz, translated by K.M. Lois Simpson, New York: Praeger, 1969. **428** From *Pre-Columbian Literatures of Mexico* by Miguel Leon-Portilla. Copyright © 1969 by the University of Oklahoma Press. Reprinted by permission of the University of Oklahoma Press. **435** From "1980 Ecological Anthropology" by Benjamin S. Orlove, in *Annual Review of Anthropology*, vol. 9, pp. 235–273. **437** From *Pre-Columbian Literatures of Mexico* by Miguel Leon-Portilla, Norman, Oklahoma: University of Oklahoma Press, 1969. **442** From *Everyday Life of the Aztecs* by Warwick Bray. Copyright © 1968 by Warwick Bray. Reprinted by permission of B.T. Datsford Ltd. **444** Excerpt from "The Legend of the Lake" in *Warriors, Gods and Spirits* by Douglas Gifford. Copyright © 1983 by Douglas Gifford. Used by permission of Eurobook. **466** From *Admiral of the Ocean Sea* by Samuel Eliot Morison, Boston: Little, Brown and Co., 1942. **486** Excerpt from "To the Assembly for Protection" in *The Journal of Madame Royale* by Elizabeth Powers. Copyright © 1976 by Elizabeth Powers. Used by permission of the Walker Publishing Company, Inc. **494** From *Victorian People and Ideas* by Richard D. Altick, New York: Norton, Publisher, 1973. **543** Pronunciation key copyright © 1985 by Houghton Mifflin Company. Adapted and reprinted by permission from *The American Heritage Dictionary* Second College Edition.

Illustrations

Literature border design by Peggy Skycraft. **Ligature** 22, 33, 132, 139, 156, 163, 188, 235, 267 (tr), 348, 357, 360, 368, 390, 418, 472, 492, 501. **Precision Graphics** 12, 30, 68, 69, 70, 82, 84, 85, 98, 153, 181, 205, 206–7, 229, 238–39, 244, 265, 304, 350, 379, 399, 441, 462–63, 465, 498. **Brian Battles** 151, 346. **John Butler** 54. **John T. Burgoyne** 14, 298. **Susan David** 12, 396. **Ebet Dudley** 406, 423. **Simon Galkin** 261, 262, 265. **Dale Glasgow** 163. **Henry Iken** 410. **Phil Jones** 184, 318. **Guy Kingsbery** 6. **Al Lorenz** 455. **Joseph Scrofani** 331, 373. **Scott Snow** 61, 111. **Gary Toressi,** 534–35. **Jean & Mou-Sien Tsen** 232. **Richard Waldrep** 233. **Brent Watkinson** 484. **Oliver Yourke** 282–83. **Other: 76–77** Illustration by Earle Goodenowe. Reprinted by permission of Grosset & Dunlap from *The Arabian Nights*, copyright © 1946, copyright renewed © 1974 by Grosset & Dunlap, Inc. **129** From *The Cow-Tail Switch and Other West African Stories* Copyright © 1947, 1975 by Harold Courlander. Illustration by Madye Lee Chastian. Reprinted by permission of Henry Holt and Company, Inc. **407** By Michael Goodman, from "Maya Writing" by David Stuart and Stephen D. Houston. Copyright © August 1989 by *Scientific American*, Inc. All rights reserved. **408** From *Atlas of Ancient Americas*. Copyright © Equinox, Oxford. (t,r). **409** From *Atlas of Ancient Americas*. Copyright © Equinox, Oxford. (tr).

Maps

R.R. Donnelley & Sons Company Cartographic Services 518–533. **Mapping Specialists** 5, 8, 9 (b), 13, 27, 36–37, 53, 67, 80–81, 87, 97, 109, 121, 137, 140, 142, 146, 150, 167, 171, 179, 183, 193, 204, 216, 217, 219, 224, 230, 257, 260, 290, 296, 299, 311, 317, 330, 347, 352, 366, 374, 378, 382–83, 397, 398, 401, 405, 412 (b), 412 (r), 423, 430, 436, 465, 470, 481. **Precision Graphics** 9 (t). **Other: 10** Based on *Parthian Stations by Isidore of Charax*, commentary by Wilfred H. Schoff, Philadelphia Commercial Museum, 1914.

Photographs

AR—Art Resource, New York; **LPW**—Laurie Platt Winfrey, Inc.; **NB**—Newsweek Books; **RHPL**—Robert Harding Picture Library, London; **RJB**—Ralph J. Brunke; **TIB**—The Image Bank, Chicago

Front Cover Peter Bosy. **Back cover** Bibliotheque Nationale, Paris. **1** SCALA, AR. **2** © Michael O'Neill, Inc. **2–3** New York Public Library, Rare Book Division. **3** © Kay Chernush, TIB (r); Bodlein Library, Oxford (b). **4** RJB (l,lc,rc,r). **6** © Dave Bartruff, FPG International. **7** © PHOTRI, MGA (t); © Ferdinando Scianna, Magnum Photos (b); © NASA, Westlight (r). **11** © George Holton, Photo Researchers,

Inc. (t); Freer Gallery of Art (b). **13** Tokyo National Museum, Wan-go H.C. Weng. **15** The Dean and Chapter of Hereford Cathedral. **16** British Museum, NB. **17** RJB (tl,br); © Comstock, Inc. (tr); © Heinz Plenge, RHPL (bl). **18** Musee de l'Armee, Paris, AR. **19** © Trustees of the British Museum. **20** © Arthur Tress, Photo Researchers, Inc. **20–21** RJB. **21** Center of American Archaeology (t); Museum of the American Indian (r). **24** AR (tl); © Ronald Sheridan, AR (cl); SuperStock (bl); SCALA (r). **25** Louvre, NB (t); SCALA, AR (b). **26** AR. **27** AR. **28** © George Gersten. **29** Landesmuseum, Trier, West Germany (t); Rheinisches Landesmuseum, Bonn, West Germany (c); © Werner Forman Archive (b). **30** © National Geographic Society (l); Dumbarton Oaks, Washington, D.C. (lc,c,r). **31** Bibliotheque Nationale, Paris. **32** The Metropolitan Museum of Art. **33** SEF, Turin, AR (t); AR (c); Isabella Stewart Gardner Museum, Boston, AR (b). **34** Bibliotheque Nationale, Giraudon, AR (t); RJB (b). **36** Royal Ontario Museum, Toronto, Wan-go H.C. Weng (l); Royal Ontario Museum, Toronto, Wan-go H. C. Weng (r). **37** Royal Ontario Museum, Ontario, Wan-go H. C. Weng. **42** Byzantium, Time-Life Books, © Time Inc. **43** SCALA, AR (tl); AR (tr,bl); Dumbarton Oaks, Washington, D.C. (c); Dumbarton Oaks, Washington, D.C. (br). **44** SCALA, AR (tl); RJB (tr,cr,bl,br); J. Claire Dean, J. Paul Getty Museum (cl); J. Claire Dean (bc). **45** © Werner Dieterich, TIB (t); Bibliotheque Nationale, Paris (c). **48–49** © Roger Wood. **50** RJB (l); SuperStock (r). **51** The Metropolitan Museum of Art (l); © Roger Wood (t); Topkapi Museum, Istanbul (r). **52** RHPL. **52–53** RHPL. **55** RHPL. **56** © John Donat (t); RJB (b). **57** AR. **58** AR. **59** British Museum, NB (t); © Ilene Perlman, Stock Boston (b). **60** The Metropolitan Museum of Art, NB. **61** © Roger Wood. **62** © Camerapix. **63** © Mehmet Biber, Photo Researchers, Inc. **64** © Roger Wood (l); © Wayne Eastep, The Stock Market (r). **65** Topkapi Museum, Istanbul. **66** British Library (l); Chester Beatty Library (r). **68** © Roger Wood. **72** British Museum (l); © Roger Wood (r). **73** © G. Mangold, TIB (t); © Marc Romanelli, TIB (c); Museo del Ejeroito Espada de Boabdil (r). **77** RJB. **78** Edinburgh University Library. **79** © G. Champlong, TIB. **83** American Numismatic Society (t,cl,c,cr,bl,bc,br). **86** SuperStock. **86–87** RJB. **88** Bibliotheque Nationale, Paris (t); © P. Breidenbach (b). **89** RJB. **90** Princeton University (l); RJB (tr,cr); Topkapi Museum, Istanbul, AR (b). **91** Freer Gallery of Art. **92** RJB (l); Alaska Division of Tourism (b). **92–93** Collection of John Ridley. **93** Private Collection, Michael Holford. **95** © Marc Romanelli, TIB. **96** © Joachim Messerschmidt, Westlight. **97** RJB (tr,bl,br); © Stuart Cohen, Comstock, Inc. (cl); SuperStock (cr). **98** SuperStock (l); © Peter Vandermark, Stock Boston (r). **99** RJB (t,c); SCALA, AR (b). **100** Royal Chapel, Granada. **104–5** © Huet, Hoa-Qui. **106** Nigerian, Yoruba people, Anago region, town of Ago Shasha, Efe/Gelede headress, late 19th-early 20th century, Gift of Mr. and Mrs. Raymond J. Weilgus by exchange, 1988.22...profile. Photograph by Alan Newman. © 1989 The Art Institute of Chicago, All Rights Reserved (l); © Victor Engelbert (r). **107** Comstock, Inc. (t); African and Oceanic Catalogue, AR (c); RJB (bl,cl,br). **108** Woodfin Camp & Associates (l); © Michael Kirtley (r). **110** Nigerian Museum, Lagos. **111** © M. & A. Kirtley, ANA. **112** © Martin Rogers. **113** © Arthur Tress. **114** RJB (tl,br); Musee de l'Institute d'Afrique Noire, Giraudon, AR (tr); © Cyril Isy-Schwart, TIB (c); © Giorgio Gualco, Bruce Coleman, Inc. (bl). **115** © P. Breidenbach (l,r); Smithsonian Institution, Museum of African Art, AR (b). **116** M. & A. Kirtley, ANA (1); © Eugene Gordon, Photo Researchers, Inc. (r). **118** Michael Kirtley. **119** RJB (t); Bibliotheque Nationale, Paris (b). **120** Bibliotheque Nationale, Paris. **121** Bibliotheque Nationale, Paris. **122** SuperStock. **123** Mike Dye, *The White Men*, Julia Blackburn, Orbis Publishing, London, © 1979, RJB (t); Nelson Gallery–Atkins Museum (Nelson Fund), Kansas City (b). **124** © Jason Laure, Woodfin Camp & Associates. **125** © Marc & Evelyne Bernheim, Woodfin Camp & Associates (t); Garfield Park Conservatory, Chicago, RJB (c); AR (b). **126** P. Breidenbach. **127** © M. & A. Kirtley, ANA. **134** British Museum, Bridgeman Art Library (1); © Leonard Lee Rue III, Bruce Coleman, Inc. (r). **135** © Rod Allin, Tom Stack & Associates (l); © Don Carl Steffen, Photo Researchers, Inc. (r). **136** © Bruce Coleman, Inc. **138** © Kim Taylor, Bruce Coleman, Inc. (t); RJB (c); © Kim Taylor, Bruce Coleman, Inc. (l); SuperStock (b). **139** British Museum, Bridgeman Art Library. **141** © Owen Franken, Stock Boston. **142** Werner Forman Archive. **143** Werner Forman Archive (l,r). **144** Hutchison Library. **145** © Sue Dorfman, Stock Boston (t); © Norman Meyers, Bruce Coleman, Inc. (b). **147** © Jason Laure (t,b). **148** Centers for Disease Control (t); National Archives of Zimbabwe (b). **149** © Eric Axelson (l); © Eric Axelson (r). **150** Zaire, Kasai Province, Mweka, Kuba People, Mask of a Mythic Royal Ancestor (Ngaang A Cyeem), late 19th-early 20th century, Restricted Gift of the American Hospital Supply Corp., The Evanston Associates of The Women's Board in honor of Mr. Wilbur Tuggle, et al., and the A.O.A. Purchase Fund, 1982.1505. © 1989 The Art Institute of Chicago, All Rights Reserved (l); American Museum of Natural History (r). **152** British Museum, Michael Holford. **153** British Museum. **154** © The Pierpont Morgan Library, 1990 (l); The Newberry Library, Chicago (r). **155** New York Public Library, Map Division (t); Zaire, Western Kasai Province, Mweka Zone, Kuba Peoples, Mukenga mask, Laura T. Magnuson Fund Income, X-Hautelet Collection 1982.1504...Photograph by Robert Hashimoto, © 1989 The Art Institute of Chicago, All Rights Reserved (b). **158–59** Wan-go H. C. Weng. **160** The Metropolitan Museum of Art (l); Bibliotheque Nationale, Paris (r). **160–61** Topkapi Museum, Istanbul. **161** Topkapi Museum, Istanbul, NB (t); Victoria & Albert Museum, London (b). **162** Topkapi Museum, Istanbul. **163** PHOTRI, MGA. **164–65** Topkapi Museum, Istanbul. **165** Topkapi Museum, Istanbul. **167** Los Angeles County Museum of Art. **168** John Massey Stewart (l); © P. Breidenbach (r). **169** Bham Museum of Art (l); Collection of the National Palace Museum, Taiwan, Republic of China (r). **170** Bibliotheque Nationale, Paris. **172** © Ara Guler, Magnum Photos (l); FPG International (r). **173** AR (t); British Museum (b). **174** University Library, Istanbul. **175** Topkapi Museum, Istanbul (t,c,b). **176** Topkapi Museum, Istanbul (l,c); Topkapi Palace, Istanbul, Giraudon, AR (r). **177** Topkapi Museum, Istanbul. **178** © Roger Wood. **180** Victoria & Albert Museum, London (l); British Museum, Michael Holford (c). **180–81** © Roger Wood. **181** Victoria & Albert Museum, NB. **182** © Helen Marcus, Photo Researchers, Inc. (l); Victoria & Albert Museum, London (r). **184** Kenneth Crossman, No credit found (cl); RJB (cr,bl); Archaeological Survey of India, Government of India, RJB (br). **185** Prince of Wales Museum, AR. **187** © Pramod Chandra. **189** © Pramod Chandra. **190** Seattle Museum, LPW (l); National Palace Museum, Taiwan, Republic of China (r); © Charles Liu, Westmont, Illinois (t). **191** Art Resource (t); © Guido Alberto Rossi, TIB (b). **192** The Water Margin, Chen Hongshou (t); The Museum of Fine Arts, Boston (c). **192–93** RJB. **194** British Museum. **195** © Private Collection, LPW. **196** SuperStock. **197** Wan-go H. C. Weng. **198** © Harald Sund, TIB (t); National Numismatic Society, Smithsonian Institution (bl,bc). **199** Xi'an Visual Art Company, China (l); © Photo R.M.N., Paris (r). **202** Wan-go H. C. Weng; Asian Art Museum of San Francisco. **203** Wan-go H. C. Weng (t); RJB (b). **206** National Maritime Museum, Greenwich, London (l); Freer Gallery of Art (r); National Numismatic Society, Smithsonian Institution (t). **207** Ontario Science Museum (t); Bibliotheque Nationale, Paris (b). **208** RJB (t); Wan-go H. C. Weng (b). **209** Biblioteca Nacional, Madrid. **210** Private Collection. **211** AR. **212** © George Holton, Photo Researchers, Inc. **213** © Edward Bower, TIB (l); From *The Western Sea Cruises of Eunuch San Pao*, by L.O. Mou-teng, 1597 (tr); RJB (c); AR (cr); © K. Wothe, TIB (bl); Chait Galleries, New York (br). **214** Wan-go H.C. Weng. **215** Wan-go H. C. Weng. **217** SuperStock. **220** © P. & G. Bowater, TIB (l); RJB (r); **221** LPW (t); Shashinka Photo (b); © Martha Cooper Guthrie, AR (r). **222** The Museum of Fine Arts, Boston. **223** © PHOTRI, MGA. **224** Shashinka Photo Library. **225** © Norma Morrison, Gartman Agency (t); Shashinka Photo Library (b). **226** Shashinka Photo Library (t); Cameramann International, Ltd. (b). **227** Shashinka Photo Library. **228** LPW. **229** AR. **231** Shashinka Photo. **234** Shashinka Photo Library (t); Japanese, Panel from Amida Triad, hanging scroll, Kamakura period, 13th century, Gift of Kate S. Buckingham, 1929.856...,© 1989 The Art Institute of Chicago, All Rights Reserved (b). **235** © Urasenke Tea Ceremony Society (l,lc); © Thomas Haar, Shasinka Photo Library (rc); © Norman Morrison, Gartman Agency (r). **236** © Mike Yamashita, Westlight (t); Werner Forman Archive (r); SuperStock (b). **237** British Museum, Michael Holford. **238** © P. Breidenbach (c); © Michael J. Howell, Stock Boston (b). **238–39** Asian Art Museum of San Francisco. **240** Shashinka Photo. **241** © Bernard G. Silberstein, SuperStock (c); LPW (b). **242** Shashinka Photo. **243** AR. **246–47** Bibliotheque Nationale, Paris, NB. **248** History Museum, Stockholm, Giraudon, AR (t); © F.H.C. Birch, Sonia Halliday Photographs (b). **249** Victoria & Albert Museum, Michael Holford (l); Private Collection, Michael Holford (c);Werner Forman Archive (r). **254** Cathedral Treasury, Aachen. **256** Trustees of the British Museum. **257** Walters Art Gallery. **258** Cathedral Treasury, Aachen, AR. **259** AR. **263** British Museum, Michael Holford. **264** Musee Conde, Chantilly, France, AR. **265** AR. **266** Musee Conde, Chantilly, France, NB. **267** RJB (cr,bl,bc,br); AR (c). **268** AR (t); Hotel Lunaret, Montpellier, France, Giraudon, AR (b). **269** Ecole des Beaux Arts, Paris, Giraudon, AR (t); © Ronald Sheridan, AR (b). **270** AR. **271** Trustees of the British Museum (t); The Granger Collection (b). **272** City of Bayeux, AR. **273** LPW **274** © Alain Choisnet, TIB. **275** RJB. **276** Joel Sackett, Michael O'Mara Books, Ltd. (c); RJB (b). **276–77** RJB. **277** RJB. **280** British Library, Bridgeman Art Library (l); Art History Museum, Vienna, NB (r). **280–81** © N. DeVore III, Bruce Coleman, Inc. **281** St. Mark's, Venice, AR. **282** British Museum. **283** SuperStock. **284** Treasury, Manza, AR (l); Vatican Palace, Rome (r). **285** AR (t); Her Majesty's Stationery Office, England (c). **286** Goya Museum, Castres, France, Giraudon, AR (tl); Musee Conde, Chantilly, France, Giraudon, AR (tr); Bibliotheque Arsenal, Paris, Giraudon, AR (c); Musee Condee, Chantilly, France, Giraudon, AR (b). **287** SCALA, AR. **288** Musee des Beaux–Arts, Angers, France, Giraudon, AR (l); © Raphael Gailarde, Gamma-Liaison (r). **289** © Michael Yamashita, Westlight (l); St. Mark's Treasury, Venice, Giraudon, AR (r). **291** © Ara Juler, NB. **292** © Nathan Benn, Stock Boston (l,r). **293** RJB. **294** The Metropolitan Museum of Art. **295** Bibliotheque Nationale, Paris. **297** La Reunion des Musees Nationaux, Cluny, France (c); Gian Berto Vanni, AR (b). **299** British Museum, London, Bridgeman Art Library. **300** Bibliotheque Nationale, Paris. **301** Bibliotheque Nationale, Paris. **306–7** SCALA, AR. **307** LPW **308** National Museum, Florence, AR (l); SCALA, AR (r). **309** SCALA, AR (t); RJB (b); AR (r). **310** Campo Santo, Pisa, AR. **311** RJB. **312** AR (t,c); © R. Kord, H. Armstrong Roberts, Inc. (b). **313** The Folger Shakespeare Library. **314** Louvre, AR (cl); RJB (cr,bl,br). **315** Accademia, Florence, SCALA, AR. **316** Victoria & Albert Museum, Bridgeman Art Library (l,r); AR (b). **317** SCALA, AR. **318** © S. Georgio Schiavoni, Venice, SCALA, AR;. **319** SCALA, AR. **320** RJB (t); AR (bl,bc). **320–21** IBM. **321** IBM (tl,c); RJB (tr); Leonardo da Vinci (bl); AR (bc). **322** © Hubatka, Mauritius, Westlight. **323** SCALA, AR (tl,tr). **324** Northwestern University Library, RJB (l); IBM (r). **325** The Cleveland Museum of Art. **326** Musee de Cluny, Paris (t); National Gallery of Art, Index of the Americas (c); SuperStock (b). **327** AR (l,r,b). **328** San Martino, Buonomini, Florence, SCALA, AR. **329** AR. **332** Musee Conde, Chantilly, France, AR (t); SCALA, AR (l). **333** The Folger Shakespeare Library. **335** RJB. **336** Isabella Stewart Gardner Museum, Boston, AR. **336-37** Tribuna di Galileo, Museum of Physics and Natural History, Florence. **337** Burndy Library (l); Galleria Palatina, Florence, AR (r). **338** Her Majesty's Stationery Office, NB (c); SEF, Turin, AR (r). **339** © Peter Menzel, Stock Boston. **340** The Folger Shakespeare Library. **341** SCALA, AR. **342** AR. **343** AR (t); Lutherhalle, Wittenberg (b). **344** Library of Congress. **345** Worms, Museum der Stadt Andreasstift (t); Rhode Island Historical Society and Massachusetts Charitable Mechanic Association, Boston (b). **349** Bibliotheque Nationale, Paris. **350** LPW **351** British Museum. **353** British Museum. **354** Northwestern University Library, RJB. **355** Northwestern University Library, RJB (l); RJB (c); British Museum, Michael Holford (r). **356** Northwestern University Library, RJB (t); New College, Oxford (r); **358** Northwestern University Library, RJB. **359** © Lou Jones, TIB (tl); © Gregory Heisler, TIB (tc); © Jay Freis, TIB (tr); © Melchior DiGiacomo, TIB (cr). **362** RJB (l); Bibliotheque Nationale, Paris (c). **363** National Maritime Museum, Michael Holford (t); Uffizi, Florence, RHPL (c). **364** New York Public Library. **364–65** © Ernst A. Jahn, TIB. **365** New York Public Library, Map Division. **366** © E.R. Degginger, Bruce Coleman, Inc. **367** RJB (tr,bl,br); Bibliotheque Nationale, Paris (cl); © Roger Wood (cr). **368** Navale Museum, Pegli, Italy, AR. **369** AR. **370** © Scott H. Zieske, Homestake Mining Company (t,c). **371** The Granger Collection. **372** © Ronald Sheridan, AR (t); New York Public Library, Prints Division (b). **373** RJB. **375** British Museum, Michael Holford. **376** RJB. **377** © Allan Eaton, Sheridan Photo Library. **378** The Granger Collection. **379** American Numismatic Society (t,c,b). **380** AR. **381** LPW **383** Bibliotheque Nationale, Paris. **386** Giraudon, AR. **392–93** The Textile Museum, Washington, D.C. **394** © Robert W. Parvin (l); LPW (r). **395** © M. Martin, TIB (t); LPW (c); Museum of the American Indian, Heye Foundation (bl,br). **397** © Jeff Foott, Tom Stack & Associates (t); © Gilcrease Institute (cr,br); LPW (bl,blc,brc). **399** RJB. **400** © Justin Kerr.

—Continued on page 548.